Evangelization
as Interreligious Dialogue

Global Perspectives on the New Evangelization

Volume 2

Series Introduction

Then he sat down and taught the crowds from the boat. After he had finished speaking, he said to Simon, "Put out into deep water and lower your nets for a catch." Simon said in reply, "Master, we have worked hard all night and have caught nothing, but at your command I will lower the nets." When they had done this, they caught a great number of fish and their nets were tearing.

Luke 5:3–6

"How beautiful upon the mountains are the feet of the one bringing good news, announcing peace, bearing good news, announcing salvation, saying to Zion, 'Your God is King!'" (Isaiah 52:7). Evangelization is something beautiful. Derived from the Greek word, *euaggelion*, evangelization means to bear a "happy/blessed message." It is safe to say that every human being longs for good news, and the entire drama of salvation history, as revealed especially in Scripture and Tradition, hinges on a claim to the best news there is. In a word, salvation through divine intimacy—Emmanuel, God with us (see Isaiah 7:14; Matthew 1:23). And as for the essence of this salvation? Isaiah's witness makes it clear: a return to goodness, peace, and the lordship of God.

The bridge of meaning between Isaiah's text and the life and teachings of Jesus of Nazareth is unmistakable: "After John had been arrested, Jesus came to Galilee proclaiming the gospel (*euaggelion*) of God: 'This is the time of fulfillment. The kingdom of God is at hand. Repent, and believe in the gospel'" (Mark 1:14–15). Jesus not only proclaims the good news indicated by Isaiah—"Your God is King!"—he manifests and embodies it. Jesus is the good news of God in person: "And the Word became flesh and made his dwelling among us" (John 1:14). In Jesus's humanity united with his divinity, the good news of God becomes sacrament through the perpetual liturgy of incarnation. Yet the totality of God's revelation in Jesus is laced with paradox. He is a servant king. His royal garments are stark nakedness. His crown is woven of thorns. His ministry is unconcerned with the accumulation of material wealth but, to the contrary, is about giving all away. His queen is a vestal virgin, the Church, *in persona Mariae*, and he reigns from a wooden throne of suffering.

In the twenty-first century, the paradoxical message of the Gospel is no less shocking than it was two thousand years ago. If anything, it is even more riveting to scientific sensibilities and to a surging expansion of secularism taking root in virtually every cultural setting of the world. As Pope Paul VI put it in his 1975 apostolic exhortation, *Evangelii nuntiandi*, we have entered definitively "a new period of evangelization (*feliciora evangelizationis tempora*)" (2). In other words, today we find ourselves in a happy and profitable season to evangelize.

This book series, *Global Perspectives on the New Evangelization*, aims to contribute to the mission field of this "New Evangelization." By offering fresh voices from a diversity of perspectives, these books put Catholic theology into dialogue with a host of conversation partners around a variety of themes. Through the principle of inculturation, rooted in that of incarnation, this series seeks to reawaken those facets of truth found in the beautiful complementarity of cultural voices as harmonized in the one, holy, catholic, and apostolic Church.

John C. Cavadini and **Donald Wallenfang,** *Series editors*

Evangelization as Interreligious Dialogue

EDITED BY

John C. Cavadini

AND

Donald Wallenfang

PICKWICK *Publications* · Eugene, Oregon

EVANGELIZATION AS INTERRELIGIOUS DIALOGUE

Global Perspectives on the New Evangelization 2

Pickwick Publications
An Imprint of Wipf and Stock Publishers
199 W. 8th Ave., Suite 3
Eugene, OR 97401

www.wipfandstock.com

PAPERBACK ISBN: 978-1-5326-5209-7
HARDCOVER ISBN: 978-1-5326-5210-3
EBOOK ISBN: 978-1-5326-5211-0

Cataloguing-in-Publication data:

Names: Cavadini, John C., editor. | Wallenfang, Donald, editor.

Title: Evangelization as interreligious dialogue / edited by John C. Cavadini and Donald Wallenfang.

Description: Eugene, OR : Pickwick Publications, 2019 | Series: Global Perspectives on the New Evangelization 2 | Includes bibliographical references and index.

Identifiers: ISBN 978-1-5326-5209-7 (paperback) | ISBN 978-1-5326-5210-3 (hardcover) | ISBN 978-1-5326-5211-0 (ebook)

Subjects: LCSH: Catholic Church—United States—History—20th century. | Catholic Church—United States. | Evangelistic work—United States. | Evangelistic work—Catholic Church. | Christianity and other religions.

Classification: BR127 .E91 2019 (paperback) | BR127 .E91 (ebook)

Manufactured in the U.S.A.   08/21/19

The editors would like to dedicate this volume to the memory and legacy of Saints Francis Xavier, SJ, and Thérèse of Lisieux, OCD, co-patrons of the missionary life of the Church. Like Jesus's friends, Martha and Mary (see Luke 10:38–42), Francis and Thérèse testify to the complementarity between the active life and the contemplative life within the mission field of evangelization. So much contemplation, so much evangelization; so much evangelization, so much contemplation.

"I have come to think that I ought to provide for their salvation even at the risk of my life. I have resolved to go there as soon as possible, and to offer my life to the risk."

Francis Xavier, *Letter from Amboyna to the Society of Jesus at Rome*, May 1546

"A scholar has said: *'Give me a lever and a fulcrum and I will lift the world.'* What Archimedes was not able to obtain, for his request was not directed by God and was only made from a material viewpoint, the saints have obtained in all its fullness. The Almighty has given them as *fulcrum*: HIMSELF ALONE; as *lever*: PRAYER which burns with a fire of love. And it is in this way that they have *lifted the world*; it is in this way that the saints still militant lift it, and that, until the end of time, the saints to come will lift it."

Thérèse of Lisieux, *Story of a Soul*, Manuscript C, 36r°–36v°

Contents

Contributors

John C. Cavadini, PhD, is a Professor in the Department of Theology at the University of Notre Dame, having served as Chair of the Department from 1997–2010 and led the Department to a top 10 ranking in the NRC rankings of doctoral programs. He is also the McGrath–Cavadini Director of the McGrath Institute for Church Life. His main areas of research and teaching are in patristic and early medieval theology, with special interests in the theology of Augustine and in the history of biblical exegesis. In 2009, he was appointed by Pope Benedict XVI to a five-year term on the International Theological Commission and was also created a member of the Equestrian Order of St. Gregory the Great, *classis civilis*, by Pope Benedict. He has served as a consultant to the USCCB Committee on Doctrine since 2006.

Richard A. Cohen, PhD, is Professor of Jewish Thought, and Professor of Philosophy, at the State University of New York at Buffalo (SUNY). Prior to Buffalo he was the Isaac Swift Distinguished Professor of Jewish Studies at the University of North Carolina at Charlotte. He is Director of the annual Levinas Philosophy Summer Seminar. His books are: *Out of Control: Confrontations between Spinoza and Levinas* (SUNY Press, 2016); *Levinasian Meditations: Ethics, Philosophy and Religion* (Duquesne University Press, 2010); *Ethics, Exegesis and Philosophy: Interpretation after Levinas* (Cambridge University Press, 2001), and *Elevations: The Height of the Good in Rosenzweig and Levinas* (University of Chicago Press, 1994). He has also edited several additional volumes and journals, introduced and translated four books by Levinas, and published numerous articles on various topics in modern and contemporary continental philosophy.

Martino Diez, PhD, is Assistant Professor of Arabic at the Catholic University of Milan and Scientific Director of the Oasis International Foundation. From January to July 2019 he was visiting member at the Institute for Advanced Study in Princeton. He is invited researcher at the PISAI (Pontifical Institute for Arabic and Islamic Studies) and member of the Advisory

Board of the Middle East Mediterranean Freethinking Platform (MEM) in Lugano, Switzerland. His publications include: *Introduzione alla lingua araba. Origini, storia e attualità* [An introduction to Arabic: Origins, History and Present] (2018), Abū l-ʿAlāʾ al-Maʿarrī, *Lepistola del perdono. Il viaggio nell'Aldilà* [The Epistle of Forgiveness. The Journey to the Afterworld] (2011), Abū t-Tayyib al-Mutanabbī, *Lemiro e il suo profeta. Odi in onore di Sayf ad-Dawla al-Hamdani* [The Emir and His Prophet: Odes in praise of Sayf ad-Dawla al-Hamdani] (2009), and *Georges Anawati, Lultimo dialogo. La mia vita incontro all'Islam* [The last dialogue. My life-long encounter with Islam] (2010).

Robert M. Gimello, PhD, is Research Professor Emeritus of Theology and of East Asian Languages and Cultures at the University of Notre Dame, and a Research Fellow of the Liu Institute for Asia & Asian Studies. He is a specialist in the history of Buddhist thought and practice in East Asia, especially the Chan (Zen), Huayan, and esoteric traditions of medieval and early modern China. In addition, Gimello works on issues in comparative philosophy of religion, comparative mysticism, and Catholic theology of religions.

Andrew Kim, PhD, is Assistant Professor of Theology at Marquette University. He received his MA from Union Theological Seminary and his doctorate from The Catholic University of America. His primary area of research concentrates on virtue ethics in the work of Thomas Aquinas. He has published articles in *Studies in Christian Ethics* and the *Journal of Moral Theology*, and he is the author of *An Introduction to Catholic Ethics Since Vatican II* (Cambridge University Press, 2016).

Francesca Aran Murphy, PhD, is Professor of Systematic Theology at the University of Notre Dame. Her research interests include theological aesthetics, the intersection between theology and the arts, ecclesiology, and the work of Hans Urs von Balthasar, Henri de Lubac, and Joseph Ratzinger. She has written and edited a dozen books, including most recently a commentary on 1 Samuel (Brazos, 2011), *Theology, University, Humanities: Initium Sapientiae Timor Domini* (Cascade, 2011), and *Illuminating Faith: Invitation to Theology* (Bloomsbury, 2014).

Cyril O'Regan, PhD, is Huisking Professor of Theology at the University of Notre Dame. He is a systematic theologian who works at the intersection of philosophy and theology. He has published monographs on Hegel, Gnosticism in modernity, and apocalyptic theology. The first book of O'Regan's

two-volume study on Hans Urs von Balthasar and his critical engage-
ments with Hegel and Heidegger is *The Anatomy of Misremembering: Von
Balthasar's Response to Philosophical Modernity* (Crossroad, 2014).

Gabriel Said Reynolds, PhD, did his doctoral work at Yale University in
Islamic Studies. Currently he researches the Qur'ān and Muslim/Christian
relations and is Professor of Islamic Studies and Theology in the Department of Theology at the University of Notre Dame. He is the author of *The
Qur'ān and Its Biblical Subtext* (Routledge, 2010) and *The Emergence of
Islam* (Fortress, 2012), the translator of ʿAbd al-Jabbar's *Critique of Christian Origins* (BYU, 2008), and editor of *The Qur'ān in Its Historical Context* (Routledge, 2008) and *New Perspectives on the Qur'ān: The Qur'ān
in Its Historical Context 2* (Routledge, 2011). In 2012–13 Prof. Reynolds
directed, along with Mehdi Azaiez, "The Qur'ān Seminar," a year-long collaborative project dedicated to encouraging dialogue among scholars of the
Qur'ān, the acts of which appeared as *The Qur'ān Seminar Commentary*
(De Gruyter, 2016). In June 2018 his most recent book, *The Qur'an and the
Bible*, was published with Yale University Press. At Notre Dame he teaches
courses on theology, Muslim/Christian Relations, and Islamic Origins.

Deepak Sarma, PhD, is Professor of Indian Religions and Philosophy at
Case Western Reserve University. He is the author of *Classical Indian Philosophy: A Reader* (2011), *Hinduism: A Reader* (2008), *Epistemologies and
the Limitations of Philosophical Inquiry: Doctrine in Madhva Vedanta* (2005)
and *An Introduction to Madhva Vedanta* (2003). He was a guest curator
of *Indian Kalighat Paintings*, an exhibition at the Cleveland Museum of Art.
He is a curatorial consultant for the Department of Asian Art of the Cleveland Museum of Art. After earning a BA in religion from Reed College,
Sarma attended the University of Chicago Divinity School, where he received a PhD in the philosophy of religions. His current reflections concern
cultural theory, racism, and post-colonialism.

Chris Seeman, PhD, is Graduate Theology Program Director and Associate
Professor of Theology at Walsh University in North Canton, Ohio. He earned
his MA in Biblical Studies from Graduate Theological Union (Berkeley) and
his doctorate in Near Eastern Religions from the University of California at
Berkeley. His research interests include biblical theology, especially the Gospel of Mark, Deuterocanonical literature, early Judaism, Hellenistic history,
and the writings of Josephus. His recent publications include *A Parabolic
Analysis of the Trial of Jesus in Mark's Gospel: How a Literary Form Shapes the
Description of an Historical Event* (Edwin Mellen, 2018), *Flavius Josephus:*

Translation and Commentary, Judean Antiquities 11 (Brill, 2017), and *Rome and Judea in Transition: Hasmonean Relations with the Roman Republic and the Evolution of the High Priesthood* (Peter Lang, 2013). Seeman co-founded the Children of Abraham, an interfaith coalition in Cedar Rapids, Iowa, and currently co-chairs the Catholic Biblical Association Task Force, "Addressing Representations of Jews and Judaism in Catholic Exegesis, Homiletics, and Catechesis." He is a member of the Catholic Biblical Association and the Society of Biblical Literature.

Donald Wallenfang, OCDS, PhD, Emmanuel Mary of the Cross, is a Secular Discalced Carmelite and Professor of Theology at Sacred Heart Major Seminary in Detroit. He received his MTS from St. Norbert College and his doctorate from Loyola University Chicago. Wallenfang specializes in metaphysics, phenomenology, hermeneutics, and philosophical theology. His research concentrates on the work of Edith Stein, Emmanuel Levinas, Paul Ricoeur, Jean-Luc Marion, and Carmelite Spirituality. His articles have appeared in several journals and book compilations. He is the author of *Metaphysics: A Basic Introduction in a Christian Key* (Cascade, 2019), *Phenomenology: A Basic Introduction in the Light of Jesus Christ* (Cascade, 2019), *Dialectical Anatomy of the Eucharist: An Étude in Phenomenology* (Cascade, 2017), and *Human and Divine Being: A Study on the Theological Anthropology of Edith Stein* (Cascade, 2017). Wallenfang is co-editor for the book series, *Global Perspectives on the New Evangelization* (Pickwick) and is a member of the Edith Stein Circle, *Société Internationale de Recherche Emmanuel Levinas*, and the North American Levinas Society.

Acknowledgments

It is a great delight to introduce the second volume of the *Global Perspectives on the New Evangelization* book series. With the second volume we now can confirm that we truly have a series of books! This project would not be possible without the continued support of the McGrath Institute for Church Life at the University of Notre Dame and, in particular, the magnanimity of Robert and Joan McGrath. Thank you, also, to President Richard and Terie Jusseaume of Walsh University and the legacy of the Brothers of Christian Instruction and the Congregation of Holy Cross, for your common mission of making Jesus Christ known, loved and served, and thus save souls. *Sed Deus dat incrementum. Ave crux, spes unica!* Thank you to Wipf and Stock Publishers, especially Charlie Collier, our series editor, and Matt Wimer, our managing editor, both of whom have been incredibly warm, helpful, patient and insightful throughout the publishing process. Finally, we would like to thank all of the contributors to this volume, especially for your sincerity, transparency and vulnerability wagered in the fruitful risk of another attempt at interreligious dialogue. May the conversation continue, even when it is admitted that conversation across the diversity of religious traditions is quite insoluble . . . but pacifically so.

Introduction

A subtle ironic hypocrisy lurks beneath every claim to be in dialogue: the collapse into yet another self-referential monologue under the guise of "dialogue." Therefore it is difficult to give a word of introduction about interreligious dialogue apart from the actual dialogue itself. Relying on the pages that follow to showcase altogether a genuine dialogue and exchange of ideas around the promise of truth, the editors nevertheless hazard a tentative word of introduction at the risk of intruding upon the unpretentious purity of the dialogue itself. After all, interreligious dialogue is not so much an exchange of ideas as it is an intersection of cultures and shared human life. The best interreligious dialogues are those that take place within the immersion of respective cultures and the shared zones of meaning that overlap among cultures. While this book cannot pretend to provide the wealth of this kind of immersion experience within the indigenous cultures of distinct religious traditions, at least it can point in that direction.

The second volume of the *Global Perspectives on the New Evangelization* series has been elected by the question of the precarious relationship between evangelization and interreligious dialogue. As the title suggests, *Evangelization as Interreligious Dialogue*, an integral relationship obtains between these two terms. For our present era one thing is certain: we live in a global village. Globalization is a certified fact of our existence today inasmuch as transportation, virtual communication, and the rise of a global economy have put us into contact with one another to a degree surpassing that of any previous generation. With globalization comes the ambivalent effect of an intersection of cultures old, new and diverse. The possibility of diversified social unity arises in spite of the temptation toward generic uniformity and cultural homogeneity. A clash of cultural difference harbors the potential for harmonious unity and peace, but also the tinder of animosity and hegemony. Hans Küng writes: "No peace among the nations without peace among the religions. No peace among the religions without dialogue between the religions. No dialogue between the religions without investigation of the foundations of the religions."[1] And this is precisely the aim of a book like *Evangelization as Interreligious Dialogue*. For instance, if the good news of Jesus of Nazareth entails the reign of interpersonal and cosmic *shalom*, then it follows that irenic interreligious dialogue serves as an indispensable way toward the realization of *shalom*.

The third line of Küng's adage insists on investigating the foundations of the world's religions as an essential element of interreligious dialogue. This is to say that true dialogue begins with listening and observation. Giving and receiving, speaking and listening, constitute the reciprocal and complementary nature of every dialogue worthy of the name. This is why one would enter into the unpredictable arena of dialogue: to learn and to share. In a word, to be enriched. In her 2013 presentation at Stanford University, entitled "Vatican II and Other Religions: A Milestone?," Catherine Cornille proposes some key points for fostering an interreligious attitude:

- To learn not just about other religious traditions, but to learn from other religious traditions.

- Dialogue is not just an exchange of information but it is mutual witnessing to truth and tradition.

- Through interreligious dialogue we reinterpret what we already knew through the lens of the other.[2]

Cornille's insights broaden the scope of interreligious dialogue in extending beyond mere information transfer to character transformation. Openness to receive benefit from the other is always a prerequisite. Digital databases can just as well (if not better) transfer information—facts and figures, definitions and derivations; but it takes persons to witness to truth and to encounter meanings in a spiritual way. One of the cardinal fruits of interreligious dialogue is the invitation to reinterpret our most cherished beliefs and convictions in light of those of another. Social solidarity itself is the result of communal encounter and mutual enrichment. By taking Cornille's claims to heart, the heart is opened to encounter the heart of the other who faces the self. The remainder of this introduction will attempt to situate interreligious dialogue even further according to the exigencies of (1) inclusive

---

1. Küng, *Islam*, xxiii. Cf. Sacks, *Not In God's Name*. See Dupuis, *Toward a Christian Theology*, 11: "Disregard leads to contempt; acquaintance to critical evaluation."

2. Cornille, "Vatican II and Other Religions." See Whaling, *Christian Theology and World Religions*, 94: "Just as the dialogue with the rediscovered Aristotle enabled Aquinas to deepen his theological understanding and to recast Christian theology in the medieval situation, so too can the dialogue with Hindus, Buddhists, Muslims, Jews, and so on, in different parts of the world, enable us to deepen our theological understanding and to recast some of our theological ideas in the modern situation."

anthropology, (2) objective truth, (3) the soteriological question, and (4) rules for effective dialogue. By laying out this framework for interreligious dialogue, the reader will be better positioned to investigate the foundations of the world's religions.

Inclusive Anthropology

Anthropology first. This is an important general rule from which to commence profitable interreligious dialogue. After all, dialogue is a human activity—an activity that transpires between the agencies of persons. There is a sameness among us, all the while there is difference. The Second Vatican Council reiterates this point in its breakthrough Declaration on the Relation of the Church to Non-Christian Religions, *Nostra aetate*: "Humanity forms but one community. . . . We cannot truly pray to God the Father of all if we treat any people as other than sisters and brothers, for all are created in God's image."[3] Religion is a human phenomenon. From its Latin root, *re-ligare* ("to bind together again"), the term *religion* signifies that which one regards to be of ultimate concern and value in life (Tillich). Religion indicates the most central meaning and source of meaningfulness in one's life. Religion, therefore, is the centerpiece of culture as it is the greatest *cultus* among all the rest. We engage in interreligious dialogue as human beings even if the ultimate point of reference in this dialogue is not ourselves but divinity.

In both the 1984 document of the Secretariat for Non-Christians (now called the Pontifical Council for Interreligious Dialogue), *The Attitude of the Church Towards the Followers of Other Religions: Reflections and Orientations on Dialogue and Mission*, and the 1991 document of the Pontifical Council for Interreligious Dialogue, *Dialogue and Proclamation: Reflections and Orientations on Interreligious Dialogue and the Proclamation of the Gospel of Jesus Christ*, four distinct types of interreligious dialogue are identified: (1) the dialogue of life, (2) the dialogue of action, (3) the dialogue of theological exchange, and (4) the dialogue of religious experience.[4] The first of these types of dialogue is most pertinent for the claim of anthropology first: "(Interreligious) dialogue is in first place a conversation about human existence."[5] Insofar as we are all human, we all share in common life experiences, such as joy and hope, grief and anguish.[6] It is these experiences that

3. Vatican II, "*Nostra aetate*," 1, 5.

4. See Secretariat for Non-Christians, *Dialogue and Mission*, 29–35; Pontifical Council for Interreligious Dialogue, "Dialogue and Proclamation," 42.

5. Francis, "*Evangelii gaudium*," 250.

6. See Vatican II, "*Gaudium et spes*," 1.

serve as a steady point of departure for those entering into the charitable fray of interreligious dialogue.

Child psychologist, Daniel Stern, in analyzing the peculiar intersubjective life of the infant, speaks of the primordial relation of human interdependence and intimacy as *communal attunement*.[7] This differs from common forms of communication, such as those expressed in and through syntactical language, in that it is "a sharing of experience and does not attempt to alter another's belief or action system. Prior to communication mother and child experience an affective continuum through shared, meaningful, lived situations, out of which communication, and with it the acquisition of language, arise."[8] The originary relationship between mother and child may serve as a model through which to perceive the dialogue of life. There is a syntax of affectivity, stemming from our experience of life in our mother's womb, long before a syntax of nouns, verbs, adjectives, etc. develops.

Making a similar point, but from within a different context, namely non-Western modes of dialogue, Jacques Dupuis suggests that "the limitations of the categories currently used in the debate on the theology of religions betray 'theoretical approaches to the faith of other people,' issuing 'from a monoreligiocultural society and a mere academic and speculative point of view. . . . We would rather approach the issues from a different perspective,' that, namely, of a live encounter and dialogue."[9] This juxtaposition between a monoreligiocultural academic and speculative point of view on the one hand, and a live encounter and non-conformist dialogue on the other, helps to alleviate the undue pressures of cultural dominance and imperialism. By unmasking the hegemonic tendencies of some elitist worldviews that only want to talk and not listen, the healthy play and unexpected horizons of interreligious dialogue are reopened for new seasons of discovery. Going beyond a trite "theology *for* dialogue," we are able to create anew a "theology *of* dialogue." According to Michael Barnes, "the first demand of such a theology is to accept that all dialogue is established precisely in asymmetry, that is to say by the difference between the partners. Community or communality has yet to be established: this is the phenomenon which governs all faith encounter."[10] A posture of humility welcomes the

7. See Stern, *Interpersonal World of the Infant*, 149–61.

8. Simms, "Infant's Experience of the World," 38.

9. Dupuis, *Toward a Christian Theology*, 199. Here, Dupuis quotes from the 1989 statement of the Thirteenth Annual Meeting of the Indian Theological Association, entitled "Towards an Indian Christian Theology of Religious Pluralism."

10. Barnes quoted in Dupuis, *Toward a Christian Theology*, 200. Here, Dupuis quotes from Barnes's 1994 essay, "Theology of Religions in a Post-modern World."

asymmetrical nature of the interreligious dialogue, once again prioritizing the message and experience of the other as sacred in and of themselves.

While receptivity, listening, passivity and empathy serve as conditions of possibility for encountering the other as other, there remains a third-party alterity that is not identical to any of the interlocutors in the conversation. In fact, this third party is that after which all religious traditions aim and the measure by which all human experiences are judged. This third party to which all honest dialogue is tethered is called truth. Once the principle of "anthropology first" has been established, the second principle that began to be disclosed in the first and that follows upon its heels is the transparent quest for objective truth.

Objective Truth

The concept of objective truth implies the first principle of theoretical reason, namely, the principle of non-contradiction. This self-evident first principle reminds us that something cannot both be what it is and not be what it is at the same time. In other words, certain questions present themselves to us as ultimatums: either yes or no. Questions such as, "Is God real?," "Is Jesus God incarnate?," "Do all religions essentially mean the same about God?," "Did God create the universe *ex nihilo*?," demand "yes" or "no" answers. Objective truth means truth that is entirely independent of subjective determination. Objective truth is the kind of truth that determines me, of which I am not its author or master, but its docile recipient. Objective truth insists on the fact that answers precede their questions. We ask questions of objective truth because the truth of the answers provokes the questions themselves. If there were no objective truths in relation to the questions we ask, there would be no productive point for asking the questions. Even more, as anchored in the a priori facticity of objective truth, the concept of divine revelation signifies "something not ours, not to be found in what we have, comes to me and takes me out of myself, above myself, creates something new. . . . And yet this new intervention, intruding upon our sphere of experience and our consciousness of our identity, breaking them up, brings us out into the open spaces of a greater reality and, in so doing, opens for us the possibility of overcoming pluralism and coming together."[11] Because the primary content of theology is divine revelation, interreligious dialogue maintains a privileged place of accountability to objective truth encountered through both reason and revelation. In either case, truth crashes into us from an unprogrammable elsewhere, giving and signifying itself as

11. Ratzinger, *Truth and Tolerance*, 89.

non-identical to the self or even to a community of selves. In the end, we are truth's witnesses and not its inventors. If interreligious dialogue does not insist on this fact, then may the best sophist win.

The Catholic theological tradition rests on the concept of objective truth as revealed through both reason and faith in God's self-revelation as gradually disclosed throughout salvation history along a series of covenant relationships, and ultimately through Jesus, the incarnate Word (*Logos*) of God.[12] Because the objective truth of God is revealed according to the *Logos* that is truth itself, *semina verbi* ("seeds of the Word"), or *logoi spermatikoi*, can be detected across cultures and religious traditions inasmuch as they involve the common faculty of human reason and the sincere search for truth.[13] The authors of the Second Vatican Council say as much in one of the most frequently cited passages of *Nostra aetate*: "The Catholic Church rejects nothing of what is true and holy in (other) religions. It has a high regard for the manner of life and conduct, the precepts and doctrines which, although differing in many ways from its own teaching, nevertheless often reflect a ray of that truth which enlightens all men and women. Yet it proclaims and is in duty bound to proclaim without fail, Christ who is the way, the truth and the life (John 1:6). In him, in whom God reconciled all things to himself (see 2 Cor 5:18–19), people find the fullness of their religious life" (2). This is one of the most significant passages in Catholic teaching that recognizes the fact that truth and holiness are present in the diversity of religious traditions around the world inasmuch as it is the same *Logos*, identified with God the Son in Christianity, and the same *Pneuma*, identified with God the Holy Spirit in Christianity, that are operative in relation to human beings' souls as they grope for the divine.[14]

12. See John Paul II, "*Fides et ratio*," 25, 44, 56, 66, 69, 76, 82, 90, 96. For application of the concept of objective truth within the realm of moral philosophy and theology, see John Paul II, "*Veritatis splendor*"; Kim, *Introduction to Catholic Ethics*, 13–45. Cf. International Theological Commission, "Christianity and the World Religions," 13: "To sacrifice the question of truth is incompatible with the Christian vision."

13. See International Theological Commission, "Christianity and the World Religions," 41; Vatican II, "*Ad gentes*," 11; "*Lumen gentium*," 17; "*Nostra aetate*," 2.

14. See Acts 17:22–33, esp. 26–27, NAB: "He made from one the whole human race to dwell on the entire surface of the earth, and he fixed the ordered seasons and the boundaries of their regions, so that people might seek God, even perhaps grope for him and find him, though indeed he is not far from any one of us." See also Pontifical Council for Interreligious Dialogue, "Dialogue and Proclamation," 17, 26. "*Gaudium et spes*," 22: "All this holds true not only for Christians but also for all people of good will in whose hearts grace is active invisibly. For since Christ died for everyone, and since all are in fact called to one and the same destiny, which is divine, we must hold that the holy Spirit offers to all the possibility of being made partners, in a way known to God, in the paschal mystery."

It is indicative to note the way in which Jesus's itinerant ministry of teaching and healing frequently went outside the exclusive boundaries of his own Jewish community. His universal mission was revealed in how he reached out to many people other than the fold of Israel, "opening up a new horizon, beyond the purely local, to a universality which is both Christological and Pneumatological in character."[15] In his 2013 apostolic exhortation, *Evangelii gaudium*, Pope Francis, quoting from the International Theological Commission's 1997 text, *Christianity and the World Religions*, writes that "non-Christians, by God's gracious initiative, when they are faithful to their own consciences, can live 'justified by the grace of God,' and thus be 'associated to the paschal mystery of Jesus Christ.'"[16] Nevertheless, Catholic teaching, at the same time, affirms that the fullness of divine truth and sanctifying power are given and revealed in and through Christ explicitly, that is, in and through the one, holy, catholic and apostolic Church.[17]

Even more, from a Catholic theological perspective, objective truth demands objective authentication. In other words, any truth claim in the name of objectivity must secure its right to clarity by the exigency of infallibility. Since one of the fundamental meanings of objective truth is infallible truth, this truth grants access to itself through objective and infallible means. Infallibility is a *sine qua non* of objectivity. In the latter part of the nineteenth century, John Henry Newman discovered this exigency of infallibility in his own pursuit of objective truth over and against the prevailing temptation to skepticism in his time:

> Supposing then it to be the Will of the Creator to interfere in human affairs, and to make provisions for retaining in the world a knowledge of Himself, so definite and distinct as to be proof against the energy of human scepticism, in such a case—I am far from saying that there was no other way—but there is nothing to surprise the mind, if He should think fit to introduce a power

15. Pontifical Council for Interreligious Dialogue, "Dialogue and Proclamation," 21.

16. Francis, "*Evangelii gaudium*," 254; International Theological Commission, "Christianity and the World Religions," 72. See further: "The mystery of the Church in Christ is a dynamic reality in the Holy Spirit. Although the visible expression of belonging to the Church is lacking to this spiritual union, justified non-Christians are included in the Church, 'the Mystical Body of Christ' and 'a spiritual community' (*LG* 8). In this sense the fathers of the Church were able to say that justified non-Christians belong to the *ecclesia ab Abel*. While these are reunited in the universal Church joined to the Father (*LG* 2), those who certainly belong 'to the body' but not 'to the heart' of the Church because they do not persevere in love will not be saved (*LG* 14)" (International Theological Commission, "Christianity and the World Religions," 72).

17. See John Paul II, *Catechism of the Catholic Church*, 839–48; Rahner, *Foundations of Christian Faith*, 311–21.

into the world, invested with the prerogative of infallibility in religious matters. Such a provision would be a direct, immediate, active, and prompt means of withstanding the difficulty; it would be an instrument suited to the need; and, when I find that this is the very claim of the Catholic Church, not only do I feel no difficulty in admitting the idea, but there is a fitness in it, which recommends it to my mind. And thus I am brought to speak of the Church's infallibility, as a provision, adapted by the mercy of the Creator, to preserve religion in the world, and to restrain that freedom of thought, which of course in itself is one of the greatest of our natural gifts, and to rescue it from its own suicidal excesses.[18]

Newman's conviction relates the plausibility, if not necessity, of the charism of infallibility to be granted to those persons assigned the responsibility to give authentic interpretation and application of divine revelation within the human community. A loose observation of this charism is found at work in religious authority in general, whether in the form of rabbis, imams, yogi, prophets, sages, gurus, priests, theologians, bishops or religious magisteria. Yet for Catholic belief, insofar as God became incarnate in Jesus of Nazareth, a definitive teaching authority that certifies the clarity and coherence of objective truth concerning matters of divine revelation and morality emerges as positively peremptory, absolute and unmitigated. This teaching authority resides with the bishop of Rome, as direct successor of Peter the apostle, and all bishops around the world in union with his incontestable vicarious authority due to his immediate identity as vicar and pontifex of Christ on earth.[19] Claims such as this one in the Catholic theological tradition contribute to a healthy dialogue within "a differentiated theology of the religions, which is grounded in one's own truth claim, (and) is the basis of any serious dialogue and the necessary presupposition for understanding the diversity of positions and their cultural means of expression."[20] Because genuine interreligious dialogue is tethered to the concept of objective truth, interlocutors' commitment to truth must begin with their respective theological convictions in relation to the priority of truth's objectivity toward which all personal subjective participants are accountable and subservient.

18. Newman, *Apologia Pro Vita Sua*, 244–45.

19. See Matthew 16:13–19; Isaiah 22:19–22; Matthew 18:18; Luke 22:31–32; John 21:15–17; Acts 15; Galatians 1:18–19; *Lumen gentium*, 25–29; John Paul II, *Catechism of the Catholic Church*, 880–96; Pius IX, "Profession of Faith"; "Dogmatic Constitution"; "First Dogmatic Constitution."

20. International Theological Commission, "Christianity and the World Religions," 101.

In truth, objectivity can be obscured by many covert forces, such as the desire for prestige, the fear of humiliation, the pretentiousness of certainty in all matters, and the intrigue of language games (Wittgenstein). So what gives us the assurance that interlocutors abide in the truth and are obedient to its summons? Perhaps, in the end, the most decisive criterion for truth-telling is love. Does it not stand to reason that the concept and lifestyle of sincere self-gift (love) grants us the surest path to unadulterated objectivity due to the highest degrees of disinterestedness necessary for truth's discovery? Is it not the case that "the universe is invested in wonder because its intelligibility comes from this [divine] Love" and that "we are free to be formed in the love which alone makes us truly objective observers of the world" because love removes the veils that conceal the purest forms of objectivity?[21] Is it possible that truth is the prize won by the potent impotency of self-abnegation, detachment and humility? If the floodgates of wonder were to reopen in human experience, what deed must be furnished to gain access to all that gives itself in perception? Could the logic of paradox, in which the universal is expressed in the particular, be reconsidered as paradigmatic for interreligious dialogue today?

One extension of the concept of universal divine revelation made in and through a particular cultural-historical context is the paradoxical possibility of the "Concrete Universal" (*universale concretum et personale*) in which Christ is the "whole present in the fragment" (*das Ganze im Fragment*).[22] Related to the concept of objective truth, the paradox in which the universal is manifest and proclaimed in the particular and, moreover, the great is revealed in the small, is a claim unique to Christianity in its concentrated credo wherein God becomes man in actual cosmic and human history, once and for all. The claim of the "Concrete Universal," coupled with the exigency of infallibility, promotes the play of non-reductive interreligious dialogue by preventing a facile resignation to undiscerning religious relativism, syncretism or secularism.[23] These may be the three great temptations within the "heavy lifting" of interreligious dialogue because they promise a premature conclusion that would seem to favor a happy climate of religious pluralism, only to betray the seriousness of the essential distinctions among diverse theological positions in the end. The dialectical nature of truth, as discovered always through the course of open dialogue, resists its collapse

21. Cavadini, "Anatomy of Wonder," 166.

22. Balthasar, *Das Ganze im Fragment*, 243–350, quoted in Dupuis, *Toward a Christian Theology*, 142.

23. See Congregation for the Doctrine of the Faith, "*Dominus Iesus*," 4; John Paul II, "*Novo millennio ineunte*," 54–56; Benedict XVI, "*Verbum Domini*," 117; Oakes, "Resolving the Relativity Paradox," 87–113.

in favor of either of its irreducible poles: unity and diversity, sameness and difference, singularity and plurality. Instead, unity transcends its pretentious impostures of uniformity, homogeneity and monotony, while diversity exceeds its counterfeits of irreconcilable factions, divisions and dissonance. True unity implies diversity unified, nevertheless, diversity; true diversity implies unity diversified, nonetheless, unity.

Finally, under the heading of objective truth, another important distinction must be made between theology and religious studies. Over the past several decades, an unhelpful dichotomy has emerged within higher education. On the one side, most public universities subscribe to religious studies as the only adequate means to adjudicate between diverse religious traditions. Within these contexts religious traditions are analyzed according to the standards and methods of social/behavioral sciences and comparative cultural studies. The exclusive point of reference is anthropology while in effect occluding divinity and divine revelation as primary points of reference. On the other side, many private universities (and even some exceptions among public institutions), founded under the auspices of religious congregations and traditions, go beyond the restrictions of religious studies and enter the domain of theology proper. Even though anthropology remains an important point of reference for theology, as its term suggests, divinity is regarded as the most primary point of reference. For instance, again within the Catholic theological tradition, "the foundation of the Church's commitment to dialogue is not merely anthropological but primarily theological."[24] As defined as early as Augustine of Hippo, theology is faith seeking understanding (*fides quaerens intellectum*), rather than reason looking for justification to believe at best. For all their benefits, the inherent limitations of religious studies can result in a vapid connoisseurism of things religious. On the other hand, for all their merits, theological studies can narrow into an exclusionary confessionalism that closes off to further dialogue with other theological traditions because it is convinced that all of its questions have been answered sufficiently already. The hope of the present study is that it combines the best of both worlds with an accent on theological concerns, always in relation to objective truth.

The Soteriological Question

To this end, it may come as no surprise that the most pivotal theological question within interreligious dialogue is that of salvation. What is meant by salvation both within this lifetime and the potential of eternal life beyond

---

24. Pontifical Council for Interreligious Dialogue, "Dialogue and Proclamation," 38.

death is paramount to the purpose of religion. Interpreting the human situation according to the dialogue of life propels us toward the possibility of life redeemed. In the recent history of interreligious dialogue, three general positions have developed from the perspective of Christian theology vis-à-vis non-Christian traditions concerning the question of salvation: (1) exclusivism/ecclesiocentrism, (2) inclusivism/Christocentrism, and (3) pluralism/theocentrism.[25] To summarize briefly, the first position applies the hard and fast rule of *extra ecclesiam nulla salus* ("outside the Church, no salvation") to posit the necessity of baptism and explicit confession of salvation through Christ. This position can recoil upon itself as a borderline fundamentalism, resulting in a blissful complacent confidence in its own self-referential terms and conditions. The second position, while insisting on salvation through Christ alone, envisions the possibility of the merits of Christ extending beyond the visible confines of the Church through the activity of God the Holy Spirit and the *semina verbi* operative in the diversity of world religions.[26] Of the three positions, this one most adequately accounts for the dialectical nature of truth and includes an element of paradox. The third position begins with the global context of religious pluralism and immediately reaches for the lowest common denominator among all world religions: divinity (*theos*). By seeking an ultra-inclusivist worldview, this position perhaps exchanges one extreme for another, namely, trading an exclusivist fundamentalism for an inclusivist fundamentalism in which Christ is one mediator of salvation among many.

The title of this book, *Evangelization as Interreligious Dialogue*, suggests an intimate link between the proclamation of the Christian kerygma and the open disposition to dialogue with people of other religious traditions as a means to humanize one another and to encounter further facets of truth. This title does not intend to imply the conflation of proclamation and dialogue from a Catholic standpoint. Rather, "these two elements must maintain both their intimate connection and their distinctiveness; therefore they should not be confused, manipulated or regarded as identical, as though they were interchangeable."[27] Yet again, there remains the possibility of "a healthy pluralism" in which there exists "an essential bond between dialogue and proclamation" since "evangelization and interreligious dialogue, far from being opposed, mutually support and nourish one another."[28] Further,

25. See International Theological Commission, "Christianity and the World Religions," 9; Dupuis, *Toward a Christian Theology*, 180–201; Knitter, *Introducing Theologies of Religions*.

26. See John Paul II, *Catechism of the Catholic Church*, 846–48, 1257–61.

27. John Paul II, "*Redemptoris missio*," 55.

28. Francis, "*Evangelii gaudium*," 255, 251.

interreligious dialogue, as a process of mutual conversion, "does not replace, but rather accompanies the *missio ad gentes*" wherein "proclamation and sacramentalization represent the culmination of the evangelizing mission of the Church."[29] Just as people may begin a conversation about medical treatment in response to a physical ailment, interreligious dialogue is spawned in response to the universal malaise of creation and its entropic decline. The goal of this dialogue is not merely dialogue for dialogue's sake, but dialogue in pursuit of a collective remedy and elixir.

Driven by the force of the soteriological question, interreligious dialogue presses on in hope of discovering anew, or maybe for the first time, the meaning of life and death, and the unlimited horizon of religious experience and divine revelation. Where reason falters at the threshold of its maximum capacities, it senses the vocation to yield to a knowledge not cultivated from its own native soil. Reasonable reason assents to the exigencies of faith that abide in the domain of possibility that is never exhausted. This is why "the respect due to the agnostic or non-believing minority should not be arbitrarily imposed in a way that silences the convictions of the believing majority or ignores the wealth of religious traditions."[30] Secularism's sway has no warrant for eclipsing the fundamental right of religious liberty and the blind censure of religious expression. Any science that disqualifies possibility before conducting the experiment is no science at all. Any science that dismisses evidence simply because it cannot be quantified or placed according to predetermined categories within a limited field of investigation is only half-science. Any scientist that resists the question of being, the question of God, and the question of salvation loves "the small island of his so-called knowledge" more than "the sea of infinite mystery."[31] Given the growing cultural trend of disenchantment with things religious—even if oftentimes caused by intellectual acedia and spiritual torpor—Pope Francis recognizes that "a special place of encounter is offered by new Areopagi such as the Court of the Gentiles."[32] Oftentimes the first step of dialogue is to find ways to interest people in it, and perhaps the best strategy is to have a sincere interest in the other and his or her good.

---

29. Congregation for the Doctrine of the Faith, "*Dominus Iesus*," 2; Dupuis, *Toward a Christian Theology*, 363. Cf. Benedict XVI, "On The Occasion of Christmas Greetings"; Dupuis, *Toward a Christian Theology*, 359–60; Pontifical Council for Interreligious Dialogue, "Dialogue and Proclamation," 77, 82.

30. Francis, "*Evangelii gaudium*," 255.

31. Rahner, *Foundations of Christian Faith*, 22.

32. Francis, "*Evangelii gaudium*," 257. Cf. Acts 17:22–33.

Rules for Effective Dialogue

In order to set the stage for interreligious dialogue, it may be helpful to outline some preliminary rules or criteria. The work of David Tracy will prove exceptionally helpful for establishing these rules for effective interreligious dialogue. For conversation to do the work of horizon expansion, it cannot be left to arbitrary happenstance or unrestrained caprice. For Tracy, conversation must adhere to specific rules in order to generate new insights, understandings and attitudes. For an initial call to order, Tracy writes that "dialogue itself is first a practice (and a difficult one) before theories on dialogue or conclusions on the results of dialogue are forthcoming."[33] This is to say that, in the case of conversation, theory cannot precede praxis; rather praxis itself constructs the theory. Theories about interreligious dialogue are generated best in the fallow of actual dialogues between religious others. Let us now turn to the five specific rules Tracy develops with the goal of authentic conversation in mind.[34]

(1) First, conversation "demands the intellectual, moral, and, at the limit, religious ability to struggle to hear another and to respond."[35] This leading trait could be described as an attitude of openness and an ability to listen well. This is a struggling listening—a kind of listening that is neither presumptive nor self-assuring, but one that humbly allows one's personal horizons to be pulled and stretched in every act of listening. If I cannot enter conversation with this listening and attentive disposition, I cannot engage in authentic conversation with another unique person. Upon a first hearing, this may seem to be stating the obvious, but how often do we find ourselves in conversation even with close friends or family where our interlocutors are not listening to us truly, but rather become obsessed with what they have to say and hearing themselves speak! What violence is done to personal dignity when I dominate conversation with the hope of making some miserable point, when I refuse to listen or perhaps have never begun to learn the fine art of listening. So, step one cannot be stressed enough: listen, listen, listen . . . and listen again.

(2) Second, along with a disposition of openness, I, as a conversation partner, must "recognize the other *as* other, the different *as* different" and so "acknowledge that other world of meaning as, in some manner,

---

33. Tracy, *Dialogue with the Other*, 76.
34. Also see Wallenfang, 'Figures and Forms of Ultimacy.'
35. Tracy, *Dialogue with the Other*, 4.

a possible option for myself."[36] In order to maintain a disposition of openness in conversation, and to view conversation as a worthwhile expenditure of time and energy, I must maintain the possibility of having my mind and heart change, in a word, *meta-noia*. The possibility of further personal conversion is part and parcel of the possibility of having my theological imagination expanded through an uncanny and unpredictable encounter with another person.

(3) Third, in order for conversation to be genuine, the *question* must assume the place of primacy, itself controlling conversation according to the willingness of the interlocutors to follow the question wherever it may lead: "we learn to play the game of conversation when we allow questioning to take over. We learn when we allow the question to impose its logic, its demands, and ultimately its own rhythm upon us."[37] Rather than the question serving as an ally for one's self-determining will to power, both interlocutors must submit themselves to being tamed and mastered by the autonomous neutrality and anonymity of the question.

(4) Fourth, conversation must abide by general criteria of rationality and intelligibility in order to proffer a common ground whereby interlocutors can have any hope of making sense of one another. In particular, conversation must adhere to "the demands of reason, including the proper demands of metaphysical and transcendental reflection."[38] In so doing, an open space marked by the intelligible coordinates of language will be cleared. For conversation to be coherent, intelligible and meaningful, it must be tethered to a consistent logic, or better, *logos*. If there is no central logical anchor for conversation, then there would be no hope of mutual sense-making. Practically speaking, this means that certain rules for conversation, agreeable to both parties, must be made explicit. For example, both parties must agree to make explicit their respective employment of various forms of discourse—whether metaphoric, symbolic, poetic, scientific, etc., in order to arrive at precision and adequacy in meaning, truth and understanding.

(5) Fifth and above all, for Tracy, the task of authentic conversation is accomplished inasmuch as both parties risk themselves entirely in the play of conversation. "Dialogue demands the intellectual, moral,

---

36. Tracy, *Dialogue with the Other*, 41.

37. Tracy, *Plurality and Ambiguity*, 18.

38. Tracy, *Dialogue with the Other*, 46. Cf. Tracy, *Plurality and Ambiguity*, 19; Tracy and Cobb, *Talking About God*, 3, 7.

and, at the limit, religious ability to struggle to hear another and to respond" insofar as one is willing to put everything at risk.[39] To hazard oneself is to enter into the gauntlet we call conversation. This means that one must be willing to risk one's current pre-understandings and beliefs in each and every dialogical encounter. Practically speaking, the way in which one puts everything at risk in conversation is identified by Tracy as the analogical imagination. An analogical imagination "suggests a willingness to enter the conversation, that unveiling place where one is willing to risk all of one's present self-understanding by facing the claims to attention of the other."[40] With such a brave outlook, "differences need not become dialectical oppositions but can become analogies, that is, similarities-in-difference."[41] To recognize similarities-in-difference through the course of conversation, one identifies those commonalities between interlocutors that in turn unmask unwarranted biases and presuppositions on the part of both parties. For example, when it comes to religious convictions, all reasonable persons must admit their particular social conditioning and limitedness in their religious formation. Likewise, it is essential to recognize and discuss the role of testimony in each and every assertion of knowledge, especially that of alleged religious experience and knowledge. By naming such processes and factors that underlie any claim to (religious) truth whatsoever, conversation partners are better able to put their personal claims at arm's reach in order to open greater space for the possibility of being transformed by one other. It is decisive that conversation partners first acknowledge the role of ambiguity, language, unconscious factors, and the ambiguous otherness even within themselves in order to realize the importance of exercising an analogical imagination.[42] Tracy insists that the road to mutual understanding is traversed only through the employment of analogies—analogies that allow one to relate the narratives of another to one's own personal experiences, without reducing the other to the same. It is an analogical imagination that does not evade conflicting interpretations in conversation, but boldly maintains the hope that, through resistance and conversion, conversation may bear lasting fruit.

39. Tracy, *Dialogue with the Other*, 4, 95.
40. Tracy, *Plurality and Ambiguity*, 93.
41. Tracy, *Dialogue with the Other*, 30.
42. Tracy, *Dialogue with the Other*, 2–3.

David Tracy's pedagogy on the art of conversation offers a valuable hermeneutic toolbox from which to draw. By suggesting that within every I–Thou encounter we are introduced to some new dimension of reality, Tracy demonstrates the great potential within the prospect of sincere dialogues—dialogues that have the power for turning war not into superficial untalkative peace but into the ongoing labor of conversation.[43] Conversation entails conflict, no doubt, but by maintaining criteria of adequacy and appropriateness, one likewise maintains the hope of progress, enrichment and transformation. In the spirit of William James, Tracy recommends that when "life feels like a fight . . . why not be the Happy Warrior willing to listen to all, struggle with and for all, help all to hear other voices than the self?"[44] After all, as Tracy insists, "if any human discourse gives true testimony to Ultimate Reality, it must necessarily prove uncontrollable and unmasterable."[45] Such is the nature of interreligious and interdenominational dialogues: contests of non-competition wherein interlocutors give themselves over to the play of their conversation, itself led by the priority of the question.

Let the Dialogue Begin

This book features essays that participate in dialogue at the intersection of diverse religious traditions. The authors were asked to compose an exercise in interreligious dialogue with reference to Catholic magisterial teaching on interreligious dialogue. Catholic teaching was to serve as at least one of the conversation pieces within each essay. Scholars wrote out of their respective areas of expertise and aimed at contributing something new to the field of comparative theology. The book is divided into four sections based on the scope of the respective essays.

The first section, entitled "Catholic Approaches to Interreligious Dialogue," features the essays of three Catholic theologians who aim to calibrate a foundational methodology for going about this dialogue. John Cavadini leads off the effort with a provocative idea: "The Saints as Locus of Interreligious Dialogue." By "saints" he means the holy ones of any religious tradition. In his "proposal for a proposal" he suggests that in attending to the paradigmatic patterns of their leading adherents, religious traditions will bring more concrete and embodied material around which to converse at the table of comparative theology. Instead of talking only at the level of

43. Cf. Tracy, *Plurality and Ambiguity*, 112; Tracy, *Dialogue with the Other*, 14.

44. Tracy, *Dialogue with the Other*, 29.

45. Tracy, *Plurality and Ambiguity*, 109.

abstraction and theory, which may amount to one rival Gnosticism against another, Cavadini contends that by furnishing the evidence of faith in the form of incarnate testimony, dialogue partners will make more headway toward conciliation, mutual inspiration, and clear understanding of one another's respective traditions.[46] He employs an analysis of the saint primarily within the Catholic tradition through the lenses of Saints Thomas Aquinas and John Paul II, Pope Emeritus Benedict XVI, and the existentialism of Gabriel Marcel. Because soteriology is bound to the moral life of a human being, common ground can be found among diverse religious traditions in terms of universal moral virtue. For example, Marcel relates the meaning of belonging to and being disposable before the other. This may be a universal criterion of holiness: to be available and at the service of the other who faces me. Is this not the quintessential character of the saint? Altogether, Cavadini resets the typical optic of comparative theology by turning our attention to what holiness appears and sounds to be in the flesh.

Francesca Aran Murphy, with special reference to the groundbreaking conciliar texts, *Nostra aetate* and *Dignitatis humanae*, reminds us of the soberness of what the texts say and do not say. This soberness helps to ground interreligious dialogue in truth rather than in superficial platitudes that do not discern properly the philosophical and theological distinctions among religions. In her essay, "Not Altogether Wrong: Vatican II on Non-Christian Religions," Murphy affirms the unity of the one human family in spite of our stratified religious diversity. At the same time, she underscores the fact that *Nostra aetate* does not endorse outright high degrees of theological veracity within non-Christian religious traditions, nor does it disparage them either. Above all, she claims, the purpose of this document is a moral one: to foster greater respect for people of non-Christian religions. To round out her essay, Murphy reflects on the lasting influence of John Courtney Murray on *Dignitatis humanae* and its promotion of religious freedom—a freedom that Murphy describes as more comprehensive than pure choice but rather a positive freedom imbued with a teleological concept of the good as revealed to conscience through natural law and divine law. In the end, Murphy is careful to draw the distinction between respect for non-Christian religions and a blanket indifferentism that would regard all religions as equally valid as to their doctrines and practices in the name of an undiscerning political correctness that only serves to relativize the non-relativity of objective truth. Especially within the context of Catholic schools and colleges, this distinction remains intrinsic to the identity and mission of the Catholic Church.

---

46. See Francis, "*Gaudete et exsultate*," 35–46.

Combining two unlikely interlocutors, Thomas Aquinas and Paul Knitter, within his essay, "Virtuous Interreligious Dialogue as Authentic Evangelization," Andrew Kim proffers a helpful trajectory for interreligious dialogue as informed by the four cardinal virtues paired with four of Knitter's models of interreligious understanding. Corroborating Murphy's distinction between a positive teleological freedom on the one hand and a negative freedom of choice on the other, Kim nods to Servais Pinckaers's classic juxtaposition between a freedom for excellence and a freedom of indifference in order to set an appropriate standard for purposeful interreligious dialogue. Kim does this all the while in conversation with Pope Francis's treatment of interreligious dialogue in *Evangelii gaudium*. Kim shows how Francis roots the task of interreligious dialogue not only in the rationality of the cardinal virtues but also, and moreover, in the fidelity of the theological virtues tethered to a morality of happiness. The desire for friendship with God and friendship with one's neighbor—and, yes, even the stranger—urges the performance of interreligious dialogue not so much as a means to an end but as a virtuous end in itself. In this way Kim invites us to consider, along with Francis, interreligious dialogue as an indispensable element within the universal human vocation to love.

No stranger to the theological primacy of love, Pope Benedict XVI serves as the central figure in Cyril O'Regan's essay, "The Theology of Religions of Benedict XVI." O'Regan narrows the lens of his analysis to the essays of Benedict (Joseph Ratzinger) between the years 1990–2000 dedicated to the topic of interreligious dialogue. These essays are housed primarily in his two anthologies, *Truth and Tolerance: Christian Belief and World Religions* (2003) and *Many Religions—One Covenant: Israel, the Church, and the World* (1998). O'Regan sheds light on Benedict's careful negotiation between an inclusivist soteriology, as developed by the Ressourcement theologians (Daniélou, de Lubac, von Balthasar, et al.) and essentially espoused in the teachings of Vatican II, and a rejection of pluralist soteriology as suggested by Hick, Knitter and Panikkar (in its strong forms), as well as that of Jacques Dupuis and his consorts (in its mitigated and qualified forms). O'Regan draws further conclusions on the relationship between Benedict's writings as a theologian and his dominant role in crafting the 2000 CDF document, *Dominus Iesus*, and the ancillary CDF Notifications on the work of Dupuis. Altogether, O'Regan is more than sympathetic with the theological positions of Benedict and observes the delicate distinction between dialogue and proclamation that is not to be dissolved into the insipid neutrality of relativism (pluralism) on the one hand or the hostile exclusivity of fundamentalism (sectarianism) on the other. O'Regan masterfully delineates between the hegemonic pluralist tendencies in contemporary theology of religions and the patient possibility of inclusivist Christian soteriology that is Ecclesiocentric to the degree that it is Christocentric and Pneumatocentric.

Having set the stage for necessary and responsible interreligious dialogue today, the second section of the book presses ahead into dialogues between Judaism and Christianity. Given the checkered and bloody history between these two communities of faith, and their common genealogy, it is fitting, from a Christian standpoint, to begin the dialogue here. In the first of these family of essays, "Jewish–Christian Dialogue as Re-Evangelization," Chris Seeman treats the post-conciliar magisterial output of the Church on this precarious dialogue—especially fragile as it emerges out of the unspeakable twentieth-century crime of humanity against humanity, the Holocaust. Seeman highlights the Church's validation of the covenantal autonomy of the Jewish people in relation to the Christian belief of a new covenant between YHWH and humanity through Jesus as the Messiah (Christ), as well as the Church's public pledge against antisemitism or anti-Judaism. Similar to Kim's use of Knitter's models of interreligious understanding, Seeman elects the rules of formation as defined by Katharina von Kellenbach to unmask lingering attitudes of supersessionism and religious superiority within Christianity. Seeman clarifies the aim of his essay: "to identify where the Church has not yet fully allowed its teaching to penetrate its practice, and to suggest how the process might be expedited." To this end Seeman identifies three foundational desiderata for achieving this essential bridge between theory and practice: (1) general education, (2) homiletic/liturgical reform, and (3) catechetical/intellectual formation. In sum, Seeman provides practical tools for transfiguring unwarranted attitudes about Judaism within Christianity from the pews to the parliament.

Richard Cohen's essay, "Judaism and Christianity's 'Judaism': Ending Antisemitism," features the first non-Catholic voice in the book. Here is where a genuine interreligious dialogue really begins. For if the book was comprised of only Catholic theologians talking about interreligious dialogue from only a Catholic perspective, it never would get off the ground as an authentic dialogue between religious others. Speaking directly and candidly from the Jewish context, Cohen leverages a sincere counterpoint to the covert complacency and hidden hubris of interreligious dialogue initiated and marshaled by Christians alone. His essay registers the dynamic of uncanniness that should arise and intrude within every transparent dialogue between others. Cohen faces the real and haunting history of antisemitism over the centuries of Christianity and asks, why? By raising this fundamental question and mindfulness of the guilty conscience of Christianity, Cohen deconstructs the common misrepresentations of Judaism within Christianity. Further, he illuminates the Jewish new testament counterpart to the new testament of Christianity: the Talmud. The Christian reader is struck by the ignorant negligence we have as Christians toward the treasury of rabbinic interpretation redacted in the Talmud. Even more, Cohen chides Christianity for colluding with political powers (as ancient as the Roman Empire) in forging a Christendom that systematically persecutes Jews for being Jewish. Cohen effectively creates the necessary space for Christians to understand Judaism not as the "Judaism" of Christianity but as the Judaism of the Jews. He supplies a flagrant *memoria* that should be in force in every truly interreligious dialogue: let the other be other and refuse to reduce the other to more of the same.

As a kind of implicit rejoinder to Cohen's admonition toward a hermeneutic retrieval of the Jewish genius at the heart of the religious movement called Christianity, Donald Wallenfang suggests a new theological *ressourcement* for Christian theology today in his essay "Dialectical Truth between Augustine and Pelagius: Levians and the Challenge of Responsibility to Superabundant Grace." Perhaps the *Nouvelle Théologie* of Henri de Lubac, Hans Urs von Balthasar, Jean Daniélou, Joseph Ratzinger and company did not go far back enough: to the origins of Christianity that is not so much the early Church Fathers, nor even Saint Paul and the Apostles, but Jesus the Jewish rabbi from Nazareth. Wallenfang implies that if Christianity is not an expressly Jewish Christianity, then it is not worthy of the name inasmuch as it neglects its fundamental identity as a reform movement of Judaism—a Judaism that was never meant to be cast off like a snake shedding its own crustaceous skin. We need only recall the early Marcionite heresy (circa midsecond century) to back this claim. To make his case, Wallenfang evokes the phenomenology of responsibility developed by Jewish philosopher, Emmanuel Levinas, in order to revisit the theological caricature between Augustinian grace on the one hand and Pelagian self-made virtue on the other. Wallenfang alleges, along with Levinas, that the Christian concept of grace is a dangerous one: in effect, it often can excuse its blissful recipient of mature responsibility for the other. If guaranteed absolution waits around the corner of every foul misdeed, why not? Wallenfang invites a Levinasian corrective to the theological notion of superabundant grace by pairing it with superabundant responsibility that should be its proper response.

The third section of the book moves on to another careful dialogue, especially in light of several recent global terrorist movements surfacing from various species of Islamic fundamentalism (and of course every religious tradition has its own): that between Islam and Christianity. Yet within this section two responsible scholars working at the intersection of this dialogue witness to the "hope against hope" (Rom 4:18) for conciliation and collaboration between these two Abrahamic faiths that each stem from the original

Abrahamic prototype and archetype, namely, Judaism. In his essay, entitled "Islamic Christology and Muslim–Christian Dialogue," Gabriel Said Reynolds begins with the provocative question of whether or not Muslims and Christians worship the same God, and ultimately suggests that Muslims and Christians "are unified, and not divided, by theology." However, Reynolds is quick to introduce a Christological turn that inevitably will show divergence in belief between Islam and Christianity concerning the identity of Jesus. He proceeds to unearth the references to Jesus throughout the Qurʾan as a lucid demonstration of comparative theology. Reynold's comparative analysis puts in relief the important differences between (perhaps what could be called) Christology (for Christianity) and Jesusology (for Islam). He contrasts the "Muhammadan" Jesus of the Qurʾan with the "Christian" Jesus of the Gospels. Rather than endorse the Küngian hypothesis that the Qurʾan grants access to a more accurate "primitive" low Christology in which high Christology is divested of its alleged theological innovation, Reynolds draws attention to the recasting of Jesus by Muhammad according to his own strictly monotheistic theological agenda in Arabia. Reynolds concludes his study by saying that "dialogue is as much about acknowledging difference as it is about seeking commonality."

Martino Diez's essay, "The Translation of the Psalms by Mohammad al-Sadeq Hussein and Serge de Beaurecueil," showcases the fertile potential of interreligious collaboration in recounting the history behind the 1961 critical translation of the Book of Psalms into Arabic by the teamwork of a Muslim intellectual (Hussein) and a French Dominican (Beaurecueil). Though the earliest fragment of the Hebrew Scriptures in Arabic translation dates back to the eighth-century text of Psalm 77, and one of the most ancient Arabic Bibles extant is the Mount Sinai Arabic Codex 151 of the ninth century, the mid-twentieth-century translation of the Cairo publishing house, Dār as-Salām, is far from the status of an insignificant outlier in the history of Arabic biblical translation. As Diez points out, one of the most interesting traits of this 1961 translation was its interreligious origin. One of his main intents in the essay is "to illustrate how dialogue and proclamation often share a common concrete *practice*, i.e., translation." By turning our attention to the important practice of translation, Diez makes explicit a sine qua non of both interreligious dialogue and evangelization: translating doctrines and practices from one cultural milieu into another through the course of conversation. In other words, every interreligious dialogue will involve translation of some kind. By underscoring the theological inclusiveness and versatility of this particular translation of the Book of Psalms, especially for Islamic–Christian dialogue, Diez recapitulates the powerful productivity of interreligious dialogue for holistic cultural development and human flourishing.

Following its all-too-brief turn to Muslim–Christian dialogue, the book makes another all-too-brief turn to Hindu–Christian and Buddhist–Christian dialogues. An admitted shortcoming of this volume is its dearth of voices representative of non-Christian religions. However, this insufficiency is excused only by virtue of the sincerity and conviction of the Jewish (Cohen) and Hindu (Sarma) witnesses who speak herein. Deepak Sarma, in his essay "Madhva *Aetate*," relays the aporia for some forms of interreligious dialogue and exhibits one such case: the Madhva–Christian stalemate. Yet this dialogical standstill remains a dialogue, nevertheless, inasmuch as we admit the accessibility issues embroiled between distinct religious traditions. With his background in the philosophy of religion, and especially in issues of religious epistemology, Sarma accompanies us to those intercultural situations in which translation seems to be near impossible. Not only in mild protest against the social injustices committed at the hands of Christian colonizers, fueled by attitudes of religious superiority and rash prejudice, Sarma contests that at least some forms of Hinduism (such as Madhva Hinduism) resist the very idea of interreligious dialogue because they are planted firmly within a closed exclusive commentarial framework that locks-in a select and privileged insider-epistemology according to its own indigenous setting. In other words, such a tradition refuses to be indexed as just another tradition among traditions within generic and sterilizing interreligious dialogue. Madhva Hinduism is sui generis and, because of its irreducible inimitable doctrines and practices, deflects the attempt to unfold itself in the direction of another tradition only to forfeit its cohesion of identity and inherent logic of belief. Long before the stance of agreeing to disagree, the Madhva school of Vedanta sits at the threshold of interreligious dialogue with its back turned as its faithful way of dialogue. From this perspective, a Catholic magisterial text such as *Nostra aetate* betrays the reductionistic tendency within every self-enclosed religious tradition: to situate the identity of the religious other according to its own. Sarma concludes by admitting the impossibility of bypassing the Madhva restrictions according to its own self-understanding, thereby making an equitable interreligious dialogue an oxymoronic attempt at reducing religious difference to the point of deconstructing the inbuilt integrity and particularity of a distinct religious tradition. In light of Sarma's argument, perhaps some dialogues will have to take place primarily as listening to the otherness of the other without translating or reducing this otherness into more words, expressions, signs and symbols of the same.

Robert Gimello, a seasoned scholar of Buddhist–Christian dialogue, submits the final essay of the volume. Gimello supplies an erudite account of this dialogue by attending to primary texts and iconography of Buddhism—in particular, the Mahayana Buddhist tradition that exhibits a proclivity for religious expression in the form of manifestation.[47] Gimello leads with the question, "Is it possible to combine genuine respect for non-Christian religions like Buddhism, even admiration of them, with acceptance of the claim, so forcefully asserted in *Dominus Iesus*, that 'followers of other religions,' recipients though they may be of divine grace, are 'objectively speaking . . . in a gravely deficient situation in comparison with those who, in the Church, have the fullness of the means of salvation'" (22)? Ultimately answering this question in the affirmative, Gimello investigates the religious paradigm at the heart of Christianity—namely, the manifestation and proclamation of divine transcendence in and through creaturely immanence—within the reciprocal kataphatic and apophatic oscillations of Buddhist belief and practice. Gimello's research bumps up against definite kataphatic nominations and descriptions of Buddhism's inherent apophatic (a-)theology. The unconditioned as such is revealed as a trinity of personified avatars, or bodhisattvas (perhaps even ontologically stable entities or processions of the unconditioned) for Mahayana Buddhism. Gimello wonders if the recurrent discovery of contradictions within itself—especially those between denominated immanent transcendence and de-nominated super-transcendent transcendence—might serve as a kind of *Logos spermatikos* vis-à-vis Christianity, and at least provoke a bond of sympathy between Buddhists and Christians. In the end, Gimello suggests that even if the dialectical tendencies within Buddhism are not codified in doctrinal stability, at the very least they suggest a real unquenchable anthropological need for personal encounter with a personal transcendent divinity become immanent.

The real beauty of this book is the dialogue that will be ignited between the reader and these texts. The editors do not wish to offer rebuttals here to the various arguments leveraged throughout the book. Instead we leave that to you, the reader, as you wrestle with what is written here in relation to your own personal faith, informed as it is with sound reasons. After all, a primary aim of these essays is to provoke a new interreligious dialogue for the reader: a dialogue between the reader and the text and, more essentially, between the reader and the author of each essay. The nature of authentic dialogue is that it is never finished, ever open to further encounters with the gift of the other, the gift of truth, and the gift of joy. This is why the

47. See Wallenfang, "Face Off for Interreligious Dialogue," 114.

"heavy lifting" of dialogue is worth it. We form one humanity as brothers and sisters across our rich diversity of cultures and religious traditions. As Hans Urs von Balthasar asserted, "truth is symphonic," and this symphony of truth engenders a trust and a joy that "no cares could destroy."[48]

> For the sake of the joy that lay before him he endured the cross, despising its shame, and has taken his seat at the right of the throne of God.
>
> Hebrews 12:2b

Ex voto suscepto,
John C. Cavadini and Donald Wallenfang

Bibliography

Balthasar, Hans Urs von. *Truth Is Symphonic: Aspects of Christian Pluralism.* Translated by Graham Harrison. San Francisco: Ignatius, 1987.

Benedict XVI. "On The Occasion of Christmas Greetings to the Roman Curia." December 21, 2010. http://w2.vatican.va/content/benedict-xvi/en/speeches/2012/december/documents/hf_ben-xvi_spe_20121221_auguri-curia.html.

———. "*Verbum Domini.*" September 30, 2010. http://w2.vatican.va/content/benedict-xvi/en/apost_exhortations/documents/hf_ben-xvi_exh_20100930_verbum-domini.html.

Cavadini, John C. "The Anatomy of Wonder: An Augustinian Taxonomy." *Augustinian Studies* 42.2 (2011) 153–72.

———, ed. *Explorations in the Theology of Benedict XVI.* Notre Dame, IN: University of Notre Dame Press, 2012.

Cavadini, John C., and Donald Wallenfang, eds. *Pope Francis and the Event of Encounter.* Eugene, OR: Pickwick, 2018.

Congregation for the Doctrine of the Faith. "*Dominus Iesus.*" August 6, 2000. http://www.vatican.va/roman_curia/congregations/cfaith/documents/rc_con_cfaith_doc_20000806_dominus-iesus_en.html.

Coogan, Michael D., ed. *Eastern Religions: Origins, Beliefs, Practices, Holy Texts, Sacred Places.* New York: Oxford University Press, 2005.

Cornille, Catherine. "Vatican II and Other Religions: A Milestone?" May 13, 2013, Stanford University, Palo Alto, CA. YouTube video, 1:42:36. May 21, 2013. https://www.youtube.com/watch?v=WCHazdNbNg0.

Dupuis, Jacques. *Toward a Christian Theology of Religious Pluralism.* Maryknoll, NY: Orbis, 2001.

Flannery, Austin, ed. *The Basic Sixteen Documents of Vatican Council II: Constitutions, Decrees, Declarations.* Northport, NY: Costello, 1996.

---

48. See von Balthasar, *Truth Is Symphonic,* and Jan Struther's 1931 hymn, "Lord of All Hopefulness."

Francis. "*Gaudete et exsultate*." March 19, 2018. http://w2.vatican.va/content/francesco/en/apost_exhortations/documents/papa-francesco_esortazione-ap_20180319_gaudete-et-exsultate.html.

Gioia, Francesco, ed. *Interreligious Dialogue: The Official Teaching of the Catholic Church (1963–1995)*. Boston: Pauline, 1997.

International Theological Commission. "Christianity and the World Religions." 1997. http://www.vatican.va/roman_curia/congregations/cfaith/cti_documents/rc_cti_1997_cristianesimo-religioni_en.html.

John Paul II. *Catechism of the Catholic Church*. New York: Doubleday, 1995.

———. "*Fides et ratio*." September 14, 1998. http://w2.vatican.va/content/john-paul-ii/en/encyclicals/documents/hf_jp-ii_enc_14091998_fides-et-ratio.html.

———. "*Veritatis splendor*." August 6, 1993. http://w2.vatican.va/content/john-paul-ii/en/encyclicals/documents/hf_jp-ii_enc_06081993_veritatis-splendor.html.

Kim, Andrew. *An Introduction to Catholic Ethics Since Vatican II*. New York: Cambridge University Press, 2015.

Knitter, Paul F. *Introducing Theologies of Religions*. Maryknoll, NY: Orbis, 2016.

Küng, Hans. *Islam: Past, Present and Future*. Translated by John Bowden. Oxford: Oneworld, 2007.

Newman, John Henry. *Apologia pro vita sua*. New York: Longmans, Green & Co., 1890.

Oakes, Edward T. "Resolving the Relativity Paradox." In *Explorations in the Theology of Benedict XVI*, edited by John C. Cavadini, 87–113. Notre Dame, IN: University of Notre Dame Press, 2012.

Pius IX. "Dogmatic Constitution on the Catholic Faith." https://www.ewtn.com/library/councils/v1.htm.

———. "First Dogmatic Constitution on the Church of Christ." https://www.ewtn.com/library/councils/v1.htm.

———. "Profession of Faith." https://www.ewtn.com/library/councils/v1.htm.

Pontifical Council for Interreligious Dialogue. "Dialogue and Proclamation: Reflections and Orientations on Interreligious Dialogue and the Proclamation of the Gospel of Jesus Christ." May 19, 1991. http://www.vatican.va/roman_curia/pontifical_councils/interelg/documents/rc_pc_interelg_doc_19051991_dialogue-and-proclamatio_en.html.

Rahner, Karl. *Foundations of Christian Faith: An Introduction to the Idea of Christianity*. Translated by William V. Dych. New York: Crossroad, 2005.

Ratzinger, Joseph. *Truth and Tolerance: Christian Belief and World Religions*. Translated by Henry Taylor. San Francisco: Ignatius, 2005.

Sacks, Jonathan. *Not In God's Name: Confronting Religious Violence*. New York: Schocken, 2015.

Secretariat for Non-Christians (Pontifical Council for Interreligious Dialogue). "The Attitude of the Church Towards the Followers of Other Religions: Reflections and Orientations on Dialogue and Mission." 1984. http://www.vatican.va/roman_curia/pontifical_councils/interelg/documents/rc_pc_interelg_doc_19840610_dialogo-missione_po.html.

Simms, Eva-Maria. "The Infant's Experience of the World: Stern, Merleau-Ponty, and the Phenomenology of the Preverbal Self." *The Humanistic Psychologist* 21.1 (1993) 26–40.

Stern, Daniel. *The Interpersonal World of the Infant: A View from Psychoanalysis and Developmental Psychology*. New York: Basic, 1985.

Tracy, David. *The Analogical Imagination: Christian Theology and the Culture of Pluralism*. New York: Crossroad, 1981.

————. *Blessed Rage for Order: The New Pluralism in Theology*. Chicago: University of Chicago Press, 1996.

————. *Dialogue with the Other: The Inter-religious Dialogue*. Louvain: Peeters, 1990.

————. *On Naming the Present: God, Hermeneutics, and Church*. Maryknoll, NY: Orbis, 1994.

————. *Plurality and Ambiguity: Hermeneutics, Religion, Hope*. Chicago: University of Chicago Press, 1987.

Tracy, David, and John B. Cobb, Jr. *Talking About God: Doing Theology in the Context of Modern Pluralism*. New York: Seabury, 1983.

Vatican II. "*Ad gentes*." December 7, 1965. http://www.vatican.va/archive/hist_councils/ii_vatican_council/documents/vat-ii_decree_19651207_ad-gentes_en.html.

————. "*Gaudium et spes*." December 7, 1965.

http://www.vatican.va/archive/hist_councils/ii_vatican_council/documents/vat-ii_const_19651207_gaudium-et-spes_en.html.

————. "*Lumen gentium*." November 21, 1964. http://www.vatican.va/archive/hist_councils/ii_vatican_council/documents/vat-ii_const_19641121_lumen-gentium_en.html.

————. "*Nostra aetate*." October 28, 1965. http://www.vatican.va/archive/hist_councils/ii_vatican_council/documents/vat-ii_decl_19651028_nostra-aetate_en.html.

Wallenfang, Donald. "Face Off for Interreligious Dialogue: A Theology of Childhood in Jean-Luc Marion versus a Theology of Adulthood in Emmanuel Levinas." *Listening: Journal of Communication Ethics, Religion, and Culture* 50.2 (2015) 106–16.

————. "Figures and Forms of Ultimacy: Manifestation and Proclamation as Paradigms of the Sacred." *The International Journal of Religion in Spirituality and Society* 1.3 (2011) 109–14.

Catholic Approaches
to Interreligious Dialogue

CHAPTER I

The Saints as Locus
of Interreligious Dialogue

—John C. Cavadini

I n this essay I would like to make a proposal which is really a proposal
for a proposal. An actual proposal would have to be more concrete than
what I am offering here. Despite its very modest ambition, as not an actual
proposal but a proposal for a proposal, I still would like to run it up the
proverbial flagpole and see if anyone might, if not salute, at least consider
shifting their eyes in that direction however momentarily. So here it goes: I
would like to propose the lives of the saints as a potential locus for interreligious study and dialogue, maybe something like "hagiographical reasoning"
study groups on the analogy of the "scriptural reasoning" study groups that
are familiar to many. I realize that the word "saint" is contested, as would
be much of the vocabulary associated with sanctity, holiness and virtue, but
the same is true for "scripture" and that has not stopped scriptural reasoning
groups from being formed and flourishing. In fact, I think a certain loose-
ness of speech is not only allowable here but desirable. The word "saint," for
one thing, is a word of enormous potential appeal to the imagination. As
an undergraduate I was attracted to a course whose title intrigued me: "The
Buddha and the Saints." What? I thought, other religions have *saints*? Even
as a nineteen-year old I understood that the word "saints" in this context
did not mean, someone who had made his or her way through the Catholic
cursus honorum of servant of God, beatification and canonization with fully
certified miracles deluxe along the way. But it was that word that made me
want to take the course. A scheduling conflict precluded my actually enroll-
ing but the title of the course, as you can see, has, like the sacraments of
baptism and confirmation, *mutatis mutandis*, left a permanent mark on my
imagination. I believe that anything with serious power to inspire and move

the imagination also has the potential to unify in very concrete ways, even if the concept is, in a way, principally an appeal to the imagination rather than a term strictly defined according to a common agreement.

Nor do we need more than a rough and ready characterization of what a "saint" might be for the purposes of generating a proposal. Any saint worth their salt is not dependent upon definitions or precise theological distinctions to qualify him or her for admiration by people both learned and unlearned. The saints are not elitist. Far from it. Rather than restrict the term too technically, I would prefer to let it float as a kind of temptation to the imagination, and therefore a temptation to invest in the word a plenitude of meaning and a desire for a closer study.

But, lest this seem completely haphazard, towards the construction of a rough and ready understanding of what a "saint" might be in an eventual proposal, I will take a page from the process the Catholic Church uses in considering cases for beatification and canonization, namely, the category of heroic virtue. This is not necessarily a *sufficient* description of a saint, but it seems like a bare minimum that the saint be someone whose life is characterized by heroic virtue. Even if this is not a cross-cultural category, I believe the reality it refers to is cross-culturally visible and draws admiration and even devotion which can transcend cultural and religious boundaries. Beyond that, I would like to offer three ways of thematizing my proposal from a Catholic point of view. The first is Thomist, represented by Saint John Paul II; the second is Augustinian, represented by Pope Benedict XVI; and the third is existentialist, represented by Gabriel Marcel.

The Saint according to Saints Thomas Aquinas and John Paul II

First, then: in his great encyclical *Veritatis splendor,* Saint John Paul II takes up the topic of the natural moral law. In asking the question, "'*What must I do? How do I distinguish good from evil?*'" he says that "the answer is only possible thanks to the splendor of truth which shines forth deep within the human spirit."[1] Even though, "as a result of that mysterious original sin, committed at the prompting of Satan, the one who is a 'liar and the father of lies' (John 8:44)," obedience to this resplendent truth is "not always easy," and even though the very splendor of truth can itself be obscured because, under the dominion of sin, "the human capacity to know the truth is also darkened," nevertheless it is a hallmark of Catholic teaching that human nature has not been totally corrupted by sin. Thus, "no darkness of error or

---

1. John Paul II, *Veritatis splendor,* 2. Hereafter *VS.*

of sin can totally take away from man the light of God the Creator."[2] This means that no human being is totally cut off from the access to truth which belongs to them simply as part of their humanity: "The Church knows that the issue of morality is one which deeply touches every person; it involves all people, even those who do not know Christ and his Gospel or God himself. She knows that it is precisely *on the path of the moral life that the way of salvation is open to all.*"[3] John Paul cites Thomas Aquinas to further supplement his evocation of the natural law: "'the light of natural reason whereby we discern good from evil, which is the function of the natural law, is nothing else but an imprint on us of the divine light,'" an imprint which is imparted by virtue of our creation.[4]

A hallmark of the natural law is, therefore, that it points to and evokes a certain solidarity among human beings *as* human beings and, at least formally, antecedent to any culture. I say "at least formally" because human existence is irreducibly cultural, and yet that does not mean that culture gives an exhaustive account of the human. In this regard, John Paul notes, "It must certainly be admitted that man always exists in a particular culture, but it must also be admitted that man is not exhaustively defined by that same culture." If we believe that cultures can "progress" in any way—for example, from state-sponsored executions as a public spectacle to the abolition of the death penalty—then we are making a judgment on the basis of some measure that transcends a particular culture: "Moreover," John Paul continues, "the very progress of cultures demonstrates that there is something in man which transcends those cultures. This 'something' is precisely human nature: this nature is itself the measure of culture and the condition ensuring that man does not become the prisoner of any of his cultures, but asserts his personal dignity by living in accordance with the profound truth of his being."[5] Perhaps we could say that the picture of the natural law on offer here is one that is the reflection or the imprint of an idealized solidarity which is nevertheless not simply imaginary. This is what is meant when it is said that "*the natural law involves universality,*" meaning by "universality" something valid and transcending of particular cultures even though always embodied in particular cultural inflections. As John Paul puts it, evoking Thomas again, "In order to perfect himself in his specific order, the person must do good and avoid evil, be concerned for the transmission and pres-

2. John Paul II, *VS*, 1.

3. John Paul II, *VS*, 3.

4. Aquinas, *Summa theologiae*, 1–2.91.2, cited in John Paul II, *VS*, 42. See John Paul II, *VS*, 40, citing Thomas Aquinas, *In duo praecepta*, 2.129.

5. John Paul II, *VS*, 53.

ervation of life, refine and develop the riches of the material world, cultivate social life, seek truth, practice good and contemplate beauty."[6] It would be hard to think of a culture that does not try to embody all of these goods in one way or another.

It is important to note that the natural law, as construed in *Veritatis splendor,* has both positive and negative precepts and these are morally binding upon all human beings. This does not mean that there is no need "to seek out and to discover *the most adequate formulation* for universal and permanent moral norms in the light of different cultural contexts," but such would have the effect not of diluting them but of interpreting them in a given cultural context precisely so their validity shines out: the most adequate formulation would be that "most capable of ceaselessly expressing their historical relevance, of making them understood and of authentically interpreting their truth."[7] This is true above all of the positive precepts; for example, "it is always right and just, always and everywhere . . . to honor one's parents as they deserve," but the form this takes is culturally determined and the phrase "as they deserve" leaves a lot of wiggle room.[8] The feasibility of the positive precepts depends partly on circumstances. The negative precepts of the natural law, however, are different because they forbid a given action in all circumstances and always: "there are kinds of behavior which can never, in any situation, be a proper response—a response which is in conformity with the dignity of the person."[9] For example, it is never right to intentionally kill an innocent human being. People certainly argue over what these precepts might be, but for my purposes here I am not as interested in arguing about the specifics, but rather to point out that John Paul is at least saying that it would be hard to find someone who did not think that *something* qualifies as an action that is always morally wrong no matter what. Perhaps rape would be one such case. People are more likely to say, or at least imply, there is something wrong with a culture that valorizes rape, rather than to say that whether or not rape is wrong depends on your culture. And, even more to the point, it is possible to hinder someone from fulfilling the positive precepts of the moral law, but it is not possible to hinder someone from *not* doing certain things: "It is always possible that man, as the result of coercion or other circumstances, can be hindered from

6. John Paul II, *VS,* 51. See Thomas Aquinas, *Summa theologiae,* 1–2.94.2.

7. John Paul II, *VS,* 53.

8. John Paul II, *VS,* 52.

9. John Paul II, *VS,* 52.

doing certain good actions; but he can never be hindered from not doing certain actions, especially if he is prepared to die rather than to do evil."[10]

And thus natural law theory, as presented in this encyclical, and perhaps unexpectedly to some, opens itself up as a way of thematizing cross-cultural and interreligious admiration. In fact, perhaps we could say that cross-cultural admiration is one way of granting access to what "natural law" means in the first place. The possibility of heroic witness to the universal moral law by any human being is intrinsic to the theory. The heroic witness to human dignity is open to any human being simply as human. John Paul takes us through some biblical examples of such heroism to the point of death, and then notes that "the Church proposes the example of numerous Saints who bore witness to and defended moral truth even to the point of enduring martyrdom, or who preferred death to a single mortal sin."[11] The connection to human dignity is absolutely clear: "Martyrdom, accepted as an affirmation of the inviolability of the moral order, bears splendid witness both to the holiness of God's law and to the inviolability of the personal dignity of man, created in God's image and likeness."[12] Such heroic witness—"martyrdom" in the technical sense of "witness"—need not be to the point of death to qualify as heroic, though of course that is the most dramatic and final form.[13] Nor, of particular relevance here, does one have to be Catholic or Christian to qualify: "In this witness to the absoluteness of the moral good *Christians are not alone*: they are supported by the moral sense present in peoples and by the great religious and sapiential traditions of East and West, from which the interior and mysterious workings of God's Spirit are not absent."[14] John Paul cites, for example, the second-century apologist Justin Martyr's admiration for the brave witness of the Stoics to wisdom and to the "seed of the *Logos*," that is, the "seed of Reason," present in all peoples. Justin comments that "'we know that those who followed their doctrines met with hatred and were killed.'"[15] Is it really too much of a stretch to call such a person, from any religious tradition, loosely speaking a "saint?" At any rate, for the purposes of my proposal, I would like to restrict the word "saint" to someone whose martyrdom or heroic virtue, under the conditions John Paul outlines here, is undertaken *as* a member of a religious tradition and *in fidelity* to his or her formation in that tradition. It seems to me that

10. John Paul II, *VS*, 52.

11. John Paul II, *VS*, 91.

12. John Paul II, *VS*, 92.

13. See John Paul II, *VS*, 93.

14. John Paul II, *VS*, 94.

15. John Paul II, *VS*, 94, citing Justin Martyr, *Apologia* 2.2.

that is what we might legitimately, even if in a rough and ready way, call "holiness," and not just "virtue."

In invoking the word "holiness," I am not using the word to adjudicate holiness across religious traditions in a way that would make saints for other traditions, nor am I using the term to canonize anyone in the Catholic sense, for the Church or for anyone else. I am, once again, using the term because it is precise enough to invoke what natural law recognizes as the objective or public pursuit of goodness at a heroic level, when it is achieved in obedience or fidelity to one's religion. People whose lives are more or less defined by this pursuit can be and are found, living or dead, and their appeal can transcend their own culture and religion. Stories of such people are often put forward in an exemplary way by their religious tradition, and it can also be the case that people outside of the tradition have stories and memories of their own to add. Conceivably one could study such people together. Among other advantages of this approach, it has the advantage of *not* starting with doctrine. To admire someone does not necessarily mean that I accept their religion as my own or that I have become a relativist. But it is hard not to think about a religion differently, if I admire the heroic witness it inspired. Further, lives lived in and admired for their heroic virtue out of a commitment to religious teaching could be the best *interpretations* of religious doctrine possible, and thus a way to mutual understanding and respect and even affection for another's religious belief. In one of his sermons, St. Augustine, after a brief explanation of the Creed, tells his catechumens that they are not to write it down on paper, but rather on their hearts. The image of the heart inscribed with the Creed is, presents, among other things, the idea that the best interpretation of the Creed is a life lived in accordance with the Creed.[16]

The Saint according to Pope Benedict XVI

Moving on to the next pope, Benedict XVI also offers some reflections pertinent to our topic in his little collection, *Many Religions—One Covenant*, published under his own name before his election to the papacy.[17] The chapter on "The Dialogue of the Religions" takes up various possible modalities for interreligious dialogue, including what he calls "the pragmatic solution." Characterizing the pragmatic solution, as proposed by unnamed third parties, he says it means "all religions should give up the endless dispute about truth and recognize that their true essence, what they are all aiming at, is

16. See Augustine of Hippo, *On Christian Doctrine*.
17. Ratzinger, *Many Religions—One Covenant*.

found in orthopraxy."[18] Orthopraxy would mean, essentially, "the service we give to peace, justice and the protection of creation," and thus the religions "could all retain their customs and usages; all dispute would be superfluous, and yet they would be one in whatever the hour were to demand of them." The motto of this approach: "'By their fruits you shall know them.'"[19] The problem with such an approach, however, is that what will contribute to peace, justice and the protection of the environment are all matters of policy, of practical judgment, political expediency, etc. There would thus emerge a pluralism of paths which could not be resolved on religious grounds, "and if the wearying rational debate is cut short by a religiously motivated moralism that declares one path to be the only right one, religion is perverted into an ideological dictatorship, with a totalitarian passion that does not build peace but destroys it."[20] Benedict is careful to add that the refusal to turn religion into "political moralism" does not mean that education for peace, justice and protection of creation are not part of the proper concern of the religions, and in that sense, it is right to say, "By their fruits you shall know them."

This is not a rejection of the considerations from natural law that we have reviewed in John Paul's *Veritatis splendor*, but it is a warning not to allow them to be confused with a policy-based moralizing approach instead of a person-based virtue approach. When Benedict does turn to the latter approach, he appeals not to the natural law but, ironically, to the most distinctive feature of Christian revelation, the Incarnation, as a pivotal point of reflection. I take this as an Augustinian moment. Benedict notes a certain apophaticism attaching to the Incarnation, despite the fact that it teaches that "God becomes concrete, tangible in history." He goes on to explain that "this very God, become graspable, is [nevertheless] utterly mysterious. The humiliation he himself has chosen, his 'kenosis,' is in a new way, so to speak, the cloud of mystery in which he both conceals and reveals himself." This cloud of mystery is a clue for Benedict: "The Word, which the Incarnate and Crucified One is, always far surpasses human words; thus God's kenosis is the place where the religions can meet without claims of sovereignty."

Benedict shows how this directs our attention in particular to saints of poverty. This can give us a further clue to at least one kind of saint likely to be fruitful for interreligious study. Benedict comments that "Plato's Socrates . . . points us to the connection between truth and defenselessness, between truth and poverty. Socrates is credible because his commitment to 'God'

18. Ratzinger, *Many Religions—One Covenant*, 95.

19. Ratzinger, *Many Religions—One Covenant*, 96.

20. Ratzinger, *Many Religions—One Covenant*, 101–2.

brings him neither position nor possessions; on the contrary, it consigns him to poverty and ultimately to the role of an accused criminal." Socrates of course is the martyr of truth from classical Antiquity, thus connecting Benedict's discussion to the one in *Veritatis splendor*. But poverty adds another dimension, not necessarily connected with martyrdom narrowly speaking. "Poverty," Benedict concludes, "is the truly divine manifestation of truth: thus it can demand obedience without involving alienation."[21] This may explain why Saint Francis, for example, is one of the most universally admired of saints in any tradition and by people from many traditions. And perhaps why Mother Teresa of Calcutta got her own postage stamp (last I knew, the US Post Office was not noticeably Catholic). And perhaps why the Chinese Catholic jurist and philosopher, John Wu, had a special admiration for the Daoist sage Chuang Tzu, singling out with particular appreciation his voluntary poverty.[22]

The Saint according to Gabriel Marcel

Finally, my third source for thematizing an interreligious study based on the saints comes from a modern philosophical tradition, that of existentialism. Gabriel Marcel, in his essay on "Belonging and Disposability," from his book *Creative Fidelity*, offers a brief but beautiful phenomenology of admiration. Admiration is related to what Marcel calls "disposability," meaning the ability of a person to place him or herself, in an act of friendship or love, at someone else's disposal. It comes from, and also terminates in, a situation of what he calls "belonging." If I tell someone, "'Jack, I belong to you,' this means, 'I am opening an unlimited credit account in your name, you can do what you want with me, I give myself to you.' This does not mean, at least not in principle, I am your slave; on the contrary, I freely put myself in your hands."[23] Obviously there are pathologies of disposability, and degrees of both the good sort and the pathological, but for Marcel the attitude of disposability is best understood in its relation to three other existential stances, charity, hope, and admiration: "disposability is realized not only in the act of charity but also in hope, and I might add, in admiration, whose enormous spiritual and even metaphysical significance is still not recognized."[24]

21. Ratzinger, *Many Religions—One Covenant*, 108–9.

22. See Wu, *Chinese Humanism and Christian Spirituality*, 59–93, esp. 63.

23. Marcel, *Creative Fidelity*, 40.

24. Marcel, *Creative Fidelity*, 47. Passages cited in the next paragraph all come from Marcel, *Creative Fidelity*, 47–49.

Commenting on this spiritual and metaphysical significance, Marcel notes that "the function of admiration is to tear us away from ourselves and from the thoughts we have of ourselves." It implies "an active negation of inner inertia" because admiration is a kind of "irruption," and that can only occur "in a being who is not a closed or hermetic system into which nothing new can penetrate." The refusal to admire is also significant, an indication of a closed mind or even jealousy. But admiration has the power to cause the subject "to emerge from itself and realize itself primarily in the gift of oneself and in the various forms of creativity."[25] It is significant, too, that admiration is not generally caused by an antecedent act of reasoning or deliberation. It is not "caused" or "coerced" by force of logic or any other force, but rather it arises from a kind of global appeal, to which one makes a global response.

The application of this idea to an interreligious study of the saints is obvious. Admiration creates a "disposability" in the person admiring to the person admired and to his or her other admirers, one which may be followed up by reason but does not originate from it and, like faith, is not reducible to reason. Interestingly, this addresses a situation that Marcel notes in another essay from the same book, "On the Fringe of the Ecumenical." There he notes the curious fact that ecumenical (and by extension interreligious) doctrinal discussions can have a self-defeating dynamic, even when the doctrine in question is not stated polemically but simply and clearly. He was noticing the way in which, at a Catholic and Protestant dialogue he had witnessed, the attempt to present a Catholic position in a way that eliminated ambiguity—an intrinsically responsible act—had an effect on the listener opposite to the one expected. It had the effect of intensifying their intransigence. "Does this not confront us then with a real antinomy?" he goes on to ask. "What positive conclusion can we infer from this contradiction? For me at any rate, the latter is embodied in the fact that any discussion, as I have noted, is probably harmful; for whoever professes a doctrine does not have it in his power to avoid the appearance of claiming to hold it as a privilege."[26]

I am not citing this text to reinforce the claim that discussion of doctrine in these settings is necessarily harmful, though in many cases it may be, but rather to wonder if discussion of doctrine is always the best starting point. The Mahayana Buddhist doctrine of the Heart Sutra, that "form is emptiness and the very emptiness is form," seems opaque to me and I have struggled to understand it for years, but to learn the stories of the Bodhisattva of Compassion moves me and makes me want to talk about them with

---

25. Marcel, *Creative Fidelity*, 49.

26. Marcel, *Creative Fidelity*, 202.

those who venerate him (or her) and other Buddhist saints.[27] The Monks of Tibhirine, about to be beatified, seem to me better starting subjects of study for Catholic-Islamic dialogue than the doctrine of the Trinity, which has been debated since the earliest times of Islam. Anyone who knows me, will know that I am not advocating doctrinal illiteracy or lack of clarity or any kind of relativism. To the contrary! Still, here are some words from Pope Benedict again: "What we need, however, is respect for the beliefs of others and the readiness to look for the truth in what strikes us as strange or foreign; for such truth concerns us and can correct us and lead us farther along the path. What we need is the willingness to look behind the alien appearances and look for the deeper truth hidden there."[28]

What is more likely to create the openness to "look behind the alien appearances" than that which makes a religion seem less alien, namely, that admiration that is an irruption, that affirms the recognition of the non-alien, of the common humanity and reinterprets anew the dignity attaching to each person? What is more likely to create such openness than poverty and renunciation that is moving to behold across all cultural boundaries and religious borders? How best to learn not just a doctrine, but what it means, than from its embodiment and connection to someone whose witness opens the heart and creates a disposability, and indeed a belonging, that was not there before? And, far from making the doctrine irrelevant, the importance of it comes out. "Form is emptiness and emptiness is form." I wonder: does that mean that someone—the Bodhisattva—who says they are ready to sit out hell until it is empty has a compassion so large that it does not "fit" into the narrow "self" that calculates sacrifice—emptiness—by the minute instead of by the *kalpa*, "the time it would take an angel descending from heaven once a year and making one sweep of its wings across the top of a mile-high mountain to wear it down level with the ground?"[29] For hell will last at least that long. A compassion that big has very little investment in form, perhaps, except as emptiness, and an investment in emptiness, perhaps, ends up, from that compassion, as an investment in form. I am not entirely certain, only attempting to give an example.

So, to the reader: there you have it, my proposal for a proposal. If anyone is interested in working on an *actual* proposal now, I am all in.

---

27. *Heart Sutra.*

28. Ratzinger, *Many Religions—One Covenant,* 110.

29. As defined by Philip Kapleau in Kapleau, *Three Pillars of Zen,* 334.

Bibliography

Aquinas, Thomas. *Summa Theologiae*. http://www.corpusthomisticum.org/sth0000.
html.

Augustine of Hippo. *On Christian Belief*. Translated by Edmund Hill, OP. The Works of
St. Augustine: A Translation for the Twenty-First Century I/8, edited by Boniface
Ramsey. Hyde Park, NY: New City Press, 2005.

The Heart Sutra. Translated by Edward Conze. http://info.stiltij.nl/publiek/meditatie/
soetras2/heart-conze.pdf.

John Paul II. "*Veritatis splendor*." August 6, 1993. http://w2.vatican.va/content/john-
paul-ii/en/encyclicals/documents/hf_jp-ii_enc_06081993_veritatis-splendor.
html.

Kapleau, Philip. *The Three Pillars of Zen*. Boston: Beacon, 1965.

Marcel, Gabriel. *Creative Fidelity*. Translated by Robert Rosthal. New York: Crossroad,
1982.

Wu, John C. W. *Chinese Humanism and Christian Spirituality*. Edited by Paul K. T. Sih.
Kettering, OH: Angelico, 2017.

Ratzinger, Joseph. *Many Religions—One Covenant: Israel, the Church, and the World*.
Translated by Graham Harrison. San Francisco: Ignatius, 1999.

CHAPTER 2

Not Altogether Wrong

Vatican II on Non-Christian Religions

—FRANCESCA ARAN MURPHY

This essay argues that *Nostra aetate* says little that is positive about non-Christian religions and that, correlatively, *Dignitatis humanae* says nothing to authorize Catholics to give *positive* support to non-Christian religiosity either in civil society or, by extension, within Catholic institutions. Vatican II's *Declaration on Religious Freedom* powerfully and radically encourages Catholics to do nothing to restrict the religious freedom of non-Catholics, whether in the "local politics" of Catholic institutions or in the wider civic realm. The *Declaration on Religious Freedom* conceives of freedom in largely negative terms. This reflects the generous and liberal list of things which non-Christian religions have *not got wrong* in Vatican II's *Declaration on the Relation of the Church to Non-Christian Religions*. *Nostra aetate* and *Dignitatis humanae* teach that merely not getting it wrong is the prerogative of human reason, just as not being coerced is the property of the human person as a free being. On the other hand, achieving the "glorious liberty of the sons of God," positive truth and positive freedom, is a matter of *grace*. This essay focuses on the point that by saying nothing *positive* about non-Christian religions themselves (*Nostra aetate*) and therefore laying no positive responsibilities on Catholics to foster them (*Dignitatis humanae*), the Vatican II documents avoid making politicians, even including Catholic ones, play at being Gods who can dispense *the grace of salvation*. We shall claim in conclusion that, by extension, the same applies to Catholic institutional leaders or presidents.

Religious Diversity and the Unity of the Human Family

As with the constitution *Lumen gentium*, so likewise the little *Declaration on Non-Christian Religions* begins by noting the unity of the human race: the Church is envisaged as the counterpart and "microcosm" of the human race as a whole. All humanity shares a common *telos*: "One also is their final goal, God. . . . His saving design extend[s] to all men, until that time when the elect will be united in the Holy City, the city ablaze with the glory of God, where the nations will walk in his light."[1] The *Declaration* reflects on the non-Christian religions in the light of that final goal which God "design[s]" for their adherents. The non-Christian religions have been composed by people who God in "His Providence" wills to bring into the "Holy City," the heavenly Jerusalem.[2]

So, unsurprisingly, at a human level, people wonder about who they are, and try to make sense of the "meaning" and "aim" of their "life." As children of God, human beings have it in their DNA to ask "What is the road to true happiness? . . . Whence do we come, and where are we going?"[3] The *Declaration* as a whole proceeds from the lowest, most natural and anthropologically "raw" dimensions of religious engagement up to the higher reaches of human religiosity. At the bottom level, then, so to speak, there is a universal questioning about what we are here for, and where our lives are intended to take us. There is nothing *wrong* in such questioning! It has led to the recognition of a higher Being "or even of a Father." Acknowledging that there is a higher power, and, on occasion, conceiving such a power as the Progenitor of humanity, makes for deep piety, "a profound religious sense."[4] Over the centuries, Catholics have registered and responded to the near universal religiosity of mankind in numerous ways, but perhaps, by and large, most commonly in order to condemn it as idolatrous, or at least as urgently in need of evangelization and sacramental reformation. *Nostra aetate* strikes a relatively new note of respectful neutrality. Subjectively, most peoples have a deep and pervasive piety toward their gods or god: this is not in itself error.

Nostra aetate draws on the findings of primitive anthropology. In the first half of the twentieth century, scholars like Wilhelm Schmidt had argued that some form of recognition of a single Supreme Being historically precedes polytheism. Such anthropological findings, if true, strike a blow

1. Second Vatican Council, "*Nostra aetate*," 1.
2. Second Vatican Council, "*Nostra aetate*," 1.
3. Second Vatican Council, "*Nostra aetate*," 1.
4. Second Vatican Council, "*Nostra aetate*," 2.

against the reductionist narratives for which polytheistic fetishism lies at the origin of the religious impulse.[5] Schmidt had been rewarded and encouraged by Pius XII. So the tone of the opening paragraphs of *Nostra aetate* is not "*anthropocentric*" but anthropological. It is thus *theologically neutral.* Primitive peoples are *not wrong* to imagine there is a supreme Being, nor does their veneration for the Supreme Being count against them.

The following paragraph deals with "religions" springing from a more "advanced culture," that is, the two major Asiatic religions of Buddhism and Hinduism. The *Declaration* states, "the Catholic Church rejects nothing that is true and holy in these religions." *Nostra aetate* is not looking at positive contrasts from or differences with Catholic belief about God, that is, not discussing where non-Christian religions positively diverge from the Truth revealed in Jesus Christ, but at "negative similarities," or "not altogether wrongness." It presents Buddhism and Hinduism as a valiant wrestling with the problem of evil, rather than, as in some Catholic presentations, as failing to take on board the convertibility of being and goodness. Hindu sages "seek freedom from the anguish of our human condition . . . through ascetical practices or profound meditations or a flight to God with love and trust"; Buddhism "realizes the radical insufficiency of this changeable world."[6] Catholics have typically criticized the Asiatic religions for their positive answers to the problems of evil and suffering. *Nostra aetate* commends them for discovering and wrestling with that problem. The *Declaration* does not annul or render obsolete Catholic theological objections to *positive* Buddhist or Hindu solutions to the *mysterium iniquitas*: it simply "accentuates the negative," foregrounding what these religions are *not* in error about.

The many mystical paths and "ways" of life which have sought to quell the "restlessness of the human heart" with "teachings, rules, and sacred rites" naturally "differ" from the Catholic Church on the particulars of those teachings and rites: they nonetheless "often reflect a ray of that Truth which enlightens all men." As shadows and mirror images of Christ, these "religions found everywhere" present an inverted, back to front impression, like photographic negatives of the Truth.[7]

Next comes Islam, a hard-case, since it knows the Judeo-Christian biblical traditions and deliberately alters them. Here again, there is neither positive endorsement for Islam's advertent re-narrating of the Hebrew and Christian Bible nor criticism of this subversive re-narration. The *Declaration* indicates those features which the Quranic story holds in common with

5. See, for instance, Schmidt, *Origin and Grown of Religion.*

6. Second Vatican Council, "*Nostra aetate*," 2.

7. Second Vatican Council, "*Nostra aetate*," 2.

Catholicism, and where it does not deviate from Scripture as read in Western traditions. Muslims "adore the one God," and recognize that this God has "spoken with men"; they emulate Abraham's submission to the divine will; though failing to "acknowledge Jesus as God," Muslims "revere Him as a prophet." They respect Mary to the extent of praying to her and, like Christians and Jews, they have a moral-eschatological expectation of a "Day of Judgement" and direct their moral choices accordingly.[8]

At a conference on *Ut unum sint* in 2005, Charles Morerod claimed that Catholic attitudes to Christian ecumenism did not undergo a revolutionary change at the Second Vatican Council. Rather, he argued, where before the Council, Catholic attitudes to non-Catholic Christians had viewed the "glass as half empty," with the Council, Catholics began to see the glass as "half full."[9] The conciliar fathers acknowledged the same phenomenon, but described the same content differently. Likewise, instead of focusing on the positive, and differentiating claims of the non-Christian religions, *Nostra aetate* points to what in the Biblical inheritance has not been altered out of recognition by Islam, and to how Christians should *not* think about and behave toward Muslims today. Christians and Muslims alike should "forget the past" of their shared civilizational confrontations.[10]

Judaism is not a work of natural human reason and religiosity. The revelation to Moses and the Prophets is fulfilled in Jesus Christ. The *Declaration* indicates that, in some sense, revelation and its attendant covenant, still stands: *Nostra aetate* seems to walk-back on some harder versions of supersessionism. "Although the Church is the new people of God, the Jews should not be presented as rejected or accursed by God": this negative portrayal is withdrawn. "The Church" today, in the present tense, "draws substance from the root of that well-cultivated olive tree onto which have been grafted the wild shoots, the Gentiles."[11] Nonetheless, present-day Judaism, as distinct from the "religion of the Hebrew Bible" receives no positive endorsement. We learn that Jesus, Mary, and the Apostles were Jews, and that "God holds the Jews most dear for the sake of their Fathers," and not, apparently, for their own sake?[12] The God of Abraham, Moses, and the Prophets "does not repent of the gifts he makes or of the calls he issues": Judaism is still called by God, still has a place within divine providence, but one must,

8. Second Vatican Council, "*Nostra aetate*," 3.

9. Professor—and now Bishop—Charles Morerod used that metaphor in his conference talk, but it did not reappear in the paper he submitted for publication. See Morerod, "Ecumenical Meaning," 121–28.

10. Second Vatican Council, "*Nostra aetate*," 3.

11. Second Vatican Council, "*Nostra aetate*," 4.

12. Second Vatican Council, "*Nostra aetate*," 4.

perhaps reluctantly, concede, that *Nostra aetate* does not envisage its destiny as being specifically Jewish.

The underlying purpose of *Nostra aetate* seems to come from moral theology. It undertakes a neutral survey of what the non-Christian religions have not got altogether wrong in order to encourage Catholics to treat their members with respect. This comes back to the underlying conciliar theme of the unity and fraternity of the human race, and the Church as mirroring that unity. An important purpose of *Nostra aetate* is to give reasons for our viewing all non-Christians as brothers: "Man's relation to God the Father and his relation to men his brothers are so linked together that Scripture says: 'He who does not love does not know God' (1 John 4:8)." It would be outside the *Declaration's* purview to find positive value in the non-Christian religions in their positive differences from Catholic Christianity: that would be a theological undertaking that is alien to this document. The document does not look to embracing the other as other, but rather, to embracing him as a brother, a member of the single human family. The closing lines of *Nostra aetate* therefore lead straight into *Dignitatis humanae*: "No foundation . . . remains for any theory or practice that leads to discrimination between man and man . . . so far as their human dignity and the rights flowing from it are concerned. The Church reproves, as foreign to the mind of Christ, any discrimination against men . . . because of their race, color, condition of life, or religion."[13]

Nostra aetate speaks in its opening paragraphs of human religiosity as being framed by questions, especially questions about human origin, purpose and destiny. Religious questioning belongs to human nature. The human question, the question about who we are, is a religious question. The import of *Dignitatis humanae* is that human beings must be free to ask religious questions because it is a fundamental expression of our humanity to grapple with these mysteries.

Positive Freedom and Religious Freedom

Freedom is spoken of in two different ways. One is positive, the other negative. In the positive sense, freedom is conceived as a gift given to people in order to help them enlarge or fulfill their humanity. In the negative sense, freedom is thought of as non-servitude: in this negative sense, liberation is removing obstacles to self-movement. In the negative sense, freedom is the opposite of slavery; in the positive sense, "freedom," often garnished with adjectives like "true" or "authentic" is being enabled to make choices which

---

13. Second Vatican Council, "*Nostra aetate*," 5.

fulfil ones true human potential. Where freedom is used in the negative sense, the one who has received manumission is now able to choose for himself, a freed, self-moving man. In the positive sense, freedom is initiation into an ever deeper "client state," a state of ever deeper dependency upon the one who grants the liberation and thus enables one to fulfil one's potential. In the positive sense, "freedom" is a state of ever deepening tutelage; in the negative sense, freedom is a maturation into adulthood. The positive sense of freedom is ultimately, perhaps, religious, pertaining to those religions, whether primitive or Judeo-Christian, which venerate God as "Father": freedom is gracious liberation *for* an eternity of sonship, or spiritual childhood. The negative sense of freedom seems more clearly secular: at most it is the freedom of a human being to be human, or in religious parlance, of a creature *to be a creature*. In the colloquial sense, "a natural" is someone who is entirely themselves, fully self-possessed. This is the negative sense of freedom.

Dignitatis humanae takes "freedom" in the negative sense on almost every one of the multiple occasions upon which it uses the term. Modern people are, it claims, imbued with the desire to exercise "a responsible freedom, not driven by coercion but motivated by a sense of duty." "Religious freedom," without which one cannot, the *Declaration* says, "worship God," requires "immunity from coercion in civil society."[14] The "right to religious freedom" is defined, again, as meaning that "all men are to be immune from coercion on the part of . . . any human power."[15] Not only individuals but also social groups (not just individual Muslims, but entire mosques, not Jews worshipping privately, but whole synagogues, and so on) must be free to venerate God as they will: "The freedom from coercion in matters religious which is the endowment of persons as individuals is also to be recognized as their right when they act in community." Religions may spread their own message, but not in such a way as "to carry a hint of coercion or of a kind of persuasion that would be dishonorable or unworthy."[16] (Tele-evangelists take note).

Though largely the product of Americans, like John Courtney Murray, who pushed for an acknowledgement that the separation of Church and State is healthy for both, *Dignitatis humanae* does not abjure or reject the notion of an "established Church": the Council could not have called for the disestablishment of the Church in Spain and Portugal without generating an Hispanic schism that would have made the Lefebvrists look like small

---

14. Second Vatican Council, "*Dignitatis humanae*," 1.

15. Second Vatican Council, "*Dignitatis humanae*," 2.

16. Second Vatican Council, "*Dignitatis humanae*," 4.

change. Instead, the *Declaration* notes that where establishment remains, it is not to entail shackling non-jurors to the established faith: "If, in view of peculiar circumstances obtaining among peoples, special civil recognition is given to one religious community in the constitutional order of society, it is at the same time imperative that the right of all citizens and religious communities to religious freedom should be recognized and made effective in practice."[17]

Historically, that is, because of "peculiar circumstances," some countries have established churches and the *Declaration* does not advise that such legal frameworks should be dismantled. In a run-up sentence, preceding and explaining the historical fact of the existence of "special civil recognition" for "one religious community," the *Declaration* states, as a matter of fact that "government is also to help create conditions favorable to the fostering of religious life."[18] If this were not the case, it would be very ill-advised for such "special civil recognition" to exist, as it has done in various forms for a millennium and a half. Russell Hittinger reads these lines as showing that the *Declaration* maintains that "the Catholic Church did not, and does not, believe that disestablishment is a principle superior to free exercise."[19] Paragraph 6 does not give many grounds for stating *which* is preferable, establishment or non-establishment. Ian Ker may be more accurate by making the less lofty claim that, with *Dignitatis humanae*, the Church "still teaches . . . that it is legitimate for the constitutional order of society to give special recognition to one religious body such as the Catholic Church."[20] Were the *Declaration* to deny that religion can be institutionally fostered outside of, say, monasteries, it would cut the ground out from the many institutions which are miniature versions of Catholic states, like Catholic schools and colleges.

To the non-American majority at the Council, this doctrine of non-coercion in religion could sound novel. It seemed to overturn nearly two millennia of ecclesial efforts to root itself as the "religion of state" in Europe. The *Declaration on Religious Freedom* speaks delicately, at the outset, of the Council's "search[ing] into the sacred tradition and doctrine of the Church—the treasury out of which the Church continually brings forth new things that are in harmony with the things that are old."[21] John Courtney Murray, and his American episcopal supporters at the Council sought to

17. Second Vatican Council, "*Dignitatis humanae*," 6.

18. Second Vatican Council, "*Dignitatis humanae*," 6.

19. See Hittinger, "Declaration on Religious Liberty," 366.

20. Ker, "*Dignitatis Humanae*," 155.

21. Second Vatican Council, "*Dignitatis humanae*," 1.

persuade Catholics that our tradition has always latently respected religious freedom by pointing out that enforced baptism has never been permitted. Noting that Christ's words and example give no encouragement to religious compulsion, the *Declaration* indicates that although "through the vicissitudes of human history" the Church has sometimes acted in a way "hardly in accord with the spirit of the Gospel or even opposed to it. Nevertheless, the doctrine of the Church that no one is to be coerced into faith has always stood firm."[22] Baptism cannot take place under coercion: that is the bedrock in tradition on which *Dignitatis humanae* takes its stand.

John Courtney Murray and the Freedom of Faith

The principal drafter of the document, John Courtney Murray, had spent decades studying the act of faith, going back to his doctoral work on Matthias Scheeben's notion of faith. For Murray, religious freedom as non-coercion comes down to the freedom of the act of faith: faith is "my own" act, which must spring from my own inner resources as a human person. It cannot be imposed. For Murray, faith is not the act of a slave, but of a free man. As he observes many times in his dissertation, this is the teaching of Thomas Aquinas himself.[23] That document makes very clear the American's preference for Thomas's notion of faith over Scheeben's understanding of faith as "child-like obedience." The *Declaration* therefore roots the novelty of the Church's promotion of religious freedom for non-Christians and non-Catholics not only in the regulations governing baptism but also in the Church's perennial teaching concerning "the freedom of the act of Christian faith."[24] The Church must not require political or institutional power positively to inculcate faith because "It is one of the major tenets of Catholic doctrine that man's response to God in faith must be free: no one therefore is to be forced to embrace the Christian faith against his own will."[25]

The *Declaration* does not conceive of freedom as "empty liberty," that is, it does not value choice by itself, but nor does it envision freedom itself in a positive, teleological frame.[26] Rather than setting freedom in a positive frame, it thinks of human beings using freedom teleologically, to fulfill their human nature. The *Declaration* plants a negative notion of freedom as non-coercion in a positive and teleological anthropology. It is human nature, the

22. Second Vatican Council, "*Dignitatis humanae*," 11–12.

23. See Murray, *Matthias Scheeben on Faith*.

24. Second Vatican Council, "*Dignitatis humanae*," 9.

25. Second Vatican Council, "*Dignitatis humanae*," 10.

26. Hittinger, "Declaration on Religious Liberty," 368.

document says, to seek out the law of God by the light of conscience. The little light of human conscience has as its end and goal participation in the great light of divine law. That means that human beings are naturally religious, and have an innate desire to find a human path which faces toward God. Being human is, at bottom, figuring out how to be towards God. The other animals do what is natural to them without reflection or volition, but for human beings the more natural a behavior the more it requires to be understood and freely chosen. Freedom is constitutive of human nature. To prevent people, whether Christian or not, from following their conscience in religion, is to efface their humanity. The human person "is not to be forced to act in a manner contrary to his conscience. Nor . . . is he to be restrained from acting in accordance with his conscience, especially in matters religious. The reason is that the exercise of religion, of its very nature, consists before all else in those internal, voluntary and free acts whereby man sets the course of his life toward God."[27] However much it may have been embraced in practice by Christian rulers, compulsion in religion is irreligious and unchristian.

The *Declaration on Religious Freedom* takes "freedom" in its positive sense of "being actively enabled to achieve the human destiny just once," in its concluding lines which speak of divine grace: "May the God and Father of all grant that the human family, through careful observance of the principle of religious freedom in society, may be brought by the grace of Christ and the power of the Holy Spirit to the sublime and unending and 'glorious freedom of the sons of God' (Rom 8:21)."[28] Why does the document have so little to say about positive freedom, freedom as the gift and grace of human fulfillment in divine sonship? Is it inspired by a Pelagian distaste for dependency or an Americanist, classical Liberal fixation with human independence?

Dignitatis humanae was formally a product of the Vatican Secretariat for Christian Unity. It originally formed a chapter in the conciliar *Decree on Ecumenism*. Given the history of various forms of institutional, legal and civil establishment for the Catholic Church, and the current condition of the Church in 1965, where disestablishment has often been followed by governmental limitation, the *Declaration* has two tasks. On the one hand, it speaks passionately about the freedom to be religious. Here it is defending the freedom of the Church, especially in then Communist Eastern Europe. Secondly, it recognizes that *mutatis mutandis*, where Christians still have the upper hand they must grant freedom to non-Christians, to members of

27. Second Vatican Council, "*Dignitatis humanae*," 3.
28. Second Vatican Council, "*Dignitatis humanae*," 15.

non-Christian religions, and more broadly, to every kind of "conscientious objector." "Freedom" is thus conceived of negatively: secularist governments like that of then Communist Poland must not restrict or restrain the religious conscience; and likewise Catholics must not coerce our non-Christian brothers and sisters. Non-restriction, whether secularist on Catholic or Catholic on non-Catholic, is a matter of the recognition of a common humanity.

Freedom is not conceived of positively, in terms of Catholic states (as mentioned in paragraph 6), or, by analogy, Catholic institutions, directly lending support to non-Christian religions. Catholic States or Institutions which patronized and promoted non-Christian cults would reject the basic teaching of *Nostra aetate*, that the "truth" of these non-Christian faiths is negative, in not being entirely wrong or at odds with the Truth of Christ.

John Courtney Murray coached the American bishops for their conciliar debate on the draft document on religious liberty. He suggested to Bishop Primeau to emphasize two key points: "First there is an inseparable connection between the internal freedom of religious decision, which is freedom of conscience; and external freedom of religious expression in worship, observance, witness, teaching, which is free exercise of religion. Secondly, there was a need to elucidate the distinction between the notion of 'right' as an empowerment and as an immunity. He pointed out that in the *Declaration* religious freedom is called a right in the sense of an immunity from all coercion. On the ground of this distinction the charge of religious indifferentism is nullified, and the assertion can be made that the Church does not hold that all men are equally empowered by God, or conscience, to practice any religion they choose."[29] In *Nostra aetate*, the non-Christian religions are, with the exception of Judaism, *natural* "rays" of the Divine Light; they are empowered by human nature, not by God. *Dignitatis humanae* does not speak of God as empowering the non-Christian conscience. Nor does it give any grounds for Catholic States or institutions positively to empower non-Christian religions or the non-Catholic conscience. To do so would be, as Murray says, to profess "indifferentism" or agnosticism about the destiny designed for humanity by God's providence.

Comparing the *Declaration* to John Henry Newman's set of criteria for a good and true "development of doctrine," Ian Kerr argues that "before the Second Vatican Council, the condemnation of religious liberty meant that people were not free to choose whatever religion they pleased. And it is this false 'idea' of religious freedom that is also rejected by *Dignitatis humanae* when it declares that the 'one true religion subsists in the Catholic and

29. Pelotte, *John Courtney Murray*, 93.

Apostolic Church' and that 'all men are bound to seek the truth . . . and to embrace the truth . . . and to hold fast to it.' It says this obligation falls on the human conscience."[30] Human beings are obliged by their very natures, that is, by natural law, to seek the truth, but the obligation falls on the human conscience itself, not on governments. Human conscience is obliged to seek truth, but civil government is not obliged to do so on their behalf. Government can help to foster the conditions for openness to truth, and egg people on to find it, but it cannot demand the grace of faith, since it cannot give it.

"Positive" freedom treats its objects as "dependents," recipients of the gift of freedom. There *is* such a thing as positive freedom, and in fact the whole sphere of grace consists in it, just as "nature" largely revels in the negative freedom of non-coercion. Forms of Christianity which know grace but have little converse with nature, define freedom only in positive, theological terms. Here freedom becomes indistinguishable from divine coercion. These originally Christian hyper-theological conceptions of freedom have generated an immanent and political residue. It has given us theories and practices of government in which "adopted sonship" of God is replaced by becoming a "new man" at the hands of the State. Here true and authentic freedom is doing what the State tells us, or, ontologically, being the creature of the State. This political transhumanism reaches back into the nineteenth century and bore fruit in twentieth-century totalitarianism. It is not up to government to play God, *Dignitatis humanae* affirms, *in the Matter of God*. The dispensation of positive freedoms *to* enjoy human goods may be a matter for government, but *not* the dispensation of positive freedom to enjoy "the glorious liberty of the sons of God." Government may be generally pro-religious, but must not "command or inhibit acts that are religious" because human religiosity is not a secular, governable human trait, but a theologoumenon, a sign of transcendence.[31]

So, on the one hand, "religious acts whereby men . . . direct their lives to God transcend . . . the order of terrestrial and temporal affairs," that is, human religious acts of every kind, Christian and otherwise, transcend governments of all kinds, including pious Catholic ones, and, on the other hand, only God can positively empower these acts to find their home and destination in him.[32] Seeking God is the exercise of a liberated human nature; being found, galvanized and empowered by God is liberating grace and sonship in Christ.

30. Ker, "*Dignitatis Humanae*," 150–51.

31. Second Vatican Council, "*Dignitatis humanae*," 3.

32. Second Vatican Council, "*Dignitatis humanae*," 3.

We have at some points in this essay suggested that even countries like America know something analogous to the establishment of religion. Anyone who has endured a Catholic school and every alumnae of a Catholic college or university should have some intimacy with the workings of an "established Church culture." Such institutions have been led, rightly, by *Nostra aetate* and *Dignitatis humanae* to show great respect for the non-Christian conscience and non-Catholic religious traditions. For these institutions to do more than that would be for them to cross the line from freedom into indifference. There is no grounds in the teaching of the Second Vatican Council for Catholic institutions to treat non-Christian religions "on all fours with" Catholicism or to make a level playing field for Catholic and non-Catholic conscience within the "little states" of Catholic schools and colleges.

Bibliography

Hittinger, Russell. "The Declaration on Religious Liberty, *Dignitatis Humanae.*" In *Vatican II: Renewal Within Tradition*, edited by Matthew Lamb and Matthew Levering, 359–82. Oxford: Oxford University Press, 2008.

Ker, Ian. "Is *Dignitatis Humanae* a Case of Authentic Doctrinal Development?" *Logos* 11.2 (2008) 149–57.

Lamb, Matthew, and Matthew Levering, eds. *Vatican II: Renewal Within Tradition*. Oxford: Oxford University Press, 2008.

Morerod, Charles. "The Ecumenical Meaning of the Petrine Ministry." In *Ecumenism Today: The Universal Church in the Twenty-First Century*, edited by Francesca Aran Murphy and Christopher Asprey, 121–28. London: Ashgate, 2008.

Murphy, Francesca Aran, and Christopher Asprey, eds. *Ecumenism Today: The Universal Church in the Twenty-First Century*. London: Ashgate, 2008.

Murray, John Courtney. *Matthias Scheeben on Faith: The Doctoral Dissertation of John Courtney Murray*. Lewiston, NY: Edward Mellen, 1987.

Pelotte, Donald E. *John Courtney Murray: Theologian in Conflict*. New York: Paulist, 1975.

Schmidt, Wilhelm. *The Origin and Grown of Religion: Facts and Theories*. Translated by H. J. Rose. Proctorville, OH: Wythe-North, 2014.

Second Vatican Council. "*Dignitatis humanae.*" December 7, 1965. http://www.vatican.va/archive/hist_councils/ii_vatican_council/documents/vat-ii_decl_19651207_dignitatis-humanae_en.html.

———. "*Lumen gentium.*" November 21, 1964. http://www.vatican.va/archive/hist_councils/ii_vatican_council/documents/vat-ii_const_19641121_lumen-gentium_en.html.

———. "*Nostra aetate.*" October 28, 1965. http://www.vatican.va/archive/hist_councils/ii_vatican_council/documents/vat-ii_decl_19651028_nostra-aetate_en.html.

Virtuous Interreligious Dialogue as Authentic Evangelization

—Andrew Kim

This essay argues that virtue ethics can be a source of insight into the importance of interreligious dialogue for the good life. After a preliminary sketch of the distinctiveness of a morality of happiness approach within the framework of Christian ethics, the essay proceeds to examine virtuous interreligious dialogue through an analysis of the cardinal virtues of prudence, temperance, justice, and fortitude. The "models for interreligious dialogue" developed by Paul F. Knitter provide a helpful medium for reflecting upon each virtue as applied to specific questions, problems, and opportunities interreligious dialogue poses in relation to theologies of religions.[1] The essay concludes by considering the role of the theological virtues of faith, hope, and love in elevating interreligious dialogue to the level of authentic evangelization characterized by Pope Francis in *Evangelii gaudium*.

Two Approaches to Interreligious Dialogue

In *The Sources of Christian Ethics*, Servais Pinckaers observes "two broad types of organization" or "moral theories" prevalent throughout "the history of Catholic moral theology." The first kind, "characteristic of the patristic and great scholastic periods," is focused chiefly upon "the question of happiness and the virtues." The second kind, "predominate in the modern era," is primarily concerned with "theories of obligation and commandments."

---

1. Knitter, *Introducing Theologies of Religions*.

Pinckaers maintains that differences in the "internal logic animating these theories" are rooted in "varying concepts of freedom."[2]

Pinckaers refers to the concept of freedom that informs "morality of obligation" theories as "freedom of indifference." Contrary to Aquinas, William of Ockham argued "that free will *preceded* reason and will in such a way as to move them to their acts." Freedom, in this understanding, is primary and "the first fact of human experience."[3] Freedom is metaphysically defined by its unique position in the will alone and psychologically by its "indetermination" or "radical indifference" to "what reason dictated and its contrary."[4] Freedom, so understood, "*excludes natural inclinations* from the free act; they are subject to choice. In regard to these inclinations, freedom is indifferent." As a result, freedom "*has no need of virtue*, which becomes a freely used *habitude, or of finality*, which becomes one circumstance of actions."[5]

On the other hand, "freedom for excellence," which informs a "morality of happiness" approach, is firmly rooted in two principles that preceded the "Nominalist Revolution." First is the *sequi naturam*, "which was characterized by a longing for the enjoyment of the good, of truth, and of communication with others" consistent with nature. Second is the principle of "the happy life." Classical thinkers may have disagreed as to "what conformed to human nature" or how happiness was to be attained, but these two principles "formed the common basis for discussions."[6] The Church Fathers, Pinckaers notes, "not only adopted and fully maintained the two principles of *sequi naturam* and the primal longing for happiness" but also "deepened and intensified them in the light of Christian revelation"[7] In Pinckaers words, "happiness no longer consisted, for the Fathers or St. Thomas, in merely human virtue as a subjective quality, but rather in openness to the divine goodness, to the reality of God himself, through love which came to us from God, through Christ."[8]

From this brief and admittedly abbreviated sketch, then, one may observe four ways in which a morality of happiness approach as characterized by Pinckaers is capable of serving as a source for fruitful reflection upon the

---

2. Pinckaers, *Sources of Christian Ethics*, 329.

3. Pinckaers, *Sources of Christian Ethics*, 331. Pinckaers's italics reproduced throughout.

4. Pinckaers, *Sources of Christian Ethics*, 332.

5. Pinckaers, *Sources of Christian Ethics*, 375.

6. Pinckaers, *Sources of Christian Ethics*, 334.

7. Pinckaers, *Sources of Christian Ethics*, 334–35.

8. Pinckaers, *Sources of Christian Ethics*, 335.

meaning and value of interreligious dialogue. First, a morality of happiness perspective characterizes interreligious dialogue as an activity that when done virtuously shapes individuals and communities in a manner conducive to human flourishing and freedom. It should be acknowledged that, as with any virtuous activity, interreligious dialogue may at times seem like a mere obligation or duty tacked on to the moral life, directed to purely extrinsic ends, and indifferent to considerations of interiority. Indeed, one could infer such a view from Francis's statement that "interreligious dialogue is a necessary condition for peace in the world, and so it is a duty for Christians as well as other religious communities." However, Francis skillfully presents this "duty" as meaningful and intelligible in the light of larger claims regarding the interior dimension of those who are "purified and enriched" by the "mutual listening" through which one learns "to accept others and their different ways of living, thinking and speaking."[9]

Second, while able to provide a framework for reflecting upon rules and actions informing virtuous interreligious dialogue, a morality of happiness approach emphasizes the importance of the intentions driving the efforts of the participants. From this standpoint, virtuous intentions that shape the manner in which interreligious dialogue is carried out may be understood as "*rooted in the natural inclinations to the good and true,* to what has quality and perfection. It springs from an attraction to what appears true and good, and from an interest in it."[10] Francis seems to affirm this basic insight when he characterizes the "efforts" of those engaged in interreligious dialogue as expressive of a deep and universal "love for truth."[11] In this way, a focus on happiness and the virtues, while attending to the importance of rules and actions, also invites deeper reflection regarding that which integrates the various activities of interreligious dialogue "in view of an end, which unites them interiorly and insures continuity."[12]

Third, a morality of happiness approach organized around the virtues emphasizes the social or communal dimension of interreligious dialogue. As Francis eloquently states, "a dialogue which seeks social peace and justice is in itself, beyond all merely practical considerations, an ethical commitment which brings about a new social situation."[13] Virtuous interreligious dialogue, then, not only allows for but actually requires "collabora-

---

9. Francis, *Evangelii gaudium,* 250. *EG* hereafter.

10. Pinckaers, *Sources of Christian Ethics,* 375. I do not here replicate Pinckaers's ordering or full list of summative contrasts between freedom of indifference and freedom for excellence.

11. Francis, *EG,* 250.

12. Pinckaers, *Sources of Christian Ethics,* 375.

13. Francis, *EG,* 250.

tion with others for the common good and the growth of society."[14] It may seem redundant or even superfluous to point out that collaboration is a necessary ingredient for dialogue. However, as we shall see in a later section, attentiveness to the communal nature of interreligious dialogue informed by a morality of happiness approach leads to an importantly distinct set of claims and insights regarding social conditions necessary in order for virtuous interreligious dialogue to occur.

Finally, a freedom for excellence approach highlights the reality of growth in the moral life. In contrast to an approach that would differentiate only between "being free and not being free" in the sense of freedom of indifference, a freedom for excellence approach recognizes that virtue "*must be developed* through education and exercised, with discipline, through successive stages." In Pinckaers's view, this "growth is essential to freedom."[15] Interreligious dialogue, then, can be understood as the occasion to make one more free to virtuously participate in that very activity in a manner conducive to the flourishing of both the individual and the community. As Francis notes regarding interreligious dialogue between Christians and Muslims, "suitable training is essential for all involved, not only so that they can be solidly and joyfully grounded in their own identity, but so that they can also acknowledge the values of others, appreciate the concerns underlying their demands and shed light on shared beliefs."[16] Training in virtuous interreligious dialogue makes the participants more free to engage meaningfully in that activity in a manner conducive to the moral growth of the practitioners themselves.

The four emphases just described begin to shed light upon the capacity of a morality of happiness approach to supplement fruitful reflection upon the meaning and value of interreligious dialogue and correspond, very roughly, to the cardinal virtues of prudence, temperance, justice, and fortitude. Learning to "accept others and their different ways of living, thinking and speaking" can lead one to a more truthful vision of reality and accurate understanding of the way things are and so corresponds with prudence.[17] Understood as an intention driving the practice of interreligious dialogue, the innate "attraction" deep within the human heart "to what appears true and good" invites reflection upon the virtue of temperance.[18] Attentiveness to the role of interreligious dialogue as ordered to the "common good and

14. Pinckaers, *Sources of Christian Ethics*, 375.

15. Pinckaers, *Sources of Christian Ethics*, 375.

16. Francis, *EG*, 253.

17. Francis, *EG*, 250.

18. Pinckaers, *Sources of Christian Ethics*, 375.

the growth of society" provides the occasion for reflection upon the virtue of justice.[19] Lastly, the virtue of fortitude offers insight into challenges involved in progressing toward a virtuous form of interreligious dialogue that moves beyond a "facile syncretism" or "diplomatic openness which says 'yes' to everything in order to avoid problems."[20] In order to reflect more deeply upon the capacity of the virtues to offer insights into the meaning and value of interreligious dialogue a more thorough examination of each virtue as applied to specific difficulties and challenges interreligious dialogue poses can be of some use, and it is to this examination that we now turn.

Prudence and the Replacement Model

The classical tradition has often referred to prudence as the "charioteer of the virtues."[21] This metaphor reflects not only the importance of prudence but also its indispensable role in guiding and shaping the other virtues. Aquinas defines this virtue as "right reason applied to action." In order to act well in a given situation one must first "take counsel" and then assess "what one has discovered."[22] Regarding receiving counsel for the sake of discovery, Aquinas states that "reason must of necessity institute an inquiry before deciding on the objects of choice; and this inquiry is called counsel."[23] The actions of prudence, then, presuppose that "the true precedes the good."[24] As one contemporary moral theologian explains, "being a prudent person is what enables one to see rightly and translate that truthful vision into action."[25] In a broad sense, learning to "accept others and their different ways of living, thinking and speaking" in the context of interreligious dialogue may be understood as a form of taking counsel for the sake of gaining a more truthful vision of reality.[26] As Francis states, "the same Spirit everywhere brings forth various forms of practical wisdom which help people to bear suffering and to live in greater peace and harmony. As Christians, we can also benefit from these treasures built up over many centuries, which can help us better to live our own beliefs."[27]

19. Pinckaers, *Sources of Christian Ethics*, 375.

20. Francis, *EG*, 251.

21. See, for example, Aquinas, *Summa theologiae* IIa IIae q.47. *ST* hereafter.

22. Aquinas, *ST*, IIa IIae q. 47 a. 8.

23. Aquinas, *ST*, Ia IIae q. 14 a. 1.

24. Pieper, *Four Cardinal Virtues*, 2.

25. Mattison, *Introducing Moral Theology*, 97.

26. Francis, *EG*, 250.

27. Francis, *EG*, 254.

Understood generally, then, the prudent person is one who possesses "an attitude of openness in truth and in love" indispensable to authentic interreligious dialogue.[28] Francis recognizes "forms of fundamentalism on both sides" as one of the major obstacles to virtuous interreligious dialogue.[29] Though he does not offer a comprehensive definition, "fundamentalism," for Francis, seems to refer primarily to a vision of reality that is closed off to the possibility of growth in truth and understanding. Fundamentalism, then, is not to be identified solely with a particular subset of one religion or even with religion in general; it is more pervasive than that. There can even be a kind of anti-fundamentalist fundamentalism that ruthlessly enacts the very same mentality it decries, as we shall see in a later section. However, at this point, it will be helpful to examine more deeply the vision of reality fundamentalism entails.

In his influential work, *Introducing Theologies of Religions*, Paul F. Knitter defines fundamentalism within Christianity as informed by a "theology of total replacement" requiring one to regard "other faith communities as so lacking, or so aberrant, that in the end Christianity must move in and take their place."[30] Knitter argues that a "theology of total replacement," in one form or another, has "held sway over most of Christian history."[31] The historical development of Catholic doctrine regarding the link between evangelization and salvation Knitter likens to "a kind of teeter-totter" sometimes holding up and emphasizing the universality of God's love and will "to save all people" while at other times stressing the particularity of salvation accomplished only in and through Christ and the Church.[32]

According to Knitter's narrative, the "teeter-totter" is initially tilted in the universalist direction. The Church Fathers emphasized that the *logos* was "made flesh" in Christ but that the same *logos*, though "concentrated in Jesus," was also the "universally sown Word" and thus strongly affirmed "God's saving presence beyond the church."[33] The wedding of Christianity and Roman power under Emperor Constantine led to a radical shift of attitude towards those "outside the church." Knitter understands Augustine's

28. Francis, *EG*, 254.

29. Francis, *EG*, 254.

30. Knitter, *Introducing Theologies of Religions*, 23. Knitter divides the replacement model into two gradations: total and partial. While acknowledging that "the terms are frustratingly slippery," Knitter associates the total replacement perspective with "Fundamentalist" or "Evangelical" Christians and also includes "Pentecostals and Charismatics" in this grouping (Knitter, *Introducing Theologies of Religions*, 20–21).

31. Knitter, *Introducing Theologies of Religions*, 63.

32. Knitter, *Introducing Theologies of Religions*, 64.

33. Knitter, *Introducing Theologies of Religions*, 65.

insistence on salvation by grace alone as highly influential in this regard and more or less articulating the view that would hold sway until the sixteenth century: "Outside the church, no salvation *at all*."[34] Largely in response to the "discovery" of the new world, theologians such as Robert Bellarmine and Francisco Suarez, constructed a "baptism of desire" formula containing "all kinds of concepts" that made salvation attainable to those outside of the church. The main idea was that the "holy pagan" following God's voice in her or his conscience could still belong to the church even if in an "imperfect," "tendential," or "potential" way.[35]

While concepts of implicit belonging to the church may mark "a more positive attitude toward people outside the church," Knitter is quick to point out that this does not entail "a more positive attitude toward *their religions*."[36] If God draws individual members of other religions into some kind of imperfect or implicit belonging in the church by speaking directly to their consciences, then God appears to be bypassing their religions rather than making use of them "to offer grace, revelation, and salvation."[37] Thus, in Knitter's view, the "sincere and extremely imaginative efforts" of theologians around the time of the Council of Trent to give equal weight to the universal reach of God's love and the "necessary role of the church" do not move beyond the "theology of total replacement" in a meaningful way.[38]

Knitter's analysis of replacement theologies that inform a fundamentalist mindset helps elucidate the reasons why Francis regards fundamentalism as an obstacle to virtuous interreligious dialogue. There is simply no reason for anything remotely approximating a genuine dialogue if one party possesses the totality of truth and understanding that the other party utterly lacks. However, from a morality of happiness perspective, one can also reflect upon the impact that a fundamentalist mentality has on the interiority of the individual who truly regards "other faith communities as so lacking, or so aberrant, that in the end Christianity must move in and take their place."[39] Is such a mindset conducive to the flourishing of the individual who holds it? Does it enhance authentic freedom? Does it reflect a truthful vision of reality open "to the divine goodness" that Christians believe to be revealed in Christ?[40]

34. Knitter, *Introducing Theologies of Religions*, 66. His italics emphasizing the addition of *omnino* by the Fourth Lateran Council (1215).

35. Knitter, *Introducing Theologies of Religions*, 67.

36. Knitter, *Introducing Theologies of Religions*, 67.

37. Knitter, *Introducing Theologies of Religions*, 67.

38. Knitter, *Introducing Theologies of Religions*, 67.

39. Knitter, *Introducing Theologies of Religions*, 23.

40. Pinckaers, *Sources of Christian Ethics*, 335.

A fundamentalist mindset closed off to the possibility of growth in truth and understanding seems inconsistent with Paul's prayer for the Philippians that their "love may increase ever more and more in knowledge and every kind of perception, to discern what is of value, so that you may be pure and blameless for the day of Christ, filled with the fruit of righteousness that comes through Jesus Christ for the glory and praise of God" (Phil 1:8–11, NAB). The "attitude of openness in truth and in love" commended by Pope Francis may correspond on some level with Paul's understanding of Christian humility: "humbly regard others as more important than yourselves" (Phil 2:3).[41] As Pinckaers notes, "St. Paul restructured the organicity of the virtues, making them all depend on the faith, hope, and charity that bound the believer to Christ."[42]

One may discern a relationship here between, on the one hand, a morality of obligation perspective and fundamentalism, and, on the other hand, an "attitude of openness in truth and love" informed by a morality of happiness perspective. If one side possesses all of the truth and the other entirely lacks it, then the only reason for entering into dialogue would be purely out of obligation to pursue an external end detached from the dialogue itself. On the other hand, from a morality of happiness point of view, the value to be gained from interreligious dialogue is intrinsic to that activity in which both sides can grow together in truth and understanding. More specifically, through interreligious dialogue one gains a more truthful vision of reality thereby growing in the virtue of prudence. Indeed, it is the desire to advance in just such a vision that drives the fulfillment model to which we now turn.

Temperance and the Fulfillment Model

In the previous section we treated prudence very broadly as the virtue that predisposes one to a more accurate vision of reality. This section, too, does not limit the scope of temperance to the traditional categories of sensual pleasures but rather understands temperance as the name for virtuous emotions or desires. In particular, this section focuses on the desire for a greater understanding of God. One observes here the interconnectedness of temperance and prudence. This section argues that what Knitter refers to as the "fulfillment model," particularly as presented by Karl Rahner, is driven by a virtuous desire "to liberate Christians from their negative views of those outside the church and enable them to realize that God is much greater than they are."[43]

41. Cited in Francis, *EG*, 271.

42. Pinckaers, *Sources of Christian Ethics*, 130.

43. Knitter, *Introducing Theologies of Religions*, 73.

Knitter regards Rahner's theology of fulfillment as offering a virtuous alternative to replacement theology and therefore representing "something really new in the history of Christianity." While confirming the trend in Catholic theology toward a more positive attitude to members of other religions that had been maturing since Trent, Rahner "went well beyond that trend" by making the "startling" claim that "God's grace is active in the religions."[44] God's saving power "is not injected into us through some kind of spiritual transfusion" that bypasses or circumvents the "*embodied* and *social*" aspects of human experience.[45]

God's presence, then, takes many shapes throughout human history and in the variety of different religions. In the religions and in history "God meets us in physical, social forms."[46] These religions, then, can be "ways of salvation." The content of other religions does not consist merely of errors that need to be totally or partially replaced. Rather, in the non-Christian religions one can find "a positive means of gaining the right relationship to God and thus for the attaining of salvation, a means which is therefore *positively included in God's plan of salvation*."[47] Buddhists, for example, are not saved "*despite* their Buddhism, as had previously been said, but *because of* their Buddhism."[48]

At the same time, all grace is still mediated through Christ. The soul's deepest longing is for an "absolute savior" who is "truly *with us* and is so irrevocably."[49] This longing is satisfied through an experience of "God's embracing, saving love." Those who do not know Jesus can still experience this through their own religions. To have experienced this is to have experienced grace, and to have experienced grace is to be "oriented toward the Christian church."[50] Those graced in such a way in and through other religions are "Christians without the name of Christian. They are *anonymous Christians*."[51] C. S. Lewis seems to state something resembling the view of Rahner in the following passage:

44. Knitter, *Introducing Theologies of Religions*, 70.

45. Knitter, *Introducing Theologies of Religions*, 70. Here Knitter is in conversation with Karl Rahner (see Rahner, *Foundations of Christian Faith*, 178–318).

46. Knitter, *Introducing Theologies of Religions*, 71.

47. Rahner, *Foundations of Christian Faith*, 318, cited in Knitter, *Introducing Theologies of Religions*, 71.

48. Knitter, *Introducing Theologies of Religions*, 71.

49. Knitter, *Introducing Theologies of Religions*, 73.

50. Knitter, *Introducing Theologies of Religions*, 73.

51. Knitter, *Introducing Theologies of Religions*, 73.

> There are people in other religions who are being led by God's secret influence to concentrate on those parts of their religion which are in agreement with Christianity, and who thus belong to Christ without knowing it. For example, a Buddhist of good will may be led to concentrate more and more on the Buddhist teaching about mercy and to leave in the background . . . the Buddhist teaching on certain other points.[52]

As noted earlier, Knitter describes Rahner's main purpose as one of liberating "Christians from their negative views of those outside the church."[53] Returning to the "teeter-totter" metaphor, Rahner is trying to move beyond the conundrum of God's universal saving love as particularized and made known in a definitive way through Jesus of Nazareth. Dialing up the universal love seems to entail dialing down the absolutely unique revelation of God in Christ in a manner that leads one away from the saving message of the Gospel. On the other hand, dialing up the unique revelation of God in Christ seems to entail dialing down the mysterious depths of God's presence and unfailing love for the human person in a manner that leads one away from the God revealed in that very same Gospel. Rahner wants to dial up both God's universal love and the absolutely unique revelation of God in Christ. He wants to balance the teeter-totter.

Vatican II's reception of the "really new" position put forward by Rahner is, according to Knitter, ambiguous. Throughout the Council documents, particularly at various points in *Lumen gentium, Gaudium et spes, Unitatis redintegratio, Nostra aetate,* and *Ad gentes,* Knitter finds: "re-endorsement of what had been taught since the Council of Trent: that God's love and saving presence can't be locked within the walls of the church."[54] At the same time, the value of other religions, precisely in their otherness, as paths to salvation is unclear. Some have interpreted the Council documents as refusing to recognize non-Christian religions as ways of salvation.[55] Others, such as Bishop Piero Rossano, argue that Vatican II explicitly affirms that salvation can "reach the hearts of men and women through the visible, experiential signs of the various religions."[56] The primary point of contact (or compromise?) between Rahner's theology of religions and Vatican II is, in Knitter's view, to be found in the attitude to members of non-Christian religions expressed by a theology of fulfillment. Whereas a replacement mentality

---

52. Lewis, *Mere Christianity,* 209.

53. Knitter, *Introducing Theologies of Religions,* 73.

54. Knitter, *Introducing Theologies of Religions,* 76.

55. D'Costa, *Meeting of Religions and the Trinity.*

56. Rossano, "Christ's Lordship and Religious Pluralism," 102–3.

can find nothing of value in non-Christian religions, one informed by a theology of fulfillment is open to, and even looks for the truth, goodness, and beauty to be found in other religions while not forgetting that these are oriented toward "fulfillment in Christ and the church."[57]

Virtuous interreligious dialogue, then, is driven by a deep and universal "love for truth."[58] As John Paul II observes in *Fides et ratio*, "it is the nature of the human being to seek the truth. This search looks not only to the attainment of truths which are partial, empirical or scientific; nor is it only in individual acts of decision-making that people seek the true good. Their search looks toward an ultimate truth which would explain the meaning of life."[59] Seeming to echo John Paul II, Francis notes that interreligious dialogue begins "in a conversation about human existence."[60] At the same time, Christians believe that "in Jesus Christ, who is the Truth, faith recognizes the ultimate appeal to humanity, an appeal made in order that what we experience as desire and nostalgia may come to its fulfillment."[61] A question here arises: if one has already discovered the ultimate truth, then in what sense is one to go on desiring it and searching for it with a genuine openness to other views? This question is responded to more fully in the fourth section of this essay. However, a partial response may be discerned from a consideration of the virtue of justice and the mutuality model to which we now turn.

Justice and the Mutuality Model

In *Mere Christianity*, C. S. Lewis employs the metaphor of "a fleet of ships sailing in formation" in a manner illustrative of the scope of justice considered as a virtue. Lewis maintains that the "voyage will be a success" if three things occur. The first two mutually entail each other: "each ship must be seaworthy" in order to "avoid collisions." Using a different metaphor—this time that of an orchestra—Lewis notes "each player's individual instrument must be in tune and also each must come in at the right moment so as to combine with all the others." Third, is the consideration of "where the fleet is trying to get to, or what piece of music the band is trying to play."[62] With regard to interreligious dialogue, then, we may consider all three

57. Knitter, *Introducing Theologies of Religions*, 78.

58. Francis, *EG*, 250.

59. John Paul II, *Fides et ratio*, 33. *FR* hereafter.

60. Francis, *EG*, 250.

61. John Paul II, *FR*, 33.

62. Lewis, *Mere Christianity*, 71.

aspects. While the previous sections focused on prudence and temperance as interior qualities (which here may be likened to the seaworthiness of the ship or the individual instrument being in tune) conducive to genuine interreligious dialogue, the current section examines more closely the second and third components in Lewis's metaphor through an analysis of the mutuality model.

As previously mentioned, Francis recognizes "forms of fundamentalism" that depart from "true openness" as an obstacle to interreligious dialogue. Another obstacle, which may even be a form of fundamentalism in its own right, is a "facile syncretism" or "diplomatic openness which says 'yes' to everything in order to avoid problems."[63] Knitter regards John Hick as among the chief architects of a mutualist or pluralist theology that may be open to a critique of this kind. Hick proposed a "Copernican revolution" in theology that was to take place by envisioning all religions as attempts to capture in myth, metaphor, and symbol the mysterious something (or nothing) that is the true center and goal of all religions.[64] According to this view, discrepancies and variation in the specific content and teachings of the various religions result from "different human responses to the one divine Reality, embodying different perceptions which have been formed in different historical and cultural circumstances."[65]

Drawing from the philosophy of Kant, Hick distinguishes between the reality that is and the reality that human beings experience and attempt to communicate. Because the reality itself is inexhaustible and can't be fully expressed through human concepts and language, contradictions between differing religious points of view may be regarded as "an invitation to explore more deeply the richness of the Real."[66] The mysterious something (or nothing) can be described as both "loving Father and indescribable Force." In relation to this something (or nothing) we can understand ourselves as "both individuals that endure forever and pieces that lose their identity in the bigger picture."[67] Also, "whether they use personal or impersonal symbols" the end goal of all the religions has to do with "stirring and guiding their followers to change the direction of their lives from self-centeredness to Other-centeredness."[68] The efficacy of a particular religion in enacting this change is the measure of its value.

63. Francis, *EG*, 251.

64. Knitter, *Introducing Theologies of Religions*, 114.

65. Hick, *God and the Universe of Faiths*, 131.

66. Knitter, *Introducing Theologies of Religions*, 117.

67. Knitter, *Introducing Theologies of Religions*, 117.

68. Knitter, *Introducing Theologies of Religions*, 117.

While the mutuality model emphasizes the unity of religions as providing ethical imperatives related in some way to human attempts to describe the indescribable, the acceptance model, examined in the next section, is suspicious of this approach. Eagerness to find common ground can lead us to overlook or even discount genuine differences. More problematically, while the mutuality model explains the religions as all culturally and historically oriented to reality in a certain way, it seems to exempt itself from the same condition. Thus, a mutuality mentality can, perhaps even unconsciously, impose "its own particular viewpoint on all the others in the name of universality."[69] In order to gain access into the exclusive club of enlightened humanity, then, the religions must all bow the knee to the one true religion of Western modernity with its own rigid creed of "self-evident truths" and claims that "have to be taken on faith." Knitter presents the creed of Western modernity as follows:

> We believe that if there is an Infinite, it is available to all religions, but cannot be grasped fully or finally by any one of them.
>
> We believe that all religious language is symbolic and mythic.
>
> We believe that time is linear and history proceeds by evolution.
>
> We believe that for anything to be really real, it needs to be grounded in history.
>
> We believe that individual human rights take precedence over all other rights.
>
> We believe that democracy takes precedence over all other systems.
>
> We believe that "right action" (orthopraxis) takes precedence over "right belief" (orthodoxy).
>
> We believe that all religions must promote justice and human/ecological well-being.[70]

The point is not so much about the quality of the creed but rather that it is a creed and should be acknowledged as such. It is not merely sweet reason kindly setting the table for the religions to have a conversation. Rather, it is making the invitation list and arranging the seats so as to predetermine the outcome in self-serving ways or, in some cases, as Francis states, "a totalitarian gesture on the part of those who would ignore greater values of which they are not the masters."[71] In other cases, the mutuality model may be

---

69. Knitter, *Introducing Theologies of Religions*, 158.

70. Knitter, *Introducing Theologies of Religions*, 160. I added the clause "we believe."

71. Francis, *EG*, 251.

intended to "avoid collisions" by flattening out or deemphasizing ultimate truth claims adhered to by members of religious communities.

Francis is certainly not opposed to the important goals of "building consensus and agreement" in pursuit of a more "just, responsive, and inclusive society."[72] As noted earlier, Francis regards interreligious dialogue as "a necessary condition for peace in the world, and . . . a duty for Christians as well as other religious communities."[73] The goal of interreligious dialogue is "social peace and justice . . . which brings about a new social situation."[74] Virtuous interreligious dialogue, then, requires "collaboration with others for the common good and the growth of society."[75] However, Christians seek to advance these goals primarily by "preaching Jesus Christ, who is himself peace."[76] If participants in interreligious dialogue are required to leave their ultimate truth claims at the door as an entry fee into the conversation, then authentic interreligious dialogue cannot really occur. As John Paul II observed, "people seek an absolute which might give to all their searching meaning and an answer—something ultimate, which might serve as the ground of all things."[77] Right relation in the context of interreligious dialogue, then, entails bringing one's ultimate truth claims to the table in a spirit of loving friendship and openness guided by a desire to grow in understanding through collaboration with others whose ultimate truth claims are distinct at several points from one's own. This brings us to the acceptance model.

Fortitude and the Acceptance Model

Fortitude is the virtue of facing hardships well. It presupposes the other virtues and in particular prudence. As observed in the previous section, to require participants in interreligious dialogue to subscribe to the view that all religions are at bottom the same and do not make ultimate truth claims that conflict is an attempt to avoid the difficulties that accompany difference by flattening them out or pretending as though they do not really exist. But differences do exist, and virtuous interreligious dialogue provides a context to face them honestly and learn from one another. Truly accepting differences, then, is the starting point for the acceptance model.

72. Francis, *EG*, 239.

73. Francis, *EG*, 250.

74. Francis, *EG*, 250.

75. Pinckaers, *Sources of Christian Ethics*, 375.

76. Francis, *EG*, 239.

77. John Paul II, *FR*, 27.

According to Knitter, proponents of the acceptance model resist the "vague and amorphous" conception of religious truth espoused by the mutuality model.[78] Interreligious dialogue, then, takes the form of "swapping stories" or apologetics.[79] Agreeing with George Lindbeck that "every religious viewpoint or claim is, by its very nature and self-definition, *comprehensive*," Paul Griffiths makes his "apology for apologetics."[80] The measure of comprehensiveness appears to be explanatory power. A comprehensive truth is capable of "including or explaining everything else but not able to be included or surpassed by anything else."[81] Facing the difficulty of real difference and trying to find constructive ways of attending to those difficulties is the occasion for fortitude.

The acceptance model entails not only accepting the real differences between the religions, but also the comprehensive and central role religions play in the lives of believers. One should accept that, whatever he might say, he really does believe his religion to be the most true (which is why he believes it), but also that his dialogue partner feels the same about her or his religion (which is why she or he believes it). Having accepted these facts, instead of pretending them away for the sake of niceness, the dialogue partners may then proceed "dialectically, through opposing ideas" to make their respective cases.[82] The Christian approach to "interreligious apology" commended by Griffiths may again be reflected in the work of C. S. Lewis who, while acknowledging that Christians "do not have to believe that all the other religions are simply wrong all through," nevertheless went on to affirm that Christians do have to think "that where Christianity differs from other religions, Christianity is right and they are wrong." Lewis uses the analogy of arithmetic to further clarify his position: "there is only one right answer to a sum, and all other answers are wrong; but some of the wrong answers are much nearer being right than others."[83] The intention driving the activity here is not "the pleasure of knocking out the other opponents. Rather, it is a matter of ethical duty, for if I believe that the comprehensive, saving religious truth granted to me is not just for me but can and should transform the lives of all, I want to share it."[84]

---

78. Knitter, *Introducing Theologies of Religions*, 114.

79. Knitter, *Introducing Theologies of Religions*, 185.

80. Knitter, *Introducing Theologies of Religions*, 185. See Griffiths, *Apology for Apologetics*. See also Lindbeck, "Gospel's Uniqueness."

81. Knitter, *Introducing Theologies of Religions*, 185.

82. Knitter, *Introducing Theologies of Religions*, 186.

83. Lewis, *Mere Christianity*, 35.

84. Knitter, *Introducing Theologies of Religions*, 186.

While importantly distinct from the replacement model, the acceptance model does recognize that hearing and responding to the Gospel entails turning away "from, some of the practices or attitudes that [one] previously did not question. There will, in other words, be some form, some degree, of *replacement*."[85] At the same time, one can maintain "an attitude of openness in truth and love" to one's dialogue partner since, as Knitter observes, "interreligious dialogue is meant to be a truly *mutual* dialogue. Everything that Christians believe can happen to other believers in the dialogue can also happen to Christians. When Christians open themselves up to others in interreligious conversations, they too must be ready to be 'upset,' maybe turned around, challenged to replace certain beliefs or practices that they never before questioned."[86]

Sharing the Gospel in a spirit of "openness in truth and love" entails willing the good of the other: "Advocates of [the acceptance] model remind other Christians of something they too easily forget: you can't really love your neighbor unless you accept, really accept, her/his otherness."[87]

In this way, the various models "can serve as a dynamic interplay of checks and balances for each other."[88] In a similar fashion, the "dynamic interplay" of the virtues can help illuminate these models, or so I have argued. By way of conclusion, it is worthwhile to make explicit that which has been implicit throughout the current essay, namely, the integral role of the theological virtues in elevating interreligious dialogue to the level of authentic evangelization characterized by Pope Francis in *Evangelii gaudium*.

Interreligious Dialogue as Authentic Evangelization

The purpose of this concluding section is to analyze the relationship of the theological virtues to interreligious dialogue and, by extension, authentic evangelization. A morality of happiness approach helps elucidate the intrinsic connection between interreligious dialogue considered as a practice and communal and individual flourishing. At the same time, attention to the ways that the theological virtues shape and elevate the cardinal virtues examined heretofore clarifies the interplay between sharing the truth clung to in faith and the seeking out of greater understanding in love and openness to the other.

---

85. Knitter, *Introducing Theologies of Religions*, 240.

86. Knitter, *Introducing Theologies of Religions*, 241.

87. Knitter, *Introducing Theologies of Religions*, 241.

88. Knitter, *Introducing Theologies of Religions*, 239.

Aquinas understands charity as friendship with God.[89] One of the ways that this love is lived out is through willing the good of the other: "Goodwill properly speaking is that act of the will whereby we wish well to another."[90] However, Aquinas thinks this definition incomplete, since "to love, considered as an act of charity, includes goodwill, but such dilection or love adds union of affections, wherefore the Philosopher says that goodwill is a beginning of friendship."[91] Thus, love "extends not only to the love of God, but also to the love of our neighbor."[92]

Friendship with God also informs Aquinas's understanding of the "living hope . . . whereby man hopes to obtain good from God as from a friend."[93] Also connected with friendship, Aquinas defines faith as "certainty of the mind about absent things which surpasses opinion but falls short of science."[94] He goes on to note that this faith, caused by grace, "is always working man's justification, even as the sun is always lighting up the air." Aquinas, then, clarifies on this basis that "grace is not less effective when it comes to a believer than when it comes to an unbeliever: since it causes faith in both, in the former by confirming and perfecting it, in the latter by creating it anew."[95]

Francis also makes clear the indispensable role of the theological virtues in interreligious dialogue understood here as an aspect of authentic evangelization. Echoing Aquinas at several points, Francis notes that evangelization is "sustained by our own constantly renewed experience of savoring Christ's friendship and his message."[96] Inviting others into this friendship is constitutive of seeking true fulfillment of one's desires: "We do so not from a sense of obligation, not as a burdensome duty, but as the result of a personal decision which brings us joy and gives meaning to our lives."[97] Love simultaneously entails "seeking the good of others" while remaining open to "learning something new about God" in our encounters with them. Francis defines "loving others [as] a spiritual force drawing us to union with God."[98]

---

89. Aquinas, *ST*, IIa IIae q. 23 a. 1. I use the words "charity" and "love" interchangeably.

90. Aquinas, *ST*, IIa IIae q. 27 a. 2.

91. Aquinas, *ST*, IIa IIae q. 27 a. 2.

92. Aquinas, *ST*, IIa IIae q. 25 a. 1.

93. Aquinas, *ST*, IIa IIae q. 17 a. 8 ad. 2.

94. Aquinas, *ST*, IIa IIae q. 4 a. 1.

95. Aquinas, *ST*, IIa IIae q. 4 a. 4.

96. Francis, *EG*, 266.

97. Francis, *EG*, 269.

98. Francis, *EG*, 272.

Continuing with his analysis of the theological virtues applied to authentic evangelization, Francis notes that we are to give "reasons for our hope . . . not as an enemy who critiques and condemns" but rather with "gentleness and reverence" (1 Pet 3:15).[99] Francis seems to echo Rahner noting that "Jesus does not want us to be grandees who look down upon others."[100] Hope is nourished by loving others since a self-centered approach to evangelization that seeks quick results that provide us with "recognition, applause, rewards, and status" will disappoint and lead to despair. Francis refers to this as "careerism" and warns that "the resurrection is not there."[101]

Faith is "an interior certainty, a conviction that God is able to act in every situation, even amid apparent setbacks."[102] To have faith is to believe that "God truly loves us, that he is alive, that he is mysteriously capable of intervening, that he does not abandon us and that he brings good out of evil by his power and infinite creativity."[103] It is by means of this gift of faith that one persists in weakness and perseveres even when one's efforts appear not to be bearing any fruit and therefore in vain. One recognizes here a conceptual link between fortitude and the unity of the virtues. In Francis's account, the theological virtues seem to operate as the root of the cardinal virtues elevating and redirecting them to the end of a self-emptying love directed to the other.

From this analysis, it becomes clear that, for Francis, interreligious dialogue, as an aspect of authentic evangelization, is not a mere duty or obligation ordered solely to inner-worldly ends. Rather, it is shaped by the character of the human person engaging in interreligious dialogue motivated by love and the desire for friendship. As Francis notes, this mission is "not an 'extra' or just another moment in life. Instead, it is something I cannot uproot from my being without destroying my very self."[104] Francis's account of interreligious dialogue as an aspect of authentic evangelization is most intelligible from the standpoint of a morality of happiness approach specified by the virtues and the question of what it means to live a truly fulfilling life. Out of love for God one seeks greater understanding of God through friendship with others who may view the purpose of human existence in radically divergent ways. Entering into friendship not only with those who

99. Francis, *EG*, 271.

100. Francis, *EG*, 271.

101. Francis, *EG*, 277.

102. Francis, *EG*, 279.

103. Francis, *EG*, 278.

104. Francis, *EG*, 273.

already agree with us on every point but also with those who see the world very differently is entailed by the Christian life and intrinsic to the good life.

Bibliography

Anderson, Gerald H., and Thomas F. Stransky, eds. *Christ's Lordship and Religious Pluralism*. Maryknoll, NY: Orbis, 1981.

Aquinas, Thomas. *Summa theologiae*. http://www.corpusthomisticum.org/sth0000.html.

D'Costa, Gavin. *The Meeting of Religions and the Trinity*. Maryknoll, NY: Orbis, 2000.

Francis. "*Evangelii gaudium*." November 24, 2013. https://w2.vatican.va/content/francesco/en/apost_exhortations/documents/papa-francesco_esortazione-ap_20131124_evangelii-gaudium.html.

Griffiths, Paul. *An Apology for Apologetics: A Study in the Logic of Interreligious Dialogue*. Maryknoll, NY: Orbis, 1991.

Hick, John. *God and the Universe of Faiths*. New York: St. Martin's, 1973.

John Paul II. "*Fides et ratio*." September 14, 1998. http://w2.vatican.va/content/john-paul-ii/en/encyclicals/documents/hf_jp-ii_enc_14091998_fides-et-ratio.html.

Knitter, Paul. *Introducing Theologies of Religions*. Maryknoll, NY: Orbis, 2002.

Lewis, C. S. *Mere Christianity*. San Francisco: Harper Collins, 1952.

Lindbeck, George. "The Gospel's Uniqueness: Election and Untranslatability." *Modern Theology* 13 (1997) 423–50.

Mattison, William C., III. *Introducing Moral Theology: True Happiness and the Virtues*. Grand Rapids, MI: Brazos, 2008.

Pieper, Josef. *The Four Cardinal Virtues*. Notre Dame, IN: University of Notre Dame, 1966.

Pinckaers, Servais. *The Sources of Christian Ethics*. Translated by Mary Thomas Noble. Washington, DC: Catholic University of America Press, 1995.

Rahner, Karl. *Foundations of Christian Faith: An Introduction to the Idea of Christianity*. Translated by William V. Dych. New York: Crossroad, 1978.

Rossano, Piero. "Christ's Lordship and Religious Pluralism in Roman Catholic Perspective." In *Christ's Lordship and Religious Pluralism*, edited by Gerald H. Anderson and Thomas F. Stransky, 102–3. Maryknoll, NY: Orbis, 1981.

CHAPTER 4

The Theology of Religions of Benedict XVI[1]

—Cyril O'Regan

J̲ust as Christian identity has been a concern of Benedict XVI since the beginning of his sixty-year-long theological career, so also has been the concern as how properly to parse the relation between Christianity and other religions that respects long-standing Christian claims of uniqueness in terms of both revelation and salvation, while at the same time acknowledging the positive value of other religions regarding their constitutive symbols, practices, and forms of life. While accepting that there necessarily will be tension between these two aims, nonetheless, Benedict was convinced (at least since the time he was *peritus* at Vatican II) of the necessity to keep the balance between these two concerns and to refuse to tilt either in an exclusivist direction that denied the goodness and holiness manifested in other religions or in a pluralist direction that evacuates claims regarding the definitiveness of the incarnation, passion, death, and resurrection of Christ. It is, arguably, the case that over the past few decades Benedict XVI has been at once the most insistent and consistent voice regarding the necessity of balance in a theological environment that has decisively shifted in a pluralist direction. As is true of all of his theology, the view that Benedict has argued for self-consciously eschews originality. It is an expression of a theological mind and soul that is quintessentially ecclesial. He is convinced that the balanced position that he publically articulates is the position of the Church from the earliest centuries, the fundamental option of his beloved

---

1. Although many—if not most—of the texts that come under consideration in this essay were produced by Benedict XVI before he came Pope, thus under his own name of Joseph Ratzinger, in this essay, I will not use this distinction and will attribute writings made prior to his holding papal office to Benedict XVI.

Ressourcement theologians, Jean Daniélou, Henri de Lubac, and Hans Urs von Balthasar, and the proper interpretation in both spirit and letter of Vatican II. Yet if the articulation of a broadly inclusivist position in theology of religions is in many respects an act of catechesis to a public largely confused on the Church's stance towards other religions, still it cannot be denied that Benedict's statement and restatement of what he takes to be the traditional Catholic view of the matter regarding other religions represents an intervention in a post-Conciliar discussion as to whether Catholicism can or should stretch far more in a pluralist direction than it has thus far either by dropping claims of Christian uniqueness or considerably softening them, come to favor inter-religious dialogue over proclamation, and cease to introduce obstacles to cooperation with other religions, not only in working for justice and the common good, but also in worship and prayer services. Benedict resists all of these calls, even as he warns against Catholicism exhuming a full-blown exclusivist position or even devaluing other religions, which he considers to be sites of profound existential questioning and questing and authentic holiness, and draws attention to the common task of all religions, that is, to resist an aggressive secular modernity whose neutrality is armed.

In presenting Benedict's theology of religions I have made three methodological decisions. First, rather than outlining the main options in theology of religions in the post-Conciliar period, and fitting Benedict into this larger discussion, I focus on the texts of Benedict and point to the larger conversation and argument in and through my presentation of his views. Second, the texts that come in for discussion are almost exclusively post-1990, although I note that while they develop earlier views, they really do not depart from them. Third, I treat the CDF document *Dominus Iesus* (2000) as representing Benedict's position whether or not he is in the strict sense the author of the document. The essay is divided into two parts. In the first part, I offer a close reading of two volumes of essays, *Truth and Tolerance* and *Many Religions—One Covenant*,[2] both of which represent at once a kind of catechesis of the Catholic Church's stance on other religions and an intervention into an ongoing conversation within and without the Church in which pluralism has emerged as the default option. In the second part, I offer a sympathetic reading of *Dominus Jesus* that attempts to make sense of the tone as well as the substance of a document that not only seems to be directed against strong forms of pluralism, but softer forms of pluralism which, if they show respect for official Church positions on the religions, attenuate Christian claims of uniqueness, recommend against proclamation,

---

2. Hereafter I will use the abbreviations TT and MR, respectively.

and advocate consistently for cooperation between religions when it comes to worship and prayer. Suggesting that the exemplary instance of the softer version of pluralism that I take to be an implied target in *Dominus Iesus* is the work of Jacques Dupuis, on the basis of a reading of *Towards a Christian Theology of Religious Pluralism* (1997),[3] which received a Notification from the CDF, I attempt to show what is at stake between Benedict XVI and Dupuis in terms of fundamental option, the status of Ressourcement thinkers on the theology of religions, and the reception of Vatican II.

Benedict on Asian Religions and the Specialness of Judaism

In the first part of this essay I discuss two texts, that is, those essays gathered together in *Truth and Tolerance*, which focus equally on the general principles of a theology of religions and Christianity's relations to Asian religions, and *Many Religions—One Covenant* which, if it illuminates important aspects of Benedict's view of the relation between Christianity and Asian religions, very deliberately elevates the relation between Christianity and Judaism. It is along these investigative axes that Benedict self-consciously attempts to be faithful to Vatican II (*Nostra aetate*, and *Lumen gentium*, 16–17, *Ad gentes*) as well as his own inchoate judgments at the Council regarding the proper way to conceive the relation between Christianity and other religions. I should say at the outset that I will spend considerably more time on the first text, and use the second mainly to confirm and fill out lacunae in the first.

With respect to the essays gathered together in *Truth and Tolerance* I make two decisions in terms of approach: first, I concentrate on those essays that are written in the 1990s and recur to the opening essay, written in 1964,[4] only at the conclusion of my treatment of the text; second, although fully recognizing the integrity of the essays and accepting that they were produced for particular purposes on particular occasions, I treat these essays as elaborating a cohesive theology of religions. Speaking very broadly, *Truth and Tolerance* critically engages the pluralistic option in the theology of religions which has it that no religion, and especially Christianity, can make a claim to ultimate and definitive truth. For Benedict, the pluralist

3. Hereafter I will use the abbreviation TRP. This text demonstrates not only a command of all contemporary theology of religions in modern European languages, but experiential knowledge of Asian religions, as well as an encyclopedic grasp of the Catholic tradition. I will also be referencing—although not discussing—Dupuis's more popular version of his 1997 text, *Christianity and the Religions: From Confrontation to Dialogue.*

4. TT, 15–44.

option, both at the level of assumption and reflective argument, has come
to operate as a kind of default in the contemporary world and has significantly infiltrated Catholic self-understanding. While this essay elaborates
the general principles of relation between Christianity and other religions
in *Truth and Tolerance*, it also attends more specifically to what Benedict
says about Christianity's relation to Asian religions, especially Hinduism
and Buddhism. Stipulating that these religions are at least partial bearers
of truth, Benedict, nonetheless, asserts that Christianity's claim to be the
definitive disclosure of truth cannot be reneged on, and suggests that the
need to assert this claim shows the extraordinary circumstances in which
Christianity finds itself, since this claim is ineluctable and is mandated by
scripture, the theological tradition, and the magisterium.

Benedict makes it clear in *Truth and Tolerance* that now more than at
any time in Western history, with the possible exception of the early centuries in which Christianity was being inculturated into Greek and Latin-
speaking cultures, it is necessary for Christianity to make the claim to truth.
It is not a presumption but rather a duty.[5] Christianity after all, he argues,
is grounded in revelation as the unanticipated self-communication of God
in Christ, who is rendered in scripture and tradition and received in the
ongoing history of the Church. Christ is a singularity: he is neither avatar
nor symbol.[6] Not only is revelation not simply one disclosure among others, neither is it a discursive correlative to the experience of a charismatic
individual or a particular group or both. Rather, it is an event,[7] a breaking
into history of a personal God who gives meaning, direction and truth to
the "people of God" in and through history. Although Benedict does make
the point thematic, he seems to support a restricted view of revelation as
applying only to the self-communication of God, rendered in the biblical
text, and which receives its apogee in God's self-manifestation in Christ.
One assumes that Benedict thinks that this represents a proper reading of
Vatican II, a plausible reading of the post-Vatican II encyclicals of Paul VI
and John Paul II,[8] and a critical response to a significant tendency in the
theology of religions literature that would suggest that all religions belong
to the one order of revelation.

5. TT, 57, 67.

6. TT, 94–96, 104. A position explicitly argued for by Raimundo Panikkar, but,
of course, implied by the likes of Hick and Knitter. See especially Panikkar, *Unknown
Christ of Hinduism*.

7. TT, 88–89.

8. Especially important are Paul VI, *Evangelii nuntiandi* (1975), and John Paul II,
Redemptoris hominis (1979) and *Redemptoris missio* (1990). Also relevant, but perhaps
to a lesser extent, is John Paul II, *Dominum et vivificantem* (1986).

Crucially, however, the preeminence of Christianity is not based on its monopoly of salvation. Benedict queries: "Do we necessarily have to invent a theory about how God can save people without abandoning the uniqueness of Christ ?"[9] Benedict does not subscribe to the view that there is no salvation outside the church. There is nothing of the radical in Benedict's disavowal of the proposition enunciated in at the Council of Florence (1442), but anticipated in the Fourth Lateran Council (1215), and a determinate feature of Catholic Christianity from the time of Cyprian.[10] At the same time, in *Truth and Tolerance* Benedict resists elaborating specific theological criteria whereby the members of non-Christian religions might share in salvation. There are two related lines to his resistance: the first is epistemic, the second has to do with the benefits that accrue to being a member of the Church as the body of Christ that do not specifically have to do with one's situation in the afterlife. From the epistemic point of view, no one can see into God's design or charity with regard to salvation which in the final analysis is gratuitous. We can have no adequate grasp of the why or how. With regards to the second, Benedict has serious reservations regarding exclusivity or even parsing the difference between Catholic Christianity and other religions in terms of salvation.[11] Instead, Benedict broadly situates himself within the line of influence of Ressourcement theology in thinking that in the Catholic Church persons are conformed to Christ in the Holy Spirit and thereby come into relation with the Father. Thus without prejudice to the salvation of persons in other religions Benedict suggests that persons in the Catholic Church are already in a direct and fructifying relation with the triune God—a relation constitutive of the eschatological state. The junction between assertion of Christian preeminence and downplaying salvation as the criterion of preeminence puts Benedict at odds with such pluralists as John Hick,[12] Paul Knitter,[13] and their German equivalents,[14] while bringing him close to the position suggested by the

9. TT, 53.

10. The proposition "no salvation outside the Church" has Patristic ancestry. While Cyprian, Augustine, and prominent followers of Augustine—such as Prosper of Aquitaine and Fulgentius of Ruspe—have versions, it is at best inchoate in early Christian thinkers who are far more interested in denying salvation to heretics than to members of other religions.

11. TT, 55.

12. TT, 52, 119–21, 126, 131.

13. TT, 52, 113, 126, 131.

14. TT, 52. Benedict cites Hick, *Christian Theology of Religions*; Knitter, *No Other Name!* The German theologian whom Benedict picks out for particular attention in *Truth and Tolerance* is Bertram Stubenrauch. He praises his *Dialogische Dogma: Der christliche Auftrag zur interreligiösen Begegnung*. See TT, 52, for references.

post-Liberal theologian George Lindbeck and fully elaborated by Joseph Di-Noia.[15] It also associates him with the position advocated by Gavin D'Costa whose theology of religions reflections are,[16] arguably, more academically rigorous than that of Benedict and whose knowledge of world religions is truly expert in the way that Benedict's is not.

For Benedict, it follows that if Christianity is the reception of revelation, then it is obliged to proclaim the good news boldly.[17] The mandate is biblical and it is incised in the mission *ad gentes* ("to the nations") that is definitional of Christianity. To systematically proscribe or programmatically discourage mission is, therefore, from Benedict's point of view, historically out of joint and definitionally aberrant. Benedict is insistent on this point in the core essays in *Truth and Tolerance*. Given that Benedict is making this point in essays he conceives as interventions, it would be unreasonable to expect him to go into detail regarding the biblical, theological and magisterial warrants. At the same time by no means does Benedict suggest that mission and proclamation at all times and in every circumstance trump witness and dialogue. Again, in *Truth and Tolerance* it is not, however, his brief to provide criteria as to when and where proclamation and mission come to the fore. His object is the very narrow (although very important) one of re-establishing as a matter of principle that proclamation and mission are identifying features of Christianity and thus that a Christian is required to imagine some circumstances in which they come into play.

In *Truth and Tolerance* a sustained attack against the discourses of cultural and religious pluralism represents the complement to Benedict's insistence on the definitiveness of Christianity and the responsibilities of proclamation and mission.[18] Benedict sees both discourses to be infected with relativism. Naming and charting relativism is, arguably, the core task of *Truth and Tolerance*.[19] Its operation shows itself in the slide between rightfully acknowledging the plurality of cultures and religions in a complex world, many of which demonstrate a search for ultimate meaning and

---

15. See Lindbeck, *Nature of Doctrine*; DiNoia, *Diversity of Religions*. DiNoia's book is dependent in significant ways on the work of the philosopher William A. Christian. See Christian, *Doctrines of Religious Communities*.

16. Gavin D'Costa has been a major presence in the field of theology of religions who has opposed the pluralist view. Among his many book contributions, see D'Costa, *Christian Uniqueness Reconsidered*; *Meeting of Religions*; *Christianity and World Religions*.

17. TT, 57, 105.

18. TT, 67, 105.

19. TT, 70–71, 117–19, 162–63, 178, *inter alia*.

value,[20] and ruling out the possibility that one religion may be first among equals. In terms therefore of the distinction between commitment to pluralism in fact or in principle, Benedict resolutely affirms the former and refuses the latter. He understands that his choice will be controversial in an age in which there has been a shift in the other direction. For Benedict, the emerging proscription against Christianity asserting any form of superiority occurs in significant part at the level of the modern social unconscious,[21] or what Charles Taylor would refer to as the modern "social imaginary." Thus, the proscription is intrinsically dogmatic in character.[22] It is illuminating in this regard to imagine Benedict proposing a specific version of a more general point that Newman made in the *Oxford University Sermons*, (1826–43) that is, key features of modern thought such as tolerance, democracy, and the primacy of reason have come to be assumptions that moderns do not feel compelled to argue for. At the same time, it should be said that Benedict does not ignore the reflective forms of cultural and religious pluralism.[23] Doubtless, Benedict thinks that the liberal principles of tolerance and democracy play an important role in reflective pluralistic constructions at least as background assumptions. In *Truth and Tolerance* by and large Benedict tends to underscore the epistemological argument routinely adduced by those who advocate the pluralist position in theology of religions. While there are a number of epistemological strategies available to Christian thinkers to relativize truth claims, the one highlighted by Benedict is that of Kant,[24] who demonstrated the impossibility of redeeming truth claims concerning the nature and existence of God on the grounds that God exceeds human beings' finite cognitive capacities. Kantian epistemology is effectively ground zero, for example, in the case of Hick in his argument against Christian claims to definitiveness and truth.[25]

20. TT, 82, 230.

21. TT, 106, 119–21.

22. TT, 70–71, 106.

23. See TT, 52–53, 71–72. Benedict makes it abundantly clear that he is opposing the likes of Hick and Knitter. Interestingly, he gives qualified approval to Dupuis. The approval is rendered after the resolution of the CDF querying of Dupuis, *Towards a Christian Theology*.

24. TT, 131–37. See also TT, 83–84.

25. Hick's theology of religions depends explicitly on Kant's epistemology and especially on the distinction between appearance and the thing-in-itself. This is no less true of Hick's many other books in the area of theology of religions than it is with regard to Hick, *Christian Theology of Religions*. Now, three things should be noted: (a) Kant himself in all likelihood would not license the use of his epistemology in theology of religions, since it seems to suggest various orders of adequacy in signification regarding a reality that by definition transcends the order of signification; (b) in Hick's theology

Now while pluralism can be asserted generically, it can also be asserted with regard to a particular group of religions. In the case of *Truth and Tolerance* the relevant group of religions are Asian and more specifically Hinduism and Buddhism. Benedict identifies two areas of concern. The first and broader concern has more to do with Western interest in fashioning a synthesis between Christianity and Hinduism and Buddhism than with these religions themselves. From Benedict's points of view, the danger is a superficial syncretism that does justice neither to Christianity, nor to Hinduism or Buddhism. Thus the problem with interreligious prayer services on more than an exceptional basis, since one cannot assume that the addressee of prayer is identical in the case of Christianity, Hinduism, and Buddhism, or that there is in fact an addressee.[26] For Benedict, the embargo against artificial blending of Christianity, Hinduism, and Buddhism specifies the general principle of the non-interchangeability of religions.[27] The respect due the integrity of Christianity is, therefore, but a derivative of the general principle. Benedict's second and more narrow and specific concern has to do with the tendency in these major world religions—at least as picked out by their Western admirers—to emphasize a form of divine mystery that has its correlative in the inadequacy of all symbolization.[28] Thus the legitimation not only of the fact of plurality in matters of religion, but the necessity

of religions a Kantian epistemology does not provide the motivation for thinking of the divine as the signified that escapes all signification, but rather the warrant for thinking of the divine as not fully graspable in our language, concepts, and symbols; (c) even in the case of pluralists such as Hick, the initial relativization of all religions and thus equalization is not necessarily sustained over the long run. Hick, in *Christian Theology of Religions* (and elsewhere), often proceeds towards a ranking. This performative contradiction is, however, not something that Benedict points out.

26. Sticking merely to Hinduism and Buddhism, there are two main kinds of difficulty. Although Hinduism is extraordinarily ramified and has theistic as well as pantheistic inflections, there is a radical non-dualist element that has its origin in the *Upanishads* and makes its way into the non-dualist (*advaita*) philosophy of Sankara. Of course, there is also a theistic streak in the *Upanishads* that flowers in the *Bhagavad Gita* with the god Krishna and continually reappears in the Bhakti or love tradition in Hinduism that lasts down to the contemporary period. In its non-dualist trajectory the aim is the abolition of the distinction between the self and the divine, Atman and Brahman, respectively. On the other hand, the initial form of Buddhism, Theravada or Hinayana Buddhism, in contrast to Mahayana Buddhism, which imagines a world of semi-divine bodhisattvas, speaks only to states of consciousness and especially the overcoming of passion. Nirvana is related to *nibbana*, which in Sanskrit means "quenching" with the particular sense of the quenching of desire. In Hinayana Buddhism there is neither I nor Thou. With regard to his knowledge of Hinduism in particular, Benedict seems to depend to a considerable extent on R. C. Zaehner.

27. TT, 109.

28. TT, 121–25.

of plurality and the principled equality of religious approaches. In the field of theology of religions, Hinduism and Buddhism are not simply two major world religions with whom Christianity can and should enter dialogue and with respect to which it is compelled to take a stance, but in their presumptive reflection on symbolic inadequacy these religions become nothing less than parables of how Christianity should understand its own symbols and doctrines. To be truly open to other religions then means that we can be instructed by their epistemological modesty and their inherent pluralism and convert from the default exclusivism that has been an objectionable feature of Christian history.[29]

While there are many reasons to question the accuracy of the profile offered in the pluralist literature concerning these religions that seemed to be relaxed when it comes to truth claims, Benedict does not feel in a position to adjudicate. In any event, as already indicated, Benedict is more interested in Western and more specifically Christian construction of these religions and how it bears on making the case that Christianity should cease to make the claim to truth that hither to fore provides much of the energy for Christian mission. Without drawing attention to particular figures or specific texts, Benedict also wishes to cut off a line of pluralist argument that would link the so-called relativism of the symbolic systems of Hinduism and Buddhism with the Christian mystical tradition with its apparatus of negative theology.[30] In the hands of some unnamed thinkers with pluralist tendencies, the Christian mystical tradition provides an internal correlative of what Christianity comes upon in Asian religions,[31] and thus doubles the incentive and energy to get rid of the shibboleth of an absolutist claim that does not rhyme with Christianity's better, non-dogmatic self. As a scholar of

29. With respect to Hinduism, this style of argument is used by Panikkar, whose work is known to Benedict. With respect to the relationship between Christianity and Buddhism this style of argument is used by the self-consciously postmodern Irish theologian, Joseph Steven O'Leary. See his very interesting *Religious Pluralism and Christian Truth* in which he conjugates a Buddhist logic of negation with Christian negative theology and Derridian deconstruction. Robert M. Gimello focuses on the Buddhist–Christian connection on this point in his fine essay, Gimello, "Depth of Otherness," 114–41.

30. TT, 176–77, 179. This analysis, although often provided by Western assimilators of Hinduism, as Benedict indicates, can also be made from within. See TT, 24–25, 29–30 where Benedict names Radhakhrishnan.

31. Joseph O'Leary's book provides perhaps one of the more sophisticated forms of this form of comparative mysticism. But popular religious figures like Suzuki were for the longest time connecting Christian mysticism with both *advaita* forms of Hinduism and Buddhism. It is interesting that Meister Eckhart, who is the most radical negative theology thinker in the Christian mystical tradition, was used as the Christian *comparandum*.

Augustine and Bonaventure,[32] Benedict is not inclined to accept, that as it functions in the mystical tradition, suggestions of lack of absolute adequacy in symbol and concept are intended to relativize the fundamental Christological, Trinitarian, anthropological, and eschatological claims of Christianity. Their function, he believes, is simply to chasten our presumption of a complete grasp of a personal divine that exceeds us. Part of the problem, according to Benedict, is the failure in pluralist thinkers to recognize the vast difference between the kind of Neoplatonic mysticism that one observes in a non-Christian thinker such as Porphyry and a Christian thinker such as Augustine.[33] In making his point about the function of negation in Christian mysticism in contradistinction to its function outside, Benedict is (as usual) both economic and pragmatic. Nonetheless, it can be said with a fair degree of certainty that his understanding of the Christian apophatic tradition is very much in line not only with his beloved Ressourcement theologians,[34] but also with the best scholarship in the Christian mystical tradition.[35]

32. Benedict's dissertation (1954) was on Augustine's notion of the Church with particular attention to *City of God*; his Habilitation on the topic of theology of history in Bonaventure. See Ratzinger, *Volk und Haus Gottes*; *Die Geschichtstheologie des heiligen Bonaventura* (1959).

33. TT, 175. For example, in *De doctrina christiana* (1.6) and *De Trinitate* (Book 8), Augustine makes it clear that apophasis neither abolishes the givens of revelation or doctrine, but humbles the intellect before a God who exceeds signification. Of course, the influence of Augustine, who was the subject of Benedict's dissertation (1954), is everywhere in Benedict, especially in the areas of the understanding of the Church, human person, last things, and the nature of the theological task that is both polemical and constructive. For general coverage of the influence of Augustine on Benedict's thought, see O'Regan, "Benedict the Augustinian," 21–60. Of course, this very same point can be made with respect to Bonaventure, on whom Benedict wrote his Habilitation (1959). Although the level of negative theology is high in the Franciscan theologian, he does not think that he is speaking of a penultimate reality when he is speaking of the Trinity and Christ. This becomes especially clear in Bonaventure, *Itinerarium mentis ad Deum*.

34. To take just one example, this is the view of von Balthasar in this 1942 book on Gregory of Nyssa, and for that matter, his view in his book on Maximus the Confessor around the same period. We know that Benedict has read the Nyssa book. For an analysis of von Balthasar's stance on negative theology, see O'Regan, "Von Balthasar and Eckhart"; "Von Balthasar and Thick Retrieval." Although it has to be said that, of the Ressourcement theologians, it is de Lubac who exercises the greatest influence, von Balthasar is a fairly close second. See Benedict's early review essay, "Christian Universalism" (1961). A translation of this review essay by Adrian J. Walker can be found in Walker, *Unity of the Church*, 131–43.

35. Perhaps the best example is the work of Denys Turner, who, in both historical and philosophical registers, reflects on Christian grammar and the role that negative predication plays in it. See especially Turner, *Darkness of God*. In that book, while Turner covers a variety of mystical figures—including Meister Eckhart, who is a favorite in comparative mysticism—he spends considerable time on Benedict's two favorites, Augustine (50–101) and Bonaventure (102–34).

There are two other important ideological supports of the pluralist view that Benedict questions in *Truth and Tolerance*, namely (a) the view of the inviolable integrity of non-Western cultures and non-Christian religions such that any attempt to transform them is wrongheaded, and also (b) the view of the deep linkage between Christianity and violence that renders ethically suspect any attempt by Christianity to evangelize. Benedict does not think that a concern for the integrity of a culture and religion is entirely misplaced.[36] This amounts to more than a polite concession in his case, since Benedict basically thinks of Christianity as itself a culture with specific density rather than an ethereal faith floating above all culture.[37] At the same time Benedict does not feel that the assumption of the complete inviolability or "impenetrability"—and by implication incommensurability—of culture is justified. Nor is he persuaded that the arguments made against evangelization are valid. Now, on the level of assumption and reflection, the view of the absolute integrity of cultures and religions is supported by two suppositions neither of which, Benedict is convinced, can survive critical scrutiny. The first of these is the supposition that cultures and religions are static rather than dynamic[38]; the second is that any change brought to a culture and/or religion from the outside necessarily degrades them, and, more specifically, that as a religion with a determinate European stamp, Christianity cannot avoid facilitating the colonizing process.[39] For Benedict, the first view represents a denial of history and procedurally amounts to a form of Platonism. In his view, the second supposition confounds integrity with aboriginal goodness and thereby immunizes any given state of affairs regarding beliefs (however vicious) and practices (however dehumanizing) from criticism.

This is to state matters perhaps in too lapidary a manner. For Benedict any given culture or religion is a historical product, and its integrity is complex and ramified rather than simple. What is the case with regard to Christianity's emergence from Judaism[40] is repeatable with regard to other religions. Certainly, Benedict could make the point about the emergence of Buddhism from a complex form of Hinduism in which myth and ritual lived alongside philosophical inquiry into the relation between soul (Atman) and the foundation of reality (Brahman), and more erotic and affective avowal of a relationship between human being and a personal divine once

36. TT, 69.
37. TT, 67, 69.
38. TT, 59–60.
39. TT, 85–89.
40. TT, 83.

the veil of illusion has been pierced.[41] Like Christianity's complex relation of separation, continuity, and reformatting of biblical Judaism, such is also the case with regard to the relation between Buddhism and Hinduism. To insist, therefore, on a form of integrity immune to influence and change is essentially to make a culture or religion an exhibit in a museum. Moreover, the prescription of purity is mischievous as well as idle when it comes to the contemporary world in which Western capitalism is the main agent of breakdown of culture and religion world-wide.[42]

To insist on the purity of all cultures and non-Christian religions is, from Benedict's point of view, apriorist. Benedict does not indulge in genealogical reflection with regard to the provenance of this view in the Enlightenment, nor attempt to excavate the anti-Christianity that might be fueling this idea. It is sufficient for him to suggest that such claims necessarily have to be phenomenologically or empirically verified. Benedict is persuaded that should the rules of evidence be followed, then one would quite likely find that cultures and religions may have vicious beliefs and have correspondingly bad practices. The Aztec religion, for example, demonized outside groups and supported human sacrifice.[43] Although in his discussions of Hinduism in *Truth and Tolerance* Benedict does not inventory beliefs or practices that might be questionable, on the basis of other texts, which could be associated with Benedict, it seems safe to assume that Benedict thinks that the beliefs that support the caste system are wrongheaded and that the practice of a widow immolating herself on the pyre with her husband is objectionable.[44] All of this is simply to say that even the most well-meaning engagement with a particular culture or religion allows in principle that criticism might come into play. Whether such criticism is in fact levied depends entirely on the circumstances. Again Benedict does not

41. In the last case I am speaking about the Bhakti or love tradition which receives an exemplary expression in the *Bhagavad Gita* which dates approximately to two centuries before Christ and which has Krishna, an avatar of one of the three main gods, Vishnu, as its main divine protagonist. This text, over the millennia, has exercised considerable influence in Hinduism and is responsible in particular for the more personal rather than impersonal view of the divine.

42. This point, which is often mentioned in *Truth and Tolerance*, is reiterated throughout the essays that make up Benedict, *Christianity and the Crisis of Cultures*. It is given something of an exclamation point in Benedict's encyclical *Caritas in veritate* (2009).

43. TT, 74. In *Truth and Tolerance*, Benedict also proves that he is not a fan of Voodoo (TT, 77–78).

44. See CDF, *Letters to the Bishops*. In this 1986 document, both the caste system and the practice of Sutti—the immolation of a widow on the funeral pyre—is condemned.

give an inventory of circumstances under which it would be appropriate to criticize.[45] In *Truth and Tolerance* it is more an issue of Christians avoiding confusion. Simply put, there is a law of transitivity: it is not appropriate to affirm the human dignity of all in Christianity and then to proceed to affirm the caste system in another religion; it is not appropriate to question the role of women in Christianity, while failing to think problematic the practice in Hinduism of a woman's immolation on her husband's funeral pyre. In addition, for Benedict it is not a zero-sum game between self-critique or other-critique. Benedict rules out the exclusivist position from the beginning, that is, the view that non-Christian religions, precisely because they do not in the strict sense belong to the order of revelation, are without significant value.[46]

Given the Christian claim to truth, logically speaking, the truth and value quotient of other religions cannot be absolute. As a matter of principle, therefore, there will be flaws in other religions that are variously wide and deep, even if there is spiritual questioning and quest and an orientation towards a divine horizon that Christianity proposes to be Trinitarian. Benedict also realizes that, as a matter of fact, whatever claims are made on behalf of the Church, its members are flawed. More than that Benedict does not give any evidence that he is out of sync with his predecessor, John Paul II, when it comes to the condemnation of the behavior of Christianity towards Jews throughout the centuries, the Crusades, and the ways that Christianity aided in the colonization and mistreatment of the indigenous people of Africa and the Americas. There are pathological forms of religion,[47] and Christianity is not exempt. There is a need for mindfulness of systemic Christian wrongdoing. This mindfulness should rightly chasten Christian reproof and reproach of the beliefs and practices of other cultures and religions. On pain of ceasing to hold the convictions we hold, however, acknowledgement of Christian faults can no more rule out criticism of other cultures and religions than affirmation of Christian uniqueness. Self-criticism and other-criticism, therefore, should be regarded as correlative rather than as they tend to be thought in our thoroughly "modern" age as a zero-sum game.

Benedict also wants to take out a second supporting stanchion for the pluralist case, that is, the systemic connection between Christianity's claim for definitiveness and violence.[48] Benedict is aware that the association be-

45. TT, 65–66.
46. TT, 49, 80.
47. TT, 158.
48. TT, 210–58.

tween Christianity and violence is a long-standing one that came to the fore in Enlightenment polemics against Christianity and is illustrated in a host of figures, for example, Bayle, Locke, and Voltaire. However, in *Truth and Tolerance* this supposed connection takes on new urgency due to the work Jan Assmann who argues for an intrinsic relation between monotheistic intolerance and violence.[49] Benedict's critical engagement proceeds along two tracks. The first is a refutation of Assmann's counter-positive, that is, the view that polytheistic religions are necessarily less violent than monotheistic religions.[50] Benedict has a fairly easy time calling this position to account: methodologically the position advocated by Assmann is apriorist in the extreme; substantively, it is simply wrong, given the existence of an abundance of counterfactuals, including many instances that one can come across in the history of polytheistic religions sanctioning human sacrifice.[51] Moreover, it stands to reason that, as essentially religions of particular groups, polytheistic religions are invested solely in the flourishing of their specific group, which means that the gods of other religions are tolerated only to the extent that these groups are tolerated. In an earlier essay in the collection of essays that make up *Truth and Tolerance* Benedict ascribes to Augustine this recognition in the first six books of the *City of God* were he speaks to political religions.[52] The second track is positive. Benedict argues, again on the authority of Augustine, that the God of Christianity is irrefragably a God of peace because a God of wisdom and love. While it is true that the Church has blood on its hands, and is in need of repentance, this has not to do with the Christian claim as such, which is prepared to recognize the truth and

49. For references to Jan Assmann in *Truth and Tolerance*, see TT 201–24, 221–22, also 226, 227. The text that Benedict refers to is Assmann's *Moses der Ägypter*. Leaving aside the implausible hypothesis that Jewish monotheism has its roots in the memory of a form of monotheism (better henotheism) in Egypt in the second millennium before the common era (associated with Akhenaten), Assmann's provocation is that monotheism—which goes under the rubric of the "Mosaic distinction" is intrinsically connected with violence. Although Benedict recognizes that this argument is popular in Enlightenment thinkers, Assmann has given it renewed energy by posing a genetic thesis. One can suppose that Assmann's provocation regarding the connection between violence and monotheism is being responded to in Benedict's *Regensburg Address* (2006).

50. TT, 217–21.

51. Benedict is convinced that a truly empirical study of other religions will bear out his point that a great deal of violence is displayed in non-monotheistic religions. In thinking to the contrary that monotheistic religions counterintuitively are oriented towards peace, Benedict seems to invite conversation with the philosophy of religion of René Girard.

52. TT, 1.

value adumbrated in other religions[53] as well as the essential dignity of all human persons.[54]

The essays of *Truth and Tolerance* lodge a protest against assumptive and reflective forms of pluralism in the theology of religions, especially regarding the relation between Christianity and Asian religions, while insisting on the ineluctability of the Christian claim to definitive truth. These essays also present sophisticated refutations of some of the more stock arguments in favor of religious pluralism including a relativistic epistemology, the parable of the relativism of symbolism supplied by Hinduism and Buddhism, as well as the apophaticism of the Christian mystical tradition, which functions as a Trojan horse against Christian truth claims. These essays also call out the so-called absolute integrity of cultures and religions that cannot be submitted to transformation or even criticism, and finally the intrinsic link between Christianity and violence. The only remaining question to be asked is whether the essays represent a major deviation from the Benedict who attended Vatican II as a theological expert. Fortunately, in *Truth and Tolerance* Benedict provides us with a means for testing. The first essay in *Truth and Tolerance* was written for a Festschrift for Karl Rahner in 1964.[55] Although there is a little retrospective voice-over in Benedict's insisting that, given the laudatory form of a Festschrift, he did not distance himself a great deal from Rahner and that, in addition, when he is not really talking about Rahner, he operates almost exclusively on the descriptive or "phenomenological"[56] rather than evaluative level, nonetheless, there is much in the essay that anticipates the essays gathered together in *Truth and Tolerance* from the 1990s. Four points of continuity are especially important: (i) subscription to the absolute value of Christianity vis-à-vis other religions[57]—a version of this position is, Benedict thinks, implied even in Rahner's elaboration of the "anonymous Christian"; (ii) the view that the *Zeitgeist* favors pluralism and is against mission[58]; (iii) rejection of the largely "symbolic" interpretation of religious beliefs and practices—Christianity not excepted—which suggests the equality of religions[59]; and (iv)

---

53. TT, 230.

54. For Benedict, as well as for John Paul II, the affirmation of human dignity is essential to Catholicism. See especially Benedict, *Values in a Time of Upheaval.* The affirmation of human dignity finds eloquent expression in Benedict's encyclical *Deus caritas est* (2005).

55. TT, 15–44.

56. TT, 17–18, 36.

57. TT, 19, 21, 25.

58. TT, 22–23.

59. TT, 23.

relatedly, a rejection of the prioritizing of mystical forms of religion over institutional forms of religion[60] that emphasize conceptual inadequacy and, in consequence, that all religions are equally distanced from mystery and truth as such.

This brings me to my second and final point concerning Benedict's elaboration of the theology of religions in *Truth and Tolerance*. Through-out the essays in the collection as well as his retrospective comments, while denying pluralism in the strict sense, or what he calls at one point "plural-ism in its radical form,"[61] Benedict affirms the plurality of religions and draws attention to the Patristic view of non-Christian religions as "seeds of the Word" (*logoi spermatikoi*)[62] as partial truths approximating the de-finitive truth that is identified with Christianity.[63] Benedict is not making a merely historical point. From the Christian perspective he means to exhibit the maximum generosity with respect to non-Christian religions compat-ible both with relativizing them vis-à-vis Christianity and being justified in pointing to their shortcomings when appropriate. The prioritization of Christianity is not then strictly speaking a prioritizing of the Church as such, although, in line with *Lumen gentium*, Benedict entertains a high view of the Church as sacrament of Christ who is nothing less than the definitive disclosure of God in human history. In these texts as elsewhere, however, Benedict's ecclesiocentrism is a function of his Christocentrism.

Although Benedict is well grounded in the Fathers, he is not to be blamed when he focuses on Augustine's act of rejection of various forms of religion (political religions) rather than on the Alexandrians who em-phasized more nearly proximity than distance between Christianity and other religions. The overall grammar of relation in both cases in any event is complex, and there are operative vocabularies in both of affirmation and critique. For example, the complement to the negative evaluations of other religions in *The City of God* is the positive evaluation of cultures, philosophy and religions in *On Christian Doctrine*, and while in the *Stromata* Clement of Alexandria has many positive things to say about ancient philosophies and religions, he is not short of negatives when it comes to Homeric re-ligion and Epicurean philosophy. Augustine reminds us of the prospect of idolatry in non-Christian religions as a property to be especially aware of. Augustine can be our Catholic guide even today not simply because he

---

60. TT, 26–27.

61. TT, 81.

62. TT, 81, 97, 171.

63. In adopting this Patristic view, Benedict draws some inspiration from the documents of Vatican II.

is a genius, but because he is biblically faithful. And again, for Benedict, the Augustinian note seems harsh not only because of the emergent social imaginary in which it seems to be in bad taste for Christians to claim Christian uniqueness and make negative comments about other religions, but also epistemically irresponsible in the first case and morally culpable in the second, given the Christian history of violence towards native peoples and other universal religions.[64] In addition, *Truth and Tolerance* gives evidence that the overall cast of Benedict's theology of religions was Patristic from the very beginning. In his 1964 essay in the Festschrift for Rahner, Benedict makes this point by means of his extended appreciation of Jean Daniélou on this point.[65] Arguably, the reference to Daniélou indicates two things, first, that broadly speaking Benedict's theology of religions finds its basic inspiration in Ressourcement theology which, while it encouraged large-scale encounter with other world religions, insisted on the unsurpassability of Christ and Christianity's special relation to Judaism and, second, that it accords with the literal as well as spiritual sense of the relevant documents of Vatican II, as well as the encyclicals of Paul VI and John Paul II.

I turn now to *Many Religions—One Covenant* (1999). I will be much briefer in my analysis, and will limit myself to those points that confirm, complement, or develop points made in *Truth and Tolerance*. As with *Truth and Tolerance* the essays compiled in *Many Religions—One Covenant* date from the 1990s, and thus immediately before the publication of *Dominus Iesus* (2005). There is considerable overlap between it and *Truth and Tolerance* in terms of theological agenda, but only the last essay reflects explicitly on the relation between Christianity and other religions, with most of the text taken up with elaborating an understanding of the proper relationship between Christianity and Judaism. For Benedict, as for John Paul II, this task is imperative, given Christian origins, the history of relations between the two faiths, and the Shoah. Still, overall the collection of essays can be read not only as articulating a coherent theology of religions, but also a particular reception—albeit a disputed one—of Vatican II in general and *Nostra aetate* in particular. I begin with some observations on the last essay "The Dialogue of the Religions,"[66] and then proceed to the three other essays that underscore the special relation between Christianity and Judaism.

A major overlap between the position advanced in "The Dialogue of the Religions" and that of *Truth and Tolerance* is that not only can

---

64. In his 1964 essay on Rahner, Benedict already had a taxonomy of religions that moved from primitive religions, through non-monotheistic world religions and monotheistic world religions, to Christianity.

65. TT, 39–41.

66. MR, 90–113.

Christianity claim to be the "true religion," but it is obliged to do so.[67] The obligation is not rescinded when the Christian takes account of the plurality of religions and acknowledges their value. Benedict shows in this essay that he is mindful of the evidence that over the centuries claims of preeminence have as a matter of fact fostered violence[68] and that he is not skirting the issue of whether claims of preeminence logically imply violence.[69] Benedict does not treat the Liberal objection to Christianity as a canard, and in line with his encounter with Assmann in *Truth and Tolerance*, takes it quite seriously. Benedict's general view seems to be that the Christian claim to definitive truth is grammatical, that is, it is part of the warp and woof of Christian identity. While Benedict gives no directions as to when or how the claim should be made—it can be made in martyrdom as much as proclamation—the claim is ineluctable. Moreover, from his point of view, making such a claim, or being prepared to make such a claim, is not intrinsically violent. On the one hand, in making such a claim a Christian does not abrogate the rights of other religions to make the same claim of preeminence. Rather, honest profession makes Christianity vulnerable to counterclaims. Although apologetics should not be ruled out, aggressive attempts to demonstrate the truth of Christianity should be avoided. This indicates distrust in the truth that, on the one hand, is persuasive rather than coercive and, on the other, that the vindication of the truth claim of Christianity can only be eschatological. Still, within history it is impossible altogether to rule out contest and argument. There will be certain circumstances in which it is appropriate for Christianity to critique other cultures and religions, with the caveat, however, that Christianity understand that it too can be an object of critique and also that it illustrate equal or even more negative capability with regard to self-criticism.[70] Importantly, in his schematic but, nonetheless, very rich essay, Benedict refuses the binary of interreligious dialogue and proclamation that has come to be a feature of the assumptive world in the post-Vatican II period and which has become firmly entrenched in the theology of religions literature of pluralist stamp. Benedict thinks that dialogue and proclamation can mutually "interpenetrate."[71] Christians can and should acquire the skill of balancing both. To be true to our faith in Christ cannot be excised from dialogue,[72] and proclamation is dialogical in

67. MR, 100, 109.

68. MR, 94.

69. MR, 100.

70. MR, 110–11.

71. MR, 112.

72. MR, 112.

that it invites the other a failure to understand to render who they are. Interestingly, the essay ends with a poetic evocation of dialogue: "The dialogue of religions must become more and more a listening to the Logos, who is pointing out to us in the midst of our separation and our contradictory affirmations, the unity that we share."[73]

In this essay Benedict continues his long-standing practice of distinguishing between monotheistic and mystical religions.[74] In his dealing with the latter, which he identifies with Asian religions, he challenges once again the pluralist move of invoking the inexpressibility of the divine to relativize any and all truth claims in religion and Christian truth claims in particular.[75] Similar to what we found in *Truth and Tolerance*, Benedict does not renounce all appeals to mystery. His argument is with theologians of religions in whom the appeal has skeptical or agnostic implications.[76] Benedict is convinced that the example of Christian apophasis shows that this connection is far from a necessary one. Whereas in *Truth and Tolerance* the example of Augustine was invoked, in this essay it is the great Cappadocian Gregory of Nyssa. According to Benedict, Nyssa is exemplary of the overall pattern in Christian mystical theology to understand the appeal to mystery not to obviate Christian truth claims regarding Christ, the Trinity, and the self, but rather to prevent Christian truth claims from degenerating into the idolatry of self-certifying claims that exalt human reason to such an extent as to render it pathological. In lifting the reference to Nyssa from a book by von Balthasar on the early Greek theologian,[77] once again Benedict provides more than a hint that he remains largely within the ambit of his beloved Ressourcement theology.

"The Dialogue of the Religions" reprises some of the major features of Benedict's espousal in *Truth and Tolerance* of a Christocentric theology of religions and his corresponding criticisms of pluralist forms of theology of religions he feels at best attenuate Christian belief and at worst entirely subvert it. Given its relative brevity, it would be surprising if the essay provided the kind of theological and contextual coverage to be found in *Truth and Tolerance* or reproduced all its details. At the same time, however, the essay does complement *Truth and Tolerance* in at least two important respects, that is, in insisting on Christian self-criticism—this is even more prominent

73. MR, 113.

74. MR, 91. A version of this distinction is in operation in his 1964 Festschrift essay.

75. MR, 106–7.

76. MR, 108.

77. MR, 107. The reference is to von Balthasar's *Présence et pensée*. There is now an English translation available: see von Balthasar, *Presence and Thought*.

in the other essays that make up *Many Religions—One Covenant*—and also on the role of listening in the encounter with other religions. Of course, Benedict thinks that both proclamation and dialogue are necessary and that their union represents the proper balance of *Lumen gentium* and *Gaudium et spes*. In one important area of theology of religions *Many Religions—One Covenant* is in excess of *Truth and Tolerance*. This is in its articulation of the priority of Judaism for Christianity in the relational matrix. If Benedict makes the point in "The Dialogue of the Religions," it is the theme of the other essays in the collection. Judaism is privileged above all religions in terms of Christian origins, symbolic network, basic theological construal, and figuration of God. There are two kinds of motivation, extrinsic and intrinsic. The extrinsic motivation is the history of Christian anti-Semitism,[78] the intrinsic motivation is gratitude to Judaism as the root in the order of revelation and salvation that has its term in Jesus Christ. Precisely, as the consummation of divine revelation, Jesus Christ constitutes Abraham as the father of all[79] and supports the declaration of John 4:22 to the effect that "salvation is from the Jews." Throughout the three essays devoted to articulating the proper relation between Christianity and Judaism, Benedict resists the dialectical interpretation of law and gospel that determines not only the thought of the Reformers but also Liberal Protestantism, and by osmosis makes its way into all forms of Christian theology, Catholic theology not excluded, that have been touched by rationalism and moralism. Benedict is not shy about naming Marcionism a contemporary disposition,[80] one which he accounts inimicable to Christian self-understanding and a dangerous platform for Christian–Jewish relations. This in turn provides something like a hermeneutic key with regard to a considerable portion of Benedict's work. It makes sense, for example, of the close relation between Moses and Christ in *Introduction to Christianity* and the concerted effort throughout *Jesus of Nazareth* to acknowledge the Jewishness of Jesus and to link him to Torah, covenant, and prophetic promise of the old dispensation.[81] It also makes sense of Benedict's approval of the Patristic trope of the "seeds of the Word." Of course, the anti-Marcionism is typical also of the Ressourcement theologians Benedict so admires.[82] A final point to

---

78. MR, 21–23.

79. MR, 27.

80. MR, 18.

81. See Benedict XVI, *Jesus of Nazareth*, 90–92; Ratzinger, *Introduction to Christianity*. As Benedict skillfully threads his argument in his interpretation of the Apostles' Creed throughout his most successful book, the God of Mount Sinai is the God of Jesus Christ, the One whom he addresses as Abba.

82. Von Balthasar is an especially important guide for Benedict here. Consider

complete our discussion of this text. In the first essay, in arguing for the necessary relinking of Christianity with Judaism, Benedict does not proceed according to his own theological or persuasive authority. Rather the linkage is made in and through an interpretation of the relevant sections of the Catechism.[83] This is in line with deliberate avoidance of academic style theology in which there is something of premium in being a theological virtuoso. Indeed, one can read this move as putting in stone Benedict's self-identification as a theologian who, to use von Balthasar's language, speaks "from the heart of the Church."

Benedict and *Dominus Iesus* (2000)

As head of the Congregation for the Doctrine of the Faith, Benedict oversaw the writing and presentation of *Dominus Iesus* (2005). Whatever Benedict's role in the actual writing of the text,[84] the document seems to represent views, published under his own name, which were presented in the first part of the present essay. Although unjustly reviled as backward looking, both in terms of ecumenical and interreligious dialogue, there can be no doubt that the text represents an assertive intervention in a situation which Benedict, together with Pope John Paul II, believed to be at best characterized by confusion and ambiguity and at worst by lack of fidelity to the teaching of the Church, founded on Christ and resting on the twin pillars of scripture and tradition, and characterized by an adequate reception of the teaching of Vatican II. As posed by *Dominus Iesus* there are narrower and broader dimensions to what seems to be nothing less than a looming crisis. On the narrower front, the problem has to do with an emerging proscription in Catholicism against Christian proclamation; on the broader front the problem has to do with the relativism that Benedict, as well as John Paul II, see bedeviling the area of theology of religions in which there is increased acceptance that all religions—and not simply Christianity—are sites of revelation and salvation. The connection between the narrower and broader agenda of the document is stated succinctly in paragraph 4: "The Church's

---

that when Balthasar treats the relation between biblical Judaism and Christianity in the third volume of *Herrlichkeit*, he provides the precedent for Benedict prioritizing the relation in terms of "covenant" rather than text. The immense importance of anti-Marcionism in von Balthasar has been taken up in the secondary literature. See Sciglitano, *Marcion Against Prometheus*.

83. MR, 22–46.

84. The authors of the text were reputed to be Cardinal Tarcisio Bertone and Congregation Consultor Angelo Amato who later became Prefect of the Congregation for Causes of Saints.

constant missionary proclamation is endangered today by relativist theories which seek to justify religious pluralism, not only *de facto* but also *de jure* (or "in principle"). On this account, the sidelining of proclamation and the concurrent elevation of interreligious dialogue is but an expression of the larger problem of relativism. In the document the generic accusation of relativism gets further specified in complaints against the easy appeal to the elusiveness and inexpressibility of truth, the contemporary penchant for eclecticism when it comes to Eastern and Western religions, as well as a new surge in the difficulty of accepting Christ to put the seal on revelation as complete and definitive. I will focus on the first and third of these concerns not only because they are intrinsically related as question and answer, but also because the problem of syncretism seems to be in significant part a function of a relativistic disposition both in general and in the theological community in particular that results in a lack of willingness to assent to—not to mention assert—Christian exceptionalism.

I will turn to what is said in *Dominus Iesus* concerning these two issues shortly, but before I do I think it important to note the recurring mandate throughout the document of "this must be firmly believed." Here the adverb "firmly" is crucial, and seems to suggest that there are two orders of pluralistically oriented theologies of religions that are the object of criticism. There is clearly a group of out and out pluralists or relativists. These would include, but by no means be limited to, the likes of Hick and Knitter with respect to whom Benedict shows familiarity, and would possibly include Catholic theologians such as Hans Küng and Roger Haight both of whose Christologies fail sufficiently to mark the distinction between Christ and any other savior figure.[85] The document almost certainly takes into account the work of Raimundo Panikkar who has special competence in the area of the relations between Christianity and Asian religions, especially Hinduism. At the same time, the mandate suggests the existence of another constituency, one that is not unequivocally pluralistic or relativistic, but which, arguably, holds at best to the standard Catholic position tentatively and ambiguously. As already indicated, I think that taking into account the Notification given to Jacques Dupuis by the CDC shortly after the publication of *Towards a Christian Theology of Religious Pluralism* (1997), he is, arguably, the prime example of the second group.

---

85. For Roger Haight, see especially Haight, *Jesus Symbol of God*. As indicated in the title, Jesus is but a symbol of God for Christians. Other religions sanction other symbols of God. For Hans Küng, see especially Küng, *Christianity and World Religions* (with contributions by Heinrich von Stietencron and Joseeph van Esse). In this book, Küng advocates for the Church to cease proclaiming the doctrine of the Trinity and the Incarnation.

The central Christian truth, which is not only worthy of being proclaimed, but for which there is an imperative to proclaim, is that Jesus Christ, who is witnessed to in scripture, confessed in the Catholic tradition, and consistently affirmed by the magisterium, is nothing less than the complete and definitive disclosure of the divine.[86] The phrasing is exact. It is intended to rebut pluralist positions that would argue in general that the disclosure of the divine in Christ is either relative or merely exemplary, or more particularly that Jesus of Nazareth is a particular manifestation (read *avatar*) of the divine ground of reality that can be variously—and in all cases abstractly[87]—referred to as the "Infinite," the "Absolute," or the "ultimate Mystery of God."[88] In addition, although the document does not make the point absolutely explicit, strictly speaking the disclosure of the divine in other religions, excepting Judaism, does not belong to the order of revelation as such. This is confirmed in the distinction Benedict draws between Christian scripture and the sacred texts of other religions: the biblical text is inspired; in contrast, however valuable the sacred texts of other religions are, in the strict sense they are not inspired. That is, from the Christian point of view the sacred texts of other religions cannot be cast as witnesses to the direct self-communication of God.[89] Of course, salvation and revelation are totally tied together, and logically the requirement that revelation is restricted to the self-communication of God in Christ and its adumbrations in biblical Judaism involves accepting the universality of the saving mystery of Christ.[90] If there is salvation outside the Church—and the document affirms that there is[91]—then it is Christ who saves rather than one or other of the savior figures in other religions.

Against the backdrop of the affirmation of the finality of Christ, both with respect to revelation and salvation and the critique of forms of theology of religions that would essentially equalize the field of religions when it comes to revelation and salvation, *Dominus Iesus* (section II) deals critically

---

86. CDF, "*Dominus Iesus*," §4, 8.

87. Here one could talk of the tyranny of the meta-level to match the tyranny of relativism, for what is required is that the Church and its members take the third-party view of their own claims in which they are likely to be contested and in light of this agree to an abstract protocol deliberately intended not to discriminate against any religion. Benedict holds the view that Christian belief is first-order language and that by and large it should stick to it. Other religions can make their own claims. Benedict's presumption is that Christianity in principle has internal resources to prevent violence.

88. CDF, "*Dominus Iesus*," §9.

89. CDF, "*Dominus Iesus*," §8.

90. CDF, "*Dominus Iesus*," §13–14.

91. CDF, "*Dominus Iesus*," §20.

with three theological construals that have exercised a significant influence in the post-Conciliar period. The first of these is a revisionist variant of the *Logos spermatikos* view[92] in which *after* the event of Christ, the eternal Logos exercises salvific activity in other religions without reference to Christ. Again the document does not distinguish between stronger and weaker versions of this view, although it is obviously more directed at the former than the latter. Still, the mandate for holding firmly the view that wherever salvation occurs it is through Christ also rules out weaker positions which, while they would not posit an absolute separation between the divine Word and the Word incarnate, would posit a measure of autonomy and independent revelational and salvific activity. This weaker view is once again, arguably, sanctioned by Jacques Dupuis. What requires more immediate attention is a second influential construal that is a target of criticism in *Dominus Iesus*. This concerns the way in which a particular application of the Holy Spirit to the field of theology of religions is resisted.[93] It does not surprise that Benedict, who like de Lubac and von Balthasar, is very concerned how in the post-Conciliar period the Holy Spirit has come to be leveraged against Christ as well, of course, as the Church as the sacrament of Christ, has real worries about the separation of the Holy Spirit from Christ in the theology of religions. Again, we can assume that the document is directed against both weaker and stronger forms. The strong view is simply that other religions exhibit the activity of the Holy Spirit independently of the activity of Christ. *Dominus Iesus* denies this on the grounds that such a view represents nothing less than an infraction against the grammar of Catholic faith which has it that the activity of the Spirit is always connected to the incarnation, passion, death, and resurrection of Christ.[94] The CDF document disallows any ambiguity on the matter. Therefore it rules out also the weaker version of the pneumatological view which, while it would deny that that the Holy Spirit can ever be fully separated from Christ, still allows for a measure of independence. A third position that has gained influence in the post-Conciliar period that comes under critical scrutiny in *Dominus Iesus* is the regnocentric position. This is the view that the kingdom announced by Christ is also the eschatological focus of other religions. Important consequences follow: Christ cannot be said to fully embody the kingdom and the Church cannot be regarded as the privileged vehicle of the kingdom. Here it is more the traditional view of the Church that is the central object of attack rather than Christ as the universal and definitive savior of mankind, although the

---

92. CDF, "*Dominus Iesus,*" §10.

93. CDF, "*Dominus Iesus,*" §12.

94. CDF, "*Dominus Iesus,*" §12.

document makes it clear that to attack the former is to attack the latter.[95] In reply, *Dominus Iesus* refuses the Eusebian position of identifying the kingdom and the Catholic Church, while insisting that neither can the kingdom be separated from it.[96] This, of course, is the Augustinian position to which Benedict has held from the very beginning of his career. Just as importantly, however, for Benedict is that, in his view, this is the position endorsed by *Lumen gentium*.

In the above over-brief analysis of *Dominus Iesus* I have made it a point to underscore that the document is not only set against forms of theology of religions that involve outright denials of Christ being the complete and definitive revelation of God and universal and unsurpassable savior of the world and also the associated doctrines concerning the inextricable relations of Logos, Spirit and Church to Christ, but also forms of theology of religions that can be construed to articulate weaker versions of the pluralistic position that Benedict is anxious to put out of commission. On the basis of the Notification by the CDF concerning the work of Jacques Dupuis, and the document's intimation of positions that only ambiguously endorse what the document insists to be Church's positions, I thought it reasonable to insinuate that Dupuis's work is a target throughout. Of course, in *Towards a Christian Theology of Religious Pluralism* (1997) and elsewhere, Dupuis denies that he is a pluralist.[97] Indeed, his work in general, and *Towards a Christian Theology of Religious Pluralism* in particular, indicates a forceful critical engagement with the major exponents of the pluralist position, and not only Hick and Knitter, but all the major figures in European languages and especially in French.[98] In these texts Dupuis makes it clear that he desires to sanction the view articulated in Hebrews 1 that Christ is the pinnacle of revelation.[99] With this in mind he takes exception to Hick who would deny this[100] and separates himself entirely from Panikkar's view of avatars in

95. CDF, "*Dominus Iesus*," §18.

96. CDF, "*Dominus Iesus*," §19.

97. In the first chapter of *Towards a Christian Theology*, Dupuis announces that he does not advocate for religious pluralism in the strict sense. Join this avowal together with his critique of some of the more prominent pluralists, and it is obvious that he is attempting a mediation between strong forms of pluralism and the more traditional inclusivist view of the relation between Christianity and other religions represented by the Church Fathers, on the one hand, and by Ressourcement theology on the other. The issue for Benedict is whether he is successful in such a mediation.

98. If one had to pick out one French author who exercises more than a significant degree of influence on Dupuis, it would be Claude Geffré. In particular see Geffré, *Le christianisme au risque*; "Théologie chrétienne et dialogue interreligieux."

99. TRP, 244. See also Dupuis, *Christianity and the Religions*, 14, 157–58, 161.

100. TRP, 186–89.

which Christ would be at best first among equals.[101] Relatedly, Dupuis questions the appeal to mystery as critical leverage against Christianity's claim to
absoluteness.[102] Nor does Dupuis sanction a generic view of scripture—such
that the sacred texts of other religious traditions can be put on the same
level as the biblical text[103]—or the revisionist use of the "seeds of the Word"
as bruited in the strong forms of pluralist theology of religions,[104] or finally
the pneumatological form of the pluralist view provided by a scholar such
as Knitter who argues that non-Christian religions are animated by the Holy
Spirit who reveals and saves independently of Christ.[105] It is not unfair to
say that in *Towards a Christian Theology of Religious Pluralism* Dupuis is
not quite as sharp in his opposition to the pluralist objection to the universal saving significance of the Church that finds its argument in the non-
equivalence of the Church and the kingdom. The reason here is that while
to a significant extent Dupuis feels comfortable defending some version of
a Christocentric theology of religions, he does not feel equally inclined to
defend the Ecclesiocentric form of theology of religions, which he believes
has been thoroughly discredited in the post-Conciliar period if not actually
renounced.[106]

   Neither Dupuis's superior theological erudition, his acumen in interreligious dialogue, nor his good intentions in subscribing to a Christocentric, and thus inclusivist, form of theology of religions can be denied. At
the same time, however, neither can it be denied that his support of the
more traditional Church views is replete with the kinds of cavil that both
incited Notification from the CDF and led *Dominus Iesus* to call out positions very much like what any reader can independently find in *Towards
a Christian Theology of Religions*.[107] For example, having defended against

101. TRP, 149–52.

102. TRP, 272–79.

103. TRP, 250–52.

104. TR, 70–77.

105. TRP, 83. See also Dupuis, *Christianity and the Religions*, 179

106. Dupuis, *Christianity and the Religions* is, arguably, more emphatic on this point
than *Towards a Christian Theology*.

107. Given the date, as well as content, of *Dominus Iesus* (2000), which is the same
date as the Notification served to Dupuis, and also that throughout the Notification we
find plural iterations of the mandate "to firmly believe," there can be little doubt that
the two documents are closely related. There were in fact two Notifications, with the
second and more moderate one speaking only to ambiguities rather than to errors. Not
surprisingly, *Dominus Iesus* is the more expansive document. In the Notification, there
are five queries addressed to *Towards a Christian Theology*. Three are Christological
in focus and ask whether there is whole-hearted assent to the claims that (a) Christ is
the universal mediator of salvation; (b) Christ is the complete revelation of God; (c)

Hick and Panikkar the magisterial position that Christ is the fullness of revelation in *Towards a Christian Theology of Religions*, Dupuis proceeds to qualify: in Christianity revelation is relative and incomplete,[108] and limited and imperfect.[109] Moreover, when Dupuis endorses the appeal to mystery in theology of religions, he also allows its relativist consequences in through the backdoor. While he sincerely believes that he has distanced himself from Knitter and Panikkar, he seems unaware of the relativistic implications in his assertion that no human consciousness, not even Christ's, can exhaust divine mystery.[110] In addition, as we have seen, while Dupuis supports the difference between the biblical text and the sacred texts of other religions against the strong pluralists, his stance becomes contradictory or incoherent when he suggests that that Word of God can be extended beyond the Bible to these texts.[111] And Dupuis wraps anti-pluralist views and cavils regarding the standard Catholic view in a pancake of ambiguity when he claims that the universal saving significance of Christ is neither absolute nor relative.[112] Dupuis's apparent affirmations of Church positions when it comes to the "seeds of the Word" and the activity of the Holy Spirit are attended by similar caveats. While he denies anything like structural independence of the Word from Christ, he seems to affirm some measure of independence.[113] After objections to the Pneumatocentric theology of religions of Knitter, in which the Spirit functions independently of Christ in terms of fostering

---

the resurrected Christ is always supposed in the active economy of the Holy Spirit in other religions. Two queries are essentially ecclesiological in nature and concern the claims that (d) the Catholic Church is the sign and instrument of salvation; and in consequence (e) salvation occurs in other religions and to some extent through them, but not because of them. In terms of proof-texting, *Lumen gentium* and *Redemptoris missio* (1990) are given prominence. Although in reply to the Notification, Dupuis argued for a balance between dialogue and proclamation, before his death he reverted to the priority of dialogue over proclamation and showed that he preferred something weaker than Christ being the definitive revelation of God. See Dupuis and König, "Excerpts of a Conversation."

108. TR, 249.

109. TRP, 271. See also TRP 283, 297–300. Similar caveats can be found in Dupuis, *Christianity and the Religions*, 157–58, 171.

110. TRP, 249.

111. TRP, 250–52.

112. TRP, 303.

113. TRP, 70–77. This point is made clearer in Dupuis, *Christianity and the Religions*, 140, 153, 156. There Dupuis suggests that the Word cannot be regarded as *separate* from Christ who is the Word incarnate. This does not mean that it cannot be regarded as *distinct* from it. Of course, this is not an idle semantic point. *Distinction* supports some measure of independent activity of the Word post-incarnation.

grace and holiness in other religions,[114] Dupuis almost immediately qualifies his anti-pluralist view by suggesting that we should hold in "tension" the
universal significance of the incarnation, passion, death and resurrection of
Christ and the real influence of the Holy Spirit in other religions, apparently
independent of Christ. This is ambiguous at best, and suggests that while
we should follow the protocol of referring the Holy Spirit to the Word incarnate, a Christian is entitled to posit a domain of independent activity for
the Holy Spirit in other religions. Dupuis does not clarify either the measure
of this freedom, and leaves matters confused. It is probably fair to say here,
as in the other cases cited, Dupuis appears to be confounding a conceptual
solution with a conceptual need.

Perhaps above everything else the significance of the contest between
Dominus Iesus and Dupuis has to do with a referendum on the Ressourcement theology, on the one hand, and with the reception of Vatican II on the
other. In *Towards a Christian Theology of Religious Pluralism* Dupuis makes
it clear that when it comes to the theology of religions that he sees himself
to be in opposition to Ressourcement theologians such as a Daniélou, de
Lubac, and von Balthasar,[115] or perhaps better stated, he is opposed to their
continuing influence in the post-Conciliar Church. According to Dupuis,
each of these theologians supports—albeit in different ways and to different
extents—what he calls the "fulfillment model" within the inclusivist spec-
trum of the theology of religions.[116] Christianity realizes fully what the other
religions aspire to in their questioning and quest, that is, real contact with
the divine lifts human beings beyond the brokenness of the world and the
fragility of history. Although salvation in other religions is possible, Christianity is the normative way.[117] Far from denying the close relation between
Ressourcement authors and Patristic thinkers on the fulfillment model
within the theology of religions, Dupuis accents it. In determinate respects
Ressourcement thinkers follow in the footsteps of those Church Fathers who
plotted Christianity on a historical axis that effectively made other religions
adumbrations of Christianity, which is religion in the full sense.[118] Although
Dupuis, as we have seen, argues for detaching other religions from this ad-
umbrative line which gives plenary salvific value to Christianity, he does

114. TRP, 83.

115. TRP, 133–43.

116. See also Dupuis, *Christianity and the Religions*, 47–52. While in *Towards a
Christian Theology*, Dupuis dealt equally with all three of the main Ressourcement
theologians, in *Christianity and the Religions*, he speaks mainly of de Lubac. See also,
however, Dupuis, *Christianity and the Religions*, 159–61.

117. TRP, 136.

118. TRP, 134.

not suggest that Ressourcement theologians are guilty of eisegesis. While thinking that one can construe other religions as "logophanies" that are in principle independent of the incarnation, passion, death and resurrection of Christ,[119] he concedes that most of the Church Fathers,[120] not excluding Augustine, thought that the Word was too indissolubly linked to the Christ event to function independently. At the same time, Dupuis does not think that the fact that Ressourcement theologians can refer to Patristic precedent is sufficient to warrant their view as normative.

In *Towards a Christian Theology of Religious Pluralism* there also seems to be a referendum on authentic reception of Vatican II when it comes to other religions. In a carefully constructed chapter in his watershed text, Dupuis is careful not to advance the view that *Nostra aetate, Lumen gentium* 16–17, and *Ad gentes* actually support the "soft" pluralist view for which he advocates.[121] Instead he asks the question whether there are any signs that Vatican II goes beyond the parameters of the fulfillment model.[122] He seems to concede that the fulfillment model provides the overall framework for the theology of religions at Vatican II, even as *Lumen gentium, Nostra aetate,* and *Ad gentes*[123] speak in an unprecedented way of the positive values of other religions.[124] The one real piece of evidence he feels he can adduce of a tendency to go beyond the preeminence of Christianity when it comes to revelation and salvation is *Ad gentes,*[125] which speaks to the grace and truth of other religions in a way that does not seem to make point to their realization in Christianity.[126] This leads to the very weak conclusion that Vatican II did not unequivocally support the fulfillment theory.[127] The same pattern of argument is followed in Dupuis's treatment of the encyclicals of Pope Paul VI and Pope John Paul II. *Evangelii nuntiandi* (1975) by Pope

---

119. TRP, 81–83.

120. TRP, 77–80.

121. Dupuis, *Towards a Christian Theology,* 158–79.

122. TRP, 162.

123. See Second Vatican Council, *Lumen gentium,* 16; *Nostra aetate,* 2; *Ad gentes,* 3, 9, 11.

124. Dupuis, *Christianity and the Religions,* 159–66, essentially repeats this point, but more suggests a tension between the fulfillment model and the soft pluralist model whose basis is largely found in talk of "seeds of the Word" which can be interpreted to mean separation of the activity of the Word in religions outside the incarnation, passion, death, and resurrection of Christ. Dupuis supplies no argument as to how or why this would be a good reading.

125. Second Vatican Council, *Ad gentes,* 9.

126. TRP, 168.

127. TRP, 168.

Paul VI remains within the orbit of the fulfillment model,[128] as does *Tertio millenio adveniente* (1994) by Pope John Paul II. Dupuis, however, suggests that it is possible to interpret Pope John Paul's reflections on the presence of the Holy Spirit in other religions in *Redemptoris hominis* (1975) and *Redemptoris missio* (1990) as suggesting an alternate path. The vagueness is scrupulous, since Dupuis does not explicitly argue that either encyclical is actually arguing for what he ultimately argues for, that is, that the activity of the Holy Spirit in other religions can be separated in the economy of salvation from Christ.[129] There appears then to be a real contest between Benedict and Dupuis regarding the reception of Vatican II when it comes to the theology of religions, with Benedict maintaining that Vatican II unambiguously supports the fulfillment view, and Dupuis suggesting that there elements in the documents of Vatican II that move beyond the fulfillment model, and that one of the essential tasks of theology is to retrieve and develop these elements. I have spoken already to the weakness of Dupuis's actual arguments, which depends in significant part on the hermeneutic theory of the constitutional binary of the letter and spirit of Vatican II. In addition, however, there also appears to be difference between Benedict and Dupuis concerning the status of papal encyclicals. Should encyclicals be given greater weight than documents produced by various councils and commissions? Dupuis hedges here as elsewhere.[130]

Conclusion

Over an intellectual career of more than sixty years, Benedict XVI has illustrated remarkable consistency in general theological point of view, even if from time to time his stance on particular issues has shifted slightly. This consistency is apparent in his contributions to the theology of religions, and even more so if one attends, as I have, to the period between the early 1990s and early 2000s. The theology of religions elaborated in *Truth and Tolerance*

---

128. TRP, 170.

129. Dupuis, *Towards a Christian Theology*, 170–78. See also Dupuis, *Christianity and the Religions*, 66–71. The argument concerning *Redemptoris hominis* and *Redemptoris missio* is essentially the same. They represent a promise of a new trajectory in theology of religions since they do not explicitly connect the activity of the Spirit in other religions with the salvific activity of Christ. Unfortunately, this promise is later betrayed by John Paul II.

130. See Dupuis, *Towards a Christian Theology*, 178, where Dupuis acts as if a 1991 document produced by the Pontifical Commission for Interreligious Dialogue, which stresses dialogue more than proclamation, has as much authority as encyclicals that make no such provision.

and *Many Religions—One Covenant*, on the one hand, and *Dominus Iesus*, on the other, is incredibly consistent. Together they demonstrate the aim to carry forward the Church's teaching on the religions, as this teaching is grounded in scripture and tradition, refreshed by the efforts of Ressource-ment theologians, imaginatively signposted in the documents of Vatican II, especially *Lumen gentium*[131] and *Nostra aetate*, and further explored and exposited in the encyclicals of Paul VI and John Paul II. All the texts of Benedict XVI that have come in for discussion are animated by his percep-tion of the corrosive effects of relativism in the contemporary period as this bears directly or indirectly on Christian construction of other religions and tends to inhibit proclamation. While Benedict may leave open questions as to when to proclaim Christian truth and the manner of its expression, his texts leave us in no doubt about the essential nature of such claims as Christ is the definitive revelation of God in history, is the savior of the world, and that the Church is the witness to revelation as well as participating in the sacrament of salvation that is Christ.

This is not to say there are no differences between the two collections of essays published under his own name (Cardinal Joseph Ratzinger) and *Dominus Iesus*, which is a document from the CDF of which Benedict was the longtime head. There is a palpable difference in tone. In *Truth and Toler-ance* and *Many Religions—One Covenant*, while Benedict XVI defends long-standing Catholic positions regarding the religions in the public square, he is operating in persuasive mode in a discursive situation in which ideally the better argument wins. In contrast, the tone of *Dominus Iesus* is entirely declarative as it brings the testimony of the Catholic tradition to bear criti-cally on harder and softer versions of pluralism. Of course, the difference in tone is less a difference in mood than in difference in genre: the genre of doctrinal interventions is always declarative. Its focus is narrow and repre-sents a questioning of the doctrinal probity of a particular text or an entire body of work. It does not take into account the intention of the author or the motivations for writing a theological work, however honorable they may be in certain circumstances.[132] Of course, there are also differences of theme and emphasis between *Dominus Iesus* and the other texts published under Benedict's own name. For example, in *Dominus Iesus*, relative to these works that one can directly attribute to Benedict, there is a noticeable absence of concern for the relation between violence and religion in general and vio-lence and Christianity in particular. Nor can it be truly said that the special status of Judaism, strongly sanctioned in Vatican II, is made thematic in

131. Second Vatican Council, "*Lumen gentium*," 16–17.
132. As they most obviously were in the case of Jacques Dupuis.

Dominus Iesus to anyway near the extent that it is in *Many Religions—One Covenant*. Correlatively, the systematic connection between a theology of religions and individual doctrines such as Christ, Trinity, Church, and Last Things is far more clear even within the very brief space of *Dominus Iesus* than it is in *Truth and Tolerance* and *Many Religions—One Covenant* which, as collections of essays written for particular occasions, can at best make these connections in a somewhat desultory and ad hoc manner. For example, *Dominus Iesus* explicitly links the Spirit to Christ and explicitly speaks to the privileges of the Church as the interpreter of revelation and as a privileged participant in the sacrament of salvation that is Christ, whereas in *Truth and Tolerance* and *Many Religions—One Covenant*, these are at best plausible inferences.

Despite the differences in tone, theme, and emphases in his articulation of a theology of religions, it is evident that the positions advanced in *Truth and Tolerance*, *Many Religions—One Covenant*, and *Dominus Iesus* are in essential respects complementary. At the same time it is not to be supposed that Benedict XVI presumes that he has offered a full-fledged theology of religions, rather than attempt by all means available to restore balance in a post-Conciliar situation in which the pendulum has swung decisively, and in his view for the worst, in the direction of pluralism. Benedict's contribution to the theology of religions is no more, but also no less than an anamnesis of truth claims regarding other religions that he deems vouchsafed by the Catholic tradition and affirmed in the documents of Vatican II, and the correlative uncovering of the corrosive effects of relativism which either rules out truth claims or sidelines and systematically uplifts dialogue over proclamation. Benedict thinks that he has provided the conditions of beginning a theology of religions rather than bringing it to conclusion. The theology of religions needs to be on the right track, and he is convinced that for a few decades it has either been derailed or shunted to a side track, and in any case, become incapable of meeting the opportunities as well as challenges of other religions that are sources of grace and truth. Going forward the Church and individual Christians will have to conjugate in particular situations the ratios of witness, solidarity, dialogue and proclamation of indefeasible truth claims. No equation is available, and theology of religions can only be an ongoing task. And finally, Benedict is clearly aware both in his own case and in the case of the Church as a whole that there are major lacunae: now, more urgently than ever, Christianity has to think through deeply its relation to the other monotheistic religion, Islam.

Bibliography

Assmann, Jan. *Moses der Ägypter: Entzifferung einer Gedächtnisspur.* Munich: Hanser, 1998.

Balthasar, Hans Urs von. *Presence and Thought: Essay on the Religious Philosophy of Gregory of Nyssa.* Translated by Marc Sebanc. San Francisco: Ignatius, 1995.

———. *Présence et pensée: Essai sur la philosophie religiouse de Gregoire de Nysse.* Paris: Beauchesne, 1942.

Benedict XVI. *Deus caritas est* (2005). http://w2.vatican.va/content/benedict-xvi/en/encyclicals/documents/hf_ben-xvi_enc_20051225_deus-caritas-est.html.

———. *Jesus of Nazareth: Holy Week: From the Entrance into Jerusalem to Holy Week.* Translated by Phlip J. Whitmore. San Francisco: Ignatius, 2011.

———. *Regensburg Address* (2006). http://w2.vatican.va/content/benedict-xvi/en/speeches/2006/september/documents/hf_ben-xvi_spe_20060912_university-regensburg.html.

Cavadini, John C., ed. *Explorations in the Theology of Benedict XVI.* Notre Dame, IN: University of Notre Dame Press, 2012.

Christian, William A. *Doctrines of Religious Communities: A Philosophical Study.* New Haven, CT: Yale University Press, 1987.

Congregation for the Doctrine of the Faith (CDF). "*Dominus Iesus:* On the Unicity and Salvific Universality of Jesus Christ and the Church." August 6, 2000. http://www.vatican.va/roman_curia/congregations/cfaith/documents/rc_con_cfaith_doc_20000806_dominus-iesus_en.html.

———. "Letters to the Bishops of the Catholic Church on Some Aspects of Christian Meditation." October 15, 1989. http://www.vatican.va/roman_curia/congregations/cfaith/documents/rc_con_cfaith_doc_19891015_meditazione-cristiana_en.html.

D'Costa, Gavin. *Christian Uniqueness Reconsidered: Myth of Pluralistic Theology of Religion.* New York: Orbis, 1990.

———. *Christianity and World Religions: Disputed Questions in the Theology of Religions.* Oxford: Wiley-Blackwell, 2009.

———. *The Meeting of Religions and the Trinity.* New York: Orbis, 2000.

DiNoia, Joseph A. *The Diversity of Religions: A Christian Perspective.* Washington, DC: CUA, 1992.

Dupuis, Jacques. *Christianity and the Religions: From Confrontation to Dialogue.* Translated by Phillip Berryman. New York: Orbis, 2001.

———. *Towards a Christian Theology of Religious Pluralism.* New York: Orbis, 1997.

Dupuis, Jacques, and Franz König. "Excerpts of a Conversation between Jacques Dupuis and Cardinal König." *National Catholic Reporter*, March 21, 2008. http://www.natcath.org/NCR_Online/archives2/2008a/032108/032108r.htm.

Geffré, Claude. *Le christianisme au risque de l'interpetation.* Paris: Cerf, 1983.

———. "Théologie chrétienne et dialogue interreligieux." *Revue de L'Institut Catholique de Paris* 38.1 (1992) 63–82.

Gimello, Robert M. "A Depth of Otherness: Buddhism and Benedict's Theology of Religions." In *Explorations in the Theology of Benedict XVI*, edited by John C. Cavadini, 114–41. Notre Dame, IN: University of Notre Dame Press, 2012.

Haight, Roger. *Jesus, Symbol of God.* New York: Orbis, 2000.

Hick, John. *A Christian Theology of Religions: The Rainbow of Faith*. Philadelphia: Westminster, 1995.

John Paul II. *Dominum et vivificantem*, 1986. http://w2.vatican.va/content/john-paul-ii/en/encyclicals/documents/hf_jp-ii_enc_18051986_dominum-et-vivificantem.html.

———. *Redemptoris hominis*, 1979. http://w2.vatican.va/content/john-paul-ii/en/encyclicals/documents/hf_jp-ii_enc_04031979_redemptor-hominis.html.

———. *Redemptoris missio*, 1990. http://w2.vatican.va/content/john-paul-ii/en/encyclicals/documents/hf_jp-ii_enc_07121990_redemptoris-missio.html.

———. *Tertio millenio adveniente*, 1994. https://w2.vatican.va/content/john-paul-ii/en/apost_letters/1994/documents/hf_jp-ii_apl_19941110_tertio-millennio-adveniente.html.

Knitter, Paul. *No Other Name! A Critical Survey of Christian Attitudes Toward the World Religions*. New York: Orbis, 1985.

Küng, Hans. *Christianity and World Religions*. New York: Orbis, 1993.

Lindbeck, George. *The Nature of Doctrine: Religion and Theology in a Postliberal Age*. Philadelphia: Westminster, 1984.

O'Leary, Joseph Steven. *Religious Pluralism and Christian Truth*. Edinburgh: Edinburgh University Press, 1996.

O'Regan, Cyril. "Benedict the Augustinian." In *Explorations in the Theology of Benedict XVI*, edited by John C. Cavadini, 21–60. Notre Dame, IN: University of Notre Dame Press, 2012.

———. "Von Balthasar and Eckhart: Theological Principles and Catholicity." *The Thomist* 60.2 (1996) 1–37.

———. "Von Balthasar and Thick Retrieval: Post-Chalcedonian Symphonic Theology." *Gregorianum* 77.2 (1996) 227–60.

Panikkar, Raimundo. *The Unknown Christ of Hinduism: Towards an Ecumenical Christophany*. London: Darton, Longmann & Todd, 1981.

Paul VI. *Evangelii nuntiandi*, 1975. http://w2.vatican.va/content/paul-vi/en/apost_exhortations/documents/hf_p-vi_exh_19751208_evangelii-nuntiandi.html.

Ratzinger, Joseph. *Christianity and the Crisis of Cultures*. San Francisco: Ignatius, 2006.

———. *Die Geschichtstheologie des heiligen Bonaventura*. Munich: Schnell & Steiner, 1959.

———. *Many Religions—One Covenant: Israel, The Church, and the World*. Translated by Graham Harrison. San Francisco: Ignatius, 1999.

———. *Truth and Tolerance: Christian Belief and World Religions*. Translated by Henry Taylor. San Francisco: Ignatius, 2005.

———. *Values in a Time of Upheaval*. Translated by Brian McNeil. New York: Crossroad, 2006.

———. *Volk und Haus Gottes in Augustins Lehre von der Kirche*. Munich: Eos Verlag U. Druck, 1954.

Sciglitano, Anthony. *Marcion Against Prometheus: Balthasar Against the Expulsion of Jewish Origins From Modern Religious Dialogue*. New York: Herder & Herder, 2014.

Second Vatican Council. "*Ad gentes.*" December 7, 1965. http://www.vatican.va/archive/hist_councils/ii_vatican_council/documents/vat-ii_decree_19651207_ad-gentes_en.html.

————. "*Gaudium et spes.*" December 7, 1965. http://www.vatican.va/archive/hist_councils/ii_vatican_council/documents/vat-ii_const_19651207_gaudium-et-spes_en.html.

————. "*Lumen gentium.*" December 7, 1965. http://www.vatican.va/archive/hist_councils/ii_vatican_council/documents/vat-ii_const_19651207_gaudium-et-spes_en.html.

————. "*Nostra aetate.*" October 28, 1965. http://www.vatican.va/archive/hist_councils/ii_vatican_council/documents/vat-ii_decl_19651028_nostra-aetate_en.html.

Stubenrauch, Bertram. *Dialogische Dogma: Der christliche Auftrag zur interreligiösen Begegnung.* Freiburg: Herder, 1995.

Turner, Denys. *The Darkness of God: Negativity in Christian Mysticism.* Cambridge: Cambridge University Press, 1993.

Walker, Adrian J. *The Unity of the Church.* Vol. 1 of *Joseph Ratzinger in Communio.* Grand Rapids, MI: Eerdmans, 2010.

Dialogues between Judaism and Christianity

CHAPTER 5

Jewish–Christian Dialogue as Re-Evangelization

—Chris Seeman

To speak of Jewish–Christian dialogue in the same breath as evangelization within a contemporary Roman Catholic context seems, at first glance, a category confusion. After all, hasn't the Catholic Church renounced all missionary efforts specifically targeting Jews?[1] To be sure, the architects of the New Evangelization—Paul VI, John Paul II, Benedict XVI, Francis—have all been ardent advocates of interreligious dialogue; but nowhere in their pronouncements do the two agenda coincide.

This is not surprising. The "novelty" of the New Evangelization lies precisely in its focus on re-energizing inactive *Christians*. As John Paul put it in his 1988 post-synodal exhortation, *Christifideles laici*, "a mending of the Christian fabric of society is urgently needed in all parts of the world. But for this to come about what is needed is to *first remake the Christian fabric of the ecclesial community itself* present in these countries and nations."[2] In this understanding, renewal of the Church is a necessary precondition for a more effective pursuit of the common good. As one facet of the common good, Jewish–Christian relations may well be central to the Church's mission, but they remain conceptually distinct from the Church's internal house-keeping.

Against this strategic separation of *ad intra* from *ad extra* priorities may be set another programmatic statement of John Paul's, made eight years prior to his signing of *Christifideles laici*. In an address to representatives of the Jewish community in Mainz, the pontiff declared that Jewish–Christian dialogue, "is at the same time a dialogue *within* our Church, that is to say,

---

1. CRRJ, *Gifts and Calling*, 40.
2. John Paul II, *Christifidéles laici*, 34.

between the first and the second part of her Bible."[3] He goes on to specify the objectives of this intra-ecclesial dialogue in terms of the conciliar directives for the application of *Nostra aetate*:

> The effort must be made to understand better everything in the Old Testament that has its own, permanent value . . . since this value is not wiped out by the later interpretation of the New Testament, which, on the contrary, gave the Old Testament its full meaning, so that it is a question rather of reciprocal enlightenment and explanation.[4]

The idea of reciprocity is not an innovation of the Second Vatican Council. It stretches at least as far back as Augustine, who gave the principle its classical formulation: "in the Old the New lies hidden, and in the New the Old lies open."[5] Yet throughout most of the Church's career, this dictum has been applied in a decidedly unidirectional fashion: seeing the Jewish Scriptures as mere subliminal advertising for Jesus, thus reducing Israel's life and history to an obsolescent precursor to the life and history of the Church—the seeds of supersessionism. In emphasizing "permanent value" and "reciprocal enlightenment and explanation," by contrast, the directives cited by John Paul mark a tectonic shift in the way Catholics are to engage Scripture.

The most recent curial reflection on Catholic-Jewish relations, the 2015 document of Pontifical Commission for Religious Relations with the Jews (CRRJ), *The Gifts and the Calling of God Are Irrevocable*, confirms this shift. "Dialogue between Jews and Christians," we are told, "can only be termed 'interreligious dialogue' by analogy, that is, dialogue between two intrinsically separate and different religions."[6] On the contrary, "the dialogue with Judaism occupies a unique position for Christians; Christianity is by its roots connected with Judaism as with no other religion. Therefore the Jewish–Christian dialogue can only with reservations be termed 'interreligious dialogue' in the true sense of the expression; one could however speak of a kind of 'intra-religious' or 'intra-familial' dialogue *sui generis*."[7] Consequently, "both the 'dialogue ad extra' and the 'dialogue ad intra' have led with increasing clarity to the awareness that Christians and Jews are

---

3. John Paul II, "Address," emphasis added.

4. CRRJ, *Guidelines and Suggestions*.

5. *in Vetere Novum lateat, et in Novo Vetus pateat* (*Quaestiones in Heptateuchum* 2.73).

6. CRRJ, "*Gifts and the Calling*," 15

7. CRRJ, "*Gifts and the Calling*," 20.

irrevocably inter-dependent, and that the dialogue between the two is not a matter of choice but of duty as far as theology is concerned."[8]

Again, strictly speaking, there is nothing theologically "new" about affirmations of familial affinity and interdependence; one finds them already in Paul (Rom 11:13–26). What has changed is how that interconnectedness is understood. In this essay, I wish to explore one facet of this sea-change: how Jewish–Christian dialogue has shaped Catholic interpretation of the Bible, and how this hermeneutical shift has impacted—or failed to sufficiently impact—homiletics, catechesis, and apologetics. As Catholics are re-evangelized to know and love Scripture, it is essential that what they hear and how they hear it be consonant with the dialogical gains made since Vatican II. It is also crucial to the ongoing vitality of Jewish–Christian conversation that the Church take seriously Jewish voices—especially those of Jewish biblical scholars—that call the Church to task for the subtle and not so subtle ways in which theological anti-Judaism continues to reproduce itself within Christian discourse.

Anti-Judaism Defined and Dismantled

I borrow the expression "Christian discourse" from Katharina von Kellenbach, who employs it to highlight what she calls the "rules of formation"—the ideational and rhetorical strategies Christians use to define themselves in relation to others.[9] As the Church's primordial "other," Israel has always been pivotal to this project. Von Kellenbach analyzes anti-Judaism in terms of three such rules, which she dubs *antithesis*, *scapegoat* and *prologue*. Examining each of these in turn will give focus to our discussion. We begin with the rule of antithesis:

> The first rule of formation depicts Judaism as the *antithesis* of Christian beliefs and values. It identifies Judaism with the negative side of dualistic oppositions such as "justice and love," "judgment and promise" or "law and grace." While the definitions of Christianity change Judaism is always correlated as its opposite. By rendering Judaism its negative antithesis, Christian theology asserts its difference and superiority over the rival faith.[10]

---

8. CRRJ, "*Gifts and the Calling*," 13. Cf. Francis, *Evangelii gaudium*, 247–49.

9. von Kellenbach, *Anti-Judaism*, 39.

10. von Kellenbach, *Anti-Judaism*, 41.

It bears noting that all three of the dualisms identified by von Kellenbach as fueling the teaching of contempt originate in the New Testament,[11] so there is no denying that the *ingredients* of anti-Judaism (regardless of whether they are mobilized for that purpose) are intrinsic to Christianity. It is equally important to observe that in no New Testament text is the antithesis equated with "Judaism." On the other hand, it is telling that the sole New Testament occurrence of the term *Ioudaismos* (Gal 1:13–14), where Paul describes his former hostility toward the Church, participates in von Kellenbach's second rule of formation:

> Christian theology casts Israel into the role of *scapegoat* and characterizes Jews as guilty, evil and predisposed to "deicide." Israel is blamed for evil in the world. As a punishment for her various crimes culminating in Christ's murder, Israel is rejected by God who elects the Gentile church instead as the legitimate heir of Israel's covenant with God. The portrayal of Jews as morally depraved, politically sinister and religiously ominous legitimates Christianity's replacement of Israel.[12]

Needless to say, these characterizations, like the antitheses of the first rule, are indelibly canonized in the New Testament (e.g., 1 Thess 1:14–16; Matt 27:24–25; Luke 4:20–30; John 8:44–45), and in spite of noble efforts to detoxify them through historical contextualization, they remain available for anti-Jewish use. Happily, the Second Vatican Council issued a comprehensive repudiation of both the deicide charge and its supersessionist implications.[13] By contrast, as we shall see below, the Magisterium has been noticeably more reluctant to jettison dogmatic articulations of von Kellenbach's third rule:

> This rule of formation accounts for Christianity's continuity with Israel's past by reducing Judaism to the status of a *prologue* of Christianity. Judaism is identified with the "Old" Testament and seen as a relic of ancient times rather than as a contemporary and vital religious alternative. As a result, Judaism can legitimately be incorporated as Christian prehistory.[14]

---

11. "Justice vs. love" (John 8:1–11; Eph 2:1–5; 1 Tim 1:12–17); "judgment vs. promise" (Rom 7; Gal 3–4); "law vs. grace" (John 1:17; Rom 1:5–6; 3:21–26; 4:16; 5:15–21; 6:14; Gal 5:1–6).

12. von Kellenbach, *Anti-Judaism*, 41.

13. Vatican II, *Nostra aetate*, 4.

14. von Kellenbach, *Anti-Judaism*, 41.

The value of von Kellenbach's approach lies in its refusal to allow either anti-Judaism's proponents or its critics to over-simplify the phenomenon into a single, isolatable idea, attitude, or behavior. Anti-Judaism may manifest itself through one or all of these symptoms, but is reducible to none of them; rather, it is a deep structure that has shaped Christian discourse from its inception.[15] Consequently, it is likely to elude capture so long as its systemic nature remains unacknowledged. Like racism, anti-Judaism is protean, assuming different forms at different times in order to conceal itself. To assess its persistence in the Church today, we need to be attentive to all three rules of its formation as well as how they interact with one another.

As already noted, in 1965, the Magisterium officially declared supersessionism and the deicide charge on which it rests to be null and void:

> What happened in His passion cannot be charged against all
> the Jews, without distinction, then alive, nor against the Jews of
> today. Although the Church is the new people of God, the Jews
> should not be presented as rejected or accursed by God, as if this
> followed from the Holy Scriptures.[16]

Yet by affirming Christians to be "the new people of God," the construal of Israel as "prologue" was retained, albeit now without cancelling out Jewish chosenness or emptying Jewish history and faith of intrinsic—and ongoing—significance.[17] As for antithetical construals of Judaism in relation to Christianity, these have received an equally unequivocal rebuke in the 1974 directives for implementing *Nostra aetate*:

> The Old Testament and the Jewish tradition founded upon it
> must not be set against the New Testament in such a way that
> the former seems to constitute a religion of only justice, fear and
> legalism, with no appeal to the love of God and neighbor.[18]

A second document of the CRRJ issued in 1985 takes up the antithesis problem in more detail, acknowledging the biblical rootedness of the dualities on which it is based while proposing a different way of understanding them:

> [T]he difficulty of Christian teaching about Jews and Judaism
> lies in this, that it needs to *balance* a number of pairs of ideas

15. On the role of anti-Judaism in the formation of Christian discourse, see Young, *Biblical Exegesis*, 57–69.

16. Vatican II, *Nostra aetate*, 4.

17. Cf. Vatican II, *Lumen gentium*, 9–17; *Dei verbum*, 14–15; *Sacrosanctum concilium*, 5.

18. CRRJ, *Guidelines and Suggestions*.

which express the relation between the two economies of the Old and New Testament: Promise and Fulfilment; Continuity and Newness; Singularity and Universality; Uniqueness and Exemplary Nature. This means that the theologian and the catechist who deals with the subject needs to show in his practice of teaching that: promise and fulfilment throw light on each other; newness lies *in a metamorphosis of what was there before.*[19]

To sum up: since *Nostra aetate*, both magisterial and curial documents have demonstrated an awareness of the components of anti-Judaism and have taken action to either denounce them or to reconfigure them so as to foreclose anti-Jewish readings. And there is no question that much of the impetus for this about-face has come from sustained conversation between Jews and Catholics since the Shoah, at all levels—grassroots, academic, and institutional.[20] But it is one thing to mandate theological change; it is another to bring it about. In what follows, I draw attention to specific examples of how Catholic usage of Scripture continues to be implicated in von Kellenbach's rules of formation despite the Church's formal disavowal of them.

To be clear: my aim is not to question the genuineness of the theological transformation begun by *Nostra aetate*, nor to critique its dogmatic adequacy. On the contrary, as the preceding paragraphs intimate, I believe that the magisterial and curial response to the theological underpinnings of anti-Judaism has irreversibly put into play new ways of thinking that—if taken to their logical conclusion—would effectively counteract the teaching of contempt. My goal, rather, is to identify where the Church has not yet fully allowed its teaching to penetrate its practice, and to suggest how the process might be expedited.

Judaism as Antithesis: The Progressive Jesus

The Jewish New Testament scholar, Amy-Jill Levine, has voluminously documented the manifold ways in which antithetical portrayals of Judaism are alive and well in Christian preaching, teaching, and exegesis.[21] A common thread she finds running through these stereotypes is a desire to enlist Jesus as an advocate for social reform:

19. CRRJ, *Notes*, emphasis added.

20. For the historical background of this revolution, see Connelly, *From Enemy to Brother*; Schultz, *Tri-Faith America.*

21. Her most important compendia of evidence are Levine, *Misunderstood Jew*; "Bearing False Witness."

Through a chic apologetic that seeks to make Jesus politically relevant to the twenty-first century, Christians find in Jesus the answer to whatever ails the body politic, whether it is war, ethnocentrism, an institutional religion intertwined with the state, or misogyny. In order for Jesus to serve this liberationist role, he has to have something concrete to oppose. The bad "system" then becomes, in the scholarship and in the pulpit, first-century Judaism.[22]

Levine identifies ten recurrent manifestations of this apologetic strategy, some of them rooted in classical anti-Judaism (e.g., Jews as legalistic), others reflective of more recent cultural developments (e.g., Jesus as minister to "the marginalized").[23] The scenario I wish to focus on here is that of Jesus as proto-feminist who liberates women from Jewish misogyny. I choose this in part because its history has been systematically documented by von Kellenbach, who shows how feminist theologians uncritically appropriated earlier scholarship (much of it pioneered by anti-Semites before and during World War II) to construct an "un-Jewish" Jesus who broke with patriarchal norms and promoted gender equality.[24]

This antithetical apologetic is especially relevant to the contemporary Catholic landscape because of its utility to the "new feminism" promoted by John Paul II, who deploys it enthusiastically in *Mulieris dignitatem* (1988):

> In all of Jesus' teaching, as well as in his behavior, *one can find nothing which reflects the discrimination against women prevalent in his day.* On the contrary, his words and works always express the respect and honor due to women. The woman with a stoop is called a "daughter of Abraham" (Luke 13:16), while in the whole Bible the title "son of Abraham" is used only of men. Walking the Via Dolorosa to Golgotha, Jesus will say to the women: "Daughters of Jerusalem, do not weep for me" (Luke 23:28). This way of speaking to and about women, as well as his manner of treating them, *clearly constitutes an "innovation" with respect to the prevailing custom at that time.*[25]

John Paul's insistence on the "innovative" character of Jesus's interactions with women was already fielded by the CDF in *Inter insigniores* (1976):

---

22. Levine, *Misunderstood Jew*, 118.

23. Levine, *Misunderstood Jew*, 118–66; "Bearing False Witness," 759–63.

24. von Kellenbach, *Anti-Judaism*, 57–63.

25. John Paul II, *Mulieris dignitatem*, 13, emphasis added.

Jesus Christ did not call any women to become part of the Twelve. If he acted in this way, it was not in order to conform to the customs of his time, *for his attitude towards women was quite different from that of his milieu, and he deliberately and courageously broke with it.* . . . In his itinerant ministry Jesus was accompanied not only by the Twelve but also by a group of women (Luke 8:2). *Contrary to the Jewish mentality,* which did not accord great value to the testimony of women, as Jewish law attests, it was nevertheless women who were the first to have the privilege of seeing the risen Lord, and it was they who were charged by Jesus to take the first paschal message to the Apostles themselves (Matt 28:7; Luke 24:9; John 20:11), in order to prepare the latter to become the official witnesses to the Resurrection.[26]

The apologetic motivation of these reflections is easy enough to see: to defend Catholicism against the charge of misogyny in its refusal to permit ordination of women priests, there is an impulse to argue that, although Jesus did not appoint women as apostles, *in every other conceivable way* he rejected the presumed misogyny of his time; hence, Judaism (unlike Christianity) fails to recognize women's dignity. This strategy conveniently sidesteps the apologizing institution's own history of resisting and dismissing the feminist movement. One is reminded of Mark Twain's sardonic quip that, in matters of social change, the Church "never fails to drop in at the tail of the procession—and takes credit for the correction."[27]

The point is not that first-century Palestine was an egalitarian society (it was not), but that this portrayal of Jesus is dictated by modern agendas (rather than by first-century realities) and is made at Jewish expense—thus distorting both Jesus and Judaism at a stroke.[28] Moreover, the imposition of modern apologetics onto stories involving Jesus and women tends to erase other important theological dimensions of these episodes, thus muting the Gospel message as its original audiences would have heard it and as its modern audiences need to hear it.[29] There is no reason why an authentic Christian feminism cannot co-exist with a pre-feminist Jesus, just as there is no reason why modern Christians should not condemn slavery, despite the fact that no New Testament author questions the validity of that institution.

26. CDF, *Inter insigniores,* 2, emphasis added.

27. Twain, "Bible Teaching," 73.

28. For a survey of what is known about women during the Second Temple and early Rabbinic periods (which significantly complicates blanket allegations of a misogynistic society), see Ilan, "Women."

29. Levine, *Misunderstood Jew,* 131–43; *Short Stories by Jesus,* 239–65.

Judaism as Scapegoat: Good Jews vs. Bad Jews

In 2001, the Pontifical Biblical Commission (PBC) issued a major document entitled *The Jewish People and their Sacred Scriptures in the Christian Bible*. Its stated purpose, according to Cardinal Ratzinger (then president of the PBC), was to re-examine the doctrine of the unity of the Old and New Testaments in the wake of the Shoah:

> Two main problems are posed: Can Christians, after all that has happened, still claim in good conscience to be the legitimate heirs of Israel's Bible? Have they the right to propose a Christian interpretation of this Bible, or should they not instead, respectfully and humbly, renounce any claim that, in the light of what has happened, must look like a usurpation? The second question follows from the first: In its presentation of the Jews and the Jewish people, has not the New Testament itself contributed to creating a hostility towards the Jewish people that provided a support for the ideology of those who wished to destroy Israel?[30]

To the future pontiff's relief, the PBC answered the first question in the affirmative and the second (with much nuancing) in the negative, which, in Ratzinger's view, was "of great importance for the pursuit of dialogue, but above all, for grounding the Christian faith."[31] Many biblical scholars were less sanguine about the second half of this verdict.[32]

The PBC's work was not faulted for its brevity. At more than 56,000 words, the document is the most extensive curial examination of the anti-Jewish potential of the New Testament to date. No stone was left unturned. Yet, for a work intended to foster Jewish–Christian dialogue, Jewish scholarship was conspicuously absent from its pages.[33] The result is a Christian monologue that, while fully acknowledging the problematic nature of the images of Jews and Judaism found in its sacred texts, does not always succeed in defanging those images.

One element threading itself through the PBC's discussion is Jewish rejection of or hostility toward Jesus and his followers, the flashpoint that animates the vitriol of the New Testament authors. This corresponds to von Kellenbach's "scapegoat" rule, which, as we remember, is not confined to

30. PBC, *Jewish People and their Sacred Scriptures.*

31. PBC, *Jewish People and their Sacred Scriptures.*

32. See Murphy, "Biblical Commission"; Levine, "Roland Murphy"; Levenson, "Roman Catholicism."

33. Murphy, "Biblical Commission," 147.

the deicide charge but more broadly codes Jewish antagonists as "morally depraved, politically sinister and religiously ominous."[34] The fact that such representations can be found in most New Testament texts that mention Jews is not easily explained away piecemeal. Rather, they suggest an emerging Christian discourse that treats non-Christ-believing Jews—which is to say, Jews who remain Jews—as a threatening "other" against whom the "new" people of God is to define itself.

Particularly awkward is the PBC's concluding assurance that:

> In the New Testament, the reproaches addressed to Jews are not as frequent or as virulent as the accusations against Jews in the Law and the Prophets. *Therefore, they no longer serve as a basis for anti-Jewish sentiment.* To use them for this purpose is contrary to the whole tenor of the New Testament. Real anti-Jewish feeling, that is, an attitude of contempt, hostility and persecution of the Jews as Jews, is not found in any New Testament text and is incompatible with its teaching. What is found are reproaches addressed to certain categories of Jews for religious reasons, as well as polemical texts to defend the Christian apostolate against Jews who oppose it.[35]

While one cannot but welcome *Nostra aetate*'s categorical denunciation of "hatred, persecutions, displays of anti-Semitism, directed against Jews at any time and by anyone" as being incompatible with Christian faith,[36] the PBC's declaration that the New Testament is free of "an attitude of contempt, hostility and persecution of the Jews as Jews" does not inspire confidence. The premise that most Christians for most of the past two thousand years were simply mistaken about the signals their sacred texts were sending them strains credibility.

To be sure, the PBC makes no attempt to deny the reality of Jewish–Christian disagreement; on the contrary, it faces it squarely and prescinds from fake solutions. Yet in the very same breath it seems to imply that "certain categories of Jews for religious reasons"—indeed, any who "oppose" Christianity—deserve the verbal bashing they receive. This is rather like condemning domestic violence while conceding that some spouses "had it coming to them." Such hand-washing does little to ameliorate the problem of contemporary anti-Judaism.

I am not suggesting that the PBC was being disingenuous. Rather, I am suggesting that their conclusion, *a la* von Kellenbach, is itself dictated

---

34. von Kellenbach, *Anti-Judaism*, 41.

35. PBC, *Jewish People and their Sacred Scriptures*, 87, emphasis added.

36. Vatican II, *Nostra aetate*, 4.

by the scapegoating rule they are struggling to overcome—because they are doctrinally committed to the divine inspiration of the texts under discussion. Apropos of this dynamic is Jon Levenson's observation that:

> Most of the documents of the New Testament originated in a context of polemic. They are marked by much rhetorical hyperbole, anger, and even hate. . . . The church, by defining these documents as Scripture, has, in a sense, frozen that moment of bitter separation and ensured its preservation for the last two millennia, if not for all eternity.[37]

An instructive parallel may be observed in Islam, which, on the one hand, prophetically validates Jesus and affirms those who follow his Gospel to be "People of the Book" while, by the same Qur'anic warrant, excoriates those "categories" of Christians who, "for religious reasons," believe Jesus to be the Son of God and who therefore "oppose" pure monotheism.[38] A perfectly consistent position within the framework of Islamic discourse, but impossible to compass within the framework of Christian discourse. Christians ought to be grateful to Muslims for helping them understand what it *feels* like to exist, perforce, within someone else's discourse!

Judaism as Prologue: Outside Israel No Salvation?

If Judaism is not the binary opposite of Christianity (antithesis) and if Jews are not to be demonized for challenging the claims of the new revelation (scapegoat), it becomes all the more incumbent upon the Church to explain and justify its existence: If the old is good, why was something new needed at all? If Judaism is to be understood as Christianity's prologue, what, precisely, is the *logos* it gives birth to, and how does that *logos* differ from what preceded it?

There are, of course, many ways in which the Church has attempted to answer this question over the centuries. The modality I wish to explore here is that of soteriology: the conviction that Jesus's life, death, and resurrection were redemptive and salvific. Again, there are many ways in which Christian theology has approached this mystery, but the one that has the greatest bearing on anti-Judaism is its claim to universalize the particular, to expand Israel's status as God's chosen people to non-Jews who profess faith in Jesus.

As the CRRJ's *Notes on the correct way to present Jews and Judaism in preaching and catechesis in the Roman Catholic Church* declare, "the

---

37. Levenson, "Counterpart," 245.

38. Key passages include Qur'an 4:171; 5:67–77, 116–17; 9:30–31.

singularity of the people of the Old Testament is not exclusive and is open, in the divine vision, to a universal extension."[39] Similarly, the PBC affirms, "the Church is conscious of being given a universal horizon by Christ. . . . The reign of God is no longer confined to Israel alone, but is open to all, including the pagans, with a place of honour for the poor and oppressed."[40] Again, CRRJ reiterates, "With Paul the 'Jewish Jesus movement' definitively opens up other horizons and transcends its purely Jewish origins. Gradually his concept came to prevail, that is, that a non-Jew did not have to become first a Jew in order to confess Christ."[41]

What makes these seemingly innocuous descriptions of Christianity's missionary mandate accessories to von Kellenbach's rules of formation is their presumption that "pure" Judaism, undiluted by the Gospel, equates to soteriological exclusivism. In the Gospel according to Luke, the PBC rightly notes, this exclusionary mindset is yoked to "Good Jew–Bad Jew" type-casting:

> Jesus appeals to his fellow townspeople to renounce a possessive attitude to his miracles and accept that these gifts are also for the benefit of foreigners (4:23–27). Their resentful reaction is violent; rejection and attempted murder (4:28–29). Thus Luke clarifies in advance what the repeated reaction of Jews will be to Paul's success among the Gentiles. The Jews violently oppose a preaching that sweeps away their privileges as the chosen people. Instead of opening out to the universalism of Second Isaiah, they follow Baruch's counsel not to share their privileges with strangers (Ba 4:3). Other Jews resist that temptation and generously give themselves to the service of evangelisation (Acts 18:24–26).[42]

From a Jewish perspective, however, Luke's polemical portrait of cho-senness as a zero-sum game is manifestly false, as is the assumption that Gentiles must "become Jewish" in order to "be saved." As Levenson explains with respect to the Hebrew Bible, "The difference between the chosen and the unchosen is not (as it often becomes in Christianity) the difference be-tween the saved and the damned."[43] In response to its 2001 document, he comments that:

---

39. CRRJ, *Notes on the Correct Way.*

40. PBC, *Jewish People*, 64.

41. CRRJ, *Gifts and Calling*, 15.

42. PBC, *Jewish People*, 74.

43. Levenson, "Universal Horizon," 159.

the PBC ought to have taken notice of the fact that at least the Hebrew Bible does not claim that the observance of the Torah is necessary for the salvation of non-Israelites and that the rabbinic tradition likewise maintains that the righteous of all nations have a portion in the World-to-Come. So doing would have helped the PBC avoid the mistake of projecting a Christian view of salvation onto the first testament of the Christian Bible. The Commission might also have noted that both in biblical and in subsequent Jewish tradition, salvation is not the sole, perhaps not even the dominant, motivation for the observance of Torah. It has been said that different religions don't just provide different answers; they also ask different questions. It is very dangerous to project the soteriological focus of Christianity onto non-Christian religions.[44]

In light of von Kellenbach's analysis of anti-Judaism, the danger of Israel-as-prologue (at least as conceived and presented in the documents under consideration) should be evident. Christians are fully within their rights to maintain that Jews are mistaken in thinking that Gentiles require no special grace in order to share in eschatological salvation. But to saddle Judaism with a ("bad") soteriological exclusivity it has never advocated, while simultaneously maintaining that the Church is the solution to such exclusivism, is to sacrifice truth on the altar of apologetics. It makes Christian evangelization a partner to scapegoating and antithetical identity formation.

A Way Forward

In drawing attention to the imperfections of the Catholic Church's institutional-theological response to Jewish–Christian dialogue, I do not want to give the impression that its contribution has been, on balance, counter-productive, or that we are sliding back into some dark age of willful ignorance and covert intolerance. Quite the contrary: every one of the documents I have surveyed marks a significant advance in counteracting anti-Judaism's classical manifestations and rationales. These are permanent gains.

Moreover, far from proposing some new-fangled remedy to the problem, my plea is for renewed attention to the foundational desiderata repeatedly identified by the CRRJ as well as by the International Catholic-Jewish Liaison Committee (ICJLC) since the 1970s. These desiderata all revolve around education:

---

44. Levenson, "Roman Catholicism," 180.

1. General education: "a better knowledge of the basic components of the religious tradition of Judaism . . . by what essential traits the Jews define themselves in the light of their own religious experience."[45] In other words, *not* as Christians or as the New Testament define them, *not* as a prologue but as "a contemporary and vital religious alternative."[46] This need not lead to religious indifferentism or a side-stepping of the deposit of revelation. It will, however, require that *actual* Jews and *actual* Judaism become part of the *sensus fidelium* by which the Church "constantly moves forward toward the fullness of divine truth."[47]

2. Homiletic/liturgical reform: so that the meaning of liturgical texts will not be distorted "especially when it is a question of passages which seem to show the Jewish people as such in an unfavourable light . . . which Christians, if not well informed, might misunderstand because of prejudice."[48] In particular, there needs to be a shift away from the admonitory (warning Christians how *not* to think about Jews and Judaism) to the constructive (how to creatively confront the rules of formation in the New Testament so that, by acknowledging them for what they are, Christians can begin to imagine a Gospel re-configured on the basis of the general education described above).

3. Catechetical/intellectual formation: "Among sources of information, special attention should be paid to the following: catechisms and religious textbooks; history books; the mass-media (press, radio, cinema, television). The effective use of these means presupposes the thorough formation of instructors and educators in training schools, seminaries and universities."[49] The *sine qua non* of this is that priests, deacons, and lay ecclesial ministers receive mandatory—not optional—exposure to the texts and traditions of Judaism, as well as practical training on how to integrate these perspectives into their ministries.[50]

Much has already been done in these areas; much more needs to be done.[51] If evangelization means receiving the Good News, the rhetorical

---

45. CRRJ, "Guidelines and Suggestions."

46. von Kellenbach, *Anti-Judaism*, 41.

47. Vatican II, *Dei verbum*, 8.

48. Vatican II, *Dei verbum*, 8.

49. Vatican II, *Dei verbum*, 8.

50. ICJLC, "Recommendation."

51. For a recent overview and assessment, see Levine, "*Nostra Aetate, Omnia Mutantur.*"

dynamics of anti-Judaism impede that reception. The struggle to expose and eradicate those dynamics is therefore central to the New Evangelization.

Bibliography

CDF (Congregation for the Doctrine of the Faith). *Inter insigniores: Declaration on the Question of Admission of Women to the Ministerial Priesthood*. Vatican City: Holy See, 1976.

Connelly, John. *From Enemy to Brother: The Revolution in Catholic Teaching on the Jews, 1933–771965*. Cambridge, MA: Harvard University Press, 2012.

CRRJ (Pontifical Commission for Religious Relations with the Jews). *"The Gifts and the Calling of God Are Irrevocable" (Rom 11:29)—A Reflection on Theological Questions Pertaining to Catholic-Jewish Relations on the Occasion of the Fiftieth Anniversary of "*Nostra aetate*" (no. 4)*. Vatican City: Holy See, 2015.

———. *Guidelines and Suggestions for Implementing the Conciliar Declaration* Nostra Aetate *(n. 4)*. Vatican City: Holy See, 1985.

———. *Notes on the correct way to present Jews and Judaism in preaching and catechesis in the Roman Catholic Church*. Vatican City: Holy See, 1985.

Francis. *Evangelii gaudium: On the Proclamation of the Gospel in Today's World*. Vatican City: Holy See, 2013.

ICJLC (International Catholic-Jewish Liaison Committee). "Recommendation on Education in Catholic and Jewish Seminaries and Schools of Theology." International Catholic-Jewish Liaison Committee 17th Meeting, New York City, May 4, 2001.

Ilan, Tal. "Women." In *The Eerdmans Dictionary of Early Judaism*, edited John J. Collins and Daniel C. Harlow, 1346–49. Grand Rapids, MI: Eerdmans, 2010.

John Paul II. *Address to Representatives of the Jewish Community in Mainz, West Germany November 17, 1980*. Vatican City: Holy See, 1980.

———. *Christifideles laici: On the Vocation and the Mission of the Lay Faithful in the Church and in the World*. Vatican City: Holy See, 1988.

———. *Mulieris dignitatem: On the Dignity and Vocation of Women on the Occasion of the Marian Year*. Vatican City: Holy See, 1988.

Levenson, Jon D. "Can Roman Catholicism Validate Jewish Biblical Interpretation?" *Studies in Christian-Jewish Relations* 1 (2005–6) 170–85.

———. "Is There a Counterpart in the Hebrew Bible to Antisemitism?" *Journal of Ecumenical Studies* 22 (1985) 242–60.

———. "The Universal Horizon of Biblical Particularism." In *Ethnicity and the Bible*, edited by Mark G. Brett, 143–69. Leiden: Brill, 1996.

Levine, Amy-Jill. "Bearing False Witness: Common Errors Made About Judaism." In *The Jewish Annotated New Testament*, edited by Levine, Amy-Jill and Marc Zvi Brettler, 759–63. 2nd ed. Oxford: Oxford University Press, 2017.

———. *The Misunderstood Jew: The Church and the Scandal of the Jewish Jesus*. San Francisco: HarperOne, 2006.

———. "*Nostra Aetate, Omnia Mutantur*: The Times They are a Changing." In *Righting Relations After the Holocaust and Vatican II: Essays in Honor of John Pawlikowski*, edited by Elena Procario-Foley and Robert Cathey. Mahwah, NJ: Paulist/Stimulus Foundation, forthcoming.

————. "Roland Murphy, The Pontifical Biblical Commission, Jews, and the Bible." *Biblical Theology Bulletin* 33 (2003) 104–13.

————. *Short Stories by Jesus: The Enigmatic Parables of a Controversial Rabbi.* New York: HarperCollins, 2014.

Murphy, Roland E. "The Biblical Commission, the Jews, and Scriptures." *Biblical Theology Bulletin* 32 (2002) 145–49.

PCB (Pontifical Biblical Commission). *The Jewish People and their Sacred Scriptures in the Christian Bible.* Vatican City: Holy See, 2001.

Schultz, Kevin M. *Tri-Faith America: How Catholics and Jews Held Postwar America to Its Protestant Promise.* Oxford: Oxford University Press, 2011.

Twain, Mark. "Bible Teaching and Religious Practice." 51–57 in *What Is Man? And Other Philosophical Writings*, ed. Paul Baender. Berkeley: University of California Press, 1973.

Vatican II. *Dei verbum: Dogmatic Constitution on Divine Revelation.* Vatican City: Holy See, 1965.

————. *Lumen gentium: Dogmatic Constitution on the Church.* Vatican City: Holy See, 1964.

————. *Nostra aetate: Declaration on the Relation of the Church to Non-Christian Religions.* Vatican City: Holy See, 1965.

————. *Sacrosanctum concilium: Constitution on the Sacred Liturgy.* Vatican City: Holy See, 1963.

von Kellenbach, Katharina. *Anti-Judaism in Feminist Religious Writings.* Atlanta: Scholars, 1994.

Young, Frances. *Biblical Exegesis and the Formation of Christian Culture.* Cambridge: Cambridge University Press, 1997.в

Judaism and Christianity's "Judaism"

Ending Antisemitism

—RICHARD A. COHEN

Are there no Moravians in the Moon, that not a missionary has yet visited this poor pagan planet of ours, to civilize civilization and Christianize Christendom?

HERMAN MELVILLE, *WHITE-JACKET*[1]

Peace, peace, to those far and near. (שָׁלוֹם שָׁלוֹם לָרָחוֹק וְלַקָּרוֹב).

ISAIAH 57:19

Troubling Questions

Jesus and his disciples were all Jewish. How do we explain millennia of social and theological Jew-hatred in Christendom? Why contempt? Why the slaughter of the innocents? Why not love, or at least gratitude? Jesus and his disciples were all poor, marginalized, even ostracized. Jesus spoke for the poor, the ill, the lame, "unto the least," against the selfishness and abuses of wealth and power. How do we explain Christianity's millennial support for the rich, for kings and tyrants, for the mighty? Why the ingratiation?

---

1. Melville, *White-Jacket*.

Why the validation? What means "salvation"—for anyone, for some—while humanity groans under oppression and the very earth is destroyed?

Noachide Humanity

What can a Jew say about these things? Christians are Christians, Jews are Jews. Despite the famous "Judeo-Christian" label, despite all that Christianity has appropriated from Judaism, despite its birth from out of the bowels of Judaism, what really do Jews and Christians share? Is there not an abyss dividing them, a long animosity, not to forget unspeakable crimes, by Christians against Jews, that prevent genuine dialogue, let alone the rarer possibility—as among the best of friends—of criticism? Even the term "religion"—as in "interreligious dialogue"—is for the most part a Christian construct. There is no equivalent in the Hebrew Bible, or in Jewish sacred literature. Is there good will and respect enough for such a difficult dialogue, not one-sided, not reductive, and with evangelicals not *evangelical*. Not conversion but conversation; not monologue but dialogue. Like the term "religion," do Jews and Christians understand the meaning and value of "dialogue" in sufficiently similar ways? Christianity seems to be oblivious to the fact that it is the only religion that thinks it is the only religion, the only true religion. Hence it projects, or mirrors a conversionary mission onto its interlocutors, turning potential dialogues into disputations. Let me be perfectly clear, I do not consider the Christian belief, or the same belief held by minorities within other religions, that it is the one and only true religion, I do not consider this belief to be praiseworthy. Quite the reverse, it is false, reprehensible, dangerous, and indicative of a flawed spirituality, if I may put the point boldly. There is no "evangelical" Judaism—not because it is closed and exclusive, "clannish" or "tribal" as its Christian detractors say, since in reality Judaism welcomes voluntary converts, but precisely because it is open and respectful, knowing as deeply as it lives its own covenant that there are many other legitimate paths beloved by God.

Judaism is neither exclusive nor does it have a catechism. Eschewing dogmatic conformity, it encourages its adherents to independent thinking, to questioning, inventiveness, debate, argumentation, intellectual refinement, believing that the millions of people, if I may refer to a Midrash, who were given the Torah of Mount Sinai—Jews and non-Jews, in Hebrew and other languages—each received a different portion, a unique perspective, each of which is necessary for the full revelation of Torah, a revelation that continues to unfold—in our discussions, debates, study, and so on, no doubt including interreligious dialogue—to this day. Indeed, the Talmud, the "Oral Torah," through whose lens Jews read the Bible and live their Judaism, is a compendium of thousands of discussions, debates, disagreements, majority views, minority views, fanciful tales, precise quantifications, of time, of weight, of measurements, regarding everything under the sun. This cornucopia of ideas, questions, arguments, decisions, debates, which continues to this day, is testimony to Jewish devotion, a way of life, a devotion to holiness without omniscience or infallibility. Its open-mindedness and refinement, its ability to change and grow with the times, testify not to ignorance, opportunism or iconoclasm, but rather to the height of the stakes, which is holiness itself, a life obedient to God's will. No authority, not that of a prophet, not that of the greatest rabbi, not that of God Himself, can interrupt or overrule such deliberations (which are decided by majority rule). "The Torah is no longer in heaven!" the rabbis rebuke God. Is this sort of religiosity, where God's transcendence, never re-mythologized, a transcendence some will call the "absence of God," is taken up as the full responsibility of humankind, is the holiness of such ethical exigency even remotely familiar to evangelical ears?

Ethical or religious, it is an inextricable covenant, Judaism is not *laissez-faire*, not "everything goes." Judaism is quite demanding. Demanding of itself, first of all, but demanding also on the world at large, upon all human beings and all religions. Not to become Jewish, as we have seen, but this affirmation of pluralism does not mean Judaism is indifferent, or that there even is or could be an "outside" of Judaism about which it washes its hand. Nor is the Jewish demand on the world something hidden, surreptitious, conspiratorial or mystical, for revelation abhors darkness. What then? We have said it already. The greatest most difficult transcendence is not generated by logos or pathos, thought or feeling, but by the demands of morality and justice, to be good and just. The transcendence of God is ethical, the "ought" above the "is." What do Jews require of non-Jews? *Righteousness.* Jews aver—of themselves, of everyone—a minimum standard of fundamental human dignity—what else for a being created in the "image and likeness of God," to use the biblical expression—a dignity found not in obeisance but in obedience to a *basic set of moral standards*. Just as God is merciful and just, "because I am the Lord your God," humans must be merciful and just—such is the universal holiness enjoined by Judaism. The twentieth-century Jewish German thinker Martin Buber called this ethical universalism "biblical *humanitas*."[2] It is an apt expression for an ethics that for Jews has its source in Bible and Talmud, its *Taryag Mitzvot*, the "613 Commandments" (as appropriate for a "kingdom of priests and a holy nation"[מַמְלֶכֶת כֹּהֲנִים,

2. Buber, *Israel and the World*, 247. See also Benamozegh, *Israel and Humanity.*

וְגוֹי קָדוֹשׁ; (Exod 19:6)]), but which does not depend on such sources or on any proper names, but applies to all humanity, whatever the personal or religious commitments and communities, humanity as an elevation ever elevating . . . enjoined to justice.

In a single word, then, what Judaism requires of all humans and of all religions, including Jews and Judaism, is *righteousness*. Micah 6:8: "It hath been told you, O man, what is good, and what the Lord requires of you: only to do justly, and to love mercy, and to walk humbly with your God" (הִגִּיד לְךָ אָדָם, מַה-טּוֹב; וּמָה-יְהוָה דּוֹרֵשׁ מִמְּךָ, כִּי אִם-עֲשׂוֹת מִשְׁפָּט וְאַהֲבַת חֶסֶד, וְהַצְנֵעַ לֶכֶת, עִם-אֱלֹהֶיךָ). So has its Talmud and its greatest medieval sage, Moses Maimonides (1135–1204), taught: "Righteous gentiles have a share in the world to come (*Tosefta Sandhedrin* 13:2; *Mishneh Torah*, Law of Kings, 8:11). And thus, too, the righteousness Judaism requires of all humans is elaborated in what Judaism calls the "Seven Noachide Laws" (שבע מצוות בני נח), or more simply, the Noachide Laws.

Before enumerating them, some propaedeutic words of legal theory are in order. Legal theorists distinguish between law in a purely formal or procedural sense ("Was the existing law followed or not?") and law in a prescriptive or moral sense ("Is justice served?"). They are not as easily disentangled in practice as sometimes seems in theory, not only because each case is specific, where the law hits the road, as it were, but also because ultimately the formal law has been created by legislation believing it *better* than not. The Hebrew word here translated into English as "law" is "*mitzvah*" (מִצְוָה) reflects these complexities, but stands firmly on the side of the prescriptive. "Mitzvah" is derived from a root "*tzavah*" (צָוָה) meaning "will," "order," "command," whether human or divine. This root can also mean, more broadly, "a 'connection' or a relation that we enter into."[3] A *mitzvah*—including the 613 Commandments for the Jews, and the Seven Laws of Noah for the entire world—is thus a divine command, a rule or procedure, a relation, and a good deed, all wrapped up into one. A mitzvah, then, however seemingly formal, always involves ethics. Facts and values are not neatly separated or separable. Ultimately all Jewish law *serves justice*, just as all justice ultimately *serves morality*. It is an important point we must keep in mind, even if, as always, there are dissenting minority opinions.[4]

It should not surprise us that the Seven Noachide Laws, which apply to all humankind, Jews included, are comprised for the most part of the obvious moral injunctions known to the whole world without ever having

3. Patterson, *Holocaust and the Nonrepresentable*, 25.

4. A well-known, twentieth-century formalist was the Israeli biochemist, professor and public intellectual Yeshayahu Leibowitz (1903–94).

heard of the Hebrew Bible. Stated succinctly, they are: (1) No murder; (2) No stealing; (3) No worship of false gods; (4) No sexual immorality (incest, adultery); (5) No unnecessary pain inflicted on animals (literally "do not tear off the limb of a living animal"); (6) No cursing God; and (7) Maintain courts of justice. The rabbis named these seven mitzvot after Noah because he is the ancestor of all humans, and because unlike Adam he received the law against harming animals. Here are the minimum standards of the humanity of the human. No human ever perfectly follows them, to be sure, also because we are human. But they are nonetheless universal standards, call them "ideals" if one wishes. No wonder that in dedicating the Holy Temple in Jerusalem King Solomon welcomed non-Jews and implored God to heed their prayers (1 Kgs, 8:41–43), or that the Jewish priests in addition to sacrifices made by and for Jews made sacrifices for all the nations of the world. Judaism lives in and for its holy mission, not just to save itself, but to save itself by redeeming the world.

Let us pause to consider the law about animals. With only seven basic laws, is it not remarkable that one of them is concerned to prevent animals from unduly suffering? Jews for themselves have a complicated set of dietary restrictions, the laws of "kashrut," far beyond not eating pork, laws which excludes the killing of most animals, requires that those which are slaughtered are killed in the least painful way, segregates the cooking and eating of dairy and meat products, specifies prayers before and after eating different types of food, and so on. To be sure, for a thousand years the Jews were farmers and herders in their ancient Commonwealth in Israel, so the treatment of animals was no small matter. But the matter is not only practical. More profoundly it is ethical. Certainly the way we treat animals reflects how we treat one another. But it also reflects how we treat animals, fellow sentient beings, and how we treat the entire environment, that is to say, as God's creation. Do not these lessons—care for nature, care for animals, care for humanity—drive Dostoyevsky's heart-wrenching description in *Brothers Karamazov* of a drunken peasant whipping his horse to death,[5] a horrific tale he juxtaposes to more horrifying vignettes of three children being abused, two innocent daughters aged five and seven, one an eight-year-old serf boy stripped naked in winter and torn to shreds by the Master's hounds. It is all of one piece, who we are and how we treat our fellows, how we treat animals, how we treat sentient life, how we treat the natural environment. Do we recognize or deny, respect or selfishly exploit God's creation? Surely

---

5. Dostoyevsky includes the pathetic story of the whipped horse in *Crime and Punishment* as well, in a nightmare dream of Raskolnikov.

this is the sense of John Ruskin's observation that "to preserve your eagles' nests, is to be a great nation."[6]

As for the two seemingly theological rather than ethical Noachide injunctions, not to curse God and not to worship idols, these too would be distorted if divorced from the mercy and justice Jews believe are God's most intimate attributes. Unless it be mythology or ideology, the real meaning of cursing God is slander, gossip, lies, taking advantage of or exploiting another, coupled with a fundamental indifference to their suffering or one's own guilt. So, too, the ethical meaning of idol worship: to mistake the lower for the higher, the worse for the better, to value things over people. Such, so the rabbis teach, was the "crime" of the Tower of Babel, not the labor to rise to the kingdom of God, but to think that bricks were more valuable than people in the attempt. In these two laws divinity, holiness and worship are held higher than clerical distractions, from myths and cults, mysteries and miracles, called to the higher authority of ethics, the real responsibilities of goodness and justice, uplifted by an infinite transcendence. "Everything that cannot be restored to an interhuman relation," writes Emmanuel Levinas in his magnum opus, *Totality and Infinity*, "represents not the superior form but the forever primitive form of religion."[7] And the interhuman relation is precisely and poignantly moral responsibility, one serving the other, alleviating suffering.

From such a perspective, from the ethical maturity of these heights, *from the exigencies of responsibility*, the constructions and dogmatism of *theology* itself can become distractions, obstacles, concerned more for an abstract logic or dialogic of God—deductions and dogmas—than for what holiness actually points to, namely, love of neighbor and the struggle for a just world. "Faith without works is dead" (James 2:17). Transcendence also lies in escaping the hobgoblins, the narrowness of system, the temptation or self-absorption of an ersatz rationality, rationality gone mad. Religion is not an end in itself but a means to transcendence, and transcendence, aside from childish and escapist fantasy, lies in love for the neighbor, and the struggle for justice. I have cited the New Testament, the Old, the rabbis, Maimonides, Ruskin and Levinas. Let us hear from Immanuel Kant: "there exists absolutely no salvation for man apart from the sincerest adoption of genuinely moral principles into his disposition."[8] And Levinas again: "'God is merciful,' means: 'Be merciful like Him.' The attributes of God are given not in the indicative but in the imperative. The knowledge of God comes

---

6. Letter 75 in Ruskin, *Genius of John Ruskin*, 421.

7. Levinas, *Totality and Infinity*, 79.

8. Kant, *Religion Within the Limits*, 78.

to us like a commandment, like a *Mitzvah*. To know God is to know what must be done."[9] And Levinas again: "Ethics is not simply the corollary of the religious but is, of itself, the element in which religious transcendence receives its original meaning."[10] Here we think religion as adults and for adults.

Certainly the great world religions are distinguished by considerable differences in their sacred texts, rituals, symbols, histories, holy languages, and so on, as well as in their theologies and confessions, and in much else, but these differences, which are *genuinely important to believers*, because we live on earth and not in the air, cannot—such is the judgement of Israel—replace, efface or lighten the highest or best call of transcendence, the call to universal ethical obligations. The great Mahatma Gandhi (1869–1948) summed up the point: "There is no such thing as religion overriding morality." Religion is the conscience of the world—or ought to be. "Indeed," if I may again cite John Ruskin, "to do the best for others, is finally to do the best for ourselves, but it will not do to have our eyes fixed on that issue."[11]

Judaism and Christianity's "Judaism"

Evidently, the *sine qua non* of interreligious dialogue is respect. Respect appreciates differences without assimilating, conflating or disparaging them. The more significant the differences, the greater the potential respect. Given the profundity and comprehensiveness of each of the great world religions, which aside from the natural variations produced by differing time, place and culture, differ from one another not in the contents of revelation, insight or metaphysics, that is to say, not because of any lack in these remedied by one relative to the other, but by their *differing emphases* of the same salvific wisdom known to them all. It is a sad indication, let us admit it, of the recalcitrance of human and social narrowmindedness and self-assertion, of human immaturity and fears, that interreligious dialogue has at all times proven so difficult. Furthermore, it seems to have proven most difficult for Christianity, where evangelicalism is often but imperialism by another name. So while the Hindu gratefully accepts Christ as another savior, the Christian wipes out all the Hindu avatars and obliterates Hinduism. Or as Nietzsche put it, the Greek gods died of laughter upon hearing Jesus declared the One and Only God. Unfortunately for humans such impositions are historically filled far more with blood than laughter.

9. Levinas, "Religion for Adults," 17.
10. Levinas, "On the Jewish Reading," 107.
11. Ruskin, *Genius of John Ruskin*, 293.

In any event, Christian disrespect (some Christians called it "contempt"—and embraced it) for Judaism is longstanding, deeply engrained and bloody. Christianity from its very beginnings has both misunderstood and misrepresented Judaism, and these two deviations fed on one another. Declaring itself a "religion of love," it has *hated* Jews and *despised* Judaism, over the centuries perpetrating unspeakable violence, including torture, theft, humiliation, rape, mass expulsion and murder—a veritable vale of tears, which Levinas has called "the passion of Israel." Auxiliary to its mistreatment, Christianity has subtly and grossly misrepresented its victims, distorting who Jews are and what Judaism is, in an antisemitism so deeply rooted that its hatefulness and violence continue to this day.[12] That Christianity's lies and distortions are harmful to Jews has been proven all too often. That they are harmful and unworthy of Christianity should be evident not only in the death and suffering they cause Jews but in the utter mockery they make of Christianity's purported message of love.

Not to speak in vague generalities, let us briefly consider three popular and basic but fundamentally false Christian misrepresentations of Judaism.

Christians take it for granted—and make it for granted—that the root difference between Christianity and Judaism is the difference between New Testament and Old Testament. Christianity is the religion of the New Testament; Judaism is the religion of the Old Testament. Or, to say this with greater refinement: Christianity is the religion of the New Testament supersession of the Old Testament, whereas Judaism remains the religion still stuck in the Old Testament, without its New Testament fulfillment and culmination. The "New" of New Testament means fulfillment, completion, Christianity as successful culmination of Judaism, so that "Old"—the Old without the New, i.e., Judaism—means incomplete, superseded, antiquated and obsolete. Jews are mere unenlightened remnants of a superseded past, sustained by a stubbornness whose only "explanation" is the sway of the demonic.

So where, Christians ask themselves, is the misrepresentation? New Testament, Old Testament, fulfilled, antiquated—even granting that God's covenant with the Jews remains unbroken (because God, after all, can do whatever He wants, however inexplicable really). Old Testament, New Testament; Jesus and his Church saving Christians, Jews stubbornly remaining

---

12. There are many books on the topic of Christian antisemitism, many by committed Christian authors of good will who are greatly disturbed by it, including but not limited to the following: Baum, *Jews and the Gospel*; Boys, *Has God Only One Blessing?*; van Buren, *Theology of the Jewish–Christian Reality*; Carroll, *Constantine's Sword*; Flannery, *Anguish of the Jews*; Littell, *Crucifixion of the Jews*; Soulen, *God of Israel*; Ruether, *Faith and Fratricide*.

blind. Where the lie? Everything regarding Judaism! The truth is that both Christianity and Judaism have new testaments. They are not the same new testaments, but neither is "stuck" in the Old Testament. The Christian new testament, to be sure, is the New Testament, centered on the Gospels, the life and teaching of Jesus as Christ. The Jewish new testament, however, is the Talmud, the "Oral Torah," the multi-volume encyclopedic compendium of rabbinical discussions, arguments, debates and anecdotes, beginning circa 200 BCE, dedicated to refining, making precise, quantifying if possible, the ethical life divinely commanded in the Hebrew Bible, the "Written Torah." Not only that, there are actually two Jewish new testaments, two Talmuds! One a compendium of rabbinic discussions from the Land of Israel, the so-called "Jerusalem Talmud," completed circa 300 CE, and the other, the "Babylonian Talmud," a record of the discussions of the rabbis in Babylonia, completed circa 500 CE. So the *truth* is that both Judaism and Christianity consider the Hebrew Bible to be Sacred Scripture, and both Judaism and Christianity read the Old Testament through post-biblical lenses. The essential difference defining each and differentiating each from the other, the line of demarcation between them, then, runs not between Old and New Testament, but between New Testament for Christians and Talmud for Jews. The Roman Catholic Church did not figure this out for a thousand years, at which point it began banning, editing, stealing and burning Talmuds. It seems the general Christian public has never been informed.

Because this difference is important, and because Christians seem generally unfamiliar with the existence (let alone the nature) of Talmud, and because this ignorance has historically produced painful consequences for real Jews, we will dwell on it a bit longer. Christians in characterizing Judaism as cruel and mean-spirited have made a big deal of Leviticus 24:20, which seems to define justice as "an eye for an eye and a tooth for a tooth," the infamous "law of talon," taken literally to mean that one who destroys another's eye or tooth must have their eye or tooth destroyed. Of course such mutual eye or tooth plucking would be vengefulness and not justice, but Christians seem to delight on insisting that Jews actually do confuse vengefulness with justice, and hence that Jews don't know what true justice is. Christians love, but Jews pluck out eyes. But the *truth* is otherwise. This is not how Jews read Leviticus 24:20, and this is not how Jews conceive justice. The Talmud is quite clear on this point. Bava Kamma 83b–84a, explicitly explains Leviticus 24:20 as referring to monetary compensation. So the person who wrongfully deprives another of a tooth or an eye, or inflicts other wrongful injuries, is obligated to compensate that person for a financial value equal to the damage, an eye, i.e., the monetary equivalent for the loss of the damaged eye. This equivalence would be decided by a court of impartial judges. And this, by the way, is precisely how the law works in America and in all civilized countries today. Jews never confused vengeance for justice, quite the reverse, thousands of years ago, when their neighbors were chopping off hands for hands, and plucking out eyes for eyes, they insisted on equitable compensation, on justice against the vicious claims of vengeance. To say or teach otherwise is to malign the Jews and Judaism. And sad to say the misrepresentation of the "law of talon" is but one example, albeit well known, of many. The highest concern of the Talmud is to work out in the most concrete and precise details how to live a personal and social life of righteousness which is the highest concern of the Hebrew Bible and of Judaism as a whole.

A second unfortunate (because consequential) Christian misrepresentation of Judaism is its erroneous idea that Judaism is merely tribal and parochial while Christianity, in contrast, represents an all-embracing universalism. Perhaps Christian universalism is somehow tied to Galatians 3:28: "There is neither Jew nor Gentile, neither slave nor free, nor is there male and female, for you are all one in Christ Jesus." Perhaps it is tied to the easier entry requirements and obligations of Christianity, e.g., no circumcision and non-observance of the multitudinous mitzvot. Or might it might only be a comforting but false projection to distract Christianity from its own faux universalism, whereby exclusivism confuses its exclusivity for universalism, yielding the hubristic insistence that Christianity is the only true religion? The fact is that Judaism is not tribal. One must not confuse its hereditary inclusiveness, that one can be born Jewish, as Christians are for the most part in fact born Christians (aside from the theological niceties of baptism), for exclusivity. Judaism, in any event, is open and welcoming to any and all persons who wish to sincerely convert, regardless of ethnicity, gender, nationality, age, poverty, and the like. Historically, it was not Judaism that barred converts, but rather Christianity which forbade conversion to Judaism. Furthermore, beyond the matter of conversion, Jewish universalism is expressed by the biblical prophets who in the name of God insisted that Jew and foreigner be treated alike, according to the same justice. "When a stranger sojourns with you in your land, you shall not do him wrong. You shall treat the stranger who sojourns with you as the native among you, and you shall love him as yourself, for you were strangers in the land of Egypt: I am the Lord your God" (Lev 19:33–34). It is a canard, Jewish tribalism versus Christian universalism, and an especially egregious canard inasmuch as the latter was no doubt in large measure a product of Jewish universalism, and the former characterization a product of Christian exclusivism.

A third Christian misrepresentation of Judaism propagates the erroneous idea that Jews conceive God as a harsh judge, of merciless retribution, indeed of vengeance, in contrast to the Christian God of love, mercy and forgiveness. The reality is quite otherwise. As we saw when considering the Noachide laws, Jews consider the dual attributes of *mercy and justice* to be closest to the divine nature. Love of God, so the Talmud teaches, is preferable to fear of God, but both are necessary. Indeed, for Judaism these two attributes, in God and in humans, are inseparable, because when they are divorced each turns into its opposite, mercy into indulgence and justice into cruelty. But one thing is clear, the God of the Jews, far from being vengeful or hate-filled, is a *loving* God, loving Jews, loving all humankind, and loving all of creation, and teaching love. It is no accident that the Hebrew Bible does not even begin with a Jew, but with Adam, who, like Noah later, is ancestor of all humankind.

Lies and misrepresentations are reprehensible, and very often have painful consequences. This is especially true when it comes to religion, which deals in the deepest of beliefs and worldviews. Misinterpretations can be painful to correct, as well, especially when they are deeply engrained and taken for granted. But let us turn to another question: Why? Why these and so many other toxic Christian misrepresentations of Judaism? Why—given the enormous suffering that results from its lies—is Christianity so apparently indifferent if not blithely unaware of its anti-Jewish prejudices?[13] Why is Christianity so unchristian, as it were, when it comes to Judaism? Is there perhaps something deeper, hidden and more terrible at work? What? The

---

13. Once, during an invited Sunday noon talk about the Holocaust, at a large Presbyterian Church in Charlotte, North Carolina, without mentioning the name of the author, I read from some of Luther's antisemitic writings. When I asked the audience of well mannered and attentive church goers who they thought was the author, the answer was unanimous: Adolf Hitler. When I informed them it was Martin Luther, they were both aghast and completely surprised. They had never heard of Luther's antisemitism. As if Americans could know their own history without knowing about slavery and the Civil War. But such is also, sad to say, often the case regarding the Inquisition and Crusades, whose horrors of rapacity, duplicity, murder, rape, and the like, are all too often whitewashed for a more delicate Christian consumption. Certainly I am not suggesting that Christianity, or even less, that Christians are evil or necessarily antisemitic. Christianity has its share of saints and righteous, and under its brighter lights certainly intends to inculcate a high morality along with its spiritualism, etc. This is not in question. But we must not—and this regarding all religions, Judaism included—confuse the ideal and the real. We are meant to live up to ideals, meaning that the real is *not* sufficient by itself. Judaism is no doubt unusual and perhaps even unique insofar as its Sacred Scriptures, among other things, are a record of Israel's failings and backsliding. Not to exalt them, but to remember to correct such faults. Judaism neither erases nor wallows in sin, but rather recognizes and repents its failings by striving to act better, to better strive for kindness and justice. It is a religion of responsibility toward humans, and by that route toward God. Not even God, so the holiday of Yom Kippur teaches, can forgive sins against other persons; these only the responsible Jew can and must rectify, and determine not to repeat in the future.

questions are important. They are indeed essential and propaedeutic if inter-religious dialogue between Christianity and Judaism is to be possible. Just raising them is already a step forward. To answer such questions, however, exceeds the present format. What follows, then, must be considered merely limited preliminary sketches, suggestive, it is hoped, and provocative, as is inevitable, to cast some light, to raise a modicum of self-awareness and to stimulate further questioning to pierce what is still a noxious and injurious darkness.

Birth Pangs

So let us return to beginnings, this time historical—to the Mediterranean basin in the first centuries of the Common Era. It is a time dear to Chris-tianity, and especially to Protestant Christianity which returns again and again to the Gospels of that place and time which relate the life and teach-ings of Jesus of Nazareth. Of course Christianity in all its contemporary forms returns no less, and indeed a great deal more to the life and teachings of Jesus as presented by Paul, who is the true originator of Christianity as an independent religion—a new religion independent, that is to say, from the religion of its birth, the religion of Jesus, of his disciples, and even of Paul himself, namely, the Judaism of Israel. In recognizing the constitutive significance of Paul as founder of the new religion Christianity, we are on solid scholarly ground. What I want to attend to, however, is something else, or something closely related, namely, the impact of imperial Rome, its conquest of Israel and its Mediterranean hegemony. It is my thesis, and I am not alone in saying it, that the latter, the socio-political-military Ro-man hegemony, the Roman Empire, Roman civilization, often quite harsh, that more than anything else determined the origination, self-definition and subsequent spread of Christianity in the ancient world, as also it fundamen-tally impacted, though quite differently, the contemporary re-constitution of Judaism. More than the inner theological self-interpretations, which are not surprisingly self-serving, what needs to be understood is that the New Testament and Christianity, on the one hand, and the Talmud and rab-binic Judaism, on the other, both arise as *real responses to Rome and as real responses to one another*. In other words, to grasp the actual rather than imaginary or ideological nature of Christianity and Judaism, and hence their real relationship, one must disentangle and illuminate their constitu-tive dialectic—or triangulation—with Rome, and through Rome with one another, in the early centuries of the Common Era.

Let us proceed to this triangulation then. It was a time of great turmoil—social, military, political, cultural—in the tiny far eastern Mediterranean outpost of Israel, agitated by the hegemonic central power, the superpower of Imperial Rome. What Rome subjugated when it conquered Israel was not a *religion*, which did not exist for the Jews, but a thousand-year-old Commonwealth, a sovereign Jewish state serving an independent *Jewish civilization*—a civilization, let us add, that had predated its Commonwealth by at least another thousand years. Unlike Christianity later, Rome and Israel met as equals. Not in military power, of course, because Rome far surpassed Israel militarily, but in the sense that both were sovereign civilizations. Both Israel and Rome had kings, armies, legislatures, laws, temple, sacrificial rituals, priesthoods, dietary restrictions, kinship taboos, businesses, farms, and everything else that makes up the fullness of human community, civilization. Such, in contrast, was never the case with Christianity which began and remained a *religion*. This is a very important difference, and an inaugural one for Christianity. Because it was precisely as a *religion*—and not like Israel which was an alternative *civilization*—that Christianity invented and maintained itself as an alternative to Rome and Israel. Christianity and religion arise together, are the same, and are opposed to Rome and Israel alike, though differently. Unlike Rome and Israel, Christianity would be in the world but not of it. "They are not of the world, even as I am not of it" (John 17:16).

Let us be even more specific.

Christian Flight from Rome into the Hands of Rome

To achieve military victory in Israel the better led, more numerous and better trained soldiers of the invading Roman armies killed thousands of Jewish soldiers of the Jewish armies. To maintain their rule, the Roman overlords installed sympathetic local leaders, and Roman soldiers suppressed and killed thousands of rebellious Jews. Many Jews were killed in battle, many were crucified. Such was the price of the Jews' futile rebellions against Rome. Julius Caesar, having defeating his rival Pompey in 45 BCE, became undisputed ruler of the Levant, and recognized the local Judaism as a licit, legal or tolerated religion (*religio licita*), which meant that its practitioners would be under the protection of Rome, i.e., not be persecuted as such. Such largesse, as it were, had a practical dimension inasmuch as it helped maintain the famous *pax Romana*. In addition to imposing political rulers, the Romans also imposed a tribute or tax on the defeated Jews (*fiscus Iudaicus*), a nearly universal practice of victors over the defeated in the ancient world. Roman rule was oppressive to the Jews, in part because of the overbearing personalities of their Roman-backed leaders, but also in large measure owing to their long prior experience of independent sovereignty.

In any event, after more than a century of vassalage to Rome, the Jews rebelled, twice. Of course both rebellions were crushed. The first revolt, lasting from 66–70 CE, concluded with the Roman legions under General Vespasian (soon to be Emperor) destroying the Temple in Jerusalem. The second, from 132–36 CE, led by Bar Kochbah (considered by some Jews to be the Messiah), concluded with the termination of Jewish political sovereignty in Israel, indeed with the termination of *any* independent sovereignty in Israel (a situation of non-sovereignty which continued for nearly two thousand years until the United Nations reestablished the Jewish State of Israel in 1948). It was out of and in response to this cauldron of Roman conquest and rule in the first two centuries CE that Christianity emerged, as did rabbinic Judaism.

We have seen only partly how the Jews reacted to Rome: opposition, resistance, and rebellion. But there is another side, decisive after the destruction of its Temple in 70 CE, namely, revision, transformation, renovation, the rise of rabbinic Judaism displacing the authority of priests and monarchy, holding and elevating whatever of Judaism could survive the loss of Temple worship and political sovereignty. Though defeated militarily, by means of this reconstituted *rabbinic Judaism*, each Jew would be a priest and each home a temple, preserving a now "portable civilization," based in learning and synagogue communities, founding the outer means and inner strength to survive and outlive the Roman Empire, to flourish as best it could under adverse conditions, especially the loss of sovereignty, and to continue to this day, now, today, in Israel and out. So much for the Jews: civilization remade into culture, legislation and pedagogy; self-rule lived through family and community; provisionally detached from land and king; a Judaism in exile, even in the Land of Israel, until 1948, and some would say, continuing even after 1948.

An alternative response to Rome and the contemporary crisis of the early centuries CE, the distinctively Christian response, which I have until now called "religion," is concisely summed up in a single world: *spiritualization*. Such was Paul's creative genius: Jews could not join Rome; Jews could not beat Rome; better, then, to sidestep Rome absolutely. Henceforth the "kingdom of God" would not be of this world but another. In this way Christians, unlike Jews, pre-rabbinic or rabbinic, would not be a threat to Rome. It took the Romans centuries to figure this out, but eventually, looking past the pusillanimity which disgusted them, Constantine did. Is this not what Constantine understood by his vision of the Cross bearing the motto "In this sign you will conquer" (*In hoc signo vinces*)? Christianity did not oppose Rome, it let Rome be. It would never oppose Rome. Rome could do all the conquering it wanted with no complaint from Christianity, whose "kingdom" was not of this world.

It is no accident that Rome eventually absorbed Christianity and that Christianity became Roman, the sole official religion of the Empire—not because the Emperors were "saved," saw the spiritual light, embraced love, but rather and more soberly because the Empire saw in Christianity acquiescence, the teaching of acquiescence, *obedience to the Roman lords* in this world, the only world that mattered to them If the Christians had not written it themselves, the Romans would have had to invent Mark 12:17, attributed to Jesus: "*Render unto Caesar the things that are Caesar's, and unto God the things that are God's*" (Ἀπόδοτε οὖν τὰ Καίσαρος Καίσαρι καὶ τὰ τοῦ Θεοῦ τῷ Θεῷ). It is Paul's stroke of genius, to make of flight a virtue, of escape a religion, of acquiescence in the world an otherworldly exaltation.

Nothing, however, could have been more *antithetical to Judaism*, whose mission involved a difficult struggle for redemption of and in this world, not spiritual peace but real peace, the end of war, no swords, guns, bullets, bombs, mines, drones, weapons and armies. Judaism is nothing but the absolutization of an insistence on a world of justice where morality holds sway. Despite its own loss of sovereignty under the strong arm of Rome, Judaism would always hold Rome accountable, as it would hold all sovereign powers accountable, here, now, where ethics calls us to help one another, with protection, food, shelter, comfort, and so on. Never would Judaism endorse a dualism of below and above which would leave the below to its own devices, a dualism of two kingdoms, material and spiritual, abandoning to Caesar this world, regardless of good and evil, justice or injustice. Judaism lived and breathed as the contestation of such abandonment, lived and breathed as the contestation of injustice by the claims of justice, justice sanctified as nothing less than the will of God, as holiness itself. Christianity, in contrast, would accept the status quo, and turn the hearts, minds and souls of its faithful toward another world, a spiritual "kingdom," turning its cheek to the slings, arrows and blows of Caesar.

From the point of view of political realism, so-called "realpolitik," Christian escapism represents a shrewd strategy of survival. On the other hand, retaining our ethical footing, our love of our neighbors, near and far, such a manner of survival seems highly questionable, from at least two perspectives. First, it is *cowardly*, disloyal. It turns its back and deserts the community of those who would fight evil and injustice in this world, leaving them in the lurch to fend for themselves. In breaking from Judaism for the spiritual kingdom, Christianity deserted just such a battle. Second, it is *irresponsible* in itself, serving immorality and injustice. It leaves evil and injustice to their own devices, no longer concerned because, so it claims, it cares about "higher" things, "salvation" and "the spiritual kingdom." To be sure, Christian spiritualism cannot ultimately explain how, of all things, it maintains a human solidarity, or moral responsibility or supports justice, when all such commitments are used and abused by Caesar No doubt, too, we must remind ourselves that the ordinary run of humankind is ordinarily prone neither to heroism, nor to calling out evil and injustice. But clear-headed recognition of human finitude, for human failings, which will always be with us, is no *excuse* for cowardice and irresponsibility. Furthermore, as we have seen, Judaism teaches precisely that the ultimate worth or holiness of life lies precisely in making the world better, in kindness and justice, which includes the risks, dangers and difficulties of opposing evil and injustice. Very simply, then, Christianity's response to Rome, i.e., the spiritualization of religion, translates concretely into accommodation, non-opposition, and ultimately into deference toward and complicity with evil and injustice. In spiritualizing religion, in affirming another world as the only world that truly counts, the heavenly City of God, Christianity has concomitantly endorsed the status-quo, the powers that be, the Caesars of this world. In sharp contrast to Judaism, the Christian can be—and perhaps must be—with God and Caesar at the same time, because its metaphysical dualism does not and cannot take Caesare seriously.

Does it need to be said what Christianity's metaphysical dualism—cleaving the world, and leaving the world of Caesar to Caesar—means? It is the rule of the powerful for the sake of power, of the rich for the sake of more wealth, or the propertied for the sake of more property, and so on. No matter that the mass of humanity is thereby rendered subservient, deprived and exploited. This world is the rule of the few at the expense of the many. The triumph of Christianity is the triumph of Rome. No wonder Rome—what Hannah Arendt called "the Roman trinity of religion, authority, and tradition"[14]—eventually absorbed and took over Christianity. Had Christianity not arisen, Rome would eventually have had to invent it. It is the perfect tool for Caesar's subjugation of the masses, making them indifferent, docile, and subservient. No wonder the *Roman* Catholic Church, with its Concordats with Mussolini, and Hitler, or that the Russian Orthodox Church, which fancies Moscow the new Rome, with Stalin's approval, and now Putin's. Why should we be surprised, if indeed we are surprised, that Germany's Lutherans prayed to an Aryan Jesus in the 1930s and early

14. Arendt, *Between Past and Future.*

1940s when Hitler ruled Germany?[15] Why has Christianity *not* turned itself inside out in the deepest most profound anguish and self-questioning in the aftermath of the recent extermination of six million Jews like vermin—shot, gassed, hung, starved—by mass murderers, all of whom had been baptized in Christian churches, raised by Christian parents, heard the New Testament, lived beneath church steeples hearing church bells? I am not saying Christianity is Nazi, which it is not. But I am saying, regarding the real consequences of its spiritualization of religion, that it cannot wash its hands of the Holocaust, because, as I have argued elsewhere, "the Holocaust is a Christian issue."[16] Jews, after all, were the victims. What was the Holocaust if not six million passions, the rape, plunder and mass murder of the innocent? These are not matters peripheral to Christianity, or a passing pang of conscience—they speak to its essence, and yet does Christianity even conceive of establishing a daily pray, or an annual holy day in excplicit remembrance of these Jewish victims, victims because of their Jewishness? So, indeed, I raise the challenge of Christianity's inner *stubbornness*, its inner *blindness*, its inner *obtuseness* regarding morality and justice, and regarding Jews and Judaism. Surely Christianity does not need Jews and Judaism to have its own holy conscience, or to obey it?

I turn now to Aristotle, to his notion of the mean, to help us understand Christianity's distortion of Judaism. What is relevant is his recognition that the extremes—whether excess or deficiency—distort the mean. Each extreme treats the mean as if it were the opposite extreme. Only the mean can accurately evaluate extremes as extremes. So, for instance, only a brave person recognizes the deficiency of bravery as cowardice and its excess as foolhardiness; the coward takes the brave person to be foolhardy; the foolhardy person takes the brave person to be a coward. Such is the unbalance, the extremity of the extreme, that it lumps the genuine mean with the opposite extreme. How does this model help us understand Christianity's relation to Judaism? Christianity represents an extreme of otherworldliness, what I have called spiritualization and characterized as political escapism. This is true of its relation to Rome, and it is true of its relation to Judaism, both of which are civilizations. The problem, then, from an Aristotelean point of view, is that Christianity cannot distinguish Judaism from Rome, seeing both as corrupt because overly materialistic. Jewish holiness, Jewish ethics, everything Jewish, as we saw in the case of the law of talon and as we shall see in a moment with the early Church Fathers' demeaning glosses

15. Even in the twentieth century, the majority of Christians in Nazi Germany apparently considered Jesus to be an Aryan. See Heschel, *Aryan Jesus.*

16. See Cohen, "Holocaust is a Christian Issue."

of Jewish biblical figures, is misread as materially corrupt, overly earthly, arrogant, elitist and the like. Hence the blindfolded figures symbolizing the Jew throughout European church architecture. Hence only Judas is taken to be Jewish; when in fact so too are Jesus and the rest of the Apostles. The examples are innumerable. Christianity, ensconced in the spiritual, sees and denounces Judaism as too worldly, too earthy, carnal, blind to the spiritual, dirty, grasping, and ultimately—how else explain its rejection of Jesus as Messiah?—as demonic, satanic.

Rabbi Jonathan Sacks, former Chief Rabbi of the United Hebrew Congregations of the Commonwealth of Great Britain from 1991 to 2013, in a recent book traces early Christian biblical exegetical antisemitism from Paul's displacement of the Jews who would no longer be blessed through Abraham, Isaac and Jacob, contrary to what Jews actually believe, but now and newly considered by Christianity as heirs of Ishmael, child of the slave Hagar, with Christians now taking the role of descendants of Isaac (see Gal 4:21–31); and then also the Christian recasting of Jews as descendants of Esau with Christians become the descendants of Jacob ("Jacob I loved, but Esau I hated" [Rom 9:13]); exegetical-genealogical degradations of the Jews later further advanced by Cyprian, for whom the weak-eyed Leah is the ancestor of the Jews while from the beautiful Rachel come Christians; an anti-Jewish revisionist genealogy extended and deepened by the early Church Fathers Maximinus, Tertullian, John Chrysostom and Aphrahat who, in Rabbi Sacks's words, "made the final, devastating move: that the Jews are Cain who, having murdered their brother, are now condemned to permanent exile."[17] I think we can safely say that all Jews would declare their unanimity with Rabbi Sacks's *offended* response to such exegetical-interpretive smearing: "It feels like being disinherited, violated, robbed of an identity. This is my past, my ancestry, my story, and here is Paul saying it is not mine at all, it is his and all who travel with him."[18] Christian spirituality, unbalanced, oppositional, becomes realized concretely as hatred of the Jew, and hatred of Jewish ethical opposition to Rome.

Given how much Christianity in actual history and fact owes to Judaism, given its unerasable origination out of the bowels of Judaism, should not Christians, despite their differences, rather be filled with reverence, awe and gratitude? Where is the love? Why such contempt and why the long painful history of malevolence, of persecution, of violence, rather than appreciation and praise? If God is love, if Jesus is love, why no love for the Jews?

---

17. Sacks, *Not in God's Name*, 98. See also Sacks, *Not in God's Name*, 94–98.
18. Sacks, *Not in God's Name*, 96.

Time to Grow Up

Certainly there are many answers. I will suggest one—again not my invention—by analogy with developmental child psychology. Simply put it is the idea that Christian antisemitism is the organizational and theological equivalent of adolescent rebellion and identity formation. Despite parental love, sacrifice and patience, there comes a stage in psychic maturation, adolescence, usually beginning in the early teenage years, when a child turns against its parents in order to make its own way. At that time, for a limited period of time, the young person defines himself or herself in opposition to its parents and significant childhood authority figures who are redefined negatively by that opposition. Out of the blue, so it seems, the loving parents, once figures of loving car and wisdom, become epitomes of stupidity, callousness, selfishness, narrowmindedness, restrictiveness and what have you . . . in a word ogres. In fact the parents have not changed nor has their love or good will. What is transpiring has to do not with the parents but with the child, with its development. The child is establishing its own identity, and it does so by breaking away from the identity hitherto maintained in relation to the authority of the parents, regardless of the latter's real virtues and faults. It is time for the child to become an adult, and hence it must stand on its own, free of its parents. Such adolescent rejection of parents is a step toward initiation into adulthood. Only on the hither side of adolescence, when the child has established its identity, become an adult, can that young adult begin to appreciate the true character of its parents, for better and for worse, but respecting who they truly are on their own as adults and parents, freed of its adolescent rebellious projected image of them. The Hebrew Bible says children should "honor" their parents, which suggests that the relation is never fully one of equals, and that in the best of cases, when parenting has been exemplary, children, now adults should remain grateful.

I expect the reader sees the analogy with Christian-Jewish relations, the younger religion Christianity in relation to its elder or parent religion Judaism. Antisemitism, then, would be the expression of an adolescent Christianity, still living its own fantasies in contrast to facing up to realities, in relation to Judaism. It is a reflection of Christian immaturity, upsetting and punishing its parents for faults not their own. Given how much Christianity learned and adopted from Judaism, it becomes more understandable—though not justifiable—the length and difficulty of its adolescence, its misrepresentations, distortions, and abusiveness toward Judaism. But by the same token, having now had two thousand years to establish itself, hopefully having reached its own independence, its own adult identity, it is high time—enough is enough!—for its misrepresentations and abuses to end, and perhaps even for some genuine love and honoring to emerge. Let us hope, in a spirit of ethical fellowship, that Christianity's new well-meaning commitment to "inter-religious" dialogue, such as may be found in the present volume, and in this case with Judaism specifically, where it is so needed, is driven by such maturity, and rises to it.

By now Christianity should be capable of seeing that while the model of "Judaism" that it has constructed within its own precincts to serve as an inferior and mere preparation for Christianity, it should be capable of seeing by now that that model is not the actual Judaism, which has all along, before and during Christianity's existence, had its own independent and fully mature existence. Part of that maturation of Christianity, then, must be the recognition that Jews are not Christians, that Jewish identity is fully independent of Christian identity (regardless of the asymmetries which remain in the other direction), and because Jews have their own fully mature religion, that they have little attraction to an antisemitic Christianity Jewish rejection of Christianity, therefore, has nothing to do with the demonic or satanic. Rather it represents contentment with Judaism, and genuine respect for the differences separating Judaism and Christianity, and also also the painful memory of too many past abuses. For instance, the Jewish rejection of Jesus as Messiah needs no demonic or satanic attribution. The explanation is far simpler, namely, that Jesus—however much he is the *Christian Messiah*, that is not in question—did not fulfill a single criterion of *Jewish Messiahship*. Just to name three: he was divine while the Jewish Messiah is human; he did not put an end to war and establish world peace; and he did not restore a secure Jewish sovereignty in the Land of Israel. Paul would certainly have been aware of these obstacles, from a Jewish point of view, so having embraced Jesus as Messiah he either had to become a Jewish renegade or, given his genius, create a new religion wherein Jesus was Messiah. As we know, he chose the latter path, and did so by misrepresenting, demeaning and demonizing Judaism—beginning a long history of Christian misrepresentations of Judaism and Christian antisemitism.

Of course the matter is far more complicated, as I have already suggested. Paul also devised an alternative way of dealing with Roman hegemony, namely, spiritualization. In relation to Judaism and to Rome as well, such a path naturally appears to be cowardly and irresponsible. Eventually it also proved useful to Rome, to all Romes, which helped "establish" Christianity, but also created the still unsolved problem of the "Christian Prince" or Christian politics, beyond its usual servitude to earthly power. For the same reason, however, such spiritualized escapism made Christianity even more unacceptable to Jews. Who can be surprised, then, that a fledgling Christianity in opting for spiritual salvation over the struggle for justice would have unkind words, to say the least, for the Jews who continued to pursue the latter difficult though worthy path. Who can be surprised, then, that they denigrated Jews and Judaism as too worldly, materialistic, dirty, greedy, carnal, and the like, and finally as demonic and satanic. But the time of surprise and even of forbearance is long over. Christianity is no longer a child, no longer a fledgling. It has had two thousand years to grow up, to stand on its own feet without those feet trampling the supine bodies of Jews and Judaism. Just as the flourishing of Judaism is independent of Christianity, from the side of Judaism, so too from the side of Christianity should the flourishing of Christianity finally free itself from Jew baiting.

So therein lies the basic condition for interreligious dialogue between Christianity and Judaism. Christianity must grow up! And presumably because over the past two thousand years it has grown up, it is time to own up to its own maturity not by a reverse philosemitism, but by laying off Jews and Judaism, and opening its eyes to who and what Jews and Judaism really are—no longer the "Judaism" of Christianity, but the Judaism of Jews. And to do this, Christianity must deepen its notion of spirituality, to no longer flee from righteousness but to embrace righteousness as a necessary component (if not the epitome) of holiness. It is not unlikely that Christianity, like other world religions, like all humanity, can still learn much from Judaism—true learning seeks and embraces wisdom wherever it is to be found. And in the case of Christianity, given its birth from within an already ancient Jewish community, it can, if I am not grossly mistaken, learn a great deal about its deepest cares, loves, aspirations and revelations. And again unless I am grossly mistaken, it is precisely to rise to this challenge, to be an adult religion, a religion of adults, to rise to the genuine heights of responsibility, wherein lies the real work of "Vatican II's *Nostra aetate*, the CDF's *Dominus Iesus*, the Pontifical Council on Interreligious Dialogue's *Dialogue and Proclamation*, Pope Francis's *Evangelii gaudium*, etc.," to which Donald Wallenfang has called to our attention in organizing and editing the present volume. To care for our neighbors, to care for "the near and the far," the weak no less than the strong, the poor no less than the rich, those of our community, of our faith, and those of other communities and faiths, "the widow, the orphan, the stranger," "unto this last"—such is the holiness that all religions enjoin and that joins all religions, and joins us all.

Bibliography

Arendt, Hannah. *Between Past and Future*. New York: World, 1961.

Baum, Gregory. *The Jews and the Gospel: A Re-Examination of the New Testament*. London: Bloomsbury, 1961.

Benamozegh, Elijah. *Israel and Humanity*. Translated by Maxwell Luria. New York: Paulist, 1995.

Boys, Mary. *Has God Only One Blessing? Judaism as a Source of Christian Self-Understanding*. New York: Paulist, 2000.

Buber, Martin. *Israel and the World*. 2nd ed. New York: Schocken, 1963.

Buren, Paul M. van. *A Theology of the Jewish–Christian Reality*. Lanham, MD: University Press of America, 1995.

Carroll, James. *Constantine's Sword: The Church and the Jews: A History*. New York: Houghton Mifflin, 2001.

Cohen, Richard A. "The Holocaust is a Christian Issue: Christology Revisited." *Modern Believing: Church and Society* 47.1 (2006) 28–43.

———. "L'Olocausto e una questione Cristiana." Translated by Fiorella Gabizon. *La figura nel tappeto* (2006) 125–38.

Congregation for the Doctrine of the Faith. *Dominus Iesus*, 2000. http://www.vatican.va/roman_curia/congregations/cfaith/documents/rc_con_cfaith_doc_20000806_dominus-iesus_en.html.

Flannery, Edward. *The Anguish of the Jews: Twenty-Three Centuries of Anti-Semitism*. New York: Paulist, 1985.

Heschel, Susannah. *The Aryan Jesus: Christian Theologians and the Bible in Nazi Germany*. Princeton: Princeton University Press, 2010.

Kant, Immanuel. *Religion Within the Limits of Reason Alone*. Translated by T. M. Greene and H. H. Hudson. New York: Harper & Row, 1960.

Levinas, Emmanuel. *Beyond the Verse: Talmudic Readings and Lectures*. Translated by Gary D. Mole. Bloomington: Indiana University Press, 1994.

———. *Difficult Freedom: Essays on Judaism*. Translated by Seán Hand. Baltimore: Johns Hopkins Press, 1990.

———. *Totality and Infinity: An Essay on Exteriority*. Translated by Alphonso Lingis. Pittsburgh: Duquesne University Press, 1969.

Littell, Franklin H. *The Crucifixion of the Jews: The Failure of Christians to Understand the Jewish Experience*. New York: Harper & Row, 1975.

Melville, Herman. *White-Jacket, Or the World in a Man-Of-War*. New York: US Book Company, 1892. http://www.gutenberg.org/files/10712/10712-h/10712-h.htm.

Patterson, David. *The Holocaust and the Nonrepresentable*. Albany: State University of New York Press, 2018.

Pontifical Council for Interreligious Dialogue. *Dialogue and Proclamation: Reflections and Orientations on Interreligious Dialogue and the Proclamation of the Gospel of Jesus Christ*, 1991. http://www.vatican.va/roman_curia/pontifical_councils/interelg/documents/rc_pc_interelg_doc_19051991_dialogue-and-proclamatio_en.html. Accessed 03/28/2018.

Ruether, Rosemary R. *Faith and Fratricide: The Theological Roots of Anti-Semitism*. New York: Seabury, 1974.

Ruskin, John. *The Genius of John Ruskin: Selections from His Writings*. Edited by John D. Rosenberg. New York: George Braziller, 1963.

Sacks, Jonathan. *Not in God's Name: Confronting Religious Violence*. New York: Schocken, 2015.

Second Vatican Council. *Nostra aetate*. 1965. http://www.vatican.va/archive/hist_councils/ii_vatican_council/documents/vat-ii_decl_19651028_nostra-aetate_en.html.

Soulen, R. Kendall. *The God of Israel and Christian Theology.* Minneapolis: Fortress, 1996. B

CHAPTER 7

Dialectical Truth between Augustine and Pelagius

Levinas and the Challenge of Responsibility to Superabundant Grace

—Donald Wallenfang, OCDS

Where sin increased, grace overflowed all the more, so that, as sin reigned in death, grace also might reign through justification for eternal life through Jesus Christ our Lord. What then shall we say? Shall we persist in sin that grace may abound? Of course not!

ROMANS 5:20B–6:1

Paradox of the experience. I always said to myself that the executioners of Auschwitz—Protestants or Catholics—had all probably done their catechism.

EMMANUEL LEVINAS,
1986 INTERVIEW WITH FRANÇOIS POIRIÉ[1]

The Church is enriched when she receives the values of Judaism . . . there exists a rich complementarity.

POPE FRANCIS, *EVANGELII GAUDIUM*, 252

1. See Robbins, *Is It Righteous to Be?*, 41.

Is it possible that the premier Christian theological concept of grace may be at once powerful and problematic? Is there a point at which too much reliance on divine grace may impede moral development? What can Christianity continue to learn from Judaism in order to recast the concept of grace according to its most authentic meaning? These are among the questions that will be pursued in the text to follow. By sitting face-to-face with the eminent twentieth-century Jewish philosopher, Emmanuel Levinas (1906–95), an irenic confrontation between the theological concepts of grace and responsibility for the other will ensue.

The argument is organized according to the following four corners: (1) an introduction to the problematics of grace given the backdrop of the Jewish rabbinic tradition of interpretation, (2) a direct critique of the loose Christian concept of grace and forgiveness in a post-Holocaust world, (3) an extension of this critique through a dialectical rapprochement within the classic polemic between Augustine and Pelagius on nature and grace, and (4) an application of these theological findings to a revision of the meaning of Christian discipleship. By attending to these four corners of discovery, we will observe a fortification of the concept of grace as it intersects the concept of responsibility for the other.

Coloring Outside Artificial Lines

May I continue on a more personal note? This essay is the fruit of an ongoing interreligious dialogue between Emmanuel Levinas and I that began in the year 2008. On a larger scale, this essay aims at presenting an important fruit borne from Jewish–Christian dialogue in general. If you ask me, "Are you Christian?," my answer is yes. If you ask me, "Are you Jewish?" my answer is a qualified yes. Aside from the ambiguity of my ethnicity—I was adopted at six weeks after birth without knowledge of my ethnic genealogy—this is so because I understand that my master, teacher (indeed rabbi), savior and Lord is Jewish. It is obvious and necessary to remember that Jesus is Jewish. There was never a point at which he converted to Christianity as such. His mother, Mary, was Jewish, his adoptive father, Joseph, was Jewish, and the twelve men he designated as his apostles were Jewish. Christianity is, first of all, a reform movement within Judaism. It is an outgrowth of Judaism. According to the British scholar of comparative religion, John Hinnells, "in practice the divisions between religions are sometimes artificial. It is not always the case that to believe one religion is 'right' necessarily involves believing that another is 'wrong.' . . . Religion must sometimes be studied as a regional phenomenon rather than under the conventional headings of '-isms.'"[2] And so it is the case with the Judeo-Christian tradition in which two distinct lines of tradition evolved from the common wellspring of monotheistic and ethical faith: שְׁמַע יִשְׂרָאֵל יְהוָה אֱלֹהֵינוּ יְהוָה אֶחָד (*Shema Israel: Adonai Elohinu Adonai ehad*)—"Hear, O Israel, the Lord our God is one" (Deut 6:4).

The truth is, as Hinnells goes on to say, that "there are few cold facts in the study of religions: all explanation involves interpretation."[3] Reminiscent of the Talmudic method, Hinnells suggests that interreligious dialogue reveals the play of truth through dialectical confrontation. Jewish Midrash probes the truth of a text by keeping the dialectical dance of interpretation alive. Not content with simple face-value meanings alone, Rabbinic hermeneutics unearths allegorical, parabolic, and even mystical meanings generated by the text through the interpretive stages of *P'shat*, *Remez*, *Derash*, and *Sod*. Talmudic method refuses to let the ambiguity of problems and the dialectics of truth resolve into facile solutions and singular meanings. Instead, as Levinas insists, the Talmud signifies "an eternal dialogue taking place within human consciousness."[4] Truth is spoken and heard through the plurality of conversation and unresolved dialectical discourse. Levinas observes that "the *relation* between the same and the other—upon which we seem to impose such extraordinary conditions—is language" and that "truth arises where a being separated from the other is not engulfed in him, but speaks to him."[5] Language constitutes the insoluble bridge between the self and the other. It is the field of truth-telling that maintains the irreducibility of the other to the same. Even within human consciousness, truth is announced through the infinite play of discourse between interlocutors, at least one of which is always other than the self. Levinas applies this hermeneutic of dialectical truth to the diversity of civilizations emerging throughout history and to the human vocation to tolerance: "We can tolerate the pluralism of great civilizations and even understand why they cannot merge. The very nature of truth explains how this is impossible: truth

2. Hinnells, *Penguins Handbook*, 7.

3. Hinnells, *Penguins Handbook*, 7.

4. Levinas, *Difficult Freedom*, 65.

5. Levinas, *Totality and Infinity*, 39, 62, respectively. For Levinas, the epiphany of the face appears inasmuch as it speaks, for the essence of language is the very "bond between expression and responsibility" (Levinas, *Totality and Infinity*, 200). Through language, the other becomes my teacher and master, opening new vistas of recognition by implicating me in her suffering. Whereas the "manifestation tradition" in phenomenology (represented by figures such as Jean-Luc Marion) interprets all phenomena according to the totalizing criterion of givenness, a Levinasian hermeneutics of alterity unlocks the infinite possibilities of discourse between others. See Wallenfang, *Dialectical Anatomy of the Eucharist*.

manifests itself in a way that appeals to an enormous number of human possibilities and, through them, a whole range of histories, traditions and approaches."[6] Truth cannot be packaged exclusively within a monocultural totality of expressions. Instead truth is expressed through an unlimited variety of signs, symbolic orders, and modes of communication.

This insight is crucial for the formidable task of interreligious dialogue on a global scale. According to the nature of truth itself, there must be an inherent plurality of distinct civilizations and religious traditions. The saturating host of religious traditions articulates the impossibility of manipulating truth as truth in its global epiphany of a united polyphony of voices. Today we encounter a genealogy of world religions which have evolved over the course of time in various geographical and cultural centers: Judaism and Christianity from the Mediterranean region; Zoroastrianism and Islam from Arabia and the Middle East; Hinduism, Buddhism, Jainism, and Sikhism from India; Taosim and Confucianism from China; and Shintoism from Japan. Several other religious traditions could be mentioned as well, but the point here is to set forth the first principle of interreligious dialogue as inspired by Levinas: "Truth is consequently experienced as a dialogue . . . (which) does not reach a conclusion, but constitutes the very life of truth."[7] The unresolved dialogue of truth prevents the closure and falsification of truth. If the dialogue of truth comes to an abrupt end with nothing left to say, what becomes of truth as a living and universal summons to rediscover it over and over again, let alone as a perennial call to action and responsibility?

Levinas affirms that "to respect the Other is, before all else, to refer to the Other's opinions."[8] Interreligious dialogue begins, and is sustained, by seeking to understand the other first and to affirm the seriousness of the other's religious convictions and the particular expression of those beliefs. Without the attitude of mutual respect and intellectual hospitality, the open quest for truth is reduced to a bland contest of rhetoric untethered from truth and its radical difference in identity in relation to the self. One always must be on guard against the Parmenidean distinction between truth (*aletheia*) and opinion (*doxa*) inasmuch as one would pretend to regard one's own opinion (*doxa*) to be truth (*aletheia*) and the position of the other as always and only opinion (*doxa*). Truth (*aletheia*) as such always transcends its conversation partners by definition. It maintains an otherness over and above the otherness between conversation partners and never can be

6. Levinas, *Totality and Infinity*, 52.

7. Levinas, *Totality and Infinity*, 163.

8. Levinas, *Totality and Infinity*, 239.

identified exclusively with the opinion (*doxa*) of any one of the interpreting correspondents. This does not thereby imply that truth cannot be known and spoken as such. Truth is spoken precisely in and through the play of conversation. It can be said but neither possessed nor commodified. Truth, and especially religious truth, is the elusive and enigmatic prize for the painstaking task of interreligious dialogue.

To return to my opening personal note. Yes, I have been in dialogue with Levinas over the past ten years through his written texts and transcribed and recorded interviews around many questions, both philosophical and theological. In addition, I have had the privilege of getting to know some of his closest family members personally through the North American Levinas Society's annual meetings, such as George and Simone (Levinas) Hansel, and David and Joëlle Hansel, as well as many veteran scholars who knew Levinas personally before 1995. The topic that has fascinated me above all, within the dialogue between Levinas and I, is the relationship between grace and responsibility.[9] As a practicing Roman Catholic, I try to follow the life and teachings of Jesus faithfully. There is not a day that passes that I do not feel a deeper call to conversion that would enable a lifestyle charged with higher degrees of divine love. For Catholic belief, we are empowered by divine grace as channeled above all through the sacraments of the Church, such as baptism, penance and Eucharist. However, in my encounters with the work of Levinas, I have come upon a redoubtable critique of the slippery theological concept of grace. Paul of Tarsus had recognized the fiercely ambivalent potential of the concept when he wrote with great personal transparency to the church in Rome:

> Where sin increased, grace (χάρις) overflowed all the more (ὑπερεπερισσεύω), so that, as sin reigned in death, grace also might reign through justification for eternal life through Jesus Christ our Lord. What then shall we say? Shall we persist in sin that grace may abound? Of course not! . . . We know that the law is spiritual; but I am carnal, sold into slavery to sin. What I do, I do not understand. For I do not do what I want, but I do what I hate. . . . The willing is ready at hand, but doing the good is not. For I do not do the good I want, but I do the evil I do not want. Now if [I] do what I do not want, it is no longer I who do it, but sin that dwells in me. . . . Miserable one that I am! Who will deliver me from this mortal body? Thanks be to God through

9. See Wallenfang, *Dialectical Anatomy of the Eucharist*; Wallenfang, "Levinas and Marion"; Wallenfang, "Face Off for Interreligious Dialogue." For an insightful study on the relationship between the work of Levinas and Paul Ricoeur's dialectic of love and justice, see Delgadillo, "Love."

Jesus Christ our Lord. Therefore, I myself, with my mind (νοῦς),
serve the law of God but, with my flesh (σάρξ), the law of sin.
(Rom 5:20b–6:1; 7:14–15, 18b–20, 24–25)

In Paul's examination of conscience and general confession of sin,
he seems to interpret himself as living under the spell of a psychosomatic
schizophrenia. If he knows what is good to do, why does he not do it but
instead does what he hates? Why does he go even farther and scapegoat
his moral failure on the impersonal theological concept of sin? Why does
grace increase in proportion to sin's proliferation? This seems unjust to say
the least. Why would Paul portray grace as abounding to the measure of
sin's multiplication? He recognizes that the logic of grace could lead one
to the hasty conclusion that more sin invites more grace. As if hedonism
needed more fire to add to its fury! In effect, grace could serve as license
to sin. Though this is not what Paul is arguing overall, through his frank
rhetoric we observe with Paul that this remains a nearby interpretation of
the paradoxical relationship between sin and grace: where sin increased,
grace overflowed all the more. Grace and, moreover, forgiveness as license
(or at least as insurance) to sin and to be saved in the end nevertheless.

Cheap Forgiveness

Failing to resist the sinister temptation within the hermeneutics of grace,
forgiveness quickly can become a cheap and banal word, especially when
one believes that forgiveness awaits around the corner of every guilty misdeed. If I believe that I can and will be forgiven after each and every sinful
thought, word or deed, why not have the best of both worlds? Is it really so
bad to sin if it only brings me right back to God through mercy and recon-
ciliation? Perhaps I can experience divine mercy all the more if I heap up
sin upon sin. Even Jesus seems to indicate as much when he teaches about
the prodigal privilege, whether it be the prodigal son (Luke 10:29–37), the
lost sheep (Matt 18:12–14), the tardy workers in the vineyard (Luke 15:3–7),
the contrite tax collector who places himself at a distance from the inner
sanctum of the temple (Matt 20:1–16), the one owing a greater debt (Luke
18:9–14), or the one who loves much because she has been forgiven much
(Luke 7:36–50). Are we not left with the impression that the one who does
worse is better and the one who does better is worse? What is forgiveness
worth—whether human or divine—if it is taken for granted and entitled before it is requested? In effect, do the central Christian concepts of grace and
forgiveness serve as a blissful warrant to sin? Do these concepts promote

human flourishing or do they contribute to the gravest forms of dehuman-ization to the degree that they complacently sanction it?

In his 1963 book, *Difficult Liberty*, Levinas raises a powerful and disquieting objection to the exorbitance of grace, pardon and forgiveness: "no one, not even God, can substitute himself for the victim. The world in which pardon is all-powerful becomes inhuman . . . the possibility of infinite pardon tempts us to infinite evil."[10] Enter the Shoah, perpetrated at the hands of Christians who, whether Protestant or Catholic, Levinas surmises, "had all probably done their catechism."[11] Enter 9/11, executed by men who believed they were accomplishing the divine will, shouting "Al-lah Akbar" ("God is greatest") upon the doorstep of death. Enter abortion, enacted by men and women who deny the call of the living other in the name of some alleged greater good. Enter slavery, eugenics, racism, sex-ism, classism, and all hate crimes that privilege the self over and against the other, reducing the personal other as a means to an impersonal end. Enter Donald Wallenfang, me, saying with Dostoyevsky that "each of us is guilty before everyone for everyone, and I more than the others."[12] "The world in which pardon is all-powerful becomes inhuman." Just as God does not will to save us without us, neither does God will to forgive us without us. It would be less than divine to supplant entirely the role of the human victim in his or her potential of extending forgiveness to their perpetrator. Likewise, it would be ungodly of God to bypass the free agency of the victim in granting absolution to the victimizer or not granting it. Personal account-ability, vis-à-vis transgression, is necessary for the soberness of justice, the moral exigencies of mercy, and the eschatological rendezvous of judgment. Forgiveness is not something incidental to my neighbor, not something on the side of my neighbor, but something that involves my neighbor directly, personally and incommunicably.

Levinas's corrective of absolute divine forgiveness is necessary for the Christian conscience today. If I believe that I can get away with murder, then I just might do it. However, the truth about personal justice is that just as no one can take the place of the witness, no one can take the place of the victim, not even God. It is not for God to take the place of the human victim and offer forgiveness to the victimizer in the name of the victim. It is up to the victim to do so voluntarily. Levinas goes on to say that "God cannot see to all man's sins; the sin committed against man can be pardoned only by the man who has suffered by it; God cannot pardon it. For His glory as a moral

10. Levinas, *Difficult Freedom*, 20, 139.

11. Levinas, *Is It Righteous to Be?*, 41.

12. As quoted in Levinas, *Otherwise than Being*, 146.

God and for the glory of the man who has come of age, God is powerless."[13] For Christians who believe that they simply can confess their sins against their neighbors to God and the slate can be wiped clean, Levinas points us to a decisive otherwise: "the possibility of infinite pardon tempts us to infinite evil." I must own up to my faults concerning my neighbor before the face of my neighbor. Justice demands that "the measure you give will be the measure you get" (Mark 4:24, RSV).

While forgiveness remains as one of the most powerful possibilities in the human experience, it is powerful inasmuch as it is not taken for granted as a given in the wake of every foul misdeed. Responsibility for the other holds together the fabric of human being and relationships, and forgiveness without responsibility is no forgiveness at all. Moreover, love is nothing without responsibility for the other. This is an insight with which Judaism continues to challenge Christian theology, and rightly so. To live in an authentically Christian way is to live at once in an authentically Jewish way concerning responsibility for the other. According to Levinas, ethics will remain always first philosophy. No grace without responsibility for the other who faces me.

Truth that Lies within Every Persuasive Lie: Pelagius Had a Point

For Christian theology, as the Christian scriptures (especially the New Testament) make evident, the concept of grace is at the forefront of the theological imagination. All is grace and all is ruled by grace. By grace is meant several things: (1) "*favor*, the *free and undeserved help* that God gives us to respond to his call to become children of God, adoptive sons, partakers of the divine nature and of eternal life," (2) "*participation in the life of God*. It introduces us into the intimacy of Trinitarian life," (3) "the gratuitous gift that God makes to us of his own life, infused by the Holy Spirit into our soul to heal it of sin and to sanctify it. It is the *sanctifying* or *deifying grace* received in Baptism," (4) "the gift of the Spirit who justifies and sanctifies us," and (5) that which "*escapes our experience* and cannot be known except by faith."[14] Of all these definitions, the most precise one is that grace is the gift of God the Holy Spirit, the third Person of the Most Holy Trinity, at work in a human being's soul and body to justify, heal and sanctify him or her in relation to God, other persons, and the whole of creation. God the Holy Spirit grants to the soul, first of all, an expansion of spiritual capacities

13. Levinas, *Difficult Freedom*, 54.
14. *Catechism of the Catholic Church*, 1996–2005.

for loving God and other persons. Though the operation of grace cannot be detected directly by empirical methods of physical sense verification, its effects (or fruits) can be known with certainty.[15] This is why grace maintains a sacramental character inasmuch as the hidden and invisible activity of God is manifest and proclaimed in and through the body, and is channeled through the sacramental rites of the Church. Within the history of Christian theology, the two most prominent theologians of grace were Paul of Tarsus and Augustine of Hippo.[16]

In his polemic with Pelagius, Augustine of Hippo asserted the primacy of grace and, at the same time, the corruption of human nature according to its infection of original sin originating with the primordial man, Adam, and his wife, Eve. Pelagius, in contrast, contended that human nature is essentially good and, to protect the autonomous agency of free will, claimed that (1) God would not determine any human being to total depravity and thereby retract the goodness and autonomy of free will, and (2) reason, conscience and the law of God were effective (not completely unrelated to or unaided by grace) to lead people of good will to choose the good.[17] Pelagius's concern with Augustine's position, as articulated for instance in the *Confessions*—"Give what you command, then command what you will"— was that it seemed to allay the weight of responsibility of the moral agent.[18] Was the essence of salvation pure passivity before the force of divine grace? Or did human beings have some personal ownership and responsibility for working out their salvation? Even though the respective theological positions of Augustine and Pelagius involve much nuance that must necessarily be glossed over here for the sake of brevity, suffice it to say that the Augustine–Pelagius polemic serves as a helpful corollary to Jewish–Christian

15. See *Catechism of the Catholic Church*, 2005; Gal 5:13–26.

16. For a helpful account of the evolution of the concept of grace in Augustine's writings, see Teselle, "Background," 1–13. For a consideration of the intricacies involved in the Augustine–Pelagius polemic, see Bonner, *Augustine of Hippo*, 312–93; Bonner, *Freedom and Necessity*, 66–80; Dupont, "Question of the Impact."

17. See Pelagius, *Letter to Demetrias*, 37, where Pelagius emphasizes the power of "reason and wisdom . . . intelligence and mental vigor" within human nature; Pelagius contends "that we might do his will by exercising our own . . . assisted by the aid of divine grace as well" (38–39); Pelagius emphasizes the important role of conscience for the moral life (39–40); Pelagius is concerned to "try to protect (human nature) from an unjust charge, so that we may not seem to be forced to do evil through a fault in our nature, when, in fact, we do neither good nor evil without the exercise of our will and always have the freedom to do one of the two, being always able to do either" (43, cf. Augustine, *De libero arbitrio*, II.1); and where Pelagius aims at a vision of "complete moral perfection" (54).

18. See Augustine, *Confessions*, 10.29.40, 31.45, 37.62; Hwang et al., *Grace for Grace*, 4–5.

dialogue today and the recuperation of personal moral responsibility as provoked by welcome confrontation with the dialectical nature of rabbinic Midrash and, more specifically, the critique of superabundant grace by Emmanuel Levinas.

Dialectical theology, as inspired by authentic interreligious dialogue, always is on the lookout for the reductionistic tendencies of fundamentalism and relativism alike. In the case of the question of grace, one extreme is that it is incidental at best for the pursuit of moral perfection. Pelagianism certainly moves in this direction but, as history shows, his position is taken to further extreme by others in relation to his work, such as Celestius and Julian of Eclanum, as well as the negative coloration Pelagius receives in the texts of Augustine. On the other extreme, however, is the idea that the superabundance of grace, coupled with divine election, results in a fundamentalist doctrine of predestination, and divine determinism (in the name of divine sovereignty), coupled with at least a tacit doctrine of total depravity (forward to Protestantism in the sixteenth century and Jansenism in the seventeenth century). As British theologian Harry Williams has put it, "St. Augustine took the worst of St. Paul, and Calvin the worst of St. Augustine."[19] Soteriological truth, from a Judeo-Christian standpoint, renounces both extremes—on the one hand, *sola gratia* ("grace alone"), and on the other hand, *sola operatur* ("works alone")—and insists on the dialectical relationship between the two—*non solum gratia, sed etiam operatur* ("not only grace, but also works")—even if it is necessary to concede that all is gift in relation to God (see James 2:14–26).

One meaning that emerges at the heart of Pelagius's theology is reminiscent of the fourth of Christ's beatitudes as recounted by the Gospel of Matthew: "We must . . . desire righteousness as strongly as we desire food and drink when hungry or thirsty, and to all without exception who desire the promise of eternal life we must say this."[20] Of course there is no Catholic teaching against such an exhortation and, in fact, this quote could be found in magisterial writings were it not for other things Pelagius said that pulled his work on the whole away from dialectical proximity with the fullness of the doctrine of grace. All the same, is the desire for righteousness, as advocated by Pelagius, not at the heart of the Gospel of Christ and not only a Stoic ideal of virtue? Indeed, this hunger and thirst for righteousness is an essential element of the soteriological life, that is, a living within the process

19. As quoted in Rees, *Pelagius*, 53. For a helpful essay on Augustine's emerging doctrine of predestination in his later work, see Wetzel "Snares of Truth," 124–41. For an insightful treatment of Jansenism and its aftermath, see de Lubac, *Augustinianism and Modern Theology*.

20. See Pelagius's *Letter to Demetrias* in Rees, *Pelagius*, 49.

of redemption. Even Augustine preached that "God created us without us: but he did not will to save us without us."[21] The dialectical point is this: grace yes and our free response yes.

It is the indispensable intuition of personal responsibility that remains the ethical locus of Judaism and resurfaces within the Augustine–Pelagius debate. Levinas, as representative of the Jewish philosophical and theological tradition, helps augment the doctrine of grace to recuperate the doctrine of personal responsibility within its concept. In effect, grace (as divine love and responsibility) is received to the measure that it is given in turn. Love and responsibility beget love and responsibility if they are received as such by their graced recipient. Without the ensuing soberness of responsibility, grace is ineffective in the end. The sinner who has been reconciled and forgiven, restored and healed by divine grace, and continues in the same habits of sin or worse is permitting a short-circuiting of grace within his soul. Grace is not given to enable sin but to check it. Yet only if grace is understood as impregnated within the vocation to responsibility for the other is grace then restored to the dignity and fullness of its concept. It is due to the Jewish roots of Christianity that this restoration is made possible.

Toward Responsible Christian Discipleship

Jesus, the Jewish rabbi, taught that "much will be required of the person entrusted with much, and still more will be demanded of the person entrusted with more" (Luke 12:48b, NAB). This too is the summons to responsibility, one-for-the-other. Due to a prevailing theology of superabundant grace, Christianity has strayed almost irrevocably from its Jewish roots. Beginning with the patristic period and the severely unfortunate caricature of the "Judaizers," the supersessionist attitude of Christianity vis-à-vis Judaism is unmistakable to this day, in spite of the good intentions of ecumenical and interreligious documents and occasional collaborative events. The fact of the matter is that Christians (Catholic, Orthodox and Protestant inclusively) do not read their Bibles in the tradition of Midrash or Talmud. Christianity has lost sight of the vibrant rabbinic tradition that continues in Judaism today, but is missing largely from Christian biblical hermeneutics. With this eclipse of the rabbis has come the eclipse of "a religion for adults" in which there is "a desacralization of the Sacred" because of the humanizing priority of the "liturgy of the neighbor," the "liturgy of dailiness."[22] No grace

21. Augustine, *Sermo 169*, 11.13, as quoted in the *Catechism of the Catholic Church*, 1847.

22. Levinas, *Difficult Freedom*, 11, 18; Chauvet, *Symbol and Sacrament*, 238; Chauvet, *Sacraments*, 58, 63. Cf. Bloechl, *Liturgy of the Neighbor*.

without responsibility for the other who faces me. This is a precious insight gleaned through the course of interreligious dialogue between Judaism and Christianity.

Yet this insight has even further application in serving as a most necessary corrective for at least three additional common biblical misinterpretations within Christian theology:

> (a) The first of these concerns the classic narrative of Genesis 22, the *Akedah* ("binding") of Isaac. In his book, *Proper Names*, Levinas issues a severe critique of Kierkegaardian (Christian) philosophy in its claim to surpass the domain of the ethical.[23] The narrative of Abraham's will to slay his son, Isaac, to placate the deit(ies) has been interpreted as an act of heroism and radical faith over the centuries of Christian theology, as early as the Letter to the Hebrews 11:17–19 and the Letter of James 2:21. Yet this same interpretation has given rise to the grossest forms of nominalism that have their root in the original sin, with its misinterpretation of divine sovereignty and freedom.[24] Instead, Levinas more than suggests that "perhaps Abraham's ear for hearing the voice that brought him back to the ethical order was the highest moment in this drama."[25] This intuition is corroborated by the biblical text itself upon attending to the naming of God in Hebrew throughout the narrative. The "God" who puts Abraham to the test in verse 1 is named *Eleh/Elohim*—two plural nouns for the divine that hover over the ambiguous lines of distinction between polytheism, henotheism and monotheism. The narrative begins here with this naming of the divine, but at the most decisive moment, as suggested

23. See Levinas, *Proper Names*, 72: "Violence emerges in Kierkegaard at the precise moment when, moving beyond the esthetic stage, existence can no longer limit itself to what it takes to be an ethical stage and enters the religious one, the domain of belief. . . . Thus begins the disdain for the ethical basis of being, the somehow secondary nature of all ethical phenomena that, through Nietzsche, has led us to the amoralism of the most recent philosophers."

24. See Servais Pinckaers's helpful distinction between Ockhamian "freedom of indifference" (even as related to the so-called law of parsimony) and Thomistic "freedom for excellence" in Pinckaers, *Sources of Christian Ethics*, 327–99; *Morality*, 65–81.

25. Levinas, *Proper Names*, 74, and further on 74, 77: "But death is powerless, for life receives meaning from an infinite responsibility, a fundamental *diacony* that constitutes the subjectivity of the subject—without that responsibility, completely tendered toward the Other, leaving any leisure for a return to self. . . . That (Abraham) obeyed the first voice is astonishing: that he had sufficient distance with respect to that obedience to hear the second voice—that is the essential." Cf. Laurence Bove's essay, "Unbinding the Other," 169–86; Seeskin, *Thinking about the Torah*, 51–70.

by Levinas, the return to the ethical, the tetragrammaton emerges for the first time in the narrative in verse 11 as the angle of the LORD/YHWH (מַלְאַךְ יְהוָה) commands Abraham not to harm his son Isaac. The repetition of Abraham's response, "Here I am" (in verses 1 and 11), reinforces the summons to ethical responsibility within the narrative. It seems quite clear upon further investigation that Levinas's interpretation is authentic not only to the text itself, but also to the historical-cultural context of Abraham and the conversion away from the abominable practice of child sacrifice of polytheistic tribes and a faithful return to the exigencies of ethical monotheism. Again, here is how Judaism is imperative for authentic Christian theology today. No grace without responsibility for the other who faces me.

(b) The second glaring misinterpretation of common Christian theology comes to light in the judgment scene of Matthew 25. In sum, Jesus says that "whatever you did for one of these least brothers of mine, you did for me" (Matt 25:40, NAB). A misappropriation of this text can leave Christian disciples with the impression that the corporal works of mercy should be carried out inasmuch as Christ is in the anonymous other, and not so much for the sake of the uniqueness of the created human other. However, given the greater biblical context of the *corpus mysticum Christi* ("the mystical Body of Christ"), Jesus's saying does not diminish the incommunicable uniqueness of the other person who faces me. Rather, Jesus's teaching elevates this uniqueness all the more since it makes reference to the harmonious unity of humanity in Christ—the Word made flesh—in which each unique person "is to be inserted as a flower in an eternally imperishable wreath."[26] Every person, in his or her beautiful uniqueness, is inherently loveable.[27] In other words, as a disciple of Christ, I do not care for the other person who

---

26. Stein, *Finite and Eternal Being*, 508. Cf. Stein, *Finite and Eternal Being*, 526: "Every individual human being is created to be a member of [the mystical Body of Christ]. . . . However, it is of the very essence of humankind that every individual as well as the entire human family are to become what, according to their nature, they are destined to be in a process of temporal unfolding, and that this unfolding depends on the cooperation of each individual as well as on the common effort of all."

27. See Farley, *Just Love*, 169n109, 204n52, 205n53. For example: "Love involves . . . a response to what is perceived as loveable" (Farley, *Just Love*, 205n53). Granted that this observation is in reference more so to the erotic dimensions of love, though in relation to the agapic dimensions of love. Cf. Benedict XVI, *Deus caritas est*, part 1; Seeskin, *Thinking about the Torah*, 31–50.

faces me merely because I "see Christ" in them, as if without Christ in them they would be utterly unloveable. Instead, in radical passivity before the other I can behold that which is entirely loveable in her as she is in her beautiful and unrepeatable uniqueness—a uniqueness that Jesus only wishes to unveil and reinforce to a higher degree by referencing the eschatological rendezvous of the communion of angels and saints. Levinas describes the notion of responsible love as "nonindifference" wherein the "relation to the unique" is opened.[28] No grace without responsibility for the uniquely beautiful other who faces me.

(c) The third frequent misinterpretation of Christian theology is to come to the assistance of the other solely for the sake of receiving the great reward that awaits me in heaven (e.g., Matt 5:12; 19:21; 19:29; Luke 6:23; 12:33; 14:14; 18:22). There should be no surprise that Jesus's teachings are laced with paradox as the signature logic of the rabbinic tradition. It would be too obvious to conceive of a propitious reward in heaven as the ultimate goal of hospitality, responsibility, love and perseverance in relation to the other. Rather, hidden beneath this all-too-obvious meaning is the greater meaning that interprets the drama of love and responsibility itself as the reward, that is, interpreting the shining face of the other before me—the good of the other and the promotion of this good—as my reward.[29] Levinas says as much when he writes in *Alterity and Transcendence* that "the saintliness of the human cannot be expressed on the basis of any category. Are we entering a moment in history in which the good must be loved without promises? Perhaps it is the end of all preaching. May we not be on the eve of a new form of faith, a faith without triumph, as if the only irrefutable value were saintliness, a time when the only right to a reward would be not to expect one? The first and last manifestation of God would be to be without promises."[30] Is this not the disposition of Moses and Paul as they plead with God for the salvation of their brethren

28. Robbins, *Is It Righteous to Be?*, 50.

29. See Seeskin, *Jewish Messianic Thoughts*, 101: "I cannot lie to a homeless person or use him solely as a means to achieve a greater good, because there *is* no greater good than recognizing his dignity as a human being."

30. Levinas, *Alterity and Transcendence*, 109. Cf. Levinas, *Ethics and Infinity*, 114, 118: "To be worthy of the messianic era one must admit that ethics has a meaning, even without the promises of the Messiah . . . a humanity which can do without these consolations (of religion) perhaps may not be worthy of them."

at the expense of their own blessed eternity?[31] Is this not the supreme test of heroic virtue, forgetting one's impending death because of vehement solicitude for the death of the other who faces me? Is this disposition not more to the point of the salvation revealed in Christ—perhaps even as far as "the conception of a creature who can be saved without falling into the egotism of grace . . . (by) maintaining a distance from nature" and overcoming the self-referential sway of the *conatus essendi* wherein "what is most natural becomes the most problematic"?[32] No grace without responsibility for the desperate other who faces me, even to the point of death.

In sum, Christian belief and discipleship have much to gain from the enriching and perpetual interreligious dialogue with their Jewish roots, including even the lingering and irreducible otherness of Judaism as Judaism instead of its interpretation as a mere preface to Christianity. This essay has featured some of the theological challenges of Emmanuel Levinas for the developing Christian theological tradition. The more specific claim in this essay is that Christian disciples cannot understand adequately their own beliefs and ethical prescriptions apart from their Jewish heritage. What was true for the early Church's confrontation with Marcionism is true today: "Every scribe who has been instructed in the kingdom of heaven is like the head of a household who brings from his storeroom both the new and the old" (Matt 13:52, NAB).

Bibliography

Augustine of Hippo. *Against Julian.* Translated by Matthew A. Schumacher. New York: Fathers of the Church, 1957.

———. *Anti-Pelagian Writings.* Edited by Philip Schaff. Grand Rapids, MI: Eerdmans, 1978.

———. *Four Anti-Pelagian Writings: On Nature and Grace; On the Proceedings of Pelagius; On the Predestination of the Saints; On the Gift of Perseverance.* Translated by John A. Mourant and William J. Collinge. Washington, DC: Catholic University of America Press, 1992.

———. *On Free Choice of the Will.* Translated by Anna S. Benjamin and L. H. Hackstaff. Upper Saddle River, NJ: Prentice Hall, 1964.

31. "So Moses returned to the LORD and said, 'Ah, this people has committed a grave sin in making a god of gold for themselves! Now if you would only forgive their sin! But if you will not, then blot me out of the book that you have written'" (Exod 32:31–32); "For I could wish that I myself were accursed and separated from Christ for the sake of my brothers, my kin according to the flesh" (Rom 9:3).

32. Levinas, *Difficult Freedom*, 26; *Ethics and Infinity*, 121.

Beach, Bradley, and Matthew T. Powell, eds. *Interpreting Abraham: Journeys to Moriah.* Minneapolis: Fortress, 2014.

Benedict XVI. *Deus caritas est.* 2005. http://w2.vatican.va/content/benedict-xvi/en/encyclicals/documents/hf_ben-xvi_enc_20051225_deus-caritas-est.html.

Bloechl, Jeffrey. *Liturgy of the Neighbor: Emmanuel Levinas and the Religion of Responsibility.* Pittsburgh, PA: Duquesne University Press, 2000.

Bonner, Gerald. *Freedom and Necessity: St. Augustine's Teaching on Divine Power and Human Freedom.* Washington, DC: Catholic University of America Press, 2007.

———. *St. Augustine of Hippo: Life and Controversies.* Norwich: Canterbury, 2002.

Bove, Laurence. "Unbinding the Other: Levinas, the *Akedah*, and Going beyond the Subject." In *Interpreting Abraham: Journeys to Moriah*, edited by Bradley Beach and Matthew T. Powell, 169–86. Minneapolis: Fortress, 2014.

Cavadini, John C. "Feeling Right: Augustine on the Passions and Sexual Desire." *Augustinian Studies* 36.1 (2005) 195–217.

Cavadini, John C., and Donald Wallenfang, eds. *Pope Francis and the Event of Encounter.* Eugene, OR: Pickwick, 2018.

Chauvet, Louis-Marie. *The Sacraments: The Word of God at the Mercy of the Body.* Translated by Madeleine Beaumont. Collegeville, MN: Liturgical, 2001.

———. *Symbol and Sacrament: A Sacramental Interpretation of Christian Existence.* Translated by Patrick Madigan and Madeleine Beaumont Collegeville, MN: Liturgical, 1995.

De Lubac, Henri. *Augustinianism and Modern Theology.* Translated by Lancelot Sheppard. New York: Crossroad, 2000.

Delgadillo, Jorge Medina. "Love Complement or Redundancy of Justice? A Levinasian Revisiting of Ricoeur's Dialectic of Love and Justice." *Iyyun: The Jerusalem Philosophical Quarterly* 63 (2014) 289–310.

Dodaro, Robert, and George Lawless. *Augustine and His Critics: Essays in Honor of Gerald Bonner.* New York: Routledge, 2004.

Dupont, Anthony, et al. "The Question of the Impact of Divine Grace in the Pelagian Controversy: Human *Posse, Uelle et esse* According to Pelagius, Jerome, and Augustine." *Revue d'histoire ecclésiastique* 112.3/4 (2017) 539–68.

Evans, Robert F. *Pelagius: Inquiries and Reappraisals.* New York: Seabury, 1968.

Farley, Margaret A. *Just Love: A Framework for Christian Sexual Ethics.* New York: Continuum, 2007.

Hwang, Alexander Y., Brian J. Metz, and Augustine Casiday, eds. *Grace for Grace: The Debates after Augustine and Pelagius.* Washington, DC: Catholic University of America Press, 2014.

Levinas, Emmanuel. *Alterity and Transcendence.* Translated by Michael B. Smith. New York: Columbia University Press, 1999.

———. *Beyond the Verse: Talmudic Readings and Lectures.* Translated by Gary D. Mole. Bloomington, IN: Indiana University Press, 1994.

———. *Collected Philosophical Papers.* Translated by Alphonso Lingis. Dordrecht: Martinus Nijhoff, 1987.

———. *Difficult Freedom.* Translated by Seán Hand. Baltimore: Johns Hopkins University Press, 1990.

———. *Discovering Existence with Husserl.* Translated by Richard A. Cohen and Michael B. Smith. Evanston, IL: Northwestern University Press, 1998.

———. *Emmanuel Levinas: Basic Philosophical Writings.* Edited by Adriaan T. Peperzak, Simon Critchley, Robert Bernasconi. Bloomington, IN: Indiana University Press, 1996.

———. *Entre Nous: On Thinking of the Other.* Translated by Michael B. Smith and Barbara Harshav. New York: Columbia University Press, 1998.

———. *Ethics and Infinity: Conversations with Philippe Nemo.* Translated by Richard A. Cohen. Pittsburg, PA: Duquesne University Press, 1985.

———. *Existence and Existents.* Translated by Alphonso Lingis. Pittsburgh: Duquesne University Press, 2001.

———. *God, Death, and Time.* Translated by Bettina Bergo. Stanford, CA: Stanford University Press, 2000.

———. *Humanism of the Other.* Translated by Nidra Poller. Chicago: University of Illinois Press, 2003.

———. *In the Time of the Nations.* Translated by Michael B. Smith. Bloomington, IN: Indiana University Press, 1994.

———. *The Levinas Reader.* Edited by Seán Hand. Cambridge, MA: Basil Blackwell, 1989.

———. *New Talmudic Readings.* Translated by Richard A. Cohen. Pittsburgh: Duquesne University Press, 1999.

———. *Nine Talmudic Readings.* Translated by Annette Aronowicz. Bloomington, IN: Indiana University Press, 1990.

———. *Of God Who Comes to Mind.* Translated by Bettina Bergo. Stanford, CA: Stanford University Press, 1998.

———. *On Escape.* Translated by Bettina Bergo. Stanford, CA: Stanford University Press, 2003.

———. *Otherwise than Being or Beyond Essence.* Translated by Alphonso Lingis. Pittsburgh: Duquesne University Press, 1981.

———. *Outside the Subject.* Translated by Michael B. Smith. London: Athlone, 1993.

———. *Positivité et transcendance.* Paris: Presses Universitaires de France, 2000.

———. *Proper Names.* Translated by Michael B. Smith. Stanford, CA: Stanford University Press, 1996.

———. *The Theory of Intuition in Husserl's Phenomenology.* Second Edition. Translated by Andre Orianne. Evanston, IL: Northwestern University Press, 1995.

———. *Time and the Other.* Translated by Richard A. Cohen. Pittsburgh: Duquesne University Press, 1987.

———. *Totality and Infinity: An Essay on Exteriority.* Translated by Alphonso Lingis. Pittsburgh: Duquesne University Press, 1969.

———. *Unforeseen History.* Translated by Nidra Poller. Chicago: University of Illinois Press, 2004.

Marion, Jean-Luc. *In the Self's Place: The Approach of Saint Augustine.* Translated by Jeffrey L. Kosky. Stanford, CA: Stanford University Press, 2012.

Metz, Johann Baptist. *The Emergent Church: The Future of Christianity in a Postbourgeois World.* Translated by Peter Mann. New York: Crossroad, 1981.

Pelagius. *Commentary on St. Paul's Epistle to the Romans.* Translated by Theodore de Bruyn. Oxford: Clarendon, 1998.

Pinckaers, Servais. *Morality: The Catholic View.* Translated by Michael Sherwin. South Bend, IN: St. Augustine's, 2001.

———. *The Sources of Christian Ethics*. Translated by Mary Thomas Noble. Washington, DC: Catholic University of America Press, 1995.

Rahner, Karl. *Nature and Grace: Dilemmas in the Modern Church*. Translated by Dinah Wharton. New York: Sheed & Ward, 1964.

Rees, B. R. *Pelagius: Life and Letters*. Woodbridge, UK: Boydell, 1998.

Robbins, Jill, ed. *Is It Righteous to Be?: Interviews with Emmanuel Levinas*. Stanford, CA: Stanford University Press, 2001.

Schuld, J. Joyce. *Foucault and Augustine: Reconsidering Power and Love*. Notre Dame, IN: University of Notre Dame Press, 2003.

Seeskin, Kenneth. *Jewish Messianic Thoughts in an Age of Despair*. New York: Cambridge University Press, 2012.

———. *Thinking about the Torah: A Philosopher Reads the Bible*. Philadelphia: Jewish Publication Society, 2016.

Stein, Edith. *Finite and Eternal Being: An Attempt at an Ascent to the Meaning of Being*. Translated by Kurt F. Reinhardt. Washington, DC: ICS, 2002.

Teselle, Eugene. "The Background: Augustine and the Pelagian Controversy." In *Grace for Grace: The Debates after Augustine and Pelagius*, edited by Alexander Y. Hwang, et al., 1–13. Washington, DC: Catholic University of America Press, 2014.

Wallenfang, Donald. *Dialectical Anatomy of the Eucharist: An Étude in Phenomenology*. Eugene, OR: Cascade, 2017.

———. "Face Off for Interreligious Dialogue: A Theology of Childhood in Jean-Luc Marion versus a Theology of Adulthood in Emmanuel Levinas." *Listening: Journal of Communication Ethics, Religion, and Culture* 50.2 (2015) 106–16.

———. "Figures and Forms of Ultimacy: Manifestation and Proclamation as Paradigms of the Sacred," *The International Journal of Religion in Spirituality and Society* 1.3 (2011) 109–14.

———. *Human and Divine Being: A Study on the Theological Anthropology of Edith Stein*. Eugene, OR: Cascade, 2017.

———. "Levinas and Marion on Law and Freedom: Toward a New Dialectical Theology of Justice." *Pacifica* 29.1 (2017) 71–98.

Weaver, Rebecca Harden. *Divine Grace and Human Agency: A Study of the Semi-Pelagian Controversy*. Macon, GA: Mercer University Press, 1996.

Wetzel, James. *Augustine and the Limits of Virtue*. New York: Cambridge University Press, 1992.

———. "Snares of Truth: Augustine on Free Will and Predestination." In *Augustine and His Critics: Essays in Honor of Gerald Bonner*, edited by Robert Dodaro and George Lawless, 124–41. New York: Routledge, 2004.ʙ

Dialogues between Islam and Christianity

CHAPTER 8

Islamic Christology
and Muslim–Christian Dialogue

—GABRIEL SAID REYNOLDS

I n recent years the question of whether Muslims and Christians worship the same God has generated significant interest, and not only among theologians. In early 2016 controversy flared when Larycia Hawkins, at that time an associate professor at Wheaton College, was disciplined by the evangelical Protestant institution for declaring that Muslims and Christians worship the same God. The source of the controversy was the following statement, which Hawkins posted on Facebook in December 2015:

> I stand in religious solidarity with Muslims because they, like me, a Christian, are people of the book. And as Pope Francis stated last week, we worship the same God. . . . As part of my Advent Worship, I will wear the hijab to work at Wheaton College, to play in Chi-town, in the airport and on the airplane to my home state that initiated one of the first anti-Sharia laws (read: unconstitutional and Islamophobic), and at church.[1]

1. See Hawkins, "20 December 2015." Although Hawkins writes that Muslims and Christians are both "people of the Book," from an Islamic perspective this is not strictly correct. In Islam "People of the Book" (Ar. *ahl al-kitab*) is a category reserved for pre-Islamic communities which (according to the Qur'an) received earlier revelations. In practice this category then usually is seen as including Jews and Christians (although on occasion other religious groups have been included as well). Muslims, however, as the community of faithful believers following the new revelation given to Muhammad, are considered to be in a separate category. Notably this is also a category which the *Catechism of the Catholic Church* insists is also not appropriate for Christianity. Quoting St. Bernard, the authors of the *Catechism* write, "The Christian faith is not a 'religion of the book.' Christianity is the religion of the 'Word' of God, a word which is 'not a written and mute word, but the Word which is incarnate and living'" (*Catechism of the Catholic Church*, 108).

In response to this public declaration that Muslims and Christians worship the same God Hawkins was put on administrative leave by Wheaton College (Wheaton made it clear that the issue at hand was not her decision to wear a hijab). The administration at Wheaton apparently felt that this position conflicted with the statement of Christian faith which all faculty at Wheaton are obliged to sign.[2] While Wheaton never fired Hawkins, eventually an agreement was reached by which she left the institution.

While Hawkins (an evangelical Protestant at an evangelical Protestant institution) calls on the authority of Pope Francis, it is not actually clear which statement Hawkins is alluding to (to my knowledge the pope did not make any statement on Islam and Christianity in December of 2015). Still Hawkins appeals to the Holy Father with reason. Several statements of Pope Francis suggest a conviction that Muslims and Christians worship the same God. Soon after his election to the pontificate Pope Francis declared the following in an address to leaders of churches and world religions: "I greet and thank cordially all of you, dear friends belonging to other religious traditions; firstly the Muslims, who worship the one living and merciful God, and call upon Him in prayer."[3] In this statement Pope Francis seems to invoke *Nostra aetate*, paragraph 3: "The Church regards with esteem also the Moslems. They adore the one God, living and subsisting in Himself; merciful and all-powerful, the Creator of heaven and earth, who has spoken to men."[4] Pope Francis is still more explicit in the apostolic exhortation *Evangelii gaudium*, published later in 2013. Quoting *Lumen gentium*, the Holy Father writes:

> Our relationship with the followers of Islam has taken on great importance, since they are now significantly present in many traditionally Christian countries, where they can freely worship and become fully a part of society. We must never forget that they "profess to hold the faith of Abraham, and together with us they adore the one, merciful God, who will judge humanity on the last day."[5]

2. For more detail, see Weber, "Wheaton."

3. "Saluto poi e ringrazio cordialmente tutti voi, cari amici appartenenti ad altre tradizioni religiose; innanzitutto i Musulmani, che adorano Dio unico, vivente e misericordioso, e lo invocano nella preghiera, e voi tutti" (Francis, "Audience with Representatives").

4. "Ecclesia cum aestimatione quoque Muslimos respicit qui unicum Deum adorant, viventem et subsistentem, misericordem et omnipotentem, Creatorem caeli et terrae, homines allocutum."

5. Francis, *Evangelii gaudium*, 252. The quotation of *Lumen gentium* is from paragraph 16: "In the first place amongst these there are the Muslims, who, professing to hold the faith of Abraham, along with us adore the one and merciful God, who on the

The statement from *Lumen gentium* at the end of the citation above (the key phrase in the Latin original being "nobiscum Deum adorant unicum") does not explicitly declare that Muslims and Christians worship the same God. Indeed one could argue that this statement does not go beyond the position of *Nostra aetate* that Muslims (like Christians) worship one God; in other words, the two statements might list commonalities in Catholic and Islamic doctrine on God—one of these doctrines being the teaching that God is one—but not affirm anything specific about the object of Catholic and Islamic worship. A similar cautionary note is offered by Gavin D'Costa in his review of *Allah: A Christian Response* by the Protestant theologian Miroslav Volf.[6]

On the other hand one might note the explicit statement of John Paul II in front of a crowd of Muslim youth in a soccer stadium in Casablanca, Morocco, in 1985: "We believe in the same God!"[7] The context of this statement of course, is quite different from a magisterial document, but it is not to be taken for granted.[8] Indeed this statement might offer a guide to John Paul's reading of *Lumen gentium* and *Nostra aetate*.

The question of whether Muslims and Christians worship the same God is complicated by those doctrines which each tradition holds to be known through divine revelation. They may agree on what can be said about

last day will judge mankind." "inter quos imprimis Musulmanos, qui fidem Abrahae se tenere profitentes, nobiscum Deum adorant unicum, misericordem, homines die novissimo iudicaturum."

6. See Volf, *Allah*. Volf's work is dedicated to the argument that Muslims and Christians *do* worship the same God, even if they have certain fundamental differences including Christian teachings on the Trinity and the Incarnation. See Gavin D'Costa's response in D'Costa, "Do Christians and Muslims." See also D'Costa, *Vatican II*, esp. 160–211.

7. John Paul II, "Address to Young Muslims."

8. Commenting years later on this statement of John Paul II, the Dominican Jacques Jomier sought to add some nuance to the Holy Father's declaration in a private correspondence (now published) to his friend, the White Father Maurice Borrmans by speaking of our common presence before the only God who exists: "Je me demande s'il ne faudrait pas lier cêtte question à celle du sens du mystère. Les musulmans nous reprochent de parler du mystère comme si c'était une échappatoire dans notre impuissance. Or le silence de la foi et inséparable de l'adoration prolongée en silence. Les musulmans avec leur logique claire et leur évidence qui éblouit n'y sont pas portés, mais pas de tout me semble-t-il. Nous sommes devant le même mystère de Dieu vivant, le mystère de même Dieu vivant, le seul Dieu qui existe" (letter dated December 12, 1993 in Jomier, *Confidences islamo-chrétiennes*, 403). Later, in the same letter, Jomier cites a correspondance from Daniel Massignon, son of the famous French Islamicist Louis Massignon: "Á ma remarque [écrit Daniel]: 'Au fond nous adorons le même Dieu unique?' il [son père] a répondu: 'ce n'est pas si simple, c'est bien là le cœur du problème.'"

God on the basis of reason alone, but they do not share a scripture, and their scriptures say different things about God. For Muslims the first source of revelation is the Qur'an, a scripture considered to be the *ipsissima verba Dei*, the "very words of God," brought down from heaven to earth by the angel Gabriel to the Prophet Muhammad. Muslims do recognize scriptures before Muhammad. Among other books, the Qur'an speaks of a scripture, which it names the *injil* (from Greek *euangelion*) given by God to Jesus. However, and although the Qur'anic teaching on this question is not absolutely clear,[9] Muslims generally hold that this revelation was falsified by Christians. The original scripture given to Jesus is lost and is *not* represented by the New Testament. While (according to a hadith) Muslims are to believe in *all* of the divine books given to prophets (and not only in the Qur'an),[10] the only divine book which they consider to be extant and authentic still today is the Qur'an. The Qur'an, one might say, is the only scripture that matters.[11]

The second source of revelation in Islam is not the Bible but the *hadith*, a vast body of traditions believed by Muslims to represent either the words of Muhammad or accounts of his deeds. Thus Christians teach certain things about God, especially as regards the Trinity and the Incarnation, which Muslims do not accept, because they are not found in the Qur'an or the hadith. Indeed, already the Qur'an criticizes Christianity for these teachings (see especially Qur'an 4:171; 5:17, 72, 73, 116–17; anti-Christian material in the hadith is still more vast). Similarly (and although this point is emphasized less often) Islamic scripture and tradition teach certain things about God which Christians would not accept. The Qur'an, for example, makes God "one who compels" (Arabic *qahhar*) and "avenger" (Arabic *muntaqim*)—both titles that are found in certain lists of the "beautiful" names of Allah. These are attributions that many Christians would find out of place with their theology.

However, and these complications notwithstanding, Catholic theologians are oriented by *Nostra aetate* and *Lumen gentium* to emphasize those doctrines regarding God which are common to Islam and Christianity. And

9. See further Reynolds, "On the Qur'anic Accusation."

10. This teaching is most famously articulated in the hadith "of Gabriel" in which the angel Gabriel (disguised as a figure with black hair in white clothes) asks the Prophet Muḥammad about faith (*iman*), and Muḥammad replies that one must have faith in God, His angels, His Books, His messengers, the Day of Judgment, and the predetermination of good and evil. See (in its classical form) Muslim, *Kitab al-Iman*, 1:146.

11. Of course individual Muslims throughout history, and still today, might still refer to or quote Christian scripture but the majority position remains that only the Qur'an is authentic scripture. For an interesting contemporary example of a Muslim's engagement with the New Testament see Akyol, *Islamic Jesus*.

indeed there is significant theological commonality. Muslims and Christians alike hold that God is one, creator, merciful, and judge. In this light we might confidently conclude with Saint John Paul II that Christians and Muslims worship the same God. We are unified, and not divided, by theology.

Islamic Christology

But can we say the same for Christology? It is common to hear that Muslims and Christians are joined not only by their belief in one God but also by their common recognition of Jesus as prophet and Christ. Karen Armstrong, in an editorial composed for *The Guardian*, writes: "Muslim devotion to Jesus is a remarkable example of the way in which one tradition can be enriched by another."[12] But are Christians and Muslims united by Jesus or divided over him? Who is the Jesus whom Muslims recognize as prophet and Christ, and can he be identified with the Jesus of Christianity? In other words, do Muslims and Christians believe in the same Christ? As with the question of whether Muslims and Christians share a belief in the same God, the question of whether Muslims and Christians share a belief in Christ is complicated by the sources of revelation. Indeed it is the Jesus of the Qur'an and not the Jesus of the New Testament whom Muslims know. What then can be said about this "Muslim" Jesus?

In the Qur'an Jesus is called both a prophet (Arabic *nabiy*; Q 19:30) and a messenger (Arabic *rasul*; Q 4:157, 171; 5:75; 61:6). He appears as one figure among the many prophets to whom God has spoken:

> Say: "We believe in God, and what has been sent down to us, and what has been sent down to Abraham, and Ishmael, and Isaac, and Jacob, and the tribes, and what was given to Moses and Jesus, and what was given to the prophets from their Lord. We make no distinction between any of them, and to Him we submit" (Q 2:136).[13]

With its declaration at the end of this verse ("We make no distinction"), the Qur'an seems to make the point that no prophet is above any other. Jesus was a prophet like Abraham, Ishmael, Isaac, Jacob, the tribes (of

12. Armstrong, "Muslim Prophet born in Bethlehem." It is perhaps worth asking to what extent Muslims are "devoted" to Jesus. They read the Qur'an and not the New Testament as part of their devotions. They seek to imitate Muhammad, and not Jesus. If they believe in prophetic intercession, they seek the intercession of Muhammad, and not that of Jesus. On the other hand, Jesus is acknowledged as a prophet among others, and pious Muslims include an invocation after the mention of his name.

13. All translations, unless stated otherwise, are from Droge, *Qur'an*.

Israel), and Moses before him. God spoke to all of these prophets and He said essentially the same thing to them all: Worship God alone or face divine punishment. Thus the Qur'an has Jesus declare: "'Sons of Israel! Serve God, my Lord and your Lord. Surely he who associates (anything) with God, God has forbidden him (from) the Garden, and his refuge is the Fire" (Q 5:72).

It is the reception and proclamation of this basic message, according to the Qur'an, which makes one a prophet. It is what a prophet says, not what he does, that matters. Indeed while certain prophets might be granted miraculous signs to authenticate their words (more on that below), it is ultimately their words that matter. Thus Jesus is a messenger, and inasmuch as his message was the same message given to prophets before him, he has no particular distinction.

And yet other passages in the Qur'an seem to complicate this picture, including a verse in the second Sura:

> Certainly We gave Moses the Book, and followed up after him with the messengers, and We gave Jesus, son of Mary, the clear signs, and supported him with the holy spirit. (But) whenever a messenger brought you what you yourselves did not desire, did you became arrogant, and some you called liars and some you killed? (Q 2:87).[14]

This verse *does* distinguish Jesus from other "messengers." Jesus, apparently, is set apart in two ways: he received "clear signs" and he was "supported" "with the holy spirit." The clear signs (*bayyinat*) spoken of here are apparently the miracles which the Qur'an elsewhere attributes to Jesus. A verse in Sura 3 has Jesus himself speak of these miracles:

> Surely I have brought you a sign from your Lord: I shall create for you the form of a bird from clay. Then I will breathe into it and it will become a bird by the permission of God. And I shall heal the blind and the leper, and give the dead life by the permission of God. And I shall inform you of what you may eat, and what you may store up in your houses. Surely in that is a sign indeed for you, if you are believers (Q 3:49; cf. 5:110).

Jesus is not the only prophet to perform miracles in the Qur'an (Moses, for example, is given the ability to change a staff into a serpent),[15] but

14. On the accusation (apparently made against the Jews) at the end of this verse regarding the killing of prophets see Reynolds, "On the Qur'an."

15. In his response to an anonymous letter of Christians from Cyprus, the Muslim theologian Ibn Abi Talib al-Dimashqi (d. 1327) writes about this, "The serpent into a staff is more wonderful than raising the dead" (Ebied and Thomas, *Muslim–Christian Polemic*, 387).

no other prophet in the Qur'an is said to have accomplished so many miracles, and no other prophet is said to have raised the dead. Muslim scholars of course noted these things, and felt that they needed an explanation. A popular way of explaining why Jesus performed the miracles he did is a tradition that God decided to distinguish prophets with qualities which would impress the people of their time. The people in Moses's culture, so the tradition goes, were enamored with magic and so God gave Moses nature miracles (such as turning a serpent into a staff and splitting the sea). The people of Jesus's culture were enamored with medicine, and so God gave Jesus the miracle of healing the sick and bringing the dead to life. The people of Muhammad's culture were enamored with poetry, and so God gave him the miracle of a "matchless" literary work, the Qur'an.[16]

In fact, not all of the miracles given to Jesus in the verse above have to deal with "medicine." Indeed of particular interest is the first of the miracles above, which has Jesus create a bird from clay and, breathing into the clay bird, brings it to life. This imagery has Jesus act in a manner parallel to God Himself, who (in both the Qur'an and Genesis) creates Adam from the earth and brings him to life with His breath (Gen 2:7; Q 15:29; 32:9; 38:72). There is of course, one decisive difference, Jesus performs the miracle of the clay bird, like the raising of the dead, only "with the permission of God." Thus the parallel is incomplete: Jesus's miracles do not redound to his divinity. They are only "signs" which attest to the veracity of his prophetic words. It is telling that a word for "sign" (here Arabic: *aya*) appears twice in this verse. These miracles are indeed meant to be a sign of Jesus's prophetic status. The "signs" are evidentiary miracles, but the evidence they give is of Jesus the prophet, and not Jesus the Son of God.

Something similar can be said about another miracle (which also has nothing to do with medicine) attributed to Jesus earlier in the same Sura, and elsewhere in the Qur'anic text as well, namely his speech "in the cradle." Sura 3 has the angels who announce to Mary the birth of Jesus tell her the following: "He will speak to the people (while he is still in the cradle) and in adulthood, and (he will be) one of the righteous" (Q 3:46; cf. 5:110). Elsewhere the Qur'an tells us what Jesus says while still "in the cradle." In Sura 19 we hear of how Mary's people accused her of sin on account of the child she bore (an account which seems to presume that Mary never married). Mary does not respond herself to this accusation. Instead she points to Jesus. The people respond to this with incredulity:

---

16. For a modern example of this argument, see the work of the well-known Turkish/Kurdish exegete Bediüzzaman Said Nursi (d. 1960), preserved in Bediüzzaman, *Letters*, 204.

They said, "How shall we speak to one who is in the cradle, a (mere) child?" He said, "Surely I am a servant of God. He has given me the Book and made me a prophet. He has made me blessed wherever I am, and He has charged me with the prayer and the alms as long as I live, and (to be) respectful to my mother. He has not made me a tyrant (or) miserable. Peace (be) upon me the day I was born, and the day I die, and the day I am raised up alive" (Q 19:29–33).

The point of this passage is that a child who has the miraculous ability of (eloquent) speech could also have been conceived in a miraculous way.[17] By speaking, Jesus, as an infant, has defended his mother from the charge of fornication. Yet in speaking Jesus also identifies himself. In his very first statement Jesus calls himself the "servant of God" and a "prophet." The point is not only that Jesus is a prophet, but also that he is *only* a prophet. Indeed it is telling that the end of this speech has Jesus echo words which Zechariah uses for his son John earlier in this same Sura (Q 19:15).[18] Both are prophets, and nothing more.

Much like the reports of Jesus's miraculous raising of the dead or healing of the blind and the leprous (see above Q 3:49), the story of Jesus's speech in the cradle is also found in the biblical subtext of the Qur'an, although it is found not in the canonical New Testament but rather in an apocryphal Gospel, the *Gospel of Pseudo-Matthew* (a text which likely dates to the early seventh century). What Jesus says, however, is different. In *Pseudo-Matthew* the miracle of Jesus's speech occurs during the flight of the holy family to Egypt. While the family stops to rest near a palm tree, Jesus commands the palm tree to bend down, so that his mother might pick its fruit, and asks that water might spring up from the ground to refresh them (a miracle account which also appears in the Qur'an: Q 19:24–26).[19] The point of this passage is the divine power of the infant Jesus: nature obeys his command. The point of the Qur'anic passage is quite different: the Qur'an means to present Jesus, even from his infancy, as merely a servant and prophet of God.

17. Not all Muslim scholars agree that this passage has Jesus speak as a child. Muhammad Asad (d. 1992), the Jewish convert to Islam, insists that prophets can only receive divine revelation once they reach the age of rationality, and therefore that this passage must be read as a report of what Jesus said later in his life. See Asad, *Message of the Qur'an*, 514.

18. "Peace (be) upon him the day he was born, and the day he dies, and the day he is raised alive."

19. *Gospel of Pseudo-Matthew*, 20:1–2. See Schneemelcher, *New Testament Apocrypha*, 1:462–65. Notably the Qur'anic version of this miracle has Jesus explain to his mother that it is God who has put a stream beneath her (Q 19:24).

Jesus: Spirit, Word of God and Christ

Elsewhere the Qur'an criticizes Christians, insisting that their teaching is inconsistent with the message of Christ. Qur'an 5:72 even suggests (although it does not say so explicitly) that Christians are unbelievers for what they say about Christ:

> Certainly they have disbelieved who say, "Surely God—He is the Messiah, son of Mary," when the Messiah said, "Sons of Israel! Serve God, my Lord and your Lord. Surely he who associates (anything) with God, God has forbidden him (from) the Garden, and his refuge is the Fire. The evildoers have no helpers."

Now it might be objected that this verse more caricatures than quotes Christians. Christians as a rule would not say that "God is the Messiah" but rather that "the Messiah" (or Christ) is God. Nevertheless the caricature here rather proves than disproves the point. The Qur'an is aware of Christian doctrine on Christ and means to oppose it, even by means of caricature. Indeed the Qur'an is so opposed to Christian doctrine on Christ that it suggests here that Christians will be damned to hell (although elsewhere, notably in Q 2:62; 5:69—just a few verses earlier—it seems to say the opposite). The very next verse is similar:

> Certainly they have disbelieved who say, "Surely God is the third of three," when (there is) no god but one God. If they do not stop what they are saying, a painful punishment will indeed strike those of them who disbelieve (Q 5:73).

Although this latter verse seems to allude to the Trinity (with its reference to "three") its principal message is again about Christ (the "third" of three) and the notion that he could be God.[20] Once again Christians are threatened with divine punishment for what they say about Christ.

In Sura 9 the Qur'an uses still more dramatic language: it calls on God to "fight" the Christians for their claim that Christ is the son of God (and, curiously, Jews for their claim that Ezra is the son of God):

> The Jews say, "Ezra is the son of God," and the Christians say, "The Messiah is the son of God." That is their saying with their mouths. They imitate the saying of those who disbelieved before (them). (May) God fight them. How are they (so) deluded? (Q 9:30).

---

20. On this verse, see Griffith, "Syriacisms in the Arabic Qur'ān," 83–110.

On the basis of these verses Christ does not seem to be a common figure which somehow brings together Muslims and Christians. He seems to set them apart.

And yet certain elements of Qur'anic Christology seem closer to Christian teaching on Christ. In one of the first verses we quoted above (Q 2:87) the Qur'an has God declare that He "supported" Jesus with the Holy Spirit.[21] This is only one of three occasions where the Qur'an makes the same declaration (cf. Q 2:253; 5:110). It is true that Islamic tradition tends to identify references in the Qur'an to the Holy Spirit, or to "the Spirit," with the angel Gabriel.[22] However, this is a simplification of the complicated and nuanced way in which the Qur'an refers to the Spirit. For example, it seems to contradict explicitly Q 97:4, which speaks of the Spirit *and* the angels descending from heaven.[23] Most importantly it does not seem fully to take into account the relationship of "Spirit" in the Qur'an and Jesus himself. Notably, the Qur'an has Jesus created from the Spirit of God in two passages:

> And she who guarded her private part—We breathed into her some of Our spirit, and made her and her son a sign to the worlds (Q 21:91). And Mary, daughter of 'Imran, who guarded her private part: We breathed into it some of Our spirit, and she affirmed the words of her Lord and His Books, and became one of the obedient (Q 66:12).

It is true that in three passages the Qur'an also speaks of the creation of Adam from God's spirit (Q 15:29; 32:9; 38:72). However, in another passage the Qur'an identifies Jesus himself as a "spirit" from God:

> People of the Book! Do not go beyond the limits in your religion, and do not say about God (anything) but the truth. The Messiah, Jesus, son of Mary, was only a messenger of God, and His word, which He cast into Mary, *and a spirit from Him* (Q 4:171a).

The reference to Jesus as "spirit" in this passage (which also describes Jesus as a "word," something we will discuss presently) seems to follow from the report that Jesus was created from the Spirit of God (in the passages quoted just above). This reference has interesting echoes in Islamic tradition. Jesus

21. The Qur'anic term is literally "spirit of holiness" (*ruh al-qudus*). However, that particular formation may simply be a reflection of Syriac *ruha d-qudsha*.

22. The standard Sunni Qur'an commentary, known as *Tafsir al-Jalalayn*, glosses "Holy Spirit" here simply as "that is, Gabriel" (al-Mahalli and al-Suyuti, *Tafsir al-Jalālayn*, 16).

23. "The angels and the spirit come down during it, by the permission of their Lord, on account of every command."

is often called "Spirit of God" in later narratives, particularly in those narratives which circulated among Sufis and portray Jesus as an ascetic and a wisdom figure. Still on the basis of this one reference it is difficult to know what
exactly the Qur'an's author meant by calling Jesus a "spirit from [God]." And
in any case this notion is not consistent with Christian Christology, according to which "Spirit" is not a standard description of Jesus.[24]

Yet in Q 4:171 Jesus is not only called "spirit." He is also named "Messiah" and "word."[25] The description of Jesus as the "Word" (Arabic *kalima*) of
God (something which appears also in the angelic annunciation to Mary in
Q 3:45; cf. also Q 3:39, where John is said to confirm a "word from God")[26]
is of course telling for its apparent connection with the language of Word
(*logos*) in the prologue to John's Gospel and in later Christian theology. It is
clear by now, however, that the Qur'an does not mean thereby what Christians mean. Christ in the Qur'an is not the eternal word of God which is be-
gotten of the Father. Indeed it is possible that the reference to Jesus as "word
of God" should be understood according to the standard interpretation of
Islamic tradition—that he is so called because he is created by a "word"
(the Arabic word *kun*, "Be!"; see Q 3:59).[27] In a brief reflection entitled,
"The Portrait of Jesus in the Qur'an: Reflections of a Biblical Scholar," Heikki
Räisänen, comments aptly regarding the Qur'anic notion of Jesus as "word":
"It is futile to engage in a dialogue on this point in an attempt to Christianize
the language of the Qur'an."[28]

The case of "Messiah" is similar. On eleven occasions the Qur'an refers
to Jesus as "the Messiah" or "the Christ" (Arabic *masih*). However, there is
categorically no special significance given to the title (if it is indeed a title).
The Qur'an has no particular idea of the term messiah. It never explains

---

24. Among the Church fathers, Irenaeus (d. 202; in his *Against Heresies* and else-
where) does speak of Christ as "Spirit of God." However, he seems to use the term
"Spirit" only as a euphemism for the divine nature in Christ. See further Briggman,
Irenaeus of Lyons, 191–93.

25. In addition to "spirit," "word," and "Christ," the Qur'an also refers to Jesus as
a "sign" (Ar. *aya*, see Q 19:21; 21:91; 23:50 which likewise make Mary a "sign"). This
term is used elsewhere for miracles that prophets perform, or the revelation that unveils
divine truth (hence the use of the term *aya* for a verse of the Qur'an). That Jesus (and
Mary) are *themselves* "signs" suggests that there is something in their very being which
reveals the nature of God. Muslim scholars often explain this language by insisting
that Jesus (and Mary) were signs only because of the virgin birth. See, for example,
Al-Zamakhshari (d. 1144), *Al-Kashshaf*, 3:133.

26. Q 19:34, depending on how the term is read, might include a reference to Jesus
as a "declaration (*qawl*) of the True One."

27. This is the first of three interpretations offered by Ibn al-Jawzi (d. 1200). See
Ibn al-Jawzī, *Zad al-masir fi ' ilm al-tafsir*, 1:389.

28. Räisänen, "Portrait of Jesus in the Qur'an," 127.

what it means for Jesus to be messiah. It does not ask what kind of messiah he is. Indeed it never defines messiah in any way whatsoever. In other words, all of the tension in the Gospels over whether Jesus is the messiah disappears in the Qur'an. Kenneth Cragg comments:

> The tensions which surrounded the relevance of "Messiahship" in the Gospels and the travail Jesus had in wrestling with them both inwardly and publicly are not reflected in the Qur'anic usage because of the silence which envelops the actual course of Jesus' story there.[29]

Now Cragg holds that there is still some meaning to the term "Messiah" in the Qur'an. He writes: "It belongs with Jesus' supernatural birth and designates him a prophet of the divine word."[30] I disagree. Messiah is in no way specially connected to Jesus's birth in the Qur'an, nor does one need to be "Messiah" (or Christ) to be a "prophet of the divine word." In the Qur'an Christ is used simply as a name or title for Jesus and it has no particular meaning. It adds nothing to his Qur'anic identity. The reason for the appearance of this name in the Qur'an is presumably simple: by the seventh century, Christians treated Christ as a name interchangeable with Jesus. The author of the Qur'an seems to have been familiar with this common use, but to have had no particular sense of the theologically charged meaning behind the name, or its place in Jewish and Christian theology.

Indeed one might even ask whether it is right to speak of Jesus as "Christ" or "Messiah" in Islam. He bears the name as Salvador Dali bore the name "savior." Jesus is called Messiah, but he is not the messiah. In Islam there is no messiah in the Christian sense of the term.

Hence we might turn to the Qur'an's only reference to the Crucifixion:

> and for their saying, "Surely we killed the Messiah, Jesus, son of Mary, the messenger of God"—yet they did not kill him, nor did they crucify him, but it (only) seemed like (that) to them. Surely those who differ about him are indeed in doubt about him (Q 4:157).

Notably this verse contains no allusion to (or refutation of) the Christian notion of Jesus as redeemer, even if it refers to Jesus as Christ. What the Qur'an actually means to say in this verse is difficult to know. This verse is generally interpreted in Islamic tradition to mean that Jesus did not die at all on the cross but rather that someone else (whether a friend or an enemy) died in his place while he escaped, deathless, to heaven. Elsewhere I

29. Cragg, *Jesus and the Muslim*, 31.
30. Cragg, *Jesus and the Muslim*, 31.

have argued that this interpretation appears to be mistaken in light of the full range of Qur'anic references to the death of Christ.[31] Here I would like simply to note (and this much seems clear whether or not my argument is convincing) that the Qur'an here shows no interest in soteriology or redemption.[32] It is perhaps for this reason that the Qur'an in this verse does not explicitly declare if Jesus died on the cross or not (it declares only that that the Israelites did not kill him). It is a question with no importance: it is what Jesus *says* as a prophet, and not what he *does* as a redeemer, which matters to the Qur'an.

We might even qualify the point regarding Jesus's prophetic sayings. Very little of what Jesus says in the Qur'an (and he does not say much) is in common with the things he says in the New Testament. None of Jesus's Gospel sayings, none of the parables, none of the sermons, and none of the Johannine discourses are found in the Qur'an. Indeed the closest thing to a quotation of the Jesus from the Gospels is a reference to the camel and the eye of the needle in the Qur'an. However, the Qur'an does not attribute this saying to Jesus (it makes it simply a declaration of God) and changes its focus from a rich man to one who denies God's signs:

> Surely those who call Our signs a lie, and are arrogant about it—the gates of the sky will not be opened for them, nor will they enter the Garden, until the camel passes through the eye of the needle. In this way We repay the sinners (Q 7:40; cf. Matt 19:23–24; cf. Mark 10:25; Luke 18:25).

All of this divides still farther the Muslim Jesus and the Christian Jesus. While Muslims and Christians together can affirm that Jesus was born of Mary (without the seed of an earthly father) and that he performed miracles, there is little else which joins their understanding, at least if we establish Islamic Christology on the basis of the Qur'an.

[A] The "Muḥammadan" Jesus of the Qur'ān

Indeed from our perspective it is reasonable to ask whether the Qur'anic Christ and the Christian Christ are the same characters. At some point a character's life can be retold in terms which are so radically new that the original character can no longer be recognized. Kenneth Cragg, the Anglican

31. See Reynolds, "Muslim Jesus"

32. Whether the Qur'an has any notion of redemption at all is not entirely clear. The Qur'an does refer to offerings (Q 6:162) and to the slaughter of animals at the "Sacred House" (e.g., Q 22:33), generally assumed to be the Ka'ba in Mecca (although today in the *hajj* ritual animal sacrifice takes place outside of the city in Mina). Also, the Qur'an has God "redeem" (*fadaynahu*) the son of Abraham (who is not named explicitly in the Qur'an) with a "great sacrifice" (Q 37:107).

Bishop who dedicated most of his long career to a Christian evaluation of Islam, comes to a similar conclusion. Cragg argues that the Qur'an's material on Christ reflects Muhammad's own experiences. It is as though the Jesus of Galilee and Jerusalem has been transposed to Mecca and Medina. He sees this in the way that one verse of the Qur'an has Muhammad call on his followers to be his "helpers" (Ar. *ansar*) in the way that Jesus asked his own followers to be "helpers":

> You who believe! Be the helpers of God, as Jesus, son of Mary, said to the disciples, "Who will be my helpers to God?" The disciples said, "We will be the helpers of God." One contingent of the Sons of Israel believed, and (another) contingent disbelieved. So We supported those who believed against their enemy, and they were the ones who prevailed (Q 61:14).

The scenario here of a prophet rallying his followers around him fits the context of Muhammad in Medina (where this verse, according to tradition, was initially proclaimed). In Medina Muhammad was engaged in a fierce and violent military struggle with the polytheists who still held the city of Mecca. He sought to rally his followers (some of whom, those originally from Medina, were named "helpers" [Ar. *ansar*]) around him to join in the fight against their enemies. This is precisely the sort of scenario which seems to be imagined for Jesus and his disciples, who are said to have prevailed against their "enemies" at the end of the verse. This is a scenario which hardly fits the context of Jesus in Galilee or even Jerusalem. As Cragg notes, in the Gospels Jesus does not ask his disciples to rally around him in a struggle against their enemies: "When they did respond to Jesus' call to be his 'helpers' it was as itinerant preachers summoning their hearers to repentance and to 'the kingdom of God.'"[33]

This is not the only aspect of the Qur'anic Jesus which Cragg identifies as "Muhammadan." The way in which the Qur'an has Jesus show an intense concern for the crime of "associating" something with God—that is, with paganism—also matches more the context of Mecca and Medina than the context of the Galilee and Jerusalem. It is difficult to imagine the Jesus of the Gospels being so outraged by paganism or the "association" of something with God (Ar. *shirk*) that he would say something like: "Surely he who associates (anything) with God, God has forbidden him (from) the Garden, and his refuge is the Fire. The evildoers have no helpers" (Q 5:72b). This sounds more like Muhammad in Arabia than Jesus in Palestine. Indeed the Jesus of the Gospels had various conversations with Roman pagans—as with the

---

33. Cragg, *Jesus and the Muslim*, 26.

centurion (Matt 8/Luke 7) whose servant he healed—yet he never bothered to reprimand them for the polytheism of Roman religion.

This is not to say that the Jesus of the Gospels is ambivalent about monotheism. Cragg's point is simply that the Jesus of the Gospels is not principally concerned with paganism or polytheism. He is concerned above all with the failure of those who already believe in God to live out a loving relationship with Him and their fellow children of God:

> It is all the more urgent, therefore, to set the figure of Jesus squarely in the Palestinian milieu, where the central battle was not for the unity of God against pagan idols but against the pride of privilege and the moral and spiritual compromises of the purest theism.[34]

From this perspective the Jesus of the Qur'an appears to be a literary figure, a character created and deployed in the image of Muhammad to advance the basic message of the text. There is little or no vestige of the Jesus who ate with Mary and Martha, or who told Zacchaeus to get down from a tree on the streets of Jericho. The Jesus of Palestine has disappeared, and a new Jesus appears his place.

Jesus as "Servant of God"

This construction of a new Jesus is perhaps nowhere more in evidence than in Qur'an 4:172. Whereas in Sura 19:30 the Qur'an has Jesus himself declare, "I am the servant of God," here the Qur'an comments on his "servanthood":

> The Messiah does not disdain to be a servant of God, nor will the angels, the ones brought near. Whoever disdains His service and becomes arrogant—He will gather them to Himself—all (of them).

As others have noted before me,[35] this passage is reminiscent of the famous hymn included in the second chapter of Paul's letter to the Philippians:

---

34. Cragg, *Jesus and the Muslim*, 27.

35. See Kenneth Cragg's discussion of this parallel in Cragg, *Jesus and the Muslim*, 29–31. Cragg comments: "It would be fair to say that the entire course and cost of 'not scorning to be servant' are the essence of the Gospels" (Cragg, *Jesus and the Muslim*, 31). See also the discussion of this parallel in Samir, "Theological Christian Influence," 156–57. Samir reflects on Q 4:172: "Here, as elsewhere in the Qur'an which it comes to Christ and Christian doctrine, the Qur'anic text scrupulously respects the Christian affirmation, but juxtaposes it with Qur'anic dogma" (Samir, "Theological Christian Influence," 157).

> Make your own the mind of Christ Jesus: Who, being in the
> form of God, did not count equality with God something to be
> grasped. But he emptied himself, taking the form of a slave, be-
> coming as human beings are; and being in every way like a hu-
> man being, he was humbler yet, even to accepting death, death
> on a cross (Phil 2:5–8, NJB).

Qur'an 4:172 and Philippians 2:5–8 both speak of the humility of
Christ. He is either one who did not "disdain to be a servant of God" or who
(not counting "equality with God something to be grasped") took "the form
of a slave." Yet in another sense these two passages are arguing precisely the
opposite thing. The Qur'an means to say that Christ was born a human, a
servant of God, and (presumably as a rebuke to Christians), would never
have arrogantly claimed to be more than that. All of this fits the Qur'anic
vision of the relationship between God and humans: God is Lord, and all
humans (and angels, jinn, and demons), even the prophets, are His servants.
To this end, the Qur'an declares of God: "He is the Supreme One above
His servants. He is the Wise, the Aware" (Q 6:18; cf. 6:61). Qur'an 19:93
proclaims, "(There is) no one in the heavens and the earth who comes to the
Merciful except as a servant."

The point of the Philippians passage is quite different. The hymn declares that Christ "emptied himself" (ἑαυτὸν ἐκένωσεν [Phil 2:7]). In other
words, he was more than a servant. Out of humility, however, he chose to
become one. Thus in the Qur'an the human Christ refuses to elevate himself,
but in Philippians the divine Christ agrees to humble himself. The "servanthood" of Christ in each case, then, is different.

Again it is the servanthood of Christ which the Qur'an seeks to emphasize when it has Jesus declare that he accomplishes miracles "by the
permission of God" (Q 3:49; in Q 5:110 God tells Jesus that he accomplishes
miracles "by My permission"). Cragg argues that this declaration does not
actually distinguish Qur'anic teaching on Christ, since the Gospels agree
that God acts through (or in) Christ.[36] Yet the Qur'an's insistence on add-
ing this phrase after (almost) every mention of Christ's miracles suggests
that the Qur'an's author sought intentionally to distinguish his portrayal of
Christ from that of Christian faith. Indeed while other prophets—notably
Moses—accomplish miracles in the Qur'an (although admittedly not as
many as Christ), never does the Qur'an insist that they do so "by the permission" of God. Only with Christ does this phrase appear.

36. "The divergent understanding, by Muslims and by Christians, of the person of
Jesus, therefore—wide as it is in their respective Scriptures—need not and should not
obscure for us the unifying fact that everything in Jesus was by divine authority and
leave" (Cragg, *Jesus and the Muslim*, 34).

Perhaps, then, Christians should not look at the Jesus of the Qur'an as a different take on the same person whom they know from the Gospels, but rather as a different character altogether. In other words, if Christians and Muslims believe in the same God, they do not believe in the same Christ.

This distinctiveness of the Qur'anic Jesus seems to be signaled by his name in the Qur'an. One would expect (on the basis of the Hebrew or Syriac form of the word) Jesus to be named *Yasu'* in the Qur'an. Indeed this is the name given to him in the Arabic Bible. The Qur'an, however, places the last consonant (Arabic *'ayn*) at the front of the word and names him *'Isa*. Much ink has been spilled in attempts to explain this divergence.[37] It is possible that this form of the name owes something to a desire to have Jesus's name rhyme with that of Moses (*Musa*). For our purposes, however, it is symbolically important that the Qur'an gives to Jesus a new name. Noting the problem of Jesus's name in the Qur'an, Cragg concludes: "Two names, if remotely cognate, for one *persona*: one *persona* divergently revered and received."[38] I would conclude otherwise: two names for two *personae*.

Conclusion

Karen Armstrong scolds Christians for their history of polemics against Muhammad. Noting that Muslims recognize Jesus, the central figure of Christianity, she adds: "It cannot be said that Christians returned the compliment."[39] Behind Armstrong's sentiment is the notion that Muslims recognize Jesus as a prophet, and that it is uncharitable that Christians do not recognize Muhammad as a prophet.

To this we must ask what sort of Christ Muslims recognize. The Christ of the Qur'an is stripped of his principal characteristics and teachings: he is not a divine redeemer, the lamb of God. He does not even die (at least according to the standard interpretation). Muslim recognition of Christ is actually not unlike Christian recognition of Muhammad. Most Christians acknowledge that Muhammad was a preacher, general, and statesman. Many would recognize virtue or skill in the way Muhammad carried out these roles. However, Christians strip Muhammad of his principal characteristic in Islam: prophet. The Muslim image of Christ as only a prophet (and, it must be said, one who preaches against Christianity and Christians) is no more satisfying to Christians than the Christian image of Muhammad as only a preacher, general, and statesman is to Muslims.

37. For a summary, see Anawati, "'Isa," *EI2*, 4:81a.

38. Cragg, *Jesus and the Muslim*, 38.

39. Armstrong, "Muslim Prophet born in Bethlehem."

Some scholars have argued that the Christ of the Qur'an is not a re-duction of Christ in Christianity but rather the preservation of an ancient Christology. This was the position of Hans Küng and, following Küng, the Catholic theologian Claude Geffré, in an article for the Vatican journal *Islamochristiana*,[40] argues that the Qur'an's notion of Christ as "servant of God" reflects the Christology of the primitive Semitic Christian commu-nity, a community which was eliminated later by the Hellenistic Church with its high Christology.[41]

In response, Jacques Jomier points out that Geffré's position is fun-damentally Gnostic: it empties the Christian revelation of its fundamental claim of divine kenosis, and thereby compromises the doctrine of the Incar-nation. He also believes that such a position will not contribute to dialogue with Muslims:

> Ce n'est pas du dialogue, c'est la gnose que les musulmans n'acceptent pas; mais il salueront avec joie la chute de ce qu'ils croient nos idoles, rajoutées à Dieu, les personnages de la sainte Trinité. Il crieront de joie comme lorsque, dans les foire des lan-ceurs de boules font basculer des figures grotesques (que Dieu nous pardonne la comparaison).[42]

Jomier was aware of the seriousness of the accusation against Geffré regarding gnosticism.[43] He was right, however, that compromising a funda-mental element of orthodox Christian tradition will not advance dialogue. Dialogue is as much about acknowledging difference as it is about seeking commonality.

The present study has brought to light a second problem with the ideas of Küng and Geffré: a close study of Jesus in the Qur'an reveals that he is not so much the memory of a "primitive" Christology as much as a recasting of

---

40. See Geffré, "La portée théologique."

41. His approach is not far from Mustafa Akyol in the aforementioned work, *Islamic Jesus*. Akyol, however, does not argue that Islam so much "recovered" a primi-tive Christology but rather that this primitive Christology was preserved by the Jewish Christians and thereby taken up by the Prophet in the early seventh century.

42. Jomier, 311, letter of March 10, 1993. Elsewhere in the same letter Jomier writes, "Lorsqu'il parle du Coran témoin d'une christologie primitive de Jésus selon Hans Küng, en assortissant cette phrase d'un point d'interrogation sorte de rideau de fumée qu'il étend derrière lui et qu'il lui permettra de faire demi-tour et de disparaître caché par la fumée si la situation s'avère délicate" (Jomier, 309, letter of March 10, 1993).

43. "Je sais que je porte là une accusation très grave. Que Dieu me pardonne si malgré des mois de réflexion, de souffrance, de lectures qui m'ont mené à cette position, je me trompe" (Jomier, 309, letter of March 10, 1993).

Jesus according to the figure of Muhammad. It is this recasting, above all, which distinguishes the Jesus of the Qur'an from the Jesus of the Gospels.

Bibliography

Akyol, Mustafa. *The Islamic Jesus.* New York: St. Martin's, 2017.

Al-Mahalli, Jalal al-Din, and Jalal al-Din al-Suyuti. *Tafsir al-Jalalayn.* Translated by F. Hamza. Louisville, KY: Fons Vitae, 2008.

Al-Zamakhshari. *Al-Kashshaf ʿan haqa'iq ghawamid al-tanzil.* Edited by Mustafa Husayn Ahmad. Beirut: Dar al-Kitab al-ʿArabi, 1947.

Armstrong, Karen. "Muslim Prophet born in Bethlehem." *Guardian*, December 23, 2006. https://www.theguardian.com/commentisfree/2006/dec/23/religion.christmas.

Asad, Muhammad. *The Message of the Qur'an.* London: Book Foundation, 2003.

Bar-Asher, Meir M., et al., eds. *A Word Fitly Spoken: Studies in Medieval Exegeses of the Hebrew Bible and the Qur'an.* Jerusalem: Ben-Zvi Institute, 2007.

Briggman, Anthony. *Irenaeus of Lyons and the Theology of the Holy Spirit.* Oxford: Oxford University Press, 1992.

Cragg, Kenneth. *Jesus and the Muslim.* Oxford: OneWorld, 1999.

D'Costa, Gavin. "Do Christians and Muslims Believe in the Same God? Reflections on Miroslav Volf's Allah: A Christian Response." *Islam and Christian Muslim Relations* 24 (2013), 151–60.

———. *Vatican II: Catholic Doctrines on Jews and Muslims.* Oxford: Oxford University Press, 2014.

Droge, A. J. *The Qur'an: A New Annotated Translation.* Sheffield: Equinox, 2013.

Ebied, Rifaat, and David Thomas, eds. *Muslim–Christian Polemic during the Crusades.* Leiden: Brill, 2005.

Francis. "Audience with Representatives of the Churches and Ecclesial Communities and of the Different Religions." March 20, 2013. https://w2.vatican.va/content/francesco/en/speeches/2013/march/documents/papa-francesco_20130320_delegati-fraterni.html.

———. "*Evangelii gaudium.*" Novermber 24, 2013. https://w2.vatican.va/content/francesco/en/apost_exhortations/documents/papa-francesco_esortazione-ap_20131124_evangelii-gaudium.html.

Geffré, Claude. "La portée théologique du dialogue islamo-chrétien." *Islamochristiana* 18 (1992) 1–23.

Griffith, Sidney H. "Syriacisms in the Arabic Qur'ān: Who were those who said ʿAllāh is third of three.'" In *A Word Fitly Spoken: Studies in Medieval Exegeses of the Hebrew Bible and the Qur'ān*, edited by Meir M. Bar-Asher, et al., 83–110. Jerusalem: Ben-Zvi Institute, 2007.

Hawkins, Larycia. "20 December 2015." *Facebook.com*, December 20, 2015. https://www.facebook.com/larycia/posts/10153326773658481?pnref=story

Ibn al-Hajjaj, Muslim. *Kitab al-Iman.* Vol. 1 of *Ṣaḥīḥ Muslim.* Edited by Muḥammad Fu'ad ʿAbd al-Baqi. Beirut: Dar al-Kutub al-ʿIlmiyya, 2000.

Ibn al-Jawzi. *Zad al-masir fi ʿilm al-tafsir.* Beirut: al-Maktab al-Islami, 1984.

John Paul II. "Address to Young Muslims." August 19, 1985. https://w2.vatican. va/content/john-paul-ii/en/speeches/1985/august/documents/hf_jp-ii_ spe_19850819_giovani-stadio-casablanca.html.

Jomier, Jacques. *Confidences islamo-chrétiennes*. Edited by M. Borrmans. Marseille: Chemins de Dialogue, 2016.

Nursi, Bediuzzaman Said. *The Letters: Epistles on Islamic Thought, Belief, and Life*. Translated by Hüseyin Akarsu. Somerset, NJ: The Light, 2007.

Räisänen, Heikki. "The Portrait of Jesus in the Qur'ān: Reflections of a Biblical Scholar." *The Muslim World* 70 (1980) 122–33.

Reynolds, Gabriel Said. "The Muslim Jesus: Dead or Alive?" *Bulletin of the School of Oriental and African Studies* 72 (2009) 237–58.

———. "On the Qur'an and the Theme of Jews as 'Killers of the Prophets.'" *Al-Bayān* 10.2 (2012) 9–32.

———. "On the Qur'anic Accusation of Scriptural Falsification (*taḥrif*) and Christian anti-Jewish Polemic." *JAOS* 130 (2010) 189–202.

———, ed. *The Qur'an in Its Historical Context*. London: Routledge, 2008.

Samir, S. K. "The Theological Christian Influence on the Qur'ān: A Reflection." In *The Qur'an in Its Historical Context*, edited by Gabriel Said Reynolds, 141–62. London: Routledge, 2008.

Schneemelcher, W., ed. *New Testament Apocrypha*. Translated by R. Wilson. Cambridge: J. Clarke, 1991.

Second Vatican Council. *Lumen gentium*. 1964. http://www.vatican.va/archive/ hist_councils/ii_vatican_council/documents/vat-ii_const_19641121_lumen-gentium_en.html.

———. *Nostra aetate*. 1965. http://www.vatican.va/archive/hist_councils/ii_vatican_ council/documents/vat-ii_decl_19651028_nostra-aetate_en.html.

Volf, Miroslav. *Allah: A Christian Response*. New York: HarperOne, 2011.

Weber, Jeremy. "Wheaton: What We Learned from 'Same God' Controversy with Larycia Hawkins." *Christianity Today*, October 25, 2016. https://www.christianitytoday. com/news/2016/october/wheaton-trustee-report-same-god-larycia-hawkins. html. B

The Translation of the Psalms by Mohammad al-Sadeq Hussein and Serge de Beaurecueil

—Martino Diez[1*]

"They were bewildered, because each one heard them speaking
in his own language"

ACTS 2:6

In 1961 the Cairo publishing house Dār as-Salām issued an Arabic translation of the Psalms by a Muslim intellectual, Mohammad al-Sadeq Hussein (Muḥammad aṣ-Ṣādiq Ḥusayn), with the participation of the French Dominican Serge de Beaurecueil.[2] This instance of Islamic–

---

1 * This study was first presented in Rome on May 25, 2018, at the Pontifical Oriental Institute, during an academic ceremony in honor of Father Samir Khalil Samir on his eightieth birthday. It is a tribute to the figure of this outstanding scholar, born in Cairo in 1938.

I would like to thank Fr. Jean Druel, the director of the IDEO, for kindly providing me a copy of the Psalms' translation and de Beaurecueil's article on Coptic liturgy and H. E. Msgr. Henri Teissier, H.E. Msgr. Maroun Lahham, Fr. Jean-Jacques Pérennès, Fr. Rifaat Bader and Dominique Avon for generously answering my queries.

For the Bible, the New Revised Standard Edition has been used. The Qur'an is given in the translation by Arthur J. Arberry (The Koran Interpreted). Arabic terms are in scientific transcription except for proper nouns of common use. Older transliterations, notably in MIDEO, have been normalized accordingly.

2. The exact title of the translation is: Sifr al-Mazāmīr, naqalahu ilā al-ʿarabiyya Muḥammad aṣ-Ṣādiq Ḥusayn bi-l-ištirāk maʿ al-ab S. Dī Būrakiyy [de Beaurecueil] ad-Dūminikī.

Christian biblical teamwork, in which also the future Archbishop of Algiers, Henri Teissier, was involved, is rather extraordinary in its kind, as it is the cultural atmosphere in which the project was first conceived. What is more, the translation, whose plan goes back to Serge de Beaurecueil, but whose realization was the fact of al-Sadeq Hussein, obtained the *imprimatur* of the Vicar Apostolic of Alexandria of the Latins.[3] In spite of its quite exceptional status, this translation, to my knowledge, has not been the object of any specific study.[4] In what follows, after a brief contextualization of the Arabic Bible, I shall try to explore the profile of the scholars involved in the project, the circumstances in which it saw the light, the method they followed and the reception of their translation, which I believe has still something to teach us, more than 50 years after its publication.

Through this case study, I hope to shed some light on the relation between dialogue and proclamation, two realities that are often perceived (and lived) as mutually exclusive. Rather than challenging this dualism from a theological angle, for which I have no specific skills, I hope to illustrate how dialogue and proclamation often share a common concrete *practice*, i.e., translation. This commonality is not accidental, since dialogue and proclamation are but two faces of Christian testimony, understood as the most adequate way to articulate the relation between freedom and truth while respecting the structure of divine revelation.[5]

3. The *Nihil obstat* was issued in Jerusalem by the director of the *École Biblique*, Roland de Vaux op on July 30 1961 and the *Imprimi potest* was given in Rome by the Superior General of the Dominican Order on August 16 1961, while the *imprimatur* bears the date of September 20 of the same year. The Vicar Apostolic of Alexandria was at that time the Québécois Capuchin Jean Capistran Aimé Cayer, who occupied this charge from 1949 until his death in 1978.

4. The main facts about the translation are accurately laid out in Avon, *Les frères prêcheurs en Orient. Les dominicains du Caire*, 757–58. Some references can be found also in Pérennès, *Passion Kaboul*, 74, 124.

5. Prades, "Christianity and the Need for Witnesses." For Prades, testimony is not a mere element of credibility of the Church. It has a Christological-revelational substance, which corresponds to the "co-original move of freedom together with reason" (Prades, "Christianity and the Need for Witnesses," 13). Only testimony, understood in these terms, can preserve an understanding "of Revelation as the singular and free event of the communication of God in history, which cannot be reduced to the description of a doctrinal or ethical system" (Prades, "Christianity and the Need for Witnesses," 16). See also, in the same issue of Oasis, the articles by Carbajosa, Martinelli, Salmeri, Cuypers and Samir.

Bible Translations in Arabic: A Long History

It is impossible to summarize in a few lines the history of the Arabic Bible. According to Ronny Vollandt, who recently offered an insightful *status quaestionis*,[6] this domain of research remains largely understudied. While biblical imagery and oral traditions certainly entered Pre-Islamic Arabia, it is generally assumed that written translations were only produced after the Islamic conquests.[7] The pace of Arabization in the newly conquered provinces was rapid, especially in some communities like the Melkites of Palestine, and by no later than the ninth century Arab-speaking Jews, Samaritans and Christians started to produce several Arabic versions of their own Scriptures. Their very multiplicity attests to the fact that none of them managed to impose itself as a canonical text.

Whether Classical Arabic was ever a spontaneously spoken idiom is an open question,[8] but again we can be sure that by the tenth century at latest it had become a dead language. In his encyclopedia *al-Ḫaṣāʾiṣ*, the great linguist Ibn Ǧinnī (d. 1002) had to confess: "In our days we hardly see eloquent Bedouins" (i.e., people speaking proper Arabic).[9] By that time, Arabic had therefore become classic in the double sense defined by Pierre Larcher, i.e., "of first class" and "taught in the classes."[10] In quite a number of occasions, Christians and Jews did attend the same classes as Muslims, to the point that the emergence of an interreligious humanism in the mid-Abbasid age is among the most remarkable achievements of the classical Islamic civilization. Yet, this humanism tended to take as its favorite fields sciences, medicine and philosophy, while the study of the intricacies of the Arabic language was perceived as a matter reserved to Muslims, being ul-

6. Vollandt, "*Status Quaestionis* of Research." See also Griffith, *Bible in Arabic*, who starts his book with an outright statement: "The study of the Bible in Arabic is in its infancy" (Griffith, *Bible in Arabic*, 1). This rapidly expanding field of research is now being explored by the project "Biblia Arabica," a joint initiative of Ludwig-Maximilians-Universität and Tel Aviv University.

7. See for instance Griffith, *Bible in Arabic*, 41–53, who argues for the unlikeliness of written translations before the rise of Islam, although an oral diffusion of biblical motives and imageries is attested in some pre-Islamic poets such as ʿAdī Ibn Zayd and Umayya Ibn Abī s-Ṣalṭ, and more decisively, in the Qurʾan itself. See also Shahid, "Problem of an Arabic Bible."

8. For a first introduction, see Gilliot and Larcher, "Language and Style of the Qurʾān," 109–35; Diez, *Introduzione alla lingua araba*, 117–46.

9. Ibn Ǧinnī, *al-Ḫaṣāʾis*, 2:5.

10. "L'arabe classique est donc pour moi exactement ce que son étiquette dit étymologiquement qu'il est: à la fois la variété de prestige (classique = de première classe) et la norme scolaire (classique = tel qu'il s'enseigne dans les classes)" (Larcher, *Syntaxe de l'arabe classique*, 7).

timately bound to the Qur'an, Islamic exegesis, law and theology.[11] As a result, this "division of roles" affected the linguistic quality of most translations, which were in general literal and often exhibited a limited knowledge of Classical Arabic.

The situation began to change when the Arabic speaking minorities of the Levant, who had endured severe persecutions under the Mamluks, were inserted into the Ottoman Sultanate, at the beginning of the sixteenth century. Being masters of an empire where non-Muslims constituted roughly half the subjects, the Ottomans stretched the traditional institution of Islamic "protection" (*dimma*) to its maximum; furthermore, the treaties that the Ottoman empire signed with the other European powers made commercial and cultural relations with the "Franks" relatively easy. As a result, several Catholic orders opened new missions in the Levant, with the primary aim of restoring the communion between the local churches and the Roman See.[12] Leaving aside the experience of the polyglot Bibles in Europe, the Sacred Congregation for the Propagation of Faith (*Propaganda Fide*) commissioned a full Arabic translation of the Bible with parallel Latin text according to the Vulgate, which was published in Rome in 1671 and reprinted several times.

The *Propaganda* translation, as it came to be known, was not without flaws, to say the least, and its shortcomings were deeply felt by the Protestant communities, which in turn had started to deploy a remarkable missionary activity in the Middle East.

> The meaning [of the *Propaganda*] is often not clear, and the argument of continuous passages is not unfrequently lost. In fact, the more abstruse and doctrinal parts of Paul's Epistles lose in it almost all their force. Of the prophetical and poetical portions of the Old Testament much is either without force, in bad taste, or absolutely unintelligible. The whole version is not in a classical style. The structure of the sentences is awkward, the choice of words is not select, and the rules of grammar are often transgressed. We have been ashamed to put the sacred books

11. It is telling that when Germanos Farhat (1670–1732), the famous Maronite Archbishop of Aleppo, set up to produce a grammar of Classical Arabic for his coreligionists, he profited from the immense scholarship produced by Muslim linguists, but he felt compelled to substitute all Quranic examples with passages taken from the New Testament.

12. Just to mention a symbolic fact, the first book ever printed in Arabic was not the Qur'an but the liturgy of the hours according to the Byzantine rite (*kitāb ṣalāt as-sawāʿ ī*). It was produced in 1514 in Italy, according to the colophon in the city of Fano (present-day Marche). Most researchers however believe that the breviary was printed in Venice and the false notice was meant to bypass a competitor.

of our religion, in such a dress, into the hands of a respectable Muhammedan or Druze.[13]

At first, Protestants resigned themselves to using an adaptation of the Catholic translation—printed without the Papal insignia and the Deuterocanonical books. Soon, however, did the project of a new translation gain momentum. The most active actors in it were the Anglicans and the Presbyterians. In particular, the Society for Promoting Christian Knowledge entrusted the task of producing a new Arabic translation to the British orientalist Samuel Lee (1783–1852), who worked in co-operation with the acrimonious Fāris aš-Šidyāq (1804–87), one of the great masters of the Arabic language in the nineteenth century.[14] Lee's translation, conducted on the Hebrew and Greek text, was published posthumous in 1857 but was soon obscured by a new version promoted by the American Bible Society. Although initiated by Eli Smith (1801–57), whose pointed remarks on the *Propaganda* have just been quoted, this translation is indissolubly tied to the name of Cornelius Van Dyck (1818–95), who was assisted by the two other champions of the Arab literary awakening, Buṭrus al-Bustānī (1819–83, a Maronite who had converted to Protestantism) and Naṣīf al-Yāziǧī (1800–71, a Greek-Catholic).[15] This new translation was completed in 1865 and it met with immediate success.

To counter the diffusion of the Protestant translation, the Jesuits of Beirut set out to produce a third version, under the direction of Augustin Rodet (1828–1906) and with the participation of Ibrāhīm al-Yāziǧī (1847–1906), the son of Naṣīf and his heir at the head of this dynasty of Lebanese literati. The translation was achieved in 1881. A century later, in 1988, the Jesuits published a revised version of it, which is currently the standard text for Arab Catholics. But with this last notice we have gone beyond the chronological scope of the 1961 Psalms' translation. At that time, essentially three biblical versions were available: the two "Protestant" and the Catholic, all produced in the second half of the nineteenth century.[16]

These versions had a major impact on the renewal and modernization of the Arabic language. Although differing under many respects, they shared a common instinct to shun direct competition with the Qur'anic model, which is considered by Muslims as inimitable, while still aiming

---

13. Rev. Eli Smith quoted in Grafton, *Contested Origins,* 202.

14. Born a Maronite, Šidyāq had converted to Protestantism. He was later to adhere to Islam.

15. On this translation, see Grafton, *Contested Origins.*

16. For the sake of completeness, the Dominicans of Mosul printed in 1875 a new version of the *Propaganda* Bible with corrections.

at producing a linguistically irreproachable text. Their audience was assumed to be familiar with some biblical backgrounds and the goal was to bring them as close as possible to the original, while preserving linguistic correctness. Van Dyck however decided to test his translation on a native "speaker" of Muslim faith, to make sure that it may be understandable outside Christian circles. He therefore involved in his project a Muslim scholar, Yūsuf al-Asīr (1815–89), a native of Sidon who had received his education in al-Azhar in Egypt. His participation in the Bible translation project was an unprecedented move. As the Lebanese writer Samir Kassir once acutely commented

> The fact that a prominent Muslim scholar, the shaykh Yūsuf al-Asīr, contributed to this Christian work is without any doubt one of the most significant and most eloquent signs of the humanism which characterized the *Nahḍa* age [Arabic Renaissance].[17]

The 1961 Psalms' translation can be seen as continuing along the same lines as Van Dyck's intuition, but it goes one step further, insomuch as its final linguistic interpreter is a Muslim. Let us therefore turn to the people involved in this initiative.

The Authors of the Translation

Mohammad al-Sadeq Hussein

Not much is known about this figure, apart from a brief note introducing the first sample of fifteen Psalms, published in *MIDEO* in 1957. In this article, Serge de Beaurecueil presents his Muslim partner in these terms:

> Mr. Moḥammad al-Ṣādeq Ḥussein, former student at the *École Normale* (*Madrasat al-Muʿallimīn*), started his career as a teacher. Afterwards, he quit teaching and occupied several posts in the service of the Egyptian government, including finally that of Accountant General at the Ministry of Finance. In his free time, he continued to cultivate a deep interest in Arabic literature as well as foreign publications. Besides several articles, we owe him a translation of S. Smiles, *Character*, published in Cairo in 1924 at the *Laǧnat at-taʾlīf wa-t-tarǧama* ['Commission for Composition and Translation'] under the title *Al-Aḫlāq* and an

---

17. Kassir, *Taʾammulāt fī šiqāʾ al-ʿarab*, 71.

historical study on the *Sobkī family* (*al-Bayt al-Sobkī*), Cairo, *al-Kātib al-Miṣrī* 1948.[18]

The same biographical note is reprinted at the end of the introduction to the 1961 edition.[19] Mgr. Teissier, the only living member of the translation team, contacted personally via e-mail, was not able to add any detail and a search on the Internet in Arabic did not yield further data, apart from the fact that the translation of the Psalter is still available in some public libraries and for free download, as is the case with many Arabic books.

Yet Mohammad al-Sadeq Hussein was the brother of Mohammad Kamel Hussein (Muḥammad Kāmil Ḥusayn, 1901–77), a renowned orthopedist and the former rector of the ʿAyn Shams University in Cairo, well known for his novels. In *Qarya ẓālima* (1954), he was the first Muslim author to produce a fictional work about the highly sensitive issue of Christ's Crucifixion. Deeply influenced by Tolstoy and his pacifism, Kamel Hussein builds his novel about the primacy of conscience and non-violence.[20] Assuming the point of view of the disciples, he avoids an explicit position on the controversial issue whether the crucifixion was real or apparent, as most Muslims believe with reference to Q 4:157. Interestingly, Kamel Hussein had a role in the Psalter edition too, as he ensured the final linguistic revision.

Coming back to his brother al-Sadeq Hussein, the scant biographical notes we possess suffice to suggest that he too belonged to the milieu of cultivated professionals and state officials with a double formation (traditional and Western), who played a key role in what Albert Hourani has famously defined as the liberal age of Arabic thought. Not by chance, al-Sadeq Hussein is credited with an Arabic translation of the progressive Scottish reformer Samuel Smiles, whose *Self-Help* (1859) has been called "the Bible of mid-Victorian liberalism." Although many of these Egyptian liberals were unsatisfied with the strictures of traditional ulema, they were often inhabited by a vivid religious quest, as exemplarily attested by the multi-faceted figure of Taha Hussein (1889–1973), among the greatest Arab intellectuals of the twentieth century.[21] This attitude of research led some of them to look with new eyes at Christianity, beyond the traditional controversies and polemics of the past, in general through the lenses of English Enlightenment, French Romanticism or the great Russian novelists.

18. Al-Sadeq Hussein, "Quinze psaumes," 3n1.

19. Al-Sadeq Hussein, *Sifr al-Mazāmīr*, 18n2.

20. The novel is available in English translation by K. Cragg. See Hussein, *City of Wrong*. See also Anawati, "Jésus et ses juges."

21. On his contrasted relation with al-Azhar, see his autobiography Hussein, *al-Ayyām* [*The Days*].

Politically, the liberal season in Egypt was brought to an abrupt end in 1952 by the coup of the Free Officials and the rise to power of Gamal Abdel Nasser, but its seeds continued to fecundate the Egyptian intellectual scene and has resurfaced from time to time, not lastly in the demonstrations in Tahrir Square in 2011.

Serge de Beaurecueil

In many ways, the cultural conjuncture in the Arab world was exceptional and it goes to the merits of Marie-Dominique Chenu to have grasped it. The Dominican theologian inspired the foundation of the IDEO, the Dominican Institute of Oriental Studies, which was first established in Cairo in 1944 and took its definitive form in 1953. As Chenu himself was not an Arabist nor an Islamicist, he entrusted the project to a gifted Egyptian Brother, Georges Anawati, and two younger friars, Jacques Jomier and Serge de Beaurecueil. Albeit very different in character, they will all distinguish themselves in the domain of Islamic studies: Anawati was to become a great expert of Islamic philosophy, especially Avicenna, while Jomier would concentrate on Qur'anic exegesis and de Beaurecueil on Sufism.[22]

Serge was born in Paris in 1917, the son of the count Pierre Laugier de Beaurecueil, an official of chivalry who could boast among his ancestors a Marshal of France, and Roberte de Quelen, the offspring of a family of ancient Breton nobility with several ties to the Levant. The couple was not well assorted and divorced in 1931. The mother was especially eccentric and passionate for raising hounds: according to de Beaurecueil's biographer, Jean-Jacques Pérennès, she inspired the character of Cruella de Vil in the novel (and later Walt Disney animation) *101 Dalmatians*.[23]

> There were all preconditions for an unhappy, instable child. . . .
> On the contrary, the entrance in religious life gave him a family where he felt happy and his desire of evasion and flight was

---

22. On the IDEO, see the masterly Avon, *Les Frères prêcheurs en Orient*. Fr. Pérennès has written the biographies of two of the three founders of the IDEO. See Pérennès, *Georges Anawati (1905–1994)*; *Passion Kaboul*. An English resume of Pérennès's book on Anawati has been published in *Oasis* in two installments: 9 ("The man who changed our way of looking at Islam") and 10 ("Looking until the end for the path to Islam"). A complete bibliography of Serge de Beaurecueil can be found in Pérennès, "Bibliographie de Serge de Beaurecueil." We owe Pérennès also the biography of Antonin Jaussen, the first inspirer of the IDEO (*Le Père Antonin Jaussen*).

23. Pérennès, *Passion Kaboul*, 339n23.

changed into a project. . . . It is in the East that he will spend his life.[24]

After entering the Dominican order in 1935, aged of just 18 years, Serge de Beaurecueil follows the usual course of philosophical and theological studies at Le Saulchoir (initially located in Kain, Belgium, then moved to Étiolles, France in 1938) and while attending his last year he is authorized to study Arabic at the *École Nationale de Langues Orientales Vivantes* in Paris (*Langues O*, as it was usually called) with Régis Blachère. After the vicissitudes of the war, he arrived in Cairo on June 1, 1946. He would spend 17 years in the Egyptian capital, before moving to Afghanistan in 1963.

In Cairo de Beaurecueil is deeply involved in the foundation of the IDEO. Together with Anawati and Jomier he takes lessons in Persian and soon decides to specialize in Sufism. He is initially fascinated by the "mysticism of intoxication" of Jalal ad-Din Rumi (1207–73), but following the advice of a Syrian student of al-Azhar who frequents the IDEO, Osman Yahya, he decides to specialize in the Hanbali master 'Abd Allāh Ansārī from Herat (1006–89), the champion of the "mysticism of lucidity." He publishes his first works on Ansārī and in 1955 he is granted a scholarship by the French National Center for Scientific Research, which allows him to visit Afghanistan for the first time. Meanwhile he is also active in the service of the youths, especially the scouts of Daher, a popular neighborhood in Cairo, not far from the Dominican convent. He assures several retreats for the students of the Saint-Joseph College of Khoronfish (another popular Cairo neighborhood), run by the *Frères des Écoles chrétiennes* (De La Salle Brothers).[25] Through his experience with the Egyptian youths he becomes critical of the predominant trend in the Catholic schools and colleges, aiming at creating a French-speaking, Westernized elite. Anawati himself had experienced this identity malaise. Once, after a French theatrical performance in his high school, he had been asked by a Brother: "What are you?" "I am Egyptian." "No, you are French."[26]

Very soon, de Beaurecueil took an interest in the Coptic rite and in 1947 he obtains the permission to celebrate in it. Abandoning the mixed Latin-French liturgy in use among the Latins, he starts to say Mass according to the Coptic rite for his students in Khoronfish. His choice to grow a beard and wear it like a Coptic monk raises some concerns among his brothers of an "anti-Latinism which would be at the very least out of place,"[27] but in

24. Pérennès, *Passion Kaboul*, 35.

25. The College is still well-known in Cairo. See Khoronfish, "College Saint-Joseph."

26. Anawati, "Al-Ḥiwār al-aḫīr," 162 [Anawati, *L'ultimo dialogo*, 51].

27. Letter of Anawati to Jean de Menasce, January 25, 1948, quoted in Pérennès, *Passion Kaboul*, 313n45.

fact, de Beaurecueil becomes rapidly aware of several limitations in Egypt's autochthonous Christianity. In an article that dates from 1953,[28] he sums up lucidly the situation prevailing in the Coptic church at time.[29] "Present editions of Egyptian liturgical books are always disposed in two columns, with the Arabic translation facing the original Coptic texts."[30] The celebrant is left with a large margin of freedom and some militate in favor of a rebirth of the Coptic language, while others plea for a complete Arabization. After summarizing the arguments of each party, de Beaurecueil formulates his personal opinion. He recalls that the original language of the Church in Egypt was Greek and Coptic was introduced for pastoral needs. There is nothing of sacred liturgical origins in it—something orthodox Copts are not always aware of, even today. "Greek was only kept for formulae whose meaning everybody knew (greetings, Trisagion, etc.) and which were bound to easy and popular melodies."[31] Everything else was translated, notably the parts with a didactic function and the secret prayers of the priest, where it is essential that he understands what he is saying. This choice, argues de Beaurecueil, contains a lesson for the present too. The Coptic Church cannot become a ghetto whose only concern is survival. Its minority condition is "purely accidental"[32] and cannot inspire a defense reflex but a "burning wish to enlighten the Brethren and preparing for them the welcoming environment in which they may integrate without 'expatriating' to the Mystic Body of the Church."[33]

The text is framed in the language of the influential encyclical *Mystici Corporis Christi* (1943), but the expression "expatriating," behind which there almost certainly lies the Islamic concept of *hiǧra*, betrays a consonance with the initial vision of Louis Massignon, as expressed in his *L'hégire d'Ismaël* (1935).[34] For Massignon Muslims are spiritual expatriates, the heirs of the promise made by God to Abraham through Ishmael. Their possible conversion—this seems to be de Beaurecueil's conclusion—should

---

28. De Beaurecueil, "Un problème crucial."

29. The author is referring primarily to the Coptic Orthodox Church, but he also takes account of the Coptic-Catholic Church, which had been erected as a Church *sui juris* only in 1895. The two Churches share essentially the same liturgy, although the Catholics have simplified it for the benefit of the faithful.

30. De Beaurecueil, "Un problème crucial," 9.

31. De Beaurecueil, "Un problème crucial," 10–11.

32. De Beaurecueil, "Un problème crucial," 11.

33. De Beaurecueil, "Un problème crucial," 11.

34. Now in *Les trois prières d'Abraham*. It is worth noting that Massignon's vision of Islam has significantly changed over the years.

be theologically understood more as a return home. But is the Egyptian Church, be it Orthodox or Catholic, ready to accomplish this mission?

> At present, when [Egyptian Muslims] happen to enter a church, if they are not bewildered by the ceremonies, smelling of the Bible and the land, they cannot be but confused by the use of a "foreign" language and hurt by clumsy translations which seem to insult the word of God because of their sloppiness and the way they are pronounced. For sure, it would be stupid to dream of an Egyptian liturgy in Qur'anic language; Arabic is a dangerous tool, it always risks to become an obstacle when it is too perfect, catching the mind with the fascination of its verbal magic; but one can wish for a correct, simple, transparent, comprehensible language, placing within everybody's reach the richness of liturgy and the Biblical texts from which it draws inspiration.[35]

This sharp criticism about the quality of the Coptic liturgy in Arabic was not new at all. According to Hourani, Taha Hussein himself, had deplored "the bad Arabic of the liturgies used in the eastern Churches, and is said to have offered to help in rewriting them, so that the Arab Christians could worship in good Arabic."[36] It is probably at this point that de Beaurecueil conceives his plan of a new version of the Psalter. The connection with the liturgy is indeed evident in the first sample of translations, published four years later, in 1957, as de Beaurecueil chooses for his experiment the Psalms used in the office of Nones in the Coptic rite.[37]

Henri Teissier

The 1961 translation is therefore born at the crossroads of a Muslim interest in Western culture and spiritual matters from the side of al-Sadeq Hussein and a desire for a more "inculturated" liturgy from the side of Serge de Beaurecueil. To complete the picture, a third element has to be added and it is the great renewal of biblical studies in the Catholic Church. In fact de Beaurecueil writes

> The Arabic translations we currently possess don't take into account the progress that textual criticism recently accomplished in the understanding of the original text.[38]

35. De Beaurecueil, "Un problème crucial," 11.

36. Hourani, *Arabic Thought*, 334.

37. Al-Sadeq Hussein, "Quinze psaumes," 2n2.

38. Al-Sadeq Hussein, "Quinze psaumes," 1.

In particular, the *Bible de Jérusalem*, in which the Dominicans played a major role, had just been completed in 1956[39] and the Arabic translation takes it as its explicit basis.[40] Yet, another figure is enrolled in the team to assure "a constant reference"[41] to the Hebrew original. It is Henri Teissier who, "in addition to his qualities as an enthusiastic Arabist, possesses a degree in biblical Hebrew from the School of Oriental Languages of the *Institut Catholique* of Paris."[42] Teissier, who had just obtained a second degree in Literary Arabic from *Langues O*, was actually spending the academic year as an intern at the IDEO. But the relations between France and Egypt were rapidly degrading because of the Suez war and the repression of the Algerian revolt and Teissier was forced to leave after the publication of the first fifteen Psalms.[43] He was not able to remain in contact with his partners, "because at that time even postal communication was no longer existent between France/Algeria and Egypt,"[44] and for the rest of the translation de Beaurecueil had to make appeal to the elements of biblical Hebrew he had been taught during his novitiate.[45]

Teissier also remembers that the translation team was using an ancient Arabic version of the Psalms, which he believes to have been the Jesuits' translation. This supposition is highly probable. We also know that this translation read, in Ps 42:7, *bi-ṣawt ḥarrārātik*, a rendering which is lambasted by de Beaurecueil as meaning to the modern Egyptian reader "to the bubbling of your sewers" instead of "at the thunder of your cataracts." Unfortunately I was unable to consult the 1881 edition of the Jesuits' translation to check the verse in question.

39. The Psalms were first published in a separate edition, translated by Raymond Tournay in collaboration with Raymond Schwab.

40. Similarly, the new translation of the New Testament, published by the Paulist Father Georges Fakhouri, in 1953, in Lebanon, was based on the *Bible de Jérusalem*.

41. Al-Sadeq Hussein, "Quinze psaumes," 2.

42. Al-Sadeq Hussein, "Quinze psaumes," 3n2.

43. Al-Sadeq Hussein, "Les psaumes 1 à 25," 1. It is in this strained conjuncture that the French Arabist André Miquel was imprisoned by the Nasserist regime. He still recalls Father Anawati taking the risk to attend his trial to publicly encourage him. Cf. Miquel, "Discreet Invitation," 93. These details show that the members of the IDEO were not living in an academic ivory tower.

44. Personal communication with the author, April 8, 2018.

45. According to Régis Morelon, director of IDEO between 1984 and 2008, the formation at Le Saulchoir included an initiation to Hebrew language. De Beaurecueil seems not to have proceeded any further and Mgr. Teissier, asked on this particular point, says not to remember whether the Dominican Friar knew Hebrew, but the closeness between Arabic and Hebrew makes it easy to shift from one language to the other.

A Qur'anic Translation

As we have seen, de Beaurecueil had expressed his wish for a liturgy in correct Arabic already in 1953. But the participation of a Muslim translator, and the personal maturation of de Beaurecueil through his studies of Sufism, lead him to a new step. While in 1953 he had warned about the risks inherent in the use of Qur'anic Arabic, he now openly declares:

> Far from avoiding the expressions that are current in the Islamic religious language, we have not hesitated to adopt them whenever they corresponded exactly to the original sense of the text, without however 'Islamizing' it.[46]

De Beaurecueil gives only a few examples of the lexical choices he made with al-Sadeq Hussein, but they are of great import.[47] The righteous man of the Psalms (Hebrew ṣaddīq) is not rendered as ṣiddīq, but as rašīd and mustaqīm. Ṣiddīq in fact, although phonetically close to the Hebrew word, means in the Qur'anic language whoever accepts the message of prophecy and has therefore completely different implications than its biblical quasi-homonym. A great problem in translating biblical passages into Arabic is how to express the notion of divine goodness. Many Christian Arabs resort to the term ṣāliḥ, but in the Qur'anic vision this word cannot be predicated of God as it only applies to the believer who accomplishes the "good deeds," as-ṣāliḥāt. In its place al-Sadeq Hussein and de Beaurecueil propose the word karīm, "generous, noble." Their translation also avoids to employ Rabb ("Lord") in the absolute state, preceded by the article (ar-Rabb), because in the Qur'an the term always occurs in the construct state.

Other remarks can be added to these examples given by the translators themselves. "Law" is rendered without hesitation as šarīʿa (throughout Ps 119 for instance) and the verb "to praise" is given alternatively as ḥamida and sabbaḥa instead of hallala as it can be seen for instance in the translation of Psalm 150. Hallala is an Hebraism typical of the Christian language, related to the liturgical formula "Hallelujah," but to Muslims it means "to say Lā ilāha illā 'llāh ('There is no god but God')," i.e., the first part of the Islamic profession of faith. In contrast to hallala, sabbaḥa is deeply Qur'anic and in the Muslim tradition the Suras 57, 59, 61, 62 and 64 are called al-muṣabbiḥāt, because they share the same opening formula sabbaḥa (yusabbiḥu in 62 and 64) li-llāhi mā fī s-samawāti wa-l-arḍ (wa-mā fī-l-arḍ in 62 and 64): "All that is in the heavens and the earth magnifies God." Since this universal glorification is indeed the content of Psalm 150,

46. Al-Sadeq Hussein, "Les psaumes 26 à 50," 2.

47. Al-Sadeq Hussein, "Quinze psaumes," 1–2.

the lexical choice appears to be a felicitous one. In Ps 110:4 the Messiah is said to be priest ʿalā sunnat Malkīṣādiq, "according to the Sunnah of Melchizedeq," which is both correct and profound. And the Merciful God of Ps 113:5 yaʿlū li-yastawiya ʿalā ʿaršihi, "is seated on his high throne," an expression clearly reminiscent of many Quranic passages (Q 20:5, for instance). In several instances the translation does not hesitate to employ the Qur'anic expressions al-mušrikūna, "polytheists,"[48] ahl aš-širk, "people of polytheism'"[49] or al-kāfirūna, "the unbelievers,"[50] to denote the "nations" (Hebrew gōyim) as an alternative to the more usual Arabic rendering umam, when the context is clearly one of polemics against idolatry. And similar examples could be easily multiplied.

Of course, whenever Arabic and Hebrew share a word, the translators tried to preserve the lexical kinship. There was an illustrious tradition in that sense: for instance, Saadia Gaon, the author of the most important medieval Jewish translation of the Bible, had systematically adopted this principle.[51] But in fact—it is again the testimony of Mgr. Teissier—"the evolution of words in the two languages made it difficult to employ the Hebrew root to choose the Arabic word."[52]

Therefore, rather than insisting on forcing the language of arrival on its source, it is on the stylistic level that al-Sadeq Hussein's version strives to echo the original Hebrew text. The most relevant feature in this translation is indeed the use of saǧʿ ("rhymed prose") whenever possible. The hallmark of Qur'anic style, this stylistic device is perfectly adaptable to parallelism, the formal organizing principle of most Psalms and more generally of the so-called "Semitic rhetoric."[53] While it is impossible to offer a general survey of the impact of this stylistic choice, I give here in transcription Psalm 1 in its entirety, highlighting in bold the instances of saǧʿ. Those who are familiar with the Qur'anic language will find many additional similarities in the lexicon employed.

48. The expression literally means "those who associate something to God." See, for instance, Ps 98:2.

49. For instance Ps 96:10, where also the phrase li-rabbikum al-mulk ("The Lord is king") is worth noting, as it echoes Q 67:1.

50. Literally "those who conceal [God's favors]." By way of example, see Ps 115:2.

51. For a study of Saadia's translation techniques the reader is primarily referred to the works of Tamar Zewi. Likewise, Syriac-speaking translators tended to mold their Arabic on Syriac.

52. Personal communication with the author, April 8, 2018.

53. On this concept and its possible application to the Qur'an, see Meynet, Rhetorical Analysis; Cuypers, Banquet.

1. *Ṭūbā lahu ḏāka alladī*

    La yaġšā maǧālisa l-fāsiqīn

    Wa-lā yaqūmu fī sabīli aḍ-ḍāllīn

    Wa-lā yaq' udu ma' a al-māġinīn.

2. *Bal yaġidu l-ġibṭata fī šarī' ati* Rabbih

    *yuḥāfiṭu bihā nahārahu wa-*laylah.

3. *Ka'annahu šagaratun* qā'imah

    ḥayṯu l-miyāhu ġāriyah.

4. *Tu'tī ṯimārahā fī i*bbānihā

    Wa-lan taḏwiya awrāquhā

    A' māluhu kulluhā bi-n-nuġḥi muttasimah,

    Šattāna ḏā wa-l-fāsiqūna, šattān!

    Innahum hašīm,

    taḏrūhu r-riyāḥ.

5. *Yawma l-faṣli lā maqāma li-l-*fāsiqīn

    Wa-lā li-ḍ-ḍāllīn

    Fī zumrati ṣ-ṣāliḥīn

6. *Fa-Rabbuka a' lamu bi-sabīli ṣ-ṣāliḥīn*

    Ammā sabīlu l-fasīqīn, fa-ilā l-ḥusrānī l-mubīn.

The final clause in this sample in particular is closely reminiscent of the Qur'anic style.[54] And yet, the translation does not force the text in the Islamic mold, as some had feared.[55] This is made clear already from its title, *Sifr al-Mazāmīr*. *Sifr* is an Aramaism in Arabic, used mainly by Jews and Christians for the Biblical books, whereas Muslims prefer the terms *Kutub* ("Scriptures") and *Ṣuḥuf* (literally "Sheets"). Moreover, the Qur'an employs for the Psalm the word *Zabūr*, possibly of Ethiopic or South Arabian origin, whereas *Mazāmīr* is typical of the Christian Arabic lexicon. As far as the text itself is concerned, one example will suffice. The refrain of Ps

54. I do not wish to encumber the reader with comparisons with other versions, but anyone with some knowledge of Arabic will readily grasp the point. Just by way of example, the beginning of Psalm 1 in the Ecumenical Translation (*at-tarǧama al-muštaraka*) reads: *Hanī'an li-man lā yasluku fī mašūrati l-ašrār wa-fī ṭarīqi l-ḥāṭi'īna lā yaqifu wa-fī maǧlisi l-mustahzi'īna la yaǧlisu.*

55. De Beaurecueil hints to some anonymous reservations to his choice of a Muslim translator (De Beaurecueil, "Les psaumes 26 à 50," 2).

136, *kī lə-ʿ ōlam ḥasdō* "for his steadfast love endures forever," is translated *fa-ḥubbuhu sarmadun ilā l-abad,* whereas the Muslim tradition prefers to speak about God's *riḍā* ("contentment," cf. Q 5:119, 58:22, 98:8) with the believers or his *raḥma* ("mercy," a key term in Islam) towards them, albeit not ignoring the theme of God's *ḥubb* ("love"), as in Q 3:31.

Also the introduction to the 1961 edition, penned by de Beaurecueil, is classic in its contents. It presents the literary genres in the Psalter and debates the issue of its authorship, stating in an outright way the difference between the Islamic and Christian conception of revelation. The author then discusses two teachings in the Psalms that may hurt the Christian reader, namely the idea of *Sheol* as the ultimate abode of all souls and the imprecations against the impious. In both cases, he stresses the progressivity of revelation and reminds the readers that the texts take their final meaning only with the "appearance of the Son of God on earth," whose "Last Supper, Cross, and Resurrection have taught men the infinite love of God."[56] Finally de Beaurecueil overviews the Arabic translations of the Psalter, from its first echoing in pre-Islamic poetry and the Qur'an (with a passing critical remark on the Arabic translation of the entry *Zabūr* in the *Encyclopedia of Islam,* interpolated to make it consistent with Islamic dogma), to the famous Greek-Arabic fragment of Psalm 78 discovered in Damascus by Bruno Violet[57] down to the modern versions. The *Sifr al-Mazāmīr* is thus clearly a Christian translation, faithful to the original and meant for liturgical use. This sets it apart from some contentious Islamic–Christian attempts such as *The True Meaning of the Gospel of Christ,* published in Beirut in 2008, which in many points ends up being nothing more than an Arian paraphrase of the Gospels.

Just one year before the completion of the Egyptian translation, the Lebanese priest Afif Osseïrane (ʿAfīf ʿUsīrān, 1919–88), a convert from a prominent Shiite family, published in Beirut his own version of the Psalms, of which the Egyptian team took notice only in the last minute.[58] Osseïrane too attempted a "Qur'anization" of the Psalms and de Beaurecueil's remark ("from a swift browsing, [Osseïrane's version] seems to be superior to the translations in circulation, though falling short the desired level"[59]) is not completely fair and can perhaps be understood in light of the persistent rivalry between Lebanese and Egyptians over the mastery of the true Arabic

---

56. Al-Sadeq Hussein, *Sifr al-Mazāmīr,* 14.

57. Violet, "Ein zweisprachiges Psalmfragment."

58. Afif Osseïrane's version is entitled *Mazāmīr Dāwūd an-nabī* ("Psalms of David the prophet"). Some Psalms are available on the blog. See Osseïrane, "Psalms."

59. Al-Sadeq Hussein, *Sifr al-Mazāmīr,* 17.

language. Rather than debating the comparative merits of these works, it is worth stressing their converging persuasion that the Psalter, properly translated, can strike some chords in the Muslim soul. In the case of de Beaurecueil/al-Sadeq Hussein this effect is achieved through a joint work, while Osseïrane, who had received an Islamic education, lets the Psalm resonate in his own Qur'anic background. Their almost simultaneous publication can hardly be considered a coincidence. Rather, it reveals a common cultural atmosphere.

Abat al-'arabiyya an tatanassar, "the Arabic language refuses to become Christian."[60] This traditional saying, which still gains currency in some milieus, has been proven false by the wave of translations inaugurated around the middle of the nineteenth century and among which our version (together with Osseïrane's) stands out for its deliberate adoption of a Qur'anic language.

Its Fortune

The 1961 Psalms' translation was generally well received and already before its completion Serge de Beaurecueil started to employ it for his pastoral activities. In May 1960 he preached a three-day retreat for forty-two students belonging to the last class of the Saint-Joseph College in Khoronfish. The retreat was extraordinary because it saw the participation not only of Christians of all rites, but also of some Muslim and Jewish students (with the written authorization of their parents). Four episodes in the life of Abraham were chosen for meditation and it was the new translation of the Psalms that nourished common prayer.[61]

At any rate, things changed radically with the Second Vatican Council. Already before the Council, the faithful of Latin rite in the Levant had been allowed to use Arabic language to some extent (especially for readings),[62] but now it became imperative to translate the whole liturgy and the breviary.[63] After some pioneering attempts—Msgr. Teissier recalls for example to

60. I was not able to track down its origin. In the sources I consulted it is referred to as a *qawl ma'tūr*, a "proverbial expression."

61. On this retreat see Pérennès, *Passion Kaboul*, 124–26. Jean Mohamed Abd el-Jalil, the famous Franciscan of Moroccan origins, and Louis Massignon came to know about this experience and were deeply touched by it.

62. According to the memories of Msgr. Maroun Lahham, Auxiliary Archbishop of the Latin Patriarchate Emeritus, "while the priest was saying Mass in Latin, there was always a good layman at the bottom of the Church reciting the same prayers in Arabic" (personal communication with the author, May 9, 2018).

63. In the wake of Vatican II several Eastern Catholic Churches (for instance the Maronite and the Melkite Church) also reorganized their liturgical books, in many cases enhancing the linguistic level of the texts.

have participated, just after the Council, in formulating a provisional Arabic translation of the canon of the Mass for Algeria, together with a Moroccan Muslim and a Christian professor at the University of Algiers[64]—the task was successfully carried out by the Liturgical Commission in the Latin Patriarchate of Jerusalem, which included, among others, Msgr. William Shomali, Fr. Théodore Samama, Msgr. George Saba and Msgr. Maroun Lahham. The first edition of the Missal was published in 1966 in Jerusalem, but the edition now in use goes back to 1983.[65] The Liturgical Commission also produced a breviary for the Liturgy of the Hours, adopting for the biblical text the Jesuits' version.

The "Egyptian" Psalter translation, however, continued to be employed in the Dominican convent in Cairo until around 2010, when it was replaced by the breviary of the Patriarchate of Jerusalem. According to Father Jean-Jacques Pérennès, the main reason for this change was that at that time the community was beginning to have more Egyptian postulants, "who were uncomfortable with a vocabulary full of Islamic assonances,"[66] a remark which must be understood against the backdrop of the steady rise of political Islam and Salafism in Egypt over the last decades. At the same time—adds Father Jean Druel—the community was heading towards a full Arabization of the liturgy and needed to integrate the Psalms with the antiphons and readings of the Office. "We were juggling with too many different books."[67] Also, according to Father Druel, the translation presented some linguistic difficulties, something which sounds hardly surprising as Classical Arabic is continuously losing ground to the Egyptian dialect.

In conclusion, and for the sake of completeness, just a hint toward the further existential parable of Serge de Beaurecueil. In 1963, after seventeen years spent in Cairo, he moved to Afghanistan to teach history of Sufism at Kabul University; his studies on Anṣārī had made him an authority in the field. In Afghanistan de Beaurecueil quickly abandoned research and found a new vocation in the service of disadvantaged children, especially disabled street boys. In twenty years he will give shelter to around sixty children in his home. This period marks a profound evolution in his attitude towards the problem of religious pluralism. He initially adopts an inclusive theology of intercession and substitution whose roots go back to the Egyptian period.

---

64. Personal communication with the author, April 8, 2018.

65. The 1983 Arabic edition is based on the second edition of the *Missale Romanum* (1975). A new edition is waiting for the approbation of Rome at the time this article is being drafted.

66. Personal communication with the author, April 7, 2018.

67. Personal communication with the author, April 7, 2018.

In a country where the Church is almost non-existent,[68] he thinks of his mission as consisting in taking upon himself "the joys and the hopes, the griefs and the anxieties" of the Afghan people by presenting them to God through the daily Mass he used to celebrate in his house, where he has arranged a small chapel. But little by little he starts to attach less value to the chapel, until he closes it down altogether to make more room for the children he hosts. At this stage, he considers the sharing of life as already sacred in itself, without the necessity of an explicit liturgy: "All these kids around you—he tells one day to some guests—well, whenever I take care of one of them, in these guys it is God that I find: they are for me an Epiphany of God."[69] In parallel, he continues his living relation with the mystic Anṣārī (who was never a mere academic subject to him) and is especially fascinated by the idea of the mystical extinction in God, the only existent.[70]

And yet isn't the Christian proclamation precisely that this One God has decided, out of love, to create room for the Other, in his inner, Trinitarian life and analogically in the creatures too?[71] And consequently, can we dispense of the explicit relation to the Son? Asked by Philip, "Lord, show us the Father, and we will be satisfied," Jesus answered him: "Do you not believe that I am in the Father and the Father is in me?" (John 14:8–10).

Personally, I am convinced that the complete lack of religious freedom he experienced in Afghanistan explains much in de Beaurecueil's evolution. By mutilating the communication of the self, this circumstance implies that dialogue cannot follow its natural course, as there is a portion of things that cannot be said or done. In the long run this exercise of self-censorship is likely to exert lasting psychological effects, at the unconscious level too and in the almost total absence of a tangible Christian community, one will easily be tempted by a form of undifferentiated theism as a possible common ground. And yet, in this way the event of the self-donation of God in Christ, which is not deductible from any human religious premise, risks to be lost or at least watered down in the general striving of humanity towards the divine.

---

68. The only official presence was the chapel of the Italian Embassy (which is today the see of a *Missio sui juris* erected in 2002). The Afghan government bestowed this privilege to Italy as a sign of gratitude for being the first country to recognize Afghanistan's independence in 1919.

69. Dagonet, *Les enfants de Kaboul,* 38, quoted in Pérennès, *Passion Kaboul,* 302.

70. This spiritual itinerary is described in Pérennès, *Passion Kaboul,* esp. 183–225.

71. I cannot but refer the reader to von Balthasar's *Epilogue,* 35. Christianity solves the enigma of "how a finite being can possess definitive value and ultimate dignity next to an all-being God (or Absolute)": out of love.

Whatever the case, the heroic charitable action of Serge de Beaure-cueil in Afghanistan, certainly inspired by the memories of his unhappy childhood, is stopped by the Soviet invasion of Afghanistan. In 1983 he is evacuated in a state of deep anguish. In France he will gradually recover his serenity. In 1988 he publishes a French translation of the *Munāğāt* ("Dia-logues with God"), Anṣārī's masterpiece.[72] After a last journey to the IDEO in Cairo at the end of 2003, he passed away in 2005.

> This man, longtime torn apart, ends his journey in striking se-renity and peace.[73]

Its Relevance for Today

The translation that has occupied our attention in these pages is certainly relevant for the history of the attempts for an Arabic inculturation of the biblical message. Yet, I am convinced that its importance largely exceeds this "archaeological" remembrance.

A foundational document of the Pontifical Council for Interreligious Dialogue, *The Attitude of the Catholic Church towards the Followers of Other Religious Traditions* (1984), states that dialogue can take different forms, one of which is dialogue of religious experience and spirituality (35, see also *Dialogue and Proclamation*, 42). But for an Islamic–Christian exchange at the spiritual level to take place, the issue of Scriptures is particularly chal-lenging.[74] On the one hand, the relation of the Qur'an to the biblical uni-verse is a thorny issue for Christian theology; on the other hand, Muslims, while theoretically acknowledging some previous Scriptures—basically Torah, Psalms and the Gospel—in practice do not accept them because they consider them as altered. The exact extent of the alleged alteration (*taḥrīf*) is disputed and positions range from a complete rejection of the Jewish–Christian Bible to a partial acceptance, which seems more in line with the Qur'anic passages devoted to the subject (Q 5:13 for instance). While most commentators consider the alteration to have occurred at the textual level, some influential voices believe that *taḥrīf* is essentially a matter of wrong exegesis from the Christian side.[75] At any rate, the doctrine of *taḥrīf* is a major stumbling block in dialogue and a central element of what I propose to call "the apologetic blockade" which has been obscuring (and continues

72. Anṣārî, *Cris du cœur munâjât*.

73. Pérennès, *Passion Kaboul*, 301.

74. It was discussed in GRIC, *Ces Écritures qui nous questionnent*.

75. On this subject, see Casper and Gaudeul, "Textes de la tradition."

to obscure) the constitutive relation between the Qur'an and the Jewish–Christian Bible.[76]

And yet there is *one exception*, one instance in which the Qur'an explicitly quotes a biblical passage, which therefore Muslims cannot hold as altered. It is Q 21:105: "For We have written in the Psalms, after the Remembrance, 'The earth shall be the inheritance of my righteous servants.'" The biblical passage quoted is Ps 37:29: "The righteous shall inherit the land / and live in it forever." And that is not all: the same verse is also rephrased in the Sermon on the Mount: "Blessed are the meek, for they will inherit the earth" (Matt 5:5).

The particular status of this biblical verse in Islam, as the only assured non-altered passage, did not escape al-Sadeq Hussein and de Beaurecueil, who aptly adopted the Qur'anic terms in their translation of the passage.[77] More broadly, however, this singular textual coincidence could pave the way to a reconsideration of the whole Psalter, which is among the biblical books closer to the Islamic Scripture. In the first place, the Psalter is a *corpus* of texts, exactly as the Qur'an. Secondly, it does not recount a story, but makes allusions to many and can only be understood through recourse to other biblical books. Thirdly, in its style it is essentially homiletic and many of the literary genera it employs are found also in the Qur'an. Lastly, its theology, though not identical with the Qur'anic vision, is largely non-concurrent with it. One can therefore conclude that the Psalter is the portion of Scripture, if any, more likely to receive attention in shared Islamic–Christian meditations. And perhaps even in shared prayers, under special circumstances and with prepared audiences, since Islam and Christianity, though wary of the risks of verbal expression, are not all about negative theology and in the long run we cannot imagine Muslim–Christian encounters to remain within the limits of a silent meditation in front of the mystery of God's majesty.

In this hypothesis, the existence of an Arabic translation of the Psalms done by a Muslim and bearing an ecclesial imprimatur is certainly not a minor fact. It is worth shaking the dust off of it. But also in the assumption of a persistent Muslim suspicion towards the Bible, Ps 37:29 is the only verse

76. This subject is particularly explored by Gabriel Said Reynolds in his works, including the most recent Reynold, *Qur'ān and the Bible.*

77. The Qur'anic quotation says *(anna) al-arḍa yariṯuhā 'ibādī aṣ-ṣāliḥūn*. Al-Sadeq Hussein and de Beaurecueil's translation has *ammā aṣ-ṣāliḥūn, fa-l-arḍa yariṯūn*. While the lexical items are the same, the word order is different, but it must be remembered that the Qur'anic quotation is imbedded in an *anna* phrase, followed necessarily by a noun. In both renderings, the focus is split between *al-arḍ* (the land) and *aṣ-ṣāliḥūn* (the righteous).

we have to build on a shared scriptural spirituality. It is a tiny basis, and yet an existent one. And what is more, it is eschatological in its scope.

Bibliography

Al-Sadeq Hussein, Mohammad [aṣ-Ṣādiq Ḥusayn, Muḥammad]. "Les psaumes 1 à 25 traduits en arabe." *MIDEO* 5 (1958) 1–46.

———. "Les paumes 26 à 50 traduits en arabe." *MIDEO* 6 (1959–61) 1–54.

———. "Quinze psaumes traduits en arabe." *MIDEO* 4 (1957) 1–26.

———. *Sifr al-Mazāmīr*. Naqalahu ilā al-ʿarabiyya Muḥammad aṣ-Ṣādiq Ḥusayn bi-l-ištirāk maʿ al-ab S. dī Būrakiyy [de Beaurecueil] ad-Dūminikī. al-Qāhira: Dār as-Salām, 1961.

Anawati, Georges Chehata. "Al-Ḥiwār al-aḫīr." In vol. 2 of *Abūnā Qanawātī. Mišwār al-ʿumr*, edited by Rīǧīs Mūrilūn [Régis Morelon] and Hānī Labīb, 159–211. al-Qāhira: IDEO—al-Markaz al-ʿarabī li-ṣ-ṣaḥāfa, 1998.

———. *L'ultimo dialogo. La mia vita incontro all'Islam*. Italian, translated by Martino Diez. Venezia: Marcianum, 2010.

———. "Jésus et ses juges, d'après la *Cité inique* du Dr. Kāmel Hussein." *MIDEO* 2 (1955) 71–134.

Anṣârî, Khwâdjâ ʿAbd Allâh. *Cris du cœur* munâjât. *Présentation et traduction du persan de Serge de Laugier de Beaurecueil*. With parallel Persian text. 2nd ed. Paris: Cerf, 2010.

Avon, Dominique. *Les Frères prêcheurs en Orient. Les dominicains du Caire (années 1910–années 1960)*. Paris: Cerf, 2005.

Arberry, Arthur John. *The Koran Interpreted*. Oxford: Oxford University Press, 1964.

Balthasar, Hans Urs von. *Epilog*. German. Trier: Johannes Verlag Einsiedeln, 1987.

———. *Epilogue*. Translated by Edward T. Oakes. San Francisco: Ignatius, 2004.

Beaurecueil, Serge de. "Un problème crucial: la langue liturgique." *Les Cahiers coptes* 4 (1953) 9–11.

Biblia Arabica. "Biblia Arabica: The Bible in Arabic among Jews, Christians, and Muslims." https://biblia-arabica.com.

Briggman, Anthony. *Irenaeus of Lyons and the Theology of the Holy Spirit*. Oxford Early Christian Studies. Oxford: Oxford University Press, 1992.

Caspar, Robert, and Gaudeul, Jean-Marie. "Textes de la tradition musulmane concernant le *taḥrīf* (falsification)." *Islamochristiana* 6 (1980) 61–104.

Cuypers, Michel. *The Banquet: A Reading of the Fifth sura of the Qur'an*. Miami: Convivium Press, 2009.

———. *Le Festin, Une lecture de la sourate al-Mâ'ida*. French. Paris: Lethielleux, 2007.

Diez, Martino. *Introduzione alla lingua araba. Origini storia e attualità. Nuova edizione*. Milano: Vita e Pensiero, 2018.

Gilliot, Claude, and Larcher, Pierre. "Language and Style of the Qur'ān." In *Encyclopaedia of the Qur'ān*, edited by Jane Dammen McAuliffe III, 109–35. Leiden: Brill, 2003.

Grafton, David D. *The contested origins of the 1865 Arabic Bible*. Leiden: Brill, 2015.

GRIC (Groupe de Recherches Islamo-Chrétien). *Ces Écritures qui nous questionnent. La Bible & le Coran*. Paris: Le Centurion, 1987.

Griffith, Sidney H. *The Bible in Arabic. The Scriptures of the "People of the Book" in the Language of Islam*. Princeton: Princeton University Press, 2013.

Hourani, Albert. *Arabic Thought in the Liberal Age 1798–1939*. 2nd ed. Cambridge: Cambridge University Press 1983.

Hussein, Taha [Ḥusayn, Ṭāhā]. *Al-Ayyām. Al-Aġzā' aṭ-ṭalāṯa*. Al-Qāhira. Dār al-Maʿārif, 1999.

———. *The Days. His Autobiography in Three Parts*. Translated by Evelyn H. Paxton, et al. Cairo: American University in Cairo, 1997.

Ibn Ǧinnī, Abū l-Fatḥ ʿUṯmān. *Al-Ḥaṣā'is*. Edited by Muḥammad ʿAlī an-Naǧǧār. al-Qāhira: Dār al-Kutub al-Miṣriyya, 1952–56.

Kamel Hussein, Muhammad [Kāmil Ḥusayn, Muḥammad]. *City of Wrong. A Friday in Jerusalem*. Translated from the Arabic with an Introduction by Kenneth Cragg. Oxford: Oneworld, 1994.

———. *Qarya ẓālima*. al-Qāhira: Maṭbaʿat Miṣr, 1954.

Kassir, Samir [Qaṣīr, Samīr]. *Considérations sur le malheur arabe*. Arles: Sindbad—Actes Sud, 2004.

———. *Syntaxe de l'arabe classique*. Aix-en-Provence: Publications de l'Université de Provence (PUP), 2017.

———. *Taʾammulāt fī šiqāʾ al-ʿarab*. Bayrūt: Dār an-Nahār, 2005.

Khoronfish, Joseph. "College Saint-Joseph." http://www.csjkhoronfish.org/fr.

Massignon, Louis. *Les trois prières d'Abraham*. Paris: Cerf, 1997.

Meynet, Roland. *Rhetorical Analysis. An Introduction to Biblical Rhetoric*. Sheffield: Sheffield Academic Press, 1998.

Miquel, André. "A Discreet Invitation to Enter the 'Secret Garden.'" *Oasis* 19 (2014) 89–94.

Osseïrane, Afif [ʿUsīrān, ʿAfīf]. *Mazāmīr Dāwūd an-nabī. Tarǧama ǧadīda ʿan i n-naṣṣ al-aṣlī istinādan li-d-dirāsāt al-ḥadīṯa bi-qalam ʿAfīf ʿUsīrān*. 1960. Reprint, Bayrūt: Dar El Machreq, 2008.

———. "The Psalms according to the translation of Afif Asairan." Arabic. http://psalmsosseiran.blogspot.com.

Pérennès, Jean-Jacques. "Bibliographie de Serge de Beaurecueil." *MIDEO* 27 (2008) 7–14.

———. *Georges Anawati (1905–1994), un chrétien égyptien devant le mystère de l'Islam*. Paris: Cerf, 2008.

———. *Le père Antonin Jaussen, OP. (1871–1962). Une passion pour l'Orient musulman*. Préface de Henry Laurens. Paris: Cerf, 2012.

———. "Looking until the end for the path to Islam." *Oasis* 10 (2009) 104–7.

———. "The Man who changed our way of looking at Islam." *Oasis* 9 (2009) 94–100.

———. *Passion Kaboul. Le père Serge de Beaurecueil*. Paris: Cerf, 2014.

Prades López, Javier María. "Christianity and the Need for Witnesses." *Oasis* 7 (2008) 12–16.

Reynolds, Gabriel Said. *The Qurʾān and the Bible*. New Haven, CT: Yale University Press, 2018.

Shahid, Irfan. "The Problem of an Arabic Bible and Liturgy in Pre-Islamic Times." In *Byzantium and the Arabs II (In the Fourth Century)*, 435–443. Washington: Dumbarton Oaks, 1984.

———. "The Problem of an Arabic Bible and Liturgy in Pre-Islamic Times." In *Byzantium and the Arabs III (In the Fifth Century)*, 422–429. Washington: Dumbarton Oaks, 1989.

Violet, Bruno. "Ein zweisprachiges Psalmfragment aus Damascus." *Orientalische Literaturzeitung* 4 (1901) 384–403, 425–441, 475–488.

Vollandt, Ronny. "The *Status Quaestionis* of Research of the Arabic Bible." In *Semitic Linguistics and Manuscripts: A Liber Discipulorum in Honour of Professor Geoffrey Khan*, edited by Nadia Vidro, et al., 442–67. Uppsala: Uppsala Universitet, 2018.B

Dialogues between Hinduism, Buddhism, and Christianity

Madhva *Aetate*

—Deepak Sarma

> Thus in Hinduism, men contemplate the divine mystery and
> express it through an inexhaustible abundance of myths and
> through searching philosophical inquiry. They seek freedom
> from the anguish of our human condition either through asceti-
> cal practices or profound meditation or a flight to God with love
> and trust.[1]

In Our Time

Nostra aetate is a magnificent articulation of a call for a kind of interreligious dialogue, albeit one-sided. It is also, at the same time, a proposal
of how to deal with the problems of religious diversity, namely employing a
religious inclusivism. Its breadth and intention require, perhaps demand, a
parallel response from credentialed spokespeople of the religious traditions
addressed therein. In this connection, this short essay is an attempt at offering a critical response from a particular Hindu perspective.

To this end, I will examine the intent of *Nostra aetate* from a critical and post-colonial perspective. I then will address the difficult issue of
reification and generalization that perhaps applies to many religious traditions but is exemplified by Hinduism. Next, I look at *Nostra aetate* from the
perspective of the Madhva school of Vedanta, a philosophical/ theological
community that continues to thrive in India today, having first developed
in the thirteenth and fourteenth centuries. Finally, I will problematize the
very act of engaging in an interreligious dialogue, especially as it occurs
in dialogues with specific kinds of Hindu communities, namely those that

1. *Nostra aetate*, 2.

enforce an insider-epistemology and that are, what I call, closed exclusive commentarial religions.

In this paper, I thus argue that *Nostra aetate* is only superficially beneficial to non-Catholics, and in this case, Hindus, and that it is rather a theological justification for continued exploitation and perhaps, well-intentioned, condescension.

In Whose Time?

Nostra aetate at first glance appears to acknowledge the value and partial truth of the doctrines of other religious traditions. While the affirmation of the existence and worth of these other, non-Catholic religious traditions is pleasant, it is, of course, based on a truth value system that, not surprisingly, places Catholicism at the very top of an epistemic hierarchy. To use terminology first coined by Paul Griffiths, Catholicism offers an open "inclusivism."[2] While such a position acknowledges that there is some truth to be found in alien religious traditions (traditions that are not the home tradition), truth is to be found entirely in the home tradition.

From the perspective of the philosophy of religions, such a position addresses the diversity of religious beliefs by subsuming all possibilities under one belief system, namely the one offered by the home religion. There are many complexities that arise from this if one even considers that truth, albeit limited or partial, can exist outside of the Catholic fold. Since these and related issues are internal to Catholicism, I will only mention them here rather than examine it in any more detail.

Philosophical complexities aside, there are also problems with *Nostra aetate* and all that it encompasses if one views it from a post-colonial perspective. Consider that the invention and construction of the term "religion" and its use as a taxonomic (i.e., classificatory) device is a product of imperialism (extending a country's power through military and economic force) and colonization (when a country sends a group of its citizens to another country and establishes political control over it).[3] The same complexity, of course, is implied with "religious truth." Postcolonial religion and the postcolonial study of religion both require an awareness and sensitivity to the invention, creation, and implementation of all humanly constructed categories (with a specific focus on religion, religions, and religious communities); an acceptance of their creation; and implementation as inextricably bound

2. Griffiths, *Problems of Religious Diversity*, xv.
3. See Sarma, "Postcolonial Religion."

to oppression, exploitation, and other hegemonic (when a group or country dominates and is dominant over another) agendas and social hierarchies.[4]

Colonial-based theories of religion have placed Christianity at the top of an imaginary and invented hierarchy and Catholic open inclusivism exemplifies this. The religion of the colonizers, Christianity most broadly, and Catholicism in some specific cases, was conceived as an expression and manifestation of their inherent, and perhaps even divinely ordained, superiority. This paradigm was upheld as a template, as the comparative benchmark. The degree to which a religious tradition approximated this Christian paradigm was reflected in its stature in the hierarchy. In this way, religious beliefs are linked to race and ethnicity. It is easy to see *Nostra aetate* as an exemplar of colonialism and Christian imperialism.

Types of Hinduism that more closely resemble Christianity have been deemed more civilized, whereas those that differ the most are believed to be indicative of a barbaric Indian race, or, in some cases, a wondrous mystical "eastern" tradition.[5] Injunctions against idolatry (e.g., Exod 20:3) are used to justify the denigration of certain kinds of Hindu worship. Thus, the superiority of Christianity, Caucasians, and the North American and European civilizations could be defined in contrast to the inferior colonized others. Such beliefs justify the open inclusivism as put forth in *Nostra aetate*.

Postcolonial methodologies and perspectives are bound together by a fundamental epistemological presupposition—namely, that all taxonomies and their constituents are humanly constructed and that these knowledge systems were used, and continue to be used, to colonize; to subordinate colonized groups; and to justify subjugation, colonialism, and imperialism. In this sense I am employing, to the best of my abilities, a post-colonial method here.

It is also presupposed that since their invention and implementation, these taxonomies and categories continue to perfume, pervade, and poison their current and contemporary usages. That is, even if the times have changed, the colonial or oppressive stench and flavor of such taxonomies remains. In this postcolonial view, terminology cannot be extricated from its historical past. Viewing *Nostra aetate* from this perspective is neither altogether favorable nor pleasant. It thus exemplifies two kinds of imperialism: "western" imperialism and Christian theological imperialism.

4. I am reliant upon a number of scholars for the materials in this section. These are Chidester, *Empire of Religion*; Masuzawa, *Invention of World Religions*; Nongbri, *Before Religion*.

5. See King, *Orientalism and Religion*.

Hinduism(s)?

There are a wide variety of traditions that have been deemed "Hindu," since the term was used by Christian missionaries and scholars in the nineteenth century and by western academics since the early twentieth century. The term "Hindu," in fact, encompasses so many practices and beliefs that it has become somewhat ambiguous, if not vacuous.[6] This ambiguity is present in the characterization offered in *Nostra aetate*. That is:

> Thus in Hinduism, men contemplate the divine mystery and express it through an inexhaustible abundance of myths and through searching philosophical inquiry. They seek freedom from the anguish of our human condition either through ascetical practices or profound meditation or a flight to God with love and trust.[7]

The language of *Nostra aetate* here, despite being all-inclusive, is more obscuring than it is useful. Claiming that Hinduism offers an inexhaustible abundance of myths suggests that Hinduism has an essential ambiguity and that its canon is not restricted. From this characterization it would seem as if Hinduism has no systematized or organized beliefs and practices.

There are traditions of Hinduism, such as Advaita Vedanta and Caitanya Vaisnavism,[8] that are explicit about their open inclusiveness in the same way as Catholicism. These traditions anticipate fruitful dialogues with members of other traditions and are proactively proselytizing. Their voice is important though uninteresting, given that it parallels *Nostra aetate*. They both offer Hindu voices and they make their doctrines available to anyone interested and encourage dialogue with members of other religious traditions. From both perspectives *Nostra aetate* is a lovely stepping stone towards more mutual (and self-) understanding.

For this reason, it is more valuable to look at *Nostra aetate* from the perspective of traditions of Hinduism that are neither open-inclusive, nor proselytizing. What, then, would other schools of Hinduism think of *Nostra aetate*? What happens, for example, when a tradition, Hindu or otherwise, does not allow outsiders to access or learn their doctrine, and does not ever seek interreligious dialogue? That is, *Nostra aetate* presupposes an ability to talk with or otherwise engage the texts and doctrines of other religious

---

6. For more on the range and use of the term "Hindu," see Sarma, "Hindu Leaders in North America?"

7. *Nostra aetate*, 2.

8. See, for example, Ganeri, "Catholic Encounter with Hindus"; Das, "Vaishnava Response."

traditions. But what if the potential interlocutors are not interested in having or being a part of a dialogue, or if they take great precautions to ensure that outsiders are unable to access doctrines? What happens when the communities mentioned in *Nostra aetate* do not engage or even foster dialogue with members of other religious traditions?

As I will show, the Madhva tradition of Vedanta, is founded on an insider-epistemology that does not allow outsiders access to their doctrines. This prevents Catholics from ever engaging in meaningful dialogues with Madhva adherents. This a very different reaction to the sentiment posited in *Nostra aetate* indeed.

Madhva Vedanta: Historical Context

Madhvacarya (1238–1317 CE) was born of Sivalli Brahmin parents in the village of Pajakaksetra near modern day Udupi in the Tulunadu area of southern Karnataka. Southern Karnataka was filled with a diversity of theologies and people, making it an exciting place within which to develop a new religious tradition. The majority of traditions in the area were far outside of the exclusive commentarial framework within which is found Madhva Vedanta.[9] This pluralistic environment had a significant effect on Madhvacarya. His innovations included strategies for maintaining religious identity as well as ways to maintain the existing social system that he felt was being threatened. Madhvacarya's school of Vedanta is, in part, a reaction, against the multiplicity of theologies and social structures in thirteenth and fourteenth-century Karnataka. It is likely that the closed inclusivism that Madhvacarya professed is a result of this environment.

Madhva Vedanta is found within a commentarial framework, which serves as the basis for discerning the truth and value of other religions. This framework is shared by all of the schools of Vedanta and centers around a body of texts known as the *Vedas*. According to the Madhva perspective, reflection that occurs outside of this framework is valuable only insofar as it sharpens the debate skills of Madhvas and concurrently increases the epistemic confidence that Madhvas have in the truth of their own religion.[10]

To explain, I will first characterize "commentarial frameworks" and "exclusive commentarial frameworks." I will then place Madhva Vedanta within these frameworks. My intention is to show that, for Madhvas, religions outside of the Vedanta commentarial fold have no truth whatsoever

9. More below on "commentarial frameworks."

10. For more on "epistemic confidence," see Griffiths, *Problems of Religious Diversity*.

and are valued only as living examples of proverbial "straw men" for Madhva students. Theological/ philosophical conversations with anyone outside of the framework is thus irrelevant, making it futile for Catholics seeking dialogue. The Madhva tradition, moreover, does not allow access to its doctrines, thereby making it off-limits to the kinds of study advocated in *Nostra aetate*.

Commentarial Frameworks

Religions that operate within a commentarial framework (commentarial religions) must have a body of texts that are the objects of commentary and that serve as their epistemic foundation. I will refer to these as the "root texts." Root texts may be preserved and disseminated orally or textually. These religions have virtuoso readers of the root texts whose commentaries are deemed epistemologically authoritative.[11] Their authority derives from criteria that are likely to be found in the root texts. The doctrines, teachings, and practices of religions outside of the framework of a commentarial religion (I will refer to these as alien religions)[12] could be relevant only so far as they assist (or detract from) the commentaries offered by virtuoso readers. Similarly, dialogue with members of alien religions could be valuable if it assists with readings of the root texts, if it is prescribed by the root texts themselves, if it confirms the beliefs of those of the home religion,[13] or if its content is merely descriptive of, or informative about, the home religion. It is possible that there are intrareligious disputes about the accuracy of readings. In such cases, intrareligious dialogues are between disputing virtuoso readers, who are operating within the same framework despite their disagreement. Typically, there are methods for adjudicating disputes that are found in the root texts of commentarial religions.

Insider-epistemologies and Commentary

Among religions that operate within a commentarial framework, there are religions whose root texts and commentaries are not made available to outsiders. These religions operate within an exclusive commentarial

11. For more on "virtuoso readers," see Griffiths, *Religious Reading*; Sarma, *Epistemology*.

12. I am reliant upon Griffiths's formulation of "alien" religions as found in Griffiths, *Problem of Religious Diversity*.

13. I am reliant upon Griffiths's formulation of "home" religions as found in Griffiths, *Problem of Religious Diversity*.

framework. They may limit access to books if the root texts are in written format or they may restrict attendance to oral recitations of root texts and subsequent oral commentaries offered by virtuosos if the root texts are preserved and disseminated orally. Some may allow outsiders to convert and, therefore, to obtain access to these root texts and commentaries. These are open exclusive commentarial religions. The ensuing dialogue that might occur between the new convert and a virtuoso would, of course, be an intra-religious dialogue and not an interreligious one.

There are religions that do not permit conversion and thus severely limit access to their root texts and commentaries. These are closed exclusive commentarial religions. An informed interreligious dialogue with the virtuosos of such religions becomes impossible or, if it does occur, it must be only on a superficial level. These religions are founded on highly restrictive insider-epistemologies. It is possible that members of these religions have conversations with outsiders, in which they offer simple accounts of their doctrines or merely correct misunderstandings. It is also possible that members may learn about alien religions for the purpose of finding flaws in them and, consequently, in confirming the truth of their own. This learning could occur in the context of dialogues or via texts. The value of the doctrines of alien religions, then, is merely to verify the truth of the doctrines, teachings, and practices put forth by the home religion. Such dialogues, unlikely as they are to occur, should not concern the teaching of the home religion.

The Madhva School of Vedanta is a closed exclusive commentarial religion that does not permit outsiders to access root texts and also does not permit conversion. It also places little importance on the value of alien religions, other than the pedagogical importance for students of finding their internal flaws. I will first offer a brief characterization of the school of Vedanta. I will then turn to Madhva Vedanta. After contextualizing historically, I will examine the rules that it enforces to maintain the secrecy of its root texts and to create a closed exclusive commentarial framework. This Hindu tradition, I will show, establishes strict boundaries and obstacles that prevent the implementation of the endeavors enjoined by *Nostra aetate*.

Vedanta

Madhva Vedanta identifies itself as a school of Vedanta. Its predecessors include the aforementioned Advaita (non-dualism) School, founded by Sankaracarya, in the eighth century CE, and the Visistadvaita (qualified non-dualism) School, founded by Ramanujacarya in the eleventh century CE.

Leaving aside their widely differing epistemologies and ontologies, the schools share similar core root texts. In fact, the term *vedanta*, a determinative compound (*tatpurusa*) comprised of the two terms, *veda* and *anta*, means "the culminating sections of the *Vedas.*" That Vedanta is named after this body of texts marks their importance and centrality they give to commentary. These texts are the *Vedas*, of which there are four, namely the *Rg*, *Yajur*, *Sama*, and *Atharva Vedas*. Each *Veda* can be further subdivided into the *Samhitas*, *Brahmanas*, the *Aranyakas*, and the *Upanisads*. The *Vedas* are believed to be revealed root texts (*sruti*), without human origin (*apauruseya*) and are self-valid (*svatah-pramana*). For this reason they are held to be eternal (*nitya*) and free from defects (*nirdosa*). The schools of Vedanta were not the only ones to hold the *Vedas* in such high esteem and grant them unquestioned epistemic authority. Their most important predecessor was the Mimamsa School (Jaimini composed the *Mimamsa Sutras* in circa 25 CE), which devoted the entirety of its intellectual efforts to interpreting the ritual injunctions prescribed in the *Vedas*. Much of the hermeneutic foundations of Vedanta, in fact, can be found in Mimamsa texts. The insider-epistemology that is shared by all of the schools of Vedanta also relied heavily on the writings of Mimamsa, as well as thinkers like Sabara (400 CE) and his commentators. For these reasons, Vedanta is sometimes known as Uttara Mimamsa ("Later Investigation").

Though the schools of Vedanta include the *Vedas* in their canon, each expanded its boundaries to include additional texts. Leaving aside these supplements to the canon, the *Vedas* are the primary root texts for the schools of Vedanta and are the critical objects of commentary. Above and beyond the *Vedas*, all of the schools also include the *Brahma Sutras* as a root text. The *Brahma Sutras*, composed by Badarayana (also known as Vyasa) in the fifth century CE, is regarded as a summary of the teachings of the *Vedas*, specifically the *Upanisads*, and, indirectly, an explanation of how to obtain liberation (*moksa*). In the introduction to his commentary (*bhasya*) on it, Madhvacarya explains, "He, namely Vyasa, composed the *Brahma Sutras* for the sake of the ascertaining the meaning of the *Vedas*."[14] The text is four chapters long and is comprised of 564 pithy aphorisms (*sutras*). Its brevity makes it difficult to read without the commentaries produced by the founders of each of the schools of Vedanta and the multiple sub-commentaries produced by subsequent thinkers. It is likely that the aphorisms were merely mnemonic devices used for pedagogical purposes. Whatever the reasons, the elusive nature of the *Brahma Sutras* lends itself to concealment, limits

---

14. Madhvacarya, *Brahma Sutra Bhasya*, 1.1.1. All translations are mine.

the extent to which alien religious adherents can speak with Madhvas, and is an important component in their exclusive commentarial framework.

The *Vedas* and *Brahma Sutras* were interpreted in conflicting ways by each school, and each has different theories about the nature of the liberated state and how it can be achieved. Training in Vedanta centered on close studies of these root texts, the production of new commentaries, and the careful study of old ones, where all of these activities were conducted in the confines of monasteries (*mathas*) and in other traditional teaching environments such as the residences of teachers (*gurukulas*). The importance that the schools of Vedanta gave (and still give) to commentary and commentarial activities are reminiscent of their counterparts among the scholastics in medieval Christianity.

The Madhva Closed Exclusive Commentarial Framework

As already mentioned, the significant difference between the Vedanta commentarial tradition and those of medieval Christian scholastics, is that the schools of Vedanta gave access to the root texts and commentaries only to male Brahmins. The schools of Vedanta thus operate within a closed exclusive commentarial framework. According to Madhvacarya, "Not everyone possesses the eligibility (*adhikara*)" for acquiring knowledge of the Supreme Being (*brahman*) and for obtaining release (*moksa*) from the cycle of birth and rebirth.[15] Not every enduring self (*jiva*) has full access to Madhva root texts, the source of the knowledge that is efficacious for learning about the nature of the Supreme Being, for obtaining release, and for learning the intricacies of Madhva dialectics. The Madhva insider-epistemology hinged on this restriction of access to the root texts and made possible their exclusive commentarial framework.

Madhvacarya directly addresses eligibility requirements in his gloss of the first complete word (*pada*), of the first decree (*sutra*), of the *Brahma Sutras* of Badarayana: "Then, therefore, the inquiry into *brahman*" (*athato brahmajijñasa*). The term "then" (*atha*) glosses the sequence of eligibility. The expanded passage reads "Therefore, after having met the requirements for eligibility, the inquiry into *brahman* is to be undertaken."[16] In his *Brahma Sutra Bhasya*, a commentary on the *Brahma Sutras*, Madhvacarya explicates the requirements for eligibility. He thereby establishes rules and

15. Madhvacarya, *Brahma Sutra Bhasya*, 3.4.10.

16. Madhvacarya, *Brahma Sutra Bhasya*, 1.1.1. The word "then" is used as an auspicious expression and for sequence of eligibility. The word "therefore" refers to the reason.

regulations as to who can and cannot become a virtuoso reader of Madhva root texts.[17]

Given the rich and complex ontology envisioned by Madhvacarya, he must determine the eligibility for a wide variety of sentient beings, both human and non-human. Not surprisingly, he restricts eligibility and, therefore, restricts training as a virtuoso reader to a select group of sentient beings based on gender and class (*varna*). In the human realm, initiated males of the highest three classes, the *brahmins, ksatriyas,* and *vaisyas,* also known as the twice-born (*dvijas*) have eligibility to access some texts and doctrines. Among them *brahmins* have the highest access. Only they can become virtuoso readers. Male members of lower classes and women from all classes only have limited access to summaries of Madhva doctrine conveyed orally by virtuoso readers. Their limited access does not allow them to join monasteries (*mathas*) to examine Madhva doctrine, and to obtain training as virtuoso religious readers. Only males *dvijas* who undergo the prescribed training in Madhva monasteries can become virtuosos. Thus, Madhva Vedanta is operating within a closed exclusive commentarial framework.

Madhva Vedanta also is founded upon a position of predestination. There are those qualified for release who can be liberated from suffering (*mukti-yogyas*) and those who cannot be liberated from suffering (*mukti-ayogyas*).[18] These sentient beings neither can be released from suffering, nor can they achieve liberation (*moksa*). They are further subdivided into those who are fit only for darkness (*tamo-yogyas*), and those who are eternally caught in the cycle of birth and rebirth (*nitya-samsarins,* literally, "those who remain in the journey").[19]

Who do the Madhva virtuosos speak to? Typically they speak and have spoken to others in the Vedanta commentarial fold and to other lay-Hindus, though not exclusively. Throughout history, there are numerous cases of virtuosos from the Madhva tradition engaging with the textual depiction and refutation of representations of doctrines[20] of Buddhist and Jain scholars, as well as debating with their members, though neither Buddhists nor Jains are included in the Vedanta commentarial framework.[21] So why does a tradition

---

17. For more on these virtuoso readers in Madhva Vedanta, known in the tradition as *apta-gurus,* see Sarma, *Exclusivist Strategies in Madhva Vedanta.*

18. Madhvacarya, *Tattvasamkhyana,* 5.

19. Madhvacarya, *Tattvasamkhyana,* 5.

20. Thanks to Paul J. Griffiths for this language.

21. See Sarma, *Exclusivist Strategies in Madhva Vedanta.*

that operates within an exclusive commentarial framework appear to debate with religious aliens or depict and refute representations of their doctrines?

Debate with Heretical Religions

If a religion prepares its adherents to debate with members of alien religions then it would seem that conversion of outsiders is a possibility. Depending on the topics of the debate, access to relevant doctrines may also be permitted to the debaters, regardless of class, caste, gender, etc. There are several places in Madhvacarya's corpus where he addresses issues of debate and argues against doctrines of alien religions that are outside of their commentarial framework. This interest in debate with religions outside of the commentarial framework must be explained given that they are within an exclusive commentarial framework. Why is there an interest in debating with outsiders? Why, for example, did Madhvacarya examine Buddhism and why did he summarize debates with them in his texts? What was the purpose of critically examining the doctrines of religions outside of the commentarial framework of Vedanta?

To approach these questions, I examine two locations in the Madhva corpus where such matters are discussed. First, I examine Madhvacarya's *Vadalaksana*, a text devoted to the rules and regulations surrounding debate. Then I examine several passages in Madhvacarya's *Anuvyakhyana* in connection with *Brahma Sutra* 2.1, known as *Samayavirodha*, the contradictions in (other) doctrines. Finally, I speculate as to why there are accounts in Madhvacarya's hagiography, the *Madhvavijaya*, of debate with Buddhists and other outsiders. Though this hagiographic text is not composed by Madhvacarya, it nonetheless may contain important information about the actual, rather than the ideal, community that must be addressed.

The Vadalaksana

The *Vadalaksana*, also known as the *Kathalaksana*, is a brief text in which Madhvacarya sets out the proper types of debate in which devotees can engage. Madhvacarya lists three types of appropriate debating methods. These are *vada*, *jalpa*, and *vitanda*.[22] Although this treatise on polemics is useful as a dialectical handbook for adherents who wish to debate, it does

---

22. Madhvacarya, *Vadalaksana*, 2, in *Dasaprakaranani*. The three-fold (debating methods) are *vada*, *jalpa*, and *vitanda*. *Vada* is a debate whose purpose is the pursuit of truth. *Jalpa* is a debate whose purpose is to bring fame and glory to the competitive victor. More on *vitanda* below.

not contain any explicit summaries of restrictions regarding debate with outsiders, with those who do not have eligibility (*adhikari*) to read the root texts of Vedanta and, therefore, who may not be able to become virtuoso readers. That is, Madhvacarya states the rules and regulations regarding the practice of debate but does not address any restrictions in connection with the eligibility and qualifications of each of the participants of the debate.

Several conclusions may be drawn from this. First, it may be that there are no restrictions regarding who can and who cannot participate in debate. Second, it may be that Madhvacarya has assumed that all participants have eligibility and are legitimate (and virtuoso) religious readers. In this case, there would be no need to address the eligibility and literacy of the participants. Though the first conclusion is possible, the second clearly is more likely: one must have familiarity with the Vedas and similarly restricted texts to argue with the Madhva about his own doctrines. Arguing with a Madhva about his doctrine presumes knowledge of the root texts. These root texts, as I have shown above, are restricted. If a debate were to take place between a Madhva and an outsider (*mleccha*) it would have to be one-sided as the outsider/ religious alien would not be able to partake in arguments about the proper interpretation of passages. It is thus reasonable to conclude that debate with Madhvas about Madhva doctrine can only be undertaken by those who are (or can become) skilled readers of Madhva doctrine. That is, only intrareligious dialogue is possible. Dialogue with a Madhva is as (if not more) one-sided that the envisioned dialogue with a Catholic!

Third, it also is reasonable to conclude that these debating rules could be employed by Madhvas when they argued *via reductio* against the doctrines of other schools. This way Madhvas can refute rival positions and, at the same time, need not reveal their own doctrine. To this end, Madhvacarya characterizes the *vitanda* style of argument:

> The *vitanda* argument is (characterized) for the sake of truth (when the argument is) with another (wicked opponent). The Real is hidden in this (argument style).[23]

This style is not unusual in the history of debate among South Asian religions. Nevertheless, this passage indicates that it was part and parcel of Madhva debate. It moreover provides a reasonable explanation for the occurrence of Madhva debates with debaters who are not skilled readers of Madhva texts.

---

23. Madhvacarya, *Vadalaksana*, 3. (The word) "with another" (means) along with wicked (opponents).

Brahma Sutra 2.1, Samayavirodha: The Contradictions in (Other) Doctrines

The relevance of debate with other traditions is exemplified in the introduction to *Brahma Sutra* 2.1, known as *Samayavirodha*: the contradictions in (other) doctrines. The passages in Madhvacarya's *Anuvyakhyana*, a commentary on the *Brahma Sutras*, are introductions to this series of refutations of rival positions. They are the textual depictions and refutations of representations of the doctrines of rival schools. These rival schools are the Nyaya, Vaisesika, Samkhya, Yoga, Carvaka, Buddhism, Jainism, Saiva, and, finally, the Sakta schools. Madhvacarya first states reasons as to why these doctrines exist:

> The adherence to the knowledge regarding the falseness of the world is because of ignorance, because of the scarcity of correct understanding, because of the abundance of those who have little knowledge, (and) because of the ceaseless hatred for the highest Reality and for the knowledge of the Real.[24]

He next locates the upholders of these rival doctrines in his three-fold distinction of sentients (*jīvatraividhya*) and three-fold doctrine of predestination (*svarupatraividhya*):

> The doctrines are maintained because of the fitness of the endless impressions of many demons (*asuras*) due to their being caught by foolishness.[25]

The doctrines are kept alive by those who are predestined to do so. The phrase "endless impressions" refers to their predestined status. Having thus accounted for the existence of rival traditions in his cosmology, Madhvacarya states the importance of studying and refuting these traditions:

> Therefore, those who are suitable for that which is connected with the understanding of the Lord, (who are suitable) for correct understanding, who observe the (doctrines of the) sacred texts (*agamas*), they would always destroy the darkness (that is the ignorant).[26]

He further addresses the reason why these refutations are important:

24. Madhvacarya, *Anuvyakhyana*, 551–52.
25. Madhvacarya, *Anuvyakhyana*, 553.
26. Madhvacarya, *Anuvyakhyana*, 554; Jayatirtha, *Nyaya Sudha*, 3162.

> Therefore (Vyasa) the lord of knowledge composed the refuta-
> tions of each of the (rival) doctrines for (his) own devotees for
> the purpose of establishing a sharpened intellect.[27]

Given these portions of the introductory passages, it appears that examination and refutation of the doctrines of religious aliens is primarily for the
sake of having a correct understanding of one's own position and for increasing one's mental dexterity. Neither a correct understanding nor mental
dexterity are ends in and of themselves. Both contribute to obtaining proper
knowledge of the Lord, increasing one's skill as a religious reader, and eventually obtaining liberation (*moksa*).

If this is the case, then there is no need to reveal one's own position
even if one debates with a religious alien. One can argue *vitanda* style and
employ *reductio ad absurdum* methods, find fault with the doctrines of others, yet reveal nothing about one's own position. The intent, then, is not
to convert those who are most opposed to the Madhva position. Instead,
the intent is to reaffirm the truth of one's own position for oneself through
argument with outsiders. Conversion due to loss in a debate may indeed be
possible if the interlocutor is a twice-born (*dvija*) (or former *dvija*), eligible,
and therefore can become a skilled religious reader of Madhva Vedanta.

Research has not uncovered any instances in Madhva works of responses to critiques of Madhva doctrine by those outside of the Vedanta
commentarial framework. The responses that I have discovered refer to
criticisms made by Advaita and Viśistadvaita opponents. If there were responses to external critiques then this may indicate that Madhva thinkers
permit the possibility of outsiders, twice-borns and otherwise, to understand Madhva doctrines. However, I found no cases of this type of response.

Accounts in the Madhva Vijaya

Although Narayana Panditacarya's *Madhva Vijaya* is a hagiographic text
and often contains hyperbolical anecdotes, the descriptions of successful
debates against outsiders nevertheless need to be explained. The instances
when Panditacarya states that Madhvacarya debated with Buddhists,
among others, are too numerous to be documented here. How are they to
be understood, given the doctrines that restrict access to the root texts that
Madhvacarya has set down? It is not clear whether Madhvacarya argued via
the *vitanda* style, or if his interlocutors were only twice-borns (*dvijas*). This,
however, is unlikely since, according to the hagiography, he won a debate

---

27. Madhvacarya, *Anuvyakhyana*, 555.

against a Buddhist. Buddhisagara, a Buddhist, is mentioned as a disputant encountered by Madhvacarya in Panditacarya's *Madhva Vijaya*.[28] Panditacarya may be signaling the legitimacy of the debater and, consequently, the debate when he states that his interlocutor was a twice born. In his *Bhavaprakasika*, Panditacarya states:

> He whose name is Vadisimha, the twice-born, is a knower of the essence of the Vaisesika (system).[29]

It is also not clear if the debates were conducted in Sanskrit or if they occurred in vernacular languages. These debates, though related in a hagiographical text, may indicate that the actual Madhva community was less restrictive than the one envisioned by Madhvacarya.

Loopholes?

Careful (and skeptical) readers may be wondering if it were possible to read about Madhva doctrines on their own, or even in translation, and if this would give insight into Madhva Vedanta. Though these seem like easy loopholes, they are not.

Untranslatability

"Sanskrit can never be fully translated into any other language" is a fairly common answer given by many traditional teachers when asked if they were breaking eligibility rules when they taught or published translations of Sanskrit texts to those who were ineligible. The belief is that translations can never fully communicate the essence of the texts as they are found in the Sanskrit language. The impossibility of a full translation of Sanskrit thus protects the meaning of the texts from improper transmission. Readers, then, will be limited only to the abbreviated information that is given to them by insiders. The integrity of the root texts is partly maintained thus given that Sanskrit is posited to be untranslatable.

The view that there are languages that are untranslatable is not a widely accepted one. Such arguments are based on theories about the nature of languages itself and their individual uniqueness. They are also linked with theories that a language can be independent of the community that employs it. This belief is an underlying epistemic premise held by all of the

---

28. Panditacarya, *Madhva Vijaya*, 5.8.

29. Panditacarya, *Bhavaprakasika*, 5.8.

schools of Vedanta, namely that Sanskrit is a divine language that is an intrinsic component in the very framework of the universe. Madhvacarya, for example, held that the *Vedas* (and conjointly, the Sanskrit language) are eternal and that they were still not even created by Lord Visnu.[30] The *varnas* (phonemes) of the *Vedas* themselves, he reasoned, are eternal and without a creator.[31] For Madhvacarya Sanskrit was neither constructed by humans nor even by god(s). Such a position conflicts with ones that hold that there are linguistic universals such as syntactic and semantic categories that are found in all cultures, contexts, and so on, which are the basis for effective communication between otherwise disparate groups of people. The belief that Sanskrit is untranslatable is thus based on controversial beliefs and premises. Clearly it is not patently obvious that it is true. Are there other arguments that are dependent upon leaps of faith? Are there other justifications that make sense only to insiders?

Awaiting the Apocalypse

Another explanation that is sometimes offered by traditional teachers to explain why they can no longer enforce the restrictions is based on a belief that the current era is *kali-yuga*, a period of time when *dharma* (dutiful behavior) has collapsed. That the root texts can no longer be kept concealed exemplifies this destruction of ethics and the social order. This concept of time, also shared by Madhvacarya, is based on the *Puranas*. In them, the universe is characterized as proceeding through a cycle of four ages (*yugas*). These ages, namely *krta,* the first, *treta,* the second, *dvapara,* the third, and *kali,* the fourth age, are distinguished by the degree to which the sentient beings of the universe adhere to dutiful behavior (*dharma*). In *krta-yuga,* dutiful behavior is upheld, while in *kali-yuga,* it is ignored. In the introduction to his *Brahma Sutra Bhasya,* Madhvacarya cites a passage from the *Skanda Purana* that describes the degeneration of *dharma.*[32] According to this text, the *Brahma Sutras* themselves were composed when Brahma, Rudra and other deities requested Visnu's assistance during *dvapara-yuga.*[33] At the end of each *kali-yuga,* when the universe is chaotic and filled with *adharma* (unlawful activities), Visnu will return in his incarnation (*avatsra*) as Kalki who will destroy the universe and begin the cycle anew with the *krta-yuga.*

30. Madhvacarya, *Visnutattva(vi)nirnaya.*

31. Madhvacarya, *Visnutattva(vi)nirnaya.* The term "*varna*" has a broad semantic range that includes both "class" and "phoneme."

32. Madhvacarya, *Brahma Sutra Bhasya,* 0.

33. Madhvacarya, *Brahma Sutra Bhasya,* 0.

With this sense of impending doom and apocalypse, traditional scholars can justify their inability to uphold the Madhva insider-epistemology. They explain that they are merely breaking the rules because of the looming crisis of modernity and the complexity of a situation that is beyond their control in which all traditional rules have disintegrated. They are merely following dutiful behavior in the time of extremity (*apad-dharma*), preeminently exemplified in *kali-yuga*.

Though this loophole is mentioned in *Manava-dharmasastra* and other treatises on law, it is still not altogether clear whether a loosening of the rules governing access to the root texts is permissible, no matter the extremity of the circumstances. The appeal to the apocalypse may not be defensible. For example, Manu warns:

> A priest should never, even in extremity, forge Vedic or sexual bonds with those people who have not been purified.[34]

On other hand, he also offers a method to restore purity if one were to teach the ineligible:

> The error of sacrificing or teaching (despicable men) is dispelled by chanting (the *Veda*) and making offerings into the fire.[35]

Resorting to the *kali-yuga* hermeneutic may not be a convincing explanation after all, given the ambiguities in *Manava-dharmasastra*. Either way, traditional teachers rely upon it when seeking to give good reason for their activities.

These two explanations, the sacredness of Sanskrit and the *kali-yuga* qualification, serve to justify why teaching the root texts in translations and publishing them for mass consumption does not conflict with the restrictions. They also function to justify why, when the restrictions are broken, it is legitimate given the mitigating circumstances. Such an account, for example, permits insiders to teach outsiders to read Sanskrit. In addition to these, there are other kinds of defenses that allow insiders to maintain the insider-epistemology yet make formerly restricted texts easily accessible without requiring such leaps of faith. Such justifications are based simply on the mechanics of transmission.

---

34. *Manava-dharmasastra* 2.40. See *Laws of Manu*, 21.

35. *Manava-dharmasastra* 10.111. See *Laws of Manu*, 235.

The Madhva Pedagogical Context

The importance of the oral commentarial tradition and its use as a method for enforcing restrictions cannot be underestimated. Although the root texts may be available and outsiders may have learned to read Sanskrit, the sacred texts may be sufficiently vague such that they cannot be fully understood without the assistance of traditionally trained experts. Many of the root texts are no more than mnemonic devices for teachers whose oral commentaries are essential to decode them. It is true that the Madhva tradition has made all of the root texts somewhat available to the masses. It is also true that some people who obtain the root texts may not be eligible to access them yet have sufficient abilities in Sanskrit to be able to read them. But, in light of the importance of the oral commentary, reading alone does not automatically imply accurate understanding. Consider the following hypothetical situation: the proposition "You are not that" has been kept concealed since it was first conceived but has now been published on the front page of the *New York Times* and is available to all. Though the proposition certainly is readable, its content is ambiguous without a commentary that explains each of its components and their relationships with one another: Who is "you?," What is "that,?" and so on. Similarly, the Madhva root texts require oral commentary in order to be fully comprehensible.

One may argue that many of the oral commentaries of the Madhva tradition have already been published and that a "live" commentary is unnecessary. The commentaries, however, often require sub-commentaries themselves. Without the assistance of an expert in the Madhva tradition, complete understanding of the texts simply becomes impossible. One may wonder about who determines "completeness." Surely the evaluation can only be made by an insider, and one cannot know if the insider is telling the truth. The question of degrees becomes similarly problematic, for an outsider can only know that one's knowledge has increased but cannot know how near or far s/he is from complete knowledge of the Madhva root texts.

For these reasons, the mere publication of the root texts is insufficient for outsiders to become experts. This justification is not based on theological commitments to the ontology of Sanskrit or the inevitability of the apocalypse but is based on simple logistics: "We have complete knowledge and you cannot gain that simply by studying our root texts."

Madhva Aetate

How is *Nostra aetate* viewed from a Hindu perspective? It is viewed as a futile attempt at engaging in a one-sided dialogue. To show this I briefly summarized the components that make up the Madhva insider-epistemology. I offered a stipulative characterization of "commentarial frameworks" and "exclusive commentarial frameworks." I then placed Madhva Vedanta within these frameworks. I showed that for Madhvas, religions outside of the Vedanta commentarial fold have no truth whatsoever and are valued only as living examples of proverbial "straw men" for Madhva students. I showed that there is very little of value in the doctrines, teachings, and practices of alien religions when placed in the particular religious framework within which Madhva Vedanta functions. I showed that Madhvas would not partake in dialogues with Catholics. I showed that any attempt to bypass the Madhva restrictions would not be fruitful. I thus showed that Madhvas would not facilitate a Catholic's desire to follow the injunctions enshrined in *Nostra aetate*.

More broadly *Nostra aetate* is explicitly one-sided. The Catholic interlocutor is the one who would benefit the most from the conversation unless, of course, the non-Catholic conversation partner converts. From a postcolonial perspective, it is an unfortunate example of a dominant tradition that seeks to exploit and capitalize on others.

Bibliography

Chidester, David. *Empire of Religion: Imperialism and Comparative Religion.* Chicago: University of Chicago Press, 2014.

Das, Anuttama. "A Vaishnava Response to Dr. Francis X. Clooney's Essay, 'Nostra Aetate and the Catholic Way of Openness to Other Religions.'" In *Nostra Aetate: Celebrating Fifty Years of the Catholic Church's Dialogue with Jews and Muslims,* edited by P. Valkenberg and A. Cirelli, 16–21. Washington, DC: Catholic University of America Press, 2016.

Ganeri, Martin. "Catholic Encounter with Hindus in the Twentieth Century: In Search of an Indian Christianity." *New Blackfriars* 88.1016 (2007) 410–32.

Griffiths, Paul. *Problems of Religious Diversity.* Oxford: Blackwell, 2001.

———. *Religious Reading.* Oxford: Oxford University Press, 1999.

Jayatirtha. *Nyaya Sudha.* Bangalore: Uttaradi matha, 1982.

———. *Pramana paddhati of Sri Jayatirtha: A work on Dvaita-epistemology with eight commentaries.* Bangalore: Dvaita Vedanta Studies & Research Foundation, 1991.

———. *Vadalaksanatika.* In *Dasa Prakaranani.* 4 vols. Edited by P. P. Laksminarayanopadhyaya. Bangalore: Purnaprajna Vidyapitha, 1971.

King, Richard. *Orientalism and Religion: Post-Colonial Theory, India and "The Mystical East."* New York: Routledge, 1999.

The Laws of Manu. Translated by Wendy Doniger O'Flaherty and Brian K. Smith. New York: Penguin, 1992.

Madhvacārya. *Anuvyakhyana.* Edited by Pandurangi. Bangalore: Prabha, 1991.

—————. *Brahma Sutra Bhasya.* Edited by R. Raghavendracharya. Mysore: Government Branch, 1911.

—————. *Tattvasamkhyana.* In *Sarvamulagranthah.* Edited by Govindacarya. Bangalore: Akhila Bharata Madhwa Mahamandala, 1969–74.

—————. *Vadalaksana.* Vol. 1. *Dasa Prakaranani.* 4 vols. Edited by P.P Laksminarayanopadhyaya. Bangalore: Purnaprajna Vidyapitha, 1971.

Masuzawa, Tomoko. *The Invention of World Religions.* Chicago: University of Chicago Press, 2005.

Nongbri, Brent. *Before Religion: A History of a Modern Concept.* New Haven: Yale University Press, 2015.

Pannitacarya, Narayana. *Bhavaprakasika.* In *Sumadhvavijayah, Bhavaprakasikasametah.* Edited by Prabhanjanacarya. Bangalore: Sri Man Madhwa Siddantonnahini Sabha, 1989.

—————. *Sumadhvavijayaḥ, Bhavaprakasikasametah.* Edited by Prabhanjanacarya. Bangalore: Sri Man Madhwa Siddantonnahini Sabha, 1989.

Sarma, Deepak. *Epistemology and the Limitations of Philosophical Inquiry: Doctrine in Madhva Vedanta.* Oxford: RoutledgeCurzon, 2005.

—————. "Exclusivist Strategies in Madhva Vedanta." PhD diss., University of Chicago, 1998.

—————. "Hindu Leaders in North America?" *Teaching Theology and Religion* 9.2 (2006) 115–20.

—————. "Postcolonial Religion." In *Macmillan Interdisciplinary Handbooks: Religion,* edited by Jeffrey Kripal. Farmington Hills, MI: Macmillan Reference, 2016.

Second Vatican Council. *Nostra aetate,* 1965. http://www.vatican.va/archive/hist_councils/ii_vatican_council/documents/vat-ii_decl_19651028_nostra-aetate_en.html. B

CHAPTER 11

Intimations of Presence in the Religion of Emptiness

A Proposed Focus for Buddhist–Christian Dialogue

—ROBERT M. GIMELLO

There are questions that loom especially large in modern Catholic theological encounters with non-Christian religions. Sometimes these questions are posed explicitly and forthrightly. More often, however, they are broached only diffidently or obliquely out of concern that they may be so fraught as to impede or prevent frank and charitable dialogue. I think, however, that these are questions that cannot be avoided in any honest effort to wed evangelization to the enterprise of interreligious dialogue. One such question is the following: Is it possible to combine genuine respect for non-Christian religions like Buddhism, even admiration of them, with acceptance of the claim, so forcefully asserted in Dominus Iesus, that "followers of other religions," recipients though they may be of divine grace, are "objectively speaking . . . in a gravely deficient situation in comparison with those who, in the Church, have the fullness of the means of salvation"?[1] Should the first part of the question be answered in the affirmative, given that the second must be, what form should such respectful critique take?

A premise upon which I pose this question in the present essay is one that contains the seed of an answer. It is the belief that all men, made as they are in the image and likeness of God, are in some way oriented toward God regardless of whether or not they recognize that orientation or would so describe it. As Henri de Lubac said in so many words, echoing many fathers and doctors of the Church, including Aquinas, and voicing his objection to the scholastic formula of natura pura, it is in the God-given nature of

---

1. CDF, *Dominus Iesus*, 22.

human beings that they thirst for the vision of God and that they have the capacity to receive the grace by which alone that vision is granted.[2] On this premise we are required to believe that all men aspire to what can, in the most generic terms, be called transcendence, i.e., the escape from, or triumph over, the deficiency of our imperfect, "fallen," worldly condition, this being an end that Christians know to be possible only by theosis, i.e., by communion with the triune God in whose second person human finitude and divine transcendence are uniquely united.[3] On this same premise we may reasonably hypothesize that the doctrines, values, and practices of the world's religions were born of this very orientation toward, or thirst for, the transcendent and are in fact products of the ardent desire to attain it. Note, however, that in Christianity and other theistic religions discourse about access to, or communion with, the transcendent is governed especially by the themes of gift and gratitude. When aspiration toward absorption into the divine transcendent is fulfilled, when the restless hearts of those who have been made for God find rest in him, or even when the promise of that rest is contemplated, it arouses a response of gratitude, an impulse of love in the form of gratitude, because the granted or promised transcendence is seen as gratuitous, as an infinitely precious gift which the recipients have themselves done nothing to deserve. When we search in Buddhism for a sense of transcendence as the telos of human beings we must ask also if we can find there any analogue to such gratitude, any conception of the immanence of the transcendent as a gift given rather than an end effortfully achieved.

With the intent to show that respect for Buddhism and admiration of the profundity and subtlety of its teachings are compatible with acceptance of the Church's claim that Christ alone is the definitive fullness of salvation, I propose to examine certain key themes of Buddhist thought for evidence of a search on the part of Buddhist sages—however obscure and halting that search may be—of the necessary presence of the transcendent amidst the many and dire imperfections of the human condition. Is there in Buddhism any sense that, despite the belief that the condition of sentient beings is one of inveterate and ubiquitous suffering born of deep-rooted craving and ignorance, there must be, underlying and redeeming it all, an immanence of the transcendent? Compelling evidence of such a sense may be found, I will

2. On this subject, see Feinberg, *Natural Desire to See God*. Among the "interpreters" whom Feinberg discusses is Henri de Lubac, who, in a 1932 letter to Maurice Blondel, said: "How can a conscious spirit be anything other than a desire for God." John Milbank has cited Feinberg and this quote from de Lubac in Milbank, *Suspended Middle*, viii.

3. "He was incarnate that we might be made God [Αὐτὸς γὰρ ἐνηνθρώπησεν, ἵνα ἡμεῖς θεοποιηθῶμεν]" (Athanasius, *On the Incarnation*, 167).

argue, in the persistent tension throughout the history of Buddhist thought between, on the one hand, the conviction that the ultimate truth about all things is that they are only conditional—"empty," "dependently originated," "confected," "transient," etc.—and, on the other hand, the recurrent but not always welcome suspicion that the conditionality of all things must rest upon and conceal something ineffably unconditioned, permanent, immaculate, etc.

A warning to the reader: This foray into Buddhist doctrinal controversy will broach some fairly technical topics—technical enough, perhaps, to try the patience of those little acquainted with Buddhism. I think, however, that the Buddhist–Christian dialogue has by now developed beyond the phase in which discussion only of generalities will suffice. Nor will it any longer do to assume that Buddhism is an entirely homogenous and coherent whole free of internal doctrinal conflict

At first encounter Buddhism may seem inimical to any notion of a transcendent yet also immanent unconditioned, whether it be conceived as personal or impersonal. Central to Buddhist thought, after all, is the doctrine of dependent origination (pratītyasamutpāda, 緣起 yuánqǐ) and such corollaries thereof as the doctrines of impermanence (anityatā, 無常 wúcháng), no-self (anātman, 無我 wúwǒ), emptiness (śūnyatā, 空 kōng), and unsatisfactoriness or suffering (duḥkha, 苦 kǔ). These doctrines would seem to suggest that for Buddhists the sum total of reality, including whatever is deemed maximally real, is simply conditionality itself, the complex and endlessly changing web of fleeting and fleetingly interrelated events, no one of which, nor any amalgam of such, is possessed of even the slightest independent identity. Nowhere within, nor anywhere apart from, this ever-changing web of flickering, insubstantial phenomena does there seem to be anything that might qualify as an unconditioned. Buddhists generally deny the existence of an inner redoubt or distant domain entirely detached from the defilements of suffering, craving, and ignorance. Far more often than not they reject the notion of a personal or impersonal entity that transcends conditionality by virtue of existing permanently "of itself" rather than in transient dependence upon other equally transient things. As Buddhists often say, the world consists mostly of conditioned (saṃskṛta, 有為 yǒuwéi, i.e., "confected," or "composite") things or events (dharma) and all conditioned dharmas, each in particular and the totality of them all together, are said to be like a "fault of vision" (timira, 翳 ·yì), a "magical illusion" (māyā, 幻 huàn), a "dream" (supina /svapna, 夢 mèng), an "echo" (pratiśrukta, 響 xiǎng), a "shadow" (pratibhāsa, 影 yǐng), "foam" (budbuda, 泡 pào), a "lightning flash" (suvidyu, 電光 diànguāng), a "mirage" (marīci, 焰 yàn), etc.[4] Such a world is said to be illusory or mirage-like in an especially strong sense. It is utterly without substrate or foundation and defined as a network of particular, merely apparitional things and events. Having only other particular apparitional things and events on which to depend, it lacks the support of any deeper order of substantial reality that is possessed of a greater measure of reality. And as sentient beings exist within this mirage or illusion, this web of phantom ephemera, the suffering they experience because of their compulsive craving and the ignorance, although it is part of the illusion, is nevertheless quite "real" to those who suffer. "Awakening" (bodhi, 菩提 pútí), the ultimate goal of Buddhism, sometimes called "enlightenment" but better understood as liberation (vimokṣa, 解脱 jiětuō), is said to consist not in a transit beyond or beneath this realm of illusion into some other higher or deeper dimension that is somehow more real. It is not a flight from the realm of the mutable insubstantiality into a higher or deeper realm of immutable substantiality. Rather, the ultimate end of Buddhist faith and practice is usually held to be just the realization of the world's character precisely as illusion. This discovery may seem dire and deflationary, a mere disillusionment rather than a fulfilment, but it is held actually to be a kind of release, the attainment of freedom from the enslaving compulsion to find in the world more than is actually there, to see the world as anything other than illusion, or to mistake it for the sort of illusion that may be dissolved to reveal something more real. What Buddhists regard as their ultimate goal is not a flight from an imperfect world of suffering, craving, and ignorance into a perfect world without such afflictions. Rather they aspire to a condition of disenthrallment or blissful detachment from the world. What that condition is like, of course, is ineffable. Even words like "bliss" fail to do it full justice, which is why the Buddha is said never to have tried to describe or define it in positive, constructive terms. So, Buddhists insist on the ineffability of this ultimate liberation, but they also recognize that such insistence can be dangerously disorienting. It can then tempt one to ontologize the promised freedom of nirvāṇa or bodhi by imagining it to be another world entirely. That, however, is held to be a serious mistake for, rather that extinguish the craving that causes suffering, it simply supplies craving with a new and especially seductive object of attachment.

And yet, despite all this, Buddhists do employ a term that may be, and commonly is, translated as "unconditioned" (asaṃskṛta, 無為 wúwéi, literally: "uncompounded," "unconfected," "non-composite," "non-factum"). But what is this Buddhist unconditioned, and how can anything so labelled not stand in contradiction of all else that Buddhism seems to aver? In Buddhism's

4. See Orsborn, "Something for Nothing."

scholastic discourse there are only a few "things" (i.e., dharmas or factors of interdependence) that are said to be asaṃskṛta. Foremost among them, and the one first stipulated in Buddhist literature, is just nirodha (滅 miè) or nirvāṇa (涅槃 nièpán), the utter cessation of suffering and all of the concomitants of suffering, attainment of which, of course, is the ultimate goal of Buddhism. Certain later traditions speak in finer analysis of three kinds of asaṃskṛta-dharma: (1) cessation that is the result of meditative analysis (pratisaṃkhyānirodha, 擇滅 zémiè), e.g., the cessation of the false view that there is such a thing as a permanent self, which is an annihilation of error occasioned by meditative discernment of the truth of selflessness; (2) cessation that is not the result of meditative analysis (apratisaṃkhyānirodha, 非擇滅 fēizémiè), e.g., the cessation of thirst brought about by a drink of water; and (3) space (ākāśa, 虛空 xūkōng), defined simply as the boundless vacuity which material things (rūpa, 色 sè) require as a condition or locus of their existence. But note that all three of these terms, like the generic term "asaṃskṛta" itself, are privatives. They are words expressing negation or absence, and the "unconditioned" dharmas they label are like all other conditioned dharmas insofar as they are absences rather than presences, instances of "non-arising" or "non-production" (anutpattikadharma, 無生法 wúshēng fǎ), as Buddhists sometimes say, rather than instances of "coming into being." They are, in other words, nullities rather than potencies, vacuities rather than plena, and so forth.

Note too that as negativities these unconditioned dharmas, these modes of the peculiarly Buddhist "unconditioned," seem incapable of eliciting anything like the "gratitude" that the immanent presence of the transcendent summons in theistic traditions does. Theists are moved to gratitude, a principal mode of their faith, in response to such things as God's sacrificial self-emptying (kenōsis) in the form of incarnation and even death, or God's munificent dissemination of his grace in the sacraments, or God's generosity in making a covenant with his chosen people, or God's gift of his speech to his prophet, etc. However, it simply makes no sense to speak of gratitude toward nirvāṇa. One might confess to feeling grateful for the cessation of suffering or the possibility thereof—but grateful to what or to whom? To be sure, a Buddhist might respond immediately by saying that he or she is grateful to the Buddha or his teaching (the dharma), or his community (the saṃgha, 僧伽 sēngjiā), or to "all three of these precious jewels" (triratna, 三寶 sānbǎo). Indeed, the Pure Land Buddhist tradition is based on this very foundation of unreservedly humble and grateful trust in the saving efficacy of the vow to save all sentient beings, a vow made and fulfilled by the transcendent Buddha Amitābha (阿彌陀 Āmítuó, Japanese: Amida). This is why de Lubac found Pure Land Buddhism so fascinating and so well suited to comparison with Christianity.[5] But, one might ask, to whom or to what was the Buddha (Amitābha, Śākyamuni, or any other Buddha) himself grateful for the cessation of suffering and transcendence of ignorance that he attained? Surely it is not enough to say (and in the end even the Pure Land tradition does not say) simply that the Buddha was grateful to previous Buddhas, for that would lead to the absurdity of an infinite regress—not "turtles all the way down," perhaps, but the equally unsatisfying assumption of "Buddhas all the way back."

Notwithstanding the historical importance of Pure Land Buddhism or the frequent popular displays of devotional piety focused on particular buddhas and bodhisattvas, the mainstream of the Buddhist tradition holds all things, even buddhas and buddhahood, to be empty, defining the unconditioned only as an absence or a cessation. Such is the view that most Buddhist thinkers have judged to be orthodox. And yet (again, "and yet") we do find passages in even the earliest strata of the Buddhist canon that seem to challenge or undermine purported orthodoxy on such matters by attributing to such a negatively defined unconditioned as the Buddhist asaṃskṛta (Pāli: asaṅkhata) an uncannily positive efficacy:

> atthi bhikkhave, ajātaṃ abhūtaṃ akataṃ asaṅkhataṃ. No ce taṃ bhikkhave, abhavissā ajātaṃ abūtaṃ akataṃ asaṅkhataṃ, **nayidha jātassa bhūtassa katassa saṅkhatassa nissaraṇaṃ** paññāyetha. yasmā ca kho bhikkhave, atthi ajātaṃ abhūtaṃ akataṃ asaṅkhataṃ, tasmā jātassa bhūtassa katassa saṅkhatassa nissaraṇaṃ paññāyatii.

> There is, O monks, an unborn, an unbecome, an unmade, an unconditioned. If there were not that unborn, unbecome, unmade, unconditioned, no escape from the born, the become, the made, the conditioned would be discerned. But precisely because there is an unborn, an unbecome, an unmade, an unconditioned, escape from the born, the become, the made, the conditioned is discerned.

This passage from the Udāna (VIII.3), a collection of purportedly ecstatic or inspired utterances of the Buddha,[6] is famous and arresting because it stands in apparent contradiction of so much of the rest of Buddhism. It seems to speak of the unconditioned not only as a cessation or a nullity but also as a positivity, a potent positive reality or order of reality utterly unlike

---

5. See de Lubac, *Aspects du Bouddhisme*.

6. The Udāna is a scripture belonging to the Khuddaka Nikāya (Collection of Shorter Discourses) of the Buddhist canon preserved in the Pāli language. The passage quoted is found in the Udāna's "Third Discourse about Nirvāṇa" (Tatiyanibbāna sutta☒).

(ganz andere, totaliter aliter) the conditioned order and yet able to effect, or at least enable, the transcendence of the conditioned.

What are we to make of such passages in Buddhist scripture that seem to hover or vacillate between affirmation and negation. On the one hand, the passage uses positive locutions like "There is" and "If there were not." On the other hand, we are told, so to speak, that what "is" is a "not this, not that." The affirmative purport of the passage, its use of the phrase "there is," seems to be a retreat from the more frequent Buddhist insistence that there are no exceptions to the rule of universal conditionality, but that retreat must be judged to be, at best, hesitant or reluctant because the "exception" to the rule of universal conditionality that it seems to admit, and to insist is necessary, is labelled with a series of negations—"un-such and such," "non-this or that," etc.). It is an event, in other words, of cessation (nirvāṇa) or non-occurrence (anutpada), likened to the boundless absence of space (ākāśa), etc. How to explain the fact that the standard Buddhist definition of the sum and summit of the real as just conditionality (pratītyasamutpāda) itself is sometimes undercut by such assertions of an unconditioned reality that seems to lie wholly beyond the world of conditionality, thus affording gratuitous (gift-like?) release from confinement in and by conditionality? And how, further, to make sense of the fact that this alternative to conditionality, which is asserted to be necessary, can be labelled only with negations? These puzzles, I would suggest, are themselves evidence of the tension in Buddhism with which we are here concerned, the tension between the felt need to recognize the utter emptiness of things and the persistent sense that underlies that emptiness and makes it something more than mere nothingness. Is some "non-thing" so different from the emptiness of the conditioned world that it cannot be captured in positive descriptions?

Such questions were, of course, asked by Buddhist thinkers themselves. The answers they most often gave were usually by way of a swerve from ontology to either logic and epistemology or to hermeneutics.

An example of the former is Buddhism's development of a theory of negation. Given the prevalence of negative locutions in Buddhist discourse, and in the interest of showing that, notwithstanding its penchant for negation, Buddhism is not a kind of nihilism, Buddhist thinkers examined with great care the very concept of negation (pratiṣedha) itself. In this effort they came eventually to distinguish between two kinds or degrees of negation. The weaker sort they called paryudāsa-pratiṣedha (exclusionary, implicative, or nominally-bound negation), i.e., negation that implies a countervailing affirmation (e.g., to say "this table is not red" is to imply that it must be some other color, like blue). But they also recognized a stronger kind of negation that they called prasajya-pratiṣedha (prohibitive, non-implicative, or propositionally-bound negation), i.e., negation tout court, implying no affirmative alternative (e.g., to say "this table is not an amphibious biped" is not to imply that it might be any other sort of animal). In the parlance of modern logic, the latter and stronger sort of negation would be expressed by saying, "It is not the case that." Important strains of Buddhist doctrinal discourse (e.g., the Madhyamaka tradition of Nāgārjuna and his disciples[7]) favor the stronger kind of negation. Thus, when Buddhists of this tradition speak of nirvāṇa or some such ultimate category, they usually do not say that it "is this" or "is that." Sometimes they will say that it "is not this" or "is not that." However, when they are intent on the most definitive possible exposition many will resort either to silence (the acknowledgement that definitive exposition is ultimately impossible) or to the well-known four-fold negation. In the latter case they will say something like, "it is not the case that nirvāṇa 'is x,' nor is it the case that it 'is not-x,' neither is it the case that it 'is both x and not x,' nor is it the case that it 'is neither x nor not x.'" It is significant, however, that not all strains of Buddhism are so strict as the Madhyamaka in holding to the primacy of proposition-bound (prasajya) negation. The Udāna passage given above is a case in point. It makes use of the weaker sort of negation, juxtaposing the affirmative verb "is" with a number of nouns in the form of term-bound (paryudāsa) negations. Such vacillation between affirmation, weak negation, and strong negation is yet another indication of the sort of tension within Buddhism that we are concerned here to examine.[8]

---

7. The Madhyamaka ("middle way") tradition and its founder Nāgārjuna are famous for having held emptiness (śūnyatā) to be Buddhism's ultimate teaching and to have practiced the art of negative (prasaṅgika, reductio ad absurdum) dialectic in which discourse is employed to refute false views but never to propound views that might be deemed true, for ultimate truth, they believed, is simply not linguistically expressible.

8. This Buddhist distinction between the two types of negation seems to bear some similarity to the distinction between different kinds of negation found in Neo-Platonic philosophy (e.g., in Plotinus, Proclus, etc.), and in Christian theology influenced thereby (e.g., in Pseudo-Dionyisus, Maximus the Confessor, etc.). It was Proclus, among pagan Neo-Platonists, who most thoroughly analyzed negation, identifying three kinds or levels of its intensity. First is στέρησις (stérēsis, literally: "absence" or "privation"), which is any claim that something "lacks" a certain property or "falls short of" a certain state. Next is αφαίρεσις (aphaíresis); for Proclus this is the kind of negation that implies a countervailing affirmation. Finally, there is αποφασις (apophasis), the strongest kind of negation, which implies no countervailing affirmation and which may even negate negation itself. This last, in effect, denies the pertinence to the ultimately real or the divine of any kind of discourse or imaging, whether it be positive or negative. Modern philosophers sometimes call this last sort of negation "second-order negation." Note that the use of "aphaíresis" by Aristotle differs from its use in the Platonic, Neo-Platonic, and other traditions. Aristotle uses it to mean what we call "abstraction." Boethius translated "aphaíresis" into Latin as "abstraction," i.e., the removal from a particular

In the alternative move from ontology to hermeneutics a number of Buddhist traditions invoke distinctions between different kinds of truth, different modes of discourse, different senses of scripture (the latter analogous to the different sensa of Christian scriptural exegesis[9]), or different stages in the gradual unfolding of the Buddha's pedagogy. There are some doctrines, Buddhist thinkers asserted, that are possessed of only conventional, transactional, or spiritually pragmatic truth (saṃvṛti-satya 俗諦 súdì). These doctrines are not to be taken as literally or definitively true. Rather they are pragmatically true, useful fictions (upāya, 方便 fāngbiàn, "expedient devices") that can serve to advance one further along the path until one is ready to see them as mere metaphors and to realize the recalcitrant "ultimate truth" (paramārtha-satya, 眞諦 zhēndì) that defies all discourse but has anagogical potency. Provisional or conventional truths are amenable to affirmative exposition (kataphasis, 表詮 biǎoquán), whereas ultimate truth may be conveyed only by negation (apophasis, 遮詮 zhēquán), or by the extreme of apophasis, namely silence. Allied to this distinction between two kinds of truth is a distinction between two kinds of scriptural meaning. Some scriptures or scriptural formulations are said to convey provisional, oblique, tropological, or analogical meaning (neyārtha, 不了義 bù liǎoyì). They are true, to a limited extent or in an expedient sense, but they are in need of further interpretation and are ultimately dispensable once they have served their communicative or pedagogical purpose. Other scriptural locutions, however, are held to convey definitive meaning (nītārtha 了義 liǎoyì). They are explicitly and definitively true and do not require further interpretation. To be sure, such distinctions did not settle all doctrinal disputes or resolve all doubts. Rather they only set the stage for continuing debate about

---

thing of those features of the thing that give it its particularity (e.g., size, shape, color, number, etc.). This sense of the term is related to its use in mathematics as meaning "subtraction." Pseudo-Dionysius the Areopagite (a sixth-century Syrian monk whose actual identity is not known) essentially follows Proclus in speaking of three kinds of negation and insisting that apophasis, the highest of the three (a kind of "super-negation"), is beyond affirmation (thesis or kataphasis), beyond negation-as-privation (stéresis), and beyond negation-as-the-mere-opposite-of-affirmation (aphaíresis). He also assigns to apophasis a soteriological function insofar as he holds it to be an "ascent," "conversion" (επστροφή, epistrophé, literally: "return"), a movement of "uplift" (αναγογια, anagogia), ecstasy, or subsumption into God. He also links it to the higher sort of "knowing" which is so completely unlike ordinary knowing (γνοσις, gnosis) that he calls it "unknowing" (αγνωσία, agnosía). For more on this subject see Mortley, *From Word to Silence*, esp. 2:86–127, 221–745.

9. The definitive study of which is Henri de Lubac's four-volume masterpiece, *Exégèse médiévale*. English translation of the first three of these four volumes have been published by Eerdmans and T. & T. Clark, who plan to publish the final, fourth volume soon as well.

which scriptures were provisional in meaning and which definitive, which doctrines were expediencies that merely intimated the truth by exploiting conventional categories as metaphors and which were literally, definitively, and explicitly true. Often such debates were given hagiographical or historical frames according to which the Buddha revealed his truths gradually through sequential "turnings of the wheel of the dharma," each "turning" or stage of the Buddha's teaching career coming closer to the final expression of ultimate truth. In East Asia this notion of staged progression toward the revelation of ultimate truth gave rise to systems of doctrinal classification (判教 pànjiāo) by which the doctrinal diversity of Buddhism was sorted out teleologically, i.e., as tending gradually toward a final and complete expression of a consummate teaching (圓教 yuánjiāo).

No topic drew more heavily upon such distinctions and categories (levels of truth, sense of scripture, turnings of the doctrinal wheel, schemes of doctrinal classification) than the topic with which we are here most concerned, viz., the topic of whether or not Buddhism ever admits of an eternal, transcendent unconditioned that stands apart from, yet can salvifically engage, the realm of conditionality. And one must bear in mind the fact that this disputed topic has often generated, and continues even today, to sustain a strenuous sectarian polemic. Among the controversies that have long roiled the Buddhist tradition (each one of which deserves discussion more extensive than can be undertaken here) are the following:

(a) Arguments between advocates of emptiness as the paramount teaching of the Buddha and those who find in the doctrine of emptiness only a propaedeutic, a gateway to the higher truth of inherent Buddha-nature.

(b) Disputes between those for whom emptiness is only "emptiness of self-nature" (svabhāva-śūnyatā)—the Rantongpa (rang stong pa) of Tibet—and those for whom it is emptiness only of everything "other than" Buddha-nature—the Shentongpa (gzhan stong pa).

(c) Debates between those for whom the mind is intrinsically and inviolately pure, its apparent impurity being only adventitious, superficial, and in need only of a cleansing of its surface and those for whom the mind is inveterately defiled or at best a conduit of defilement in need, not of mere "dusting" or "polishing," but of the most radical reconstitution or metanoia.

(d) Confrontations between adherents of different kinds of contemplation. On the one hand, there are those for whom the highest meditative achievement is a state of utter stasis or equipoise of mind and body (śamatha), a supremely serene yet also intense non-discursive union (samādhi) with the ultimate. On the other hand, there are those for whom the highest contemplative attainment is just the culmination of a relentless process of eliminative analysis (vipśyanā), the ruthless shedding, one after another, of all false views. Derived from this confrontation is the dispute between those adherents of Chán or Zen (禪) Buddhism who espouse a kind of quietism that is labelled "silent illumination" (默照禪 mòjiào chán), wherein one's inherent Buddhahood is allowed naturally to shine forth, and those who practice the demanding cognitive asceticism of "scrutinizing of the word" (看話kànhuà) by which the utter emptiness of all things is sharply confronted in engagement with paradoxical or confuting utterances (公案 gōng'àn, kōan).

(e) Contentions between those who maintain that liberation can be attained only by the power of one's own efforts (自力 zìlì), for example by study, contemplative cultivation, or moral discipline, and those who reject such a claim, seeing it as foolishly prideful, and insisting rather that liberation is the result only of the conferred power of a transcendent other (他力 tālì) in whom one must have faith.

(f) Disagreements between those who see awakening as a "sudden and immediate" (頓 dùn) apprehension of a truth that is radically discontinuous with worldly experience and those who rely on various kinds of mediation, i.e., means of linking the mundane with the supramundane, in pursuit of a "gradually" (漸 jiàn) attained liberation.

(g) Controversies between those who see sensuality and materiality only as obstacles or snares and those—e.g., adherents of Tantric or Esoteric Buddhism—for whom the senses, material things, vocalizations, bodily movements, and visual images may be consecrated and thereby infused with power (adhiṣṭhāna, 加持 jiāchí), not unlike sacramental grace, so as to function as guarantors or accelerants of the progress toward liberation.

And these are only a few of the many controversies within Buddhism traceable to the persistent tension between Buddhism's characteristic tendency to deny the existence of a transcendent unconditioned and the recurrent Buddhist suspicion or confession that there must nevertheless be such an unconditioned by which we transcend conditionality and that it must some-how also be immanent if it is to be of any avail.

I would suggest that distance may be helpful here, the sort of distance that separates Buddhism from other traditions. Viewed from the perspec-tive of another religion, through lenses not of Buddhism's own making, the larger contours of Buddhist doctrines and its internal conflicts or insta-bilities may be more clearly discerned. Such an approach, the analogical application of non-Buddhist categories to Buddhist themes, might seem to threaten distortion, but I would suggest that it may just as easily reveal surprising, hitherto unsuspected implications of those themes. Such a view-from-afar is, of course, the vantage point of theology of religions and com-parative theology.

One such distant but revealing perspective, I would propose, is the view from the ancient Levantine city of Chalcedon through the lens of the great event that occurred there in the year 451. Consider this most momen-tous passage from the declaration of the Council of Chalcedon:

> Following, then, the holy Fathers, we all unanimously teach that
> our Lord Jesus Christ is to us One and the same Son, the Self-
> same Perfect in Godhead, the Self-same Perfect in Manhood;
> truly God and truly Man; the Self-same of a rational soul and
> body; co-essential with the Father according to the Godhead, the
> Self-same co-essential with us according to the Manhood; like
> us in all things, sin apart; before the ages begotten of the Father
> as to the Godhead, but in the last days, the Self-same, for us and
> for our salvation (born) of Mary the Virgin Theotokos as to the
> Manhood; One and the Same Christ, Son, Lord, Only-begotten;
> acknowledged in Two Natures unconfusedly, unchangeably,
> indivisibly, inseparably (ἐν δύο φύσεσιν ἀσυγχύτως, ἀτρέπτως,
> ἀδιαιρέτως, ἀχωρίστως / in duabus naturis inconfuse, immuta-
> biliter, indivise, inseparabiliter); the difference of the Natures
> being in no way removed because of the Union, but rather the
> properties of each Nature being preserved, and (both) concur-
> ring into One Person and One Hypostasis; not as though He
> were parted or divided into Two Persons, but One and the Self-
> same Son and Only-begotten God, Word, Lord, Jesus Christ;
> even as from the beginning the prophets have taught concern-
> ing Him, and as the Lord Jesus Christ Himself hath taught us,
> and as the Symbol of the Fathers hath handed down to us.[10]

10. See Grillmeier, *Christ in Christian Tradition*, 544–54. Originally published in German in 1964, this magisterial work is not the most recent account of the issues addressed in the fourth general council, but it is still recognized as thorough and authoritative.

Here we have the classic claim, foundational to Christianity and forged out of Greek philosophical as well as New and Old Testament scriptural materials, that the incarnate Logos, God in the second person of the Trinity made man, is both transcendent and immanent—transcendent of all the worldly conditions that comprise finite human life (save sin) and yet also mysteriously and graciously fully engaged in those conditions. His divinity and his humanity are "not confusedly amalgamated" (asynchutos) in such a way that either of his two "natures" (physes, naturae) is obscured or compromised by the other. Yet "neither" are his divine and human natures "divisible" (adiaretos) in any way that might imply that Christ is two persons (hypostases / prosopa, personae) rather than one.[11] And, of course, we Christians cannot but be grateful for the inestimable gift of God's divine yet also human presence, which is what makes possible our becoming united with him, our theosis.

Is there anything at all in Buddhism like this interfusion without confusion of the transcendent and unconditioned with the conditioned, any immanence of a transcendent? To pursue this possibility I would first draw attention to an example of Buddhist "trinitarianism," not the famous trikāya or "three bodies of the Buddha" theory,[12] but something else entirely. The early ninth-century Chinese Buddhist Monk Chéngguān (澄觀), whom tradition regards as the "fourth patriarch" of the Huáyán (華嚴, Japanese: "Kegon"; Korean: "Hwaŏm") tradition of Buddhism,[13] i.e., the tradition

11. I beg the reader's indulgence of my drastic oversimplification of this boundlessly complex subject, on which whole libraries of books have been written, and I plead timidity in avoiding such especially freighted technicalities as communicatio idiomatum, the extra calvinisticum, etc.

12. For a concise summary of the "three bodies" teaching of Mahāyāna Buddhism, see the entry on "Trikāya" in Buswell Jr. and Lopez Jr., *Princeton Dictionary of Buddhism*, 923.

13. This is the tradition based on the Huáyán or Avataṃsaka Sūtra ("The Flower Ornament Scripture" or "The Scripture of Floreate Splendor"). It is a lengthy composite sūtra, an amalgamation of several originally independent scriptures. It survives only partly in the original Sanskrit but is preserved in its entirety in one Tibetan and two Chinese translations. Although revered throughout the Mahāyāna Buddhist world, it exerted its greatest influence in East Asia. For a concise but thorough summation of its contents and a discussion of its composition, see Hamar, "Buddhāvataṃsakasūtra," 115–28. A complete English translation of the second Chinese version of the scripture has been published as Cleary, Flower Ornament Scripture. This is a generally reliable translation. It will give the reader a sense of the general purport of the text, as well as an impression of its breadth and majesty, but, as it is intended for a general readership, it is careless of technicalities and entirely innocent of the sort of commentary and annotation that a scripture of this profundity needs and deserves. For a brief and general introduction to the Huáyán "School," the tradition of East Asian Buddhism based on this scripture, see the entry on "Huayan Buddhism" in Eliade, *Encyclopedia of Religion*, 6:485–90.

based on the Huáyán or Avataṃsaka Sūtra ("Flower Ornament Scripture" or "Scripture of Floreate Splendor"), noted as a peculiar feature of that sacred text. The chief protagonist of the Sūtra is the Tathāgata Vairocana (毘盧遮那如來 Pílúzhēnèrúlái), the supreme Buddha, the source and essential identity of all Buddhas. This ontologically primordial Buddha, from whom all other Buddhas and their respective worlds emanate, is understood to stand in relation to Śākyamuni, the Buddha of our world and our aeon, in something like the relationship that Meister Eckhart and others saw between "Deitas" or "Gottheit" and Deus or Gott. But Vairocana, central figure though he is, remains silent throughout this very long scripture over which he presides and this, Chéngguān thought, was significant in ways that demanded explanation. The oddity that Chénguān addressed is that all speech in this Sūtra, unlike all other scriptures, is uttered not by the Buddha himself, whose impassible silence and stillness signify his utter transcendence, but by members of the Buddha's retinue—most especially by the two great bodhisattvas, Mañjuśrī (文殊 Wénshū) and Samantabhadra (普賢 Pǔxián). These two deities, together with the Buddha Vairocana, Chéngguān called the "Three Noble or Holy Ones" and he wrote a meditation on the relations among them, a text entitled Contemplations of the Perfect Interfusion [Perichōrēsis / Circumincession?] of the Three Noble Ones (三聖圓融觀門 Sānshèng yuánróng guànmén). This short text is seen as a distillation of the vast and prodigiously prolix Avataṃsaka Sūtra into a relatively few words. And by concisely wedding the Sūtra's profound vision of the one-and-yet-multiple nature of reality to a trio of celestial persons and their vivid iconography, it renders that vision liturgically and contemplatively practicable.

The Huáyán Trinity, carved wooden statuettes intended for personal devotion
or contemplation.
Center (seated on lotus throne): Vairocana;
Left (mounted on an elephant): Samantabhadra;
Right (mounted on a lion): Mañjuśrī.

Note that the primal Buddha Vairocana is shown in monk's garb and meditation posture symbolizing his serene detachment from the world, whereas
Samantabhadra and Mañjuśrī, as bodhisattvas, are presented in the secular
raiment of princes (crowns, royal robes, jewelry), wielding instruments and
mounted on noble beasts that symbolize their engaged and exalted worldly
status as powerful agents of compassion.

Chéngguān argued that these noble (ārya, 聖shèng) beings are three
and yet also one and that in their three-ness each embodies particular qualities that are associated especially with that individual figure but are also
mysteriously shared with the other two and, ultimately, with all other sentient beings as well. One might even say that Chéngguān treated the three
"holy ones" as both an "immanent" ("ontological") and an "economic" trinity and that he was particularly interested in the communicatio idiomatum
("the communication of properties") among the three persons such that the

qualities of each are shared with the other two, and with all beings, without diminishing the particularity of each.[14]

About the Buddha, Vairocana Chéngguān has little to say in this essay because he acknowledges at the outset that Vairocana, in the "path" (mārga, 道 dào) discourse or soteriology of Buddhism, is of the order of "fruition" (phala, 果 guǒ). That is to say, he embodies or comprises in his person that to which the path ultimately leads, a condition which "utterly transcends language and thought" (超言想 chāoyánxiǎng) and which is therefore the proper subject only of either apophasis or pregnant silence. The bodhisattvas Mañjuśrī and Samantabhadra, however, are beings of the order of "cause" (hetu, 因 yīn). They, so to speak, embody aspects of the path that leads to or "causes" the fruition of awakening and, as such, they are susceptible to kataphasis. Their characters and actions may be legitimately described in concept, word, and image. So, as the path, unlike the goal, is amenable to discourse and conceptualization, Chéngguān has much to say about Mañjuśrī and Samantabhadra, the former understood to be the embodiment of wisdom or insight (prajñā, 智 zhì / 般若 bōrě), the latter understood to be the embodiment of compassionate conduct (karuṇā, 慈 cí). He proceeds to compare them, one with the other, according to a series of paired Buddhist categories. The contrasts he draws between the two bodhisattvas, according to two such pairs of categories, and especially what he says about Samantabhadra, the paragon of skillful compassion, bear directly on our present topic.[15]

> The first pair of categories is that of "faith and the object of faith": 以能信所信相對： 謂普賢表所信之法界，即在纏如來藏。故《理趣般若》云：『一切眾生皆如來藏。普賢菩薩自體遍故』。

> "Mañjuśrī and Samantabhadra may be distinguished from each other according to the distinction between faith and the object of faith: That is to say, Samantabhadra manifests the dharmadhātu ("the realm of truth") as the object of faith, the

14. The insistence on a comprehensive unity that entails no cancellation or diminishment of particularity is a hallmark of all Huáyán doctrine, which holds that every person or thing, mundane or supramundane, is essentially implicated in every other person and thing and that this mutual implication is such that each particular is "identical or coincident with" (即是, jíshì), "incorporated into" (入 rù), and "encompassing of" (攝 shè) both each and every other thing and the whole of all things, without the particularity of any one thing or person being lost in the "amalgamation," "interfusion," or "coinherence" (圓融 yuánróng).

15. For a complete translation and interpretation of this text, from which the following passages are taken, see Gimello, "Chéngguān's 澄觀 Meditations."

germ or matrix of Buddhahood (tathāgatagarbha) "entangled"
[in the afflictions of saṃsāra ("the repeating cycle of painful life
and death")]. Therefore is it said in the Liqubore (The Scripture
of Definitive Insight = Adhyardhaśatikā Prajñāpāramitā Sūtra,
i.e., The Sūtra of the Perfection of Insight in 500 Lines), that "all
sentient beings are germs or matrices of Buddhahood for they
are instinct with the essential nature of Samantabhadra."

The second pair of categories in terms of which the two bodhisattvas are
compared is that of principle and insight.

以理智相對：普賢表所證法界。即出纏如來藏。『善財童
子入其身故』。又云，『得究竟三世平等身故』。『一毛
廣大即無邊者稱法性』故。『普賢身相如虛空』故。又，
見普賢即得智波羅蜜者明依於理而發智故。

"The two holy ones may be distinguished from each other
according to the distinction between principle and insight: Samantabhadra manifests the realm/essence of truth
(dharmadhātu), which is the object of realization. This is the
germ/matrix of Buddhahood (tathāgatagarbha) disentangled
[from saṃsāra's store of afflictions]. For, [as is said in the Flower
Ornament Sūtra], "The youth Sudhana enters Samantabhadra's
body. . . . He attains a body wherein past, present, and future
are utterly identical. . . . A single strand of [Samantabhadra's]
hair is of boundless breadth, equivalent to the dharma-nature
(dharmatā) itself. . . . The body of Samantabhadra is as vast as
space." Moreover, to meet Samantabhadra is just to attain the
perfection of insight, and from this is it clear that insight arises
from principle."

A special note on the word "lǐ" 理 is in order here. Conventionally
but inadequately translated as "principle," the "lǐ" of a thing is understood
in the philosophical usage of Buddhism and in other traditions of Chinese
thought to be the inherent structure of a thing, its sustaining constitution,
its constitutive truth—or, if western analogies may be permitted, its "nature"
(φύσις), its quidditas, its essence (in the Aristotelian sense of τὸ τί ἦν εἶναι,
the "what-is-has-been-ness" of the thing). The Chinese word does not, in
this context, translate any Sanskrit word but it does bear some relationship
to concepts expressed in Sanskrit by terms like jāti-lakṣana (真相 zhēnxiàng
= "true nature," "genuine character"). Especially when used of an array of
things, or of the totality of things, "lǐ" is distantly analogous in meaning
to the "λογος" of the Stoics. In Chéngguān's usage here it is the epistemological object (ālambana, 緣 yuán) of "insight" or "wisdom" and the object

of "realization" (abhisamaya / abhisambuddha, 證 zhèng). As such "lǐ" has been understood in some strains of East Asian Buddhist thought to be a constructive enunciation of the principle of emptiness (śūnyatā, 空 kōng), i.e., the principle of insubstantiality or the absence from all things and beings of self-existence (svabhāva, 自性 zìxìng), which absence is paradoxically said to "constitute" what things and beings most essentially are. Other strains treat the word as the label of a kind of presence, the inherence of Buddhahood, or the seed thereof, in all sentient beings (all epistemological subjects) and the presence of suchness (tathatā, 真如 zhēnrú)⊠ or truth (dharmatā, 法性 fǎxìng) in all things (all epistemological objects). In the characteristic discourse of Chéngguān's Huáyán tradition a creative tension is maintained between apophasis and kataphasis such that the doctrine of emptiness and the doctrine of inherent buddha-nature or dharma-nature are understood to be two means by which to apprehend the same ultimately ineffable truth, the former seen as propaedeutic to the latter, the latter seen as culminating.

Note that in the second of the passages cited above Chéngguān does not say that insight "attains" or "discloses" principle. Rather, reversing the conventional understanding of the relationship between insight and truth, he says that it is truth or principle that generates insight. Fruition, he tells us, is what "causes" (enables) the causes of fruition, what endows the elements of the path with their causal efficacy. An inherent yet inchoate buddhahood, in other words, is somehow the anticipatory foundation of the very path that leads to it. As was explained in another text that Chéngguān knew well, The Mahāyāna Awakening of Faith (大乘起信論 Dàshèng qǐxìn lùn),[16] "incipient awakening" (始覺 shǐjué) is caused or made possible by "original awakening" (本覺 běnjué), the proleptic ("always-already"?) presence of awakening that abides in the deepest depths of sentience. If the fruition or goal of the Buddhist religious life is the unconditioned then, Chéngguān maintains, it is an agential, or at least an inherently operative and consequential, unconditioned—an unconditioned that somehow actively indwells conditionality. Its impassable yet also agential character is well captured in its triune personification as Vairocana, Mañjuśrī, and Samantabhadra.

---

16. This curious term is a combination of the adverb "tatha," (meaning "thus," "as," "such," or "so") with the nominalizing suffix "tā." That suffix, like the English suffixes "-ness" or "-ity," turns the adverb into an abstract noun. "Tathatā" ("suchness, thusness") is generally regarded the kataphatic counterpart to the apophatic term "emptiness" (śūnyatā). It signals, with a kind of positive but barely articulate verbal gesture, the ultimate ineffability of things as they truly are in their emptiness, in the face of which one can only speak of their "as-they-are-ness."

This is a crucial point, but I would draw attention now to something even more crucial to our topic, viz., the Chinese terms translated in the two passages from Chéngguān as "entangled" (在纏 zàichán) and "disentangled" (出纏 chūchán), which render respectively the Sanskrit words "avinirmuk-ta" and "vinirmukta," (literally: "not separated from" and "separated from"). These terms depict Buddhahood as something that is paradoxically both near and far, an essential ingredient of our condition as ordinary suffering sentient beings and yet also something that stands apart from and allows es-cape from that condition. They derive from a Mahāyāna Buddhist scripture entitled Śrīmālādevīsimhanāda Sūtra (The Lion's Roar of Queen Śrīmālā), a principal source of what is known as the Tathāgatagarbha[17] tradition, i.e., the tradition of thought based on the view that every sentient being harbors in the core of his or her sentience a germinal buddhahood, an inviolably pure radiance of mind that is unaccountably hidden beneath the mental grime that comprises the outwardly afflicted mind of ignorance and crav-ing. A key passage in the Śrīmālā Sūtra is its discussion of the third of the Buddha's four noble truths, i.e., the truth of cessation (nirodha), in which a sharp distinction is drawn between the misinterpretation of cessation as mere annihilation of things (dharmas), and its correct interpretation, in which it is understood to mean just the cessation of suffering and the con-comitants of suffering.

> What is called cessation of suffering is beginningless, uncre-ated, unarisen, endless, indestructible, permanently abiding, inherently pure, and free of all afflictions. This, O Lord—fully endowed with the innumerable and inconceivable qualities of Buddhahood that are inalienable, inseparable, and indifferen-tiable [from wisdom]—this we call the dharmakāya (truth-body of the Buddha).

17. The Awakening of Faith is a treatise attributed fictitiously to the Indian sage Aśvaghoṣa but actually composed anonymously, of both Indian and Chinese concep-tual materials, in sixth-century China. It is regarded as a classic in the Chinese Buddhist tradition that earned its high status by virtue of its effort to synthesize several traditions of thought commonly seen as incompatible with one another, namely the tradition of emptiness, the Tathāgatagarbha tradition of inherent buddhahood, and the tradition which holds that all things are figments of the mind, this last known as Yogācāra or the Vijñaptimātratā (唯識wéishí = "Representation-only") tradition. This treatise too, in its own way, exemplifies the Buddhist struggle to find a way of reconciling the conviction of the emptiness and conditionality of all things with the sense that amidst or underly-ing empty conditionality there is an immanent and salvifically efficacious transcendent that resides in the tainted yet also pure mind. Interestingly, this text has attracted keen interest on the part of Christian thinkers ever since the West discovered it in the late nineteenth century.

所言苦滅者，無始，無作，無起，無盡，離盡，常住，自
性清，淨離一切煩惱藏。世尊。過於恒沙，不離，不脫不
異［知慧］，不思議佛法成就，說如來法身。

/ yo’ yam, Śāriputra, tathāgatnirdiṣṭo dharmakāyaḥ, so’yam
avinirbhāgadharmā, avinirmuktajñānaguṇo, yaduta, gaṅgānadī-
vālikā-vyatikrāntais tathāgatdharmiḥ)

And when, O Lord, this dharmakāya is not disengaged from the
cache of defilements, then it is called the embryo/matrix of Buddhahood (tathāgatagarbha)”

世尊。如是如來法身不離煩惱藏名如來藏。

/   ayam   eva   ca   bhagavaṃs   tathāgatadharmakāyo
‘vinirmuktakleśakośas tathāgatagarbhaḥ sūcyate).[18]

Note here the implied redefinition of the key Buddhist term “nirodha,” the
name of the third of the Buddha’s four noble truths and thus the synonym
of “nirvāṇa.” A word that originally named an event of final nullification
or a condition of absence, specifically the end or absence of suffering and

---

18. The term “tathāgatgarbha” is composed of two words. The first, “tathāgata,”
itself a compound, is an epithet of the Buddha, the etymology of which is not really
known but has traditionally been taken to be either “tatha + gata,” meaning “thus gone”
or “tatha-agata,” meaning “thus come.” It is therefore usually translated into English as
either “Thus Gone One” or “Thus Come One.” The translation of this component of the
compound as 如來 (rúlái) indicates that East Asians understood the term in the latter
sense. The second component is the word “garbha,” which means “seed,” “germ,” “embryo,” “essence” or, alternatively, “matrix,” or “womb.” Sanskrit grammar distinguishes
among several different kinds of compound words and, depending on which kind of
compound “tathāgatgarbha” is determined to be, and which sense of the component
“garbha” is thought to be in play, the compound may mean “embryo of a Buddha,” (i.e.,
the germ of buddhahood inherent in a sentient being), or “womb of buddha” (a sentient
being who contains an embryonic buddhahood), or a being whose core is buddhahood, or (less likely) one who was born from the womb of a buddha. The translation of
“garbha” as 藏 (zàng = “storage place” or cáng = “to store” or “to conceal”) indicates that
in East Asia “tathāgatagarbha” was most commonly understood to mean “container of a
buddha or of buddhahood.” It has also been plausibly suggested that the full compound
is rooted in the tradition of Buddhist relic worship in which relics of buddhas were
ensconced in the inner chambers (also “garbha”) of stūpas (reliquary mounds, monu-
ments, or tabernacles). In this connection also the word “garbha” is shown to be closely
related to the term “dhātu” which, in its primal sense as “relic” and its derivative sense
as “essence,” also figures in the discourse of relic or stūpa worship. Indeed, the stūpa
is sometimes called a “dhātugarbha,” from which we get (via Sinhalese) the common
English term for a stūpa, “dagoba.” Note too that “dhātu” as “essence” also appears in
the compound “dharmadhātu,” which appears in the texts discussed in this essay. For
more extensive treatments of this term see Zimmermann, *Buddha Within*; Radich,
Mahāparinirvāṇa-mahāsūtra.

rebirth, has become instead the name of a timeless presence, an inherent and inexhaustible capacity. The tathāgatgarbha, then, is held to be the germ of awakening, the capacity inherent in all sentience eventually (or, according to some traditions, suddenly) to slough off adventitious impurities and attain release. It is as though the release from suffering that this capacity enables or guarantees, is, so to speak, the very telos of the tathāgatagarbha.

It is important to note that in these two passages from Chéngguān's text three related topics have been raised: the topic of tathāgatagarbha (embryo/matrix of Buddha), the topic of dharmadhātu (domain/essence of truth), and, implicitly, the topic of dharmakāya (the truth or absolute body of a Buddha). All three of these topics are related to the person of Samantabhadra (and also, of course, to the persons of Mañjuśrī and Vairocana insofar as the whole thrust of Chéngguān's treatise is to assert that the three noble ones are as much one as they are three). Chengguan tells us, remember, that Samantabhadra "manifests" (we might justifiably say that he "embodies") the dharmadhātu, the domain and essence of truth, and that he does so in two ways: He embodies the dharmadhātu insofar as the dharmadhātu is the object of faith. He also embodies the dharmadhātu insofar as the dharmadhātu is the object of insight. Moreover, the dharmadhātu that he is said to embody in these two ways is, in both ways, also the tathāgatagarbha, the germ of buddhahood ensconced in each and every sentient being.

However, as the object of faith, the embodied dharmadhātu is said to be the "entangled" tathāgatagarbha—i.e., the Buddha-nature enmeshed in the kleśas (煩惱 fánnǎo), the afflictions of saṃsāra. This we may characterize as a decidedly immanent tathāgatagarbha, whereas the embodied dharmadhātu seen as the object of insight is said to be the "disentangled" tathāgatagarbha—i.e., a tathāgatagarbha that I would dare to call, if not "transcendent," then at least "trans-immanent."

What is the background to Chéngguān's claim that Samantabhadra embodies or personifies the tathāgatagarbha? We have already seen something of his indebtedness to tathāgatagarbha texts like the Śrīmālādevī Sūtra and the Ratnagotravibhāga, but there is a deeper and more complex history, an older heritage of thought, concerning these questions, one with which Chéngguān, and many of his learned Chinese contemporaries seem to have been quite familiar. Let me offer just a few of its highlights.

First—apropos of the concept of dharmadhātu: This concept, though associated especially with the Mahāyāna, has roots even in the Pāli Canon (the earliest stratum of Buddhist scripture), in passages designed to assert the objectivity of the Buddha's teaching, its objective validity obtaining independently of him. So, in the Nidāna-vagga ("Book of Causes") of the Saṃyutta Nikāya ("Grouped Discourses") we find a passage that speaks of "the stable element" (ṭhita'va sā dhātu), i.e., the stable condition of things that "always obtains regardless of whether or not buddhas arise in the world" (uppādā vā tathāgatānam anuppādā vā tathāgatānaṃ). It is called "the stableness of things (dhammaṭṭhitatā), the fixed course of things (dhammaniyāmatā)."[19]

The often quoted Śālistamba Sūtra (大乘緣生稻喻經 Dàshèng yuánshēng dàoyú jīng, Discourse on the Simile of the Young Rice Plant),[20] a short and early (or Proto-) Mahāyāna scripture famous for its classical definition of pratītyasamutpāda ("dependent origination"), echoes and expands this characterization of the objective condition of things, the ultimate condition of all things that will come to be called the dharmadhātu ("domain or essence of truth"), by giving it eleven names, all referring to the way in which things always are as they are by virtue of their proper nature, regardless of the arising or non-arising of Buddhas:

dharmatā, 法性 (fǎxìng) = the nature of things

dharmasthititā, 法住 (fǎjù) = the stability of things

dharmaniyāmatā, 法位 (fǎwèi) = the fixed course of things

pratītyasamutpādānulomatā, 順於緣生 (shùn yú yuánshēng) = the conformity of all things to the principle dependent origination

tathatā, 真如 (zhēnrú) = suchness

avitathatā, 不顛倒如 (bù diāndǎo rú) = unperverted suchness

ananyatathatā, 不異真如 (bù yì zhēnrú) = pure suchness

bhūtatā, 實不異 (shí bùyì) = reality

19. This passage is taken from Guṇabhadra's mid-fifth-century Chinese translation of the Śrīmālādevīsiṃhanāda Sūtra (勝鬘師子吼一乘大方便方廣經 Shèngmán shīzǐhǒu yīshéng dàfangbiàn fāngguǎng jīng—The Lion's Roar of Queen Śrīmālā, T 353:12.221c7–11). For an English translation of the Śrīmālā Sūtra, based on the Tibetan and all three Chinese versions of the text, see Wayman and Wayman, Lion's Roar of Queen Śrīmālā. No Sanskrit text of this scripture survives but some passages from it, including this one, have been quoted and preserved in other extant Sanskrit texts. The Sanskrit given here is from the Ratnagotravibhāga (alias Uttaratantra)—about which more is said below. See Zuiryū 中村瑞隆, Ratnagotravibhāga-Mahātānotttaratantra-Çāstra, 3 (lines 15–17), 21 (lines 19–20). Note that Nakamura gives both the romanized Sanskrit of the treatise and, on facing pages, an edited version of Ratnamati's early fifth-century Chinese translation (Taishō 1611). See also Takasaki, Study of the Ratnagotravibhāga, 144–45, 168. One may also profitably consult the most recently published version of the Ratnagotravibhāga, which includes the original Sanskrit in Devanāgarī script along with the ancient Ratnamati Chinese translation and a translation by the editor into modern Chinese. See Bǎoshēng, Fàn-Hàn.

20. Buddha, Connected Discourses of the Buddha, 551.

satyatā, 實 (shí) = truth

aviparītatā, 不顛倒 (bù diāndǎo) = freedom from perverted views

aviparyastatā, 不錯謬 (bú cuòmiù) = freedom from falsehood[21]

The Laṅkāvatāra Sūtra, another Tathāgatagarbha scripture and one which does actually employ the compound "dharmadhātu," describes the dharmdhātu in very similar language.[22]

One cannot help but notice here that the tradition that insists on the emptiness, insubstantiality, and transience of all things, on the lack of any abiding and inherent self-nature (svabhāva, 自性zìxìng), here resorts to such locutions as "inherent nature," "stability," "fixity," etc. and prefers the kataphatic "suchness" (tathatā) to its apophatic counterpart "emptiness" (śūnyatā). Buddhist texts often seek to conceal this apparent contradiction, to render it anodyne or explain it away by repeating claims that the "true inherent nature" of things is just that they lack any inherent nature and that the true "stability" of things is just that they lack all stability, but such equivocation does not really relieve the tension between Buddhism's avowed resistance to an ontologized unconditioned and the recurrent need to admit of such a thing. Rather it only highlights and exacerbates that tension.

Note too that the Śālistamba Sūtra also says, famously:
yaḥ pratītyasamutpādaṃ paśyati sa dharmaṃ paśyati, yo dharmaṃ paśyati sa buddhaṃ paśyati
若見緣生即見法。若見法即見佛 (ruò jiàn yuánshēng jí jiàn fǎ. ruò jiàn fǎ jí jiàn fó)

"To see pratītyasamutpāda is to see the dharma; to see the dharma is to see the Buddha"[23]

In other words, to see dependent origination is to see the truth and to see the truth is to see the Buddha. This, of course, reopens a question that might seem to have been settled, namely, the question of the relation between a

21. For an amply annotated translation and study of this scripture see Schoening, Śālistamba Sūtra; Reat, Śālistamba Sūtra. The original Sanskrit of the sūtra has not survived although certain passages in Sanskrit, including those quoted here, have been preserved in various other sources. The Schoening and Reat translations are based chiefly on Tibetan renditions of the text. There are, however, five surviving Chinese translations (708–12 in the Taishō edition of the Chinese Buddhist canon). The one from which I have taken the Chinese terminology given here is that made in the eighth century by Amoghavajra (Taishō 710).

22. Schoening, Śālistamba Sūtra, 1:62; 2:702; Reat, Śālistamba Sūtra, 33.

23. See Suzuki, Studies in the Laṅkāvatāra Sūtra, 275–82.

buddha and the dharmadhātu, the domain of ultimate reality. The implication seems to be that a buddha is not simply the discoverer and teacher of the truth but is somehow its very embodiment? But how can this be? The seeing of the objective truth of things, the truth of pratītyasamutpāda, is, on the one hand, adamantly said to be independent of the arising or not arising of buddhas. But here, in the very same text, we are told that to see that objective and independent truth is in fact also to see the buddha? Is this not also in some obscure way contradictory?

Here we see an early Buddhist anticipation of the very topic immediately at hand—the question of whether the ultimate, the transcendent unconditioned, is personal or impersonal. In Buddhist terms this is the question of the relationship between the dharmadhātu (the realm or essence of truth) and the dharmakāya (the Buddha in his truth-body or ultimate identity). On this issue the Chinese Buddhist traditions, especially the Huáyán tradition (for example, Chéngguān in the passages cited above), often invoke the Ratnagotravibhāga 究竟一乘寶性論 (The Analysis of the Germ of the [Three] Jewells [i.e., A Discourse on Essential Nature of Buddhas]), where we find it said that "the dharmakāya is to be understood as two-fold (dharmakāyo dvidhā jñeya, 法身有二種 fǎshēn yǒu èr zhǒng). First, the dharmakāya is to be understood as the body of the perfectly pure dharmadhātu (dharmadhātu sunirmalaḥ, 清淨真法界身 qīngjìng zhēn fǎjiè shēn), which is both (1) the object of non-discriminative knowledge (avikalpajñānagocara, 無分別智境界 wúfèn bié zhì jìngjiè), and (2) that which the buddhas realize through introspection (tathāgatānam pratyātmâdhigamadharma, 自內身法界能證應知 zìnèishēn fǎjiè néng zhèng yìngzhī). Second, the dharmakāya is to be understood as "the natural outflow" (tanniṣyanda, 依彼習氣流 yī bǐ xíqì liú) of the perfectly pure dharmadhātu, namely, "the teachings of both the profound [truth] and the various [worldly truths]" (gāmbhīryavaicitryanaya-deśanādharma, 以深淺 義說 yǐ shēnqiǎn yì shuō) that are "the cause of the attainment" (tatpraptihetu, 得彼因 dé bǐ yīn) [of the perfectly pure dharmadhātu].[24]

Compare this, by the way, with the line in Asaṅga's Compendium of Mahāyāna (Mahāyānasaṃgraha 攝大乘論 Shè dàshèng lùn), from Xuánzàng's (玄奘) Chinese translation of the no-longer extant Sanskrit, on the topic of how the defiled ālayavijñāna (store consciousness), the deepest level of consciousness, can be purified. Asaṅga, speaking of the "puremind" (淨心 jìngxīn) or "supramundane mind" (出世心 chūshì xīn), says that it

> is born of impregnation by the seed of the hearing [of the Buddha's word], which flows from the most pure dharmadhātu

24. Schoening, *Śālistamba Sūtra*, 1:60–62, 220; Reat, *Śālistamba Sūtra*, 27.

(*suviśuddha-dharmadhātuniṣyanda-śrutavāsana-bīja 從最清
淨法界等流正聞熏習種子所生 cóng zuì qīngjìng fǎjiè děng
liú zhèng wén xūn xí zhŏngzi suŏ shēng).[25]

The Ratnagotravibhāga further notes that the dharmadhātu is two-
fold in yet another way insofar as it is both (1) yāvadbhāvikatā (盡所
有性 jìn suŏyŏu xìng)—i.e., the full range of all existents, and also (2)
athāvatbhāvikatā (如所有性 rú suŏyŏu xìng)—the state of things as they
are.[26] Thus, the dharmadhātu, seen as "the full range of all existents," is
held to be the domain of conventional truth (saṃvṛti-satya, 世俗諦 shìsú
dì). It is also held to be the object of tatpṛṣṭhalabdha-jñāna (後得智 hòudé
zhì), i.e., the practical, worldly knowledge (jñāna 智 zhì) that is said to be
"acquired after" (pṛṣṭhalabdha) the attainment of non-discriminating insight and that allows the bodhisattva, the transcended being, to, as it were,
"return to the world" so as to undertake effective compassionate action
on behalf of sentient beings. By contrast, the dharmadhātu as "the state of
things as they are" is the suchness (tathatā, 真如 zhēnrú) and emptiness
(śūnyatā, 空 kōng)—the true, insubstantial substance—of things. And this
is held to be the domain of ultimate truth (paramārtha-satya, 第一義諦
dìyīyì dì / 眞諦 zhēndì), not conventional truth (saṃvṛti-satya, 俗諦 súdì).
It is the object of non-discriminating knowledge (avikalpa-jñāna, 無分別智
wúfènbié zhì), the very knowledge that liberates the bodhisattva, as distinct
from the practical wisdom that enables the liberated bodhisattva to enact
his compassion and save others.

What these passages suggest is that the dharmakāya (the "truth-body"
of a Buddha), in its relation to the dharmadhātu (the "essential element" or
"domain" of truth), has both an impersonal and a personal dimension. In its
impersonal, immutable, and therefore quite impassable (απαθες?) dimension it is simply the way things ultimately or truly are in and of themselves,
regardless of who does or does not perceive them as such. In its relationship to persons, which is also its gnoseological dimension, it is what the
awakened being is awakened to. It is the object of the awakened being's "supramundane" (lokôttara, 出世間 chūshìjiān), "released" (vinirmukta, 解脫
jiětuō), "non-discriminating" (nirvikalpa, 無分別 wúfènbié) knowledge. It
is also the object of the already awakened being's multifarious, discriminate,
and salvifically efficacious mundane (lokiya, 世間 shìjiān) knowledge.

25. Takasaki, *Study of the Ratnagotravibhāga*, 284–85; Nakamura, *Ratnagotravibhāga-
Mahātānottaratantra-Çāstra*, 137–38; Băoshèng, *Fàn-Hàn*, 188–89.

26. Taishō 1597, 31:333C. See Lamotte, *La Somme du grand véhicule*, 65–66. Note
that this translation, by a great Catholic scholar of Buddhism, was originally published
in 1938 in *Bibliothèque du Muséon*.

But there is still more to the matter than this, for these passages also indicate that the dharmadhātu as the domain of the real, i.e., the essence of things as they objectively are—immutable and impassable though it may seem to be—is not static or inert. Rather it has generative or causative potency. Although it does not itself change, it does somehow foster or enable, in sentient beings, change of the kind that brings about their liberation. This is what is meant when the texts say that the dharmakāya, absolute buddhahood, is "the natural outflow" (tanniṣyanda, 依彼習氣流 yī bǐ xíqì liú) of the dharmadhātu, when they say that the transformative "hearing of the Buddha's revelatory word" flows from the most pure dharmadhātu (suviśuddhadharmadhātu-niṣyanda, 從最清淨法界等流 cóng zuì qīngjìng fǎjiè děngliú), and when they say that those same teachings born of the dharmadhātu are "the cause of the awakened being's attainment of the dharmadhātu" (tatpraptihetu, 得彼因 dé bǐ yīn). This amounts to saying that the truth of things, the way things truly are, naturally generates liberating gnosis, or that gnosis is just the cognitive resonance of ultimate truth.

To be sure, the concepts of "natural outflow" or salvific "causation" are hardly perspicuous. Just how it is that objective truth naturally engenders subjective liberation is not immediately clear. The very mystery of the process may account for Mahāyāna Buddhism's resort to personification, its tendency to find enhypostatic resonances in the anhypostatic truths of the dharmakāya and tathāgatagarbha. Thus, in the imaginaire of Mahāyāna Buddhism, dharmakāya and tathāgatagarbha are both personified—the one as Vairocana, the other as Samantabhadra. However, it would be a mistake to interpret these personifications as merely metaphorical. In the spirituality of Mahāyāna, in its contemplative, devotional, iconographic, and liturgical practices, these supernal beings, who are said to embody ultimate and soteriologically effective truths, are held to be real personal presences, powerful agents whom one may encounter, commune with, revere, worship, entreat, rely upon, etc. It is as though the Mahāyāna recognition of a transcendent that is also immanent—distant from the order of suffering, ignorance, and desire and yet compassionately implicated therein—led inexorably to the conception of such "trans-immanence" as somehow personal—this despite the many strains of Buddhism that, as noted above, adduce the claim that ultimate truth obtains irrespective of any persons who may or may not attain it.

Is it too much to suggest that this may be understood as Buddhism's reluctant, not fully conscious intimation of the unconditional transcendent as a divine presence, a tacit recognition that it is necessary and an expression of a kind of unacknowledged yearning for it? Why else would Buddhism, so firmly grounded in its insight into the impermanence, selflessness, and emptiness of all things—so adamant in its resistance to ontology and to the positing of transcendent entities—nevertheless be repeatedly, albeit usually reluctantly, drawn to such ontologically affirmative categories as dharmadhātu, tathāgatagarbha, Buddha-nature, etc., as well as to such personal embodiments thereof as the Buddha Vairocana and the bodhisattvas Mañjuśrī and Samantabhadra? And might it be too much for a Christian admirer of Buddhism to suggest that here we find, in the guise of Buddhist aporias, the subtle activity of the Holy Spirit or the covert efficacy of the universal Logos? Could it be that Buddhism's recurrent discovery of contradictions deep within itself, manifest in never fully resolved doctrinal controversies, serves as a kind of "Logos spermatikos"? Of course, Buddhists themselves are not likely to endorse or welcome such suggestions, but when Christians entertain them I believe they can forge a valuable bond of sympathy with Buddhism, a sympathy that is compatible with adherence to Christian truth.[27] Such suggestions, arising from the perception of tensions within Buddhism—i.e., from the perspective of study of intra-Buddhist critique and polemic rather than from the perspective of extrinsic critique and polemic—may allow Christian theologians to find in Buddhism something analogous, for example, to the struggles of the Fathers of the Church to understand how it is that Christ can be both fully human and fully divine, how it is that having "emptied himself" (ἐκένωσεν) of his divinity the Father "highly exalted" (ὑπερύψωσεν) him as perichoretically divine, and how it is that sinners can "become God" by virtue of God's sacrifice in becoming man. When Mahāyāna Buddhists speak, as they often do, of "buddhas" (佛, fó) and "sattvas" (眾生 zhòngshēng), i.e., "noble beings " (ārya, 聖shèng) and "common beings" (pṛthagjana, 凡夫 fánfū) as different (異yì) and yet also the same (同tóng), as consolidated (圓融 yuánróng) and yet separate (別 bié), when they speak of the mind of a sentient being as a slough of corruption and yet also a preserve of radiant and inviolate purity, when they describe sensuality and materiality as enthrallment but claim also that they are capable of consecration and empowerment, and so on, are they not saying, in effect, that the unconditioned transcendence of buddhahood and the imperfect, suffering condition of unawakened sentient beings are "unconfused" (ἀσυγχύτως) and yet inseparable (ἀχωρίστως)? This of course

27. Takasaki, *Study of the Ratnagotravibhāga*, 173–76; Nakamura, *Ratnagotravibhāga-Mahātānotttaratantra-Çāstra*, 27–30; Bǎoshēng, *Fàn-Hàn*, 68. Ratnamati's Chinese translation renders yathāvad-bhāvikatā and yāvad-bhāvikatā as 如實修行 (rúshí xiūxíng) and 編修行 (biān xiūxíng) respectively, but this makes no sense in context and must be the result of a misreading or a textual corruption. In Chinese translations of other texts in which these two terms appear, they are given as we have given them above.

is a far cry from the Christian doctrine of the incarnation, which speaks of the human immanence of the divine transcendent as unique to the second person of the Trinity, and not as something common to all sentient beings. However, I would suggest that we may still detect in these Buddhist paradoxes and controversies a kind of inchoate appreciation of the need for such presence in the otherwise empty world.

In any case, I can offer, by way of unsatisfactory conclusion, nothing more than these few open and sympathetic theological questions and hypotheses.

Bibliography

Asaṅga. A Compendium of Mahāyāna (Mahāyānasaṃgraha 攝大乘論 Shè dàshèng lùn): Asaṅga's Mahāyānasaṃgraha and Its Indian and Tibetan Commentaries (Tsadra). Translated by Karl Brunnholzl. Ithaca, NY: Snow Lion, 2018.

Athanasius of Alexandria. On the Incarnation of the Word (Λόγος περί της ενανθρωπήσεως του λόγου). Translated by John Behr. Popular Patristics Series 44. Yonkers, NY: St. Vladimir's Seminary Press, 2001.

Bǎoshēng, Huáng 黄宝生, ed. Fàn-Hàn duìkān Jiūjìng yīshéng bǎoxìng lùn 梵汉对勘究竟一乘宝性论. Beijing: Chinese Academy of Social Sciences Press, 2017.

Buddha, Siddhartha Gautama. The Connected Discourses of the Buddha. Translated by Bhikkhu Bodhi. Boston: Wisdom, 2000.

Buswell, Robert E., Jr., and Donald S. Lopez, Jr., eds. The Princeton Dictionary of Buddhism. Princeton: Princeton University Press, 2014.

Cleary, Thomas, trans. The Flower Ornament Scripture: A Translation of the Avataṃsaka Sūtra. Boston: Shambala, 1993.

Congregation for the Doctrine of the Faith (CDF). Dominus Iesus: On the Unicity and Salvific Universality of Jesus Christ and the Church. 2000. http://www.vatican.va/roman_curia/congregations/cfaith/documents/rc_con_cfaith_doc_20000806_dominus-iesus_en.html.

De Lubac, Henri. Aspects du Bouddhisme: Amida. Paris: Éditions du Seuil, 1955.

———. Exégèse médiévale: Les quatre sens de l'Écriture. Paris: Aubier, 1959–64.

Eliade, Mircea, ed. The Encyclopedia of Religion. Vol. 6. New York: Macmillan, 1987.

Feinberg, Lawrence. The Natural Desire to See God, According to St. Thomas and His Interpreters. Rome: Apollinaire Studi, 2001.

Gimello, Robert M. "Chéngguān's 澄觀 Meditations on the Three Holy Ones (Sānshèng guànmén 三聖觀門)." In Kegongaku ronshū: Kamata Shigeo hakase koki ki'nen 鎌田茂雄博士古希記念 [Essays in Huáyán Studies in Celebration of the Seventieth Birthday of Dr. Kamata Shigeo]. Tokyo: Daizō shuppan 大蔵出版, 1997.

Grillmeier, Aloys. From the Apostolic Age to Chalcedon (451). Vol. 1 of Christ in Christian Tradition. Translated by John Bowden. Atlanta: John Knox, 1975.

Hamar, Imre. "Buddhāvataṃsakasūtra." In Literature and Languages, edited by Oskar von Hinuber and Vincent Eltschinger, 115–28. Vol. 1 of Encyclopedia of Buddhism. Leiden: Brill, 2015.

Lamotte, Étienne, ed. La Somme du grand véhicule d'Asaṅga (Mahāyānasaṃgraha). Publications de l'Institut Orientaliste de Louvain 8. Louvain: Éditions Peeters, 1973.

Milbank, John. The Suspended Middle: Henri de Lubac and the Debate Concerning the Supernatural. Grand Rapids, MI: Eerdmans, 2005.

Mortley, Raoul. From Word to Silence, II. The way of negation, Christian and Greek. Theophaneia Bd 31. Hanstein: Bonn, 1986.

Orsborn, Matthew. "Something for Nothing: Cognitive Metaphors for Emptiness in the *Upadeśa (大智度論Dàzhìdùlùn)." Journal of Chinese Buddhist Studies 31 (2018) 171–222.

Radich, Michael. The Mahāparinirvāṇa-mahāsūtra and the Emergence of the Tathāgatagarbha Doctrine. Hamburg Buddhist Studies 5. Hamburg: Hamburg University Press, 2015.

Reat, N. Ross, ed. The Śālistamba Sūtra. Delhi: Motilal Banarsidass, 1993.

Schoening, Jeffrey D. The Śālistamba Sūtra and Its Indian Commentaries. 2 vols. Wiener Studien zur Tibetologie und Buddhismuskunde, Heft 35.1–2. Vienna: Arbeitskreis für Tibetische und Buddhistische Studien, Universität Wien, 1995.

Suzuki, Daisetz Teitaro. Studies in the Laṅkāvatāra Sūtra. London: Routledge & Kegan Paul, 1930.

Takasaki, Jikidō. A Study of the Ratnagotravibhāga (Uttaratantra), Being a Treatise on the Tathāgatgarbha Theory of Mahāyāna Buddhism. Rome: Istituto Italiano per il Medio ed Estremo Oriente, 1966.

von Hinuber, Oskar, and Vincent Eltschinger, eds. Literature and Languages. Vol. 1 of Encyclopedia of Buddhism. Leiden: Brill, 2015.

Wayman, Alex, and Hideko Wayman, trans. The Lion's Roar of Queen Śrīmālā: A Buddhist Scripture on the Tathāgatagarbha Theory. New York: Columbia University Press, 1974.

Zimmermann, Michael. A Buddha Within: The Tathāgatagarbhasūtra, the Earliest Exposition of the Buddha-Nature Teaching in India. Bibliotheca Philologica et Philosophica 6. Tokyo: The International Research Institute for Advanced Buddhology, Soka University, 2002.

Zuiryū, Nakamura. 中村瑞隆 The Ratnagotravibhāga-Mahātānotttaratantra-Çāstra (Sanskrit with Chinese). Tokyo: Sankibo Busshorin, 1961.

Index